W9-DBA-281

Productivity and American Leadership

Productivity and American Leadership

The Long View

William J. Baumol,
Sue Anne Batey Blackman, and
Edward N. Wolff

The MIT Press
Cambridge, Massachusetts
London, England

First MIT Press paperback edition, 1991

© 1989 Massachusetts Institute of Technology

This book was set in Palatino by Asco Trade Typesetting Ltd., Hong Kong, and printed and bound by Halliday Lithograph in the United States of America.

Library of Congress Cataloging-in-Publication Data

Baumol, William J.
    Productivity and American leadership: the long view/William J. Baumol, Sue Anne Batey Blackman, and Edward N. Wolff.
    p.   cm.
    Includes index.
    ISBN 0-262-02293-1 (hb), 0-262-52163-6 (pb)
    1. Labor productivity—United States. I. Blackman, Sue Anne Batey. II. Wolff, Edward N. III. Title.
HC110.L3B38   1989
331.11′8′0973—dc19   88-37204
                                                                               CIP

Contents

Preface   ix

1   Why the Long Run?   1

2   Why Productivity Matters—and Why It Does Not   9

3   A Century of Productivity Improvement: Revolution in American Living Standards   29

4   Long-Run Growth in U.S. Productivity: Is There a Slowdown?   65

5   International Convergence: The Comparative U.S. Productivity Lag   85

6   The Service-Economy Prognosis: Cost-Disease Illusions   115

7   Is the United States Becoming an Information Economy?   143

8   Savings, Investment, and Productivity Growth   163

9   Education and the "Convergence Club": Lessons for Less Developed Countries   195

10   Depletion of Natural Resources: Must Economic Growth Mortgage the Future?   211

11   Productivity Yardsticks: Alternative Measures and Their Appropriate Uses   225

12 Toward Policy for the Longer Term 251

Appendix to Chapter 4   287
Appendix to Chapter 5   301
Appendix to Chapter 6   313
Appendix to Chapter 7   325
Appendix to Chapter 8   329
Appendix to Chapter 9   341
Appendix to Chapter 10   357
Appendix to Chapter 11   359
References   365
Index   381

Preface

This book is perhaps most easily summed up as a compendium of evidence demonstrating the error of our previous ways. The obvious self-satisfaction with which this confession is offered merely reflects a happy accident: The views previously expressed by us in print (which the facts have forced us to abandon, albeit slowly and reluctantly) bear witness that this book is not a collection of observations (possibly unintentionally) selected to support a conclusion arrived at in advance. Our opinions did not determine our choice of facts—rather, quite the reverse is true.

In many respects this book is stamped by the circumstances of its inception. Its immediate origin is the day its (chronologically) senior author was approached by the president of the Committee for Economic Development (an organization of business executives and academics seeking to formulate responsible positions on important policy issues). The president said, in effect, that the CED had undertaken to prepare a statement on productivity policy for the United States, and was seeking for the requisite research a director whose ignorance of the subject ensured that the statement would not merely recapitulate the accepted shibboleths. On that criterion, this coauthor of the present book was eminently qualified for the post. Two years of work on that policy statement ensued, involving, in one way or another, all three authors of this volume. But the time was too short to answer all of the questions left in our minds. This book contains many of the results of the subsequent research to which these residual questions impelled us.

There was, however, a second and earlier influence that colored our work: the enlightening emphasis upon the importance of the long run, which was a major focus of Jacob Viner's *Weltanschauung*. That brilliant, erudite, and delightful scholar repeatedly emphasized the danger of excessive preoccupation with transitory phenomena, either in research or in the design of policy. We trust this volume indicates that we learned the lesson well.

The main change that was forced upon our views by careful examination of the long-run data was abandonment of our earlier gloomy assessment of American productivity performance. It has been replaced by the guarded optimism that pervades this book. This does *not* mean that we believe retention of American leadership will be automatic or easy. Yet the statistical evidence did drive us to conclude that the many writers who have suggested that the demise of America's traditional position has already occurred or was close at hand were, like the author of Mark Twain's obituary, a bit premature. We are fully prepared to face up to the risk that this conclusion will undercut our standing as dismal scientists, since the evidence seems to have left us little choice in the matter. It should, incidentally, be acknowledged that a number of distinguished economists have also been driven to a similar evaluation, and we shall acknowledge their work at appropriate points in the text.

When the creditor has the proper qualifications, even indebtedness can be a pleasure. Such is our debt to Vacharee Devakula and Ilga Rosenberg, whose intelligent and reliable contributions to completion of our study are deeply appreciated by us. Phyllis Durepos provided her usual excellent assistance. We also owe debts of gratitude to Wayne Farel and Maury Gittleman for their valuable research assistance, and to Dermot Gately for patient help with the graphics when the computer program rebelled against our ministrations, as well as for the provision of data on energy developments. Profound comments on the substance of our arguments as well as invaluable data were contributed by Moses Abramovitz, Martin Baily, Paul David, David Dollar, Bradford De Long, Peggy Heim, David Landes, Mike MacDowell, Ken McLennan, Scott Miller, Lawrence Stone, and Gordon Tullock, none of whom, of course, bears any guilt for the final product. For our statistical foundations we were obviously entirely dependent on the work of Angus Maddison, Robert Summers, and Alan Heston, who went well out of their way in providing the data to us.

Aside from them, our profound thanks are owed to the several agencies that have generously and patiently funded our research over the years it has required. Chief among these is the National Science Foundation's Information Technology and Organizations Program in the Division of Information, Robotics, and Intelligent Systems. Generous support was also provided by Exxon Education Foundation, the Joint Council on Economic Education, the University of Pennsylvania's Fishman-Davidson Center for the Study of the Service Sector, and New York University's C. V. Starr Center for Applied Economics.

Productivity and
American Leadership

1   Why the Long Run?

Productivity growth is a vital subject that has, unfortunately, fallen into the hands of macroeconomists. This is not to deny that macroeconomists have made important contributions to our discipline; but it is nevertheless true that the surrender of productivity analysis to the field of macrotheory is, in some ways, regrettable. For productivity growth is essentially a long-run issue. Indeed, it can be said without exaggeration that in the long run probably nothing is as important for economic welfare as the rate of productivity growth. Yet, macroanalysts have been shaped by their training to a short-run orientation, which suits them poorly to the study of what may well be the most important implications of productivity.

1.1   The Short Run versus the Long Run in Economic Tradition

Until the Keynesian revolution, preoccupation with the long run was the hallmark of academic economists. This is what distinguished them from politicians, businesspersons, and others interested in economic issues. The economic literature was framed in terms of long-run tendencies, long-run equilibria, and what one of us once called "the magnificent dynamics," which encompasses the secular expansion or decline of entire nations and societies over protracted periods. Policy practitioners who must deal constantly with crises and fight brushfires cannot and could not then devote the time needed to study economic developments distant in time. This left a gap in policy discussions that our academic predecessors were predisposed to fill.

The birth of macrotheory changed all that. John Maynard Keynes's felicitously phrased reminder that beyond the short run the grim reaper awaits us all was followed by Abba Lerner's almost equally devastating, "In the long run we find ourselves in another short run." A time of great depression or rampaging inflation is not particularly propitious for careful study of prospective developments in the far future. We do not mean to suggest by any of this that concern over short-run issues was ill-advised. On the contrary, the problems studied by "the new economics" were of the utmost importance, and their previous relative neglect was certainly not to our credit. But we do believe that the pendulum has now swung too far in the other direction.

It still remains true that politicians seeking reelection every 2, 4, or 6 years cannot spend much time on the far future and are naturally reluctant to ask voters for current sacrifices in return for great benefits promised at distant dates. And businesspeople report that their job performance is judged to a considerable degree by the prices of the securities of their companies, which they believe are disproportionately influenced by the firm's immediate prospects. Thus, to them concern with the long run is also an expensive luxury. Who then, if not the academic economist, is to deal with the economy's long-run problems? Who is to advocate the courageous steps needed to head off threatening but still-distant disasters? To deal with such matters we do not have to turn our backs on important short-run issues in order to avoid neglect of the long.

These remarks are very pertinent for productivity growth, which macro-economists tend to transform into a short-run issue. For example, they study the effect of the stage of the business cycle on the rate of productivity growth, noting why growth characteristically slows down with the onset of a downturn in the cycle and why productivity suddenly rises with the beginning of the upturn. Similarly, macroeconomists examine whether a stimulus to productivity growth is a promising means to fight a decade-long inflation. These two matters are obviously important, but for productivity, its major implications, and the means to influence its long-run course, these are side issues.

It is only in the long run that productivity growth makes a big difference to the welfare of the populace, and it is only in the long run that productivity growth is subject to fundamental changes. Examples that are discussed in more detail in chapter 2 will bring out this point. Since the beginning of the nineteenth century average labor productivity growth in the United States probably was a bit more than $1\frac{1}{2}\%$ per year, yet that was sufficient to produce an estimated twentyfold increase in total productivity and in living standards, a figure so large that it is difficult to comprehend. A second example is the historians' judgment that less than a 1 percentage point lag in productivity growth for one century was sufficient to transform the United Kingdom from the world's undisputed industrial leader into the third-rate economy that it is today. It was also sufficient to cut real wages in the United Kingdom from about $1\frac{1}{2}$ times that in other leading European economies to about two-thirds of the real wages in those countries today. All of this shows that now is the time to worry about America's standing in productivity growth and that, in particular, it is the time to worry about that standing half a century hence. Fifty years from now the deed may have been done. It may then simply be too late to do much about it.

1.2 Investment and Growth in Labor Productivity

As an illustration of what can be shown by the long-run point of view, we may comment in a very preliminary way on one side of the determinants of relative productivity growth and, hence, of the relative wealth of different nations. There is considerable dispute about the causes of what is regarded as a major U.S. productivity problem: the lag in U.S. labor productivity growth behind that of Japan. While the reasons are far from settled, a look at the widely published data immediately calls attention to the explanatory power of what appears to be one great and consistent disparity in the behavior of the Japanese and American economies. For most of the postwar period Japan's savings rate was, apparently, quite consistently some two to three times as large as ours. Between 1970 and 1980, for example, net saving (measured in the conventional manner) was approximately 8% of net disposable income in the United States and a bit more than 25% in Japan. Incidentally, the average for the member countries of the Organization for Economic Cooperation and Development (OECD) was approximately 16%. The reported differences in investment rates were comparable. For example, net fixed investment as a percent of gross national product between 1971 and 1980 was reported to be about 7% in the United States, in Germany and France some 12–13%, and in Japan 20%. Investment in manufacturing in the 1960s was 9% of output in the United States, 16% in Germany, and 30% in Japan. It is also noteworthy that the absolute differences range from about 15 to 20 percentage points.

The point is that even such huge disparities in saving and investment rates, if they go on only for a very few years, make little difference for the relative productive capacities of two countries. But if they persist for any considerable period of time the phenomenon of *compounding* makes their influence enormous. An example will make the point. Consider two imaginary economies, call them J and U, and assume that in 1950 U starts off with 10 times as much capital (plant and equipment) per worker as J. Assume also that in U capital equipment per worker expands at 10% per year, compounded, while that in J increases at a compound rate of 20%. Then the arithmetic tells us that 5 years later (in 1955) the relative positions of the two economies will hardly have become threatening to U. Capital equipment per worker in J will have risen from 10% of U's to 16% of the latter. But by the time 25 years have passed, in 1975, J's capital equipment per worker will have attained 88% of U's, and 10 years after that, in 1985, J will have leaped ahead of U with more than twice the real value of capital equipment per worker as that in U. This powerful arithmetic force, which we have referred to elsewhere as "the tyranny of compounding," manifests its full powers only in longer periods. That is the main moral of the preceding arithmetic example, which shows why the long view can sometimes be so crucial.

We see, then, that persistent compounded differences in savings and investment rates, such as those reported for the United States and Japan (if they turn out not to be illusory), can go far to explain the differences in productivity performance. On such grounds, a study by J. R. Norsworthy and David H. Malmquist [1985] suggests that a substantial part of the superior performance of Japanese growth in labor productivity may be ascribable not to increasing efficiency but to the accumulation of capital. As the authors remark, "The results of this method of analysis should do much to dispel the aura of mystery that surrounds some discussions of productivity growth in Japan. In the main, we believe that rapid growth in the capital stock, which can be viewed as raising the workers' capacity to process a great volume of materials, is a major source of Japanese growth. And although this rapid growth in capital and materials inputs can be thought of as representing substantial technological change, the overall efficiency of Japanese manufacturing as measured by growth in the productivity of all inputs has not shown remarkable progress relative to that of U.S. manufacturing" (p. 66).

As a matter of fact, as will be reported in chapter 8, a recent study by two respected economists indicates that the true disparity between U.S. and Japanese investment rates may well be considerably smaller than it is usually reported to be, and there is also some evidence that Japanese savings rates seem to be declining. That is now seen to be the correct issue. The long-run viewpoint has shown us that real differences in savings and investment *do* matter a great deal if the period involved is substantial and if the differences persist.

This is not inconsistent with historical experience elsewhere. Another example will also lend support to the point. The United Kingdom between 1760 and 1982 had a fairly low savings rate (about 9–10% per year, compared to the 20% average for the Third World today, but a number very close to that of the United States currently). In addition, Great Britain had a very low investment rate in the period 1790–1820, a phenomenon largely attributed by at least one economic historian to "crowding out" by government expenditure on the Napoleonic wars. As a result, most of the labor productivity gains of the early Industrial Revolution presumably must be ascribed to the "wave of gadgets"—the burst of innovation that characterized the general period—not to the deepening of capital. These new inventions were sensational enough, including the appearance of the improved steam engine, the ship's chronometer (which for the first time enabled a ship's personnel to calculate longitude, thereby speeding voyages and reducing the danger of shipwreck) and the well-known improvements in textile manufacturing. Yet, despite these dramatic innovations, British per-capita income during this period grew only about 0.33% per year, as far as one can judge today from the poor data that are available. It is note-worthy that this figure is about one-tenth of the rate of growth of per-capita income in the Third World in the 1970s, despite all the unfavorable developments of that decade. This disappointing early growth record of British labor productivity and per-capita income, which occurred despite the enormous outburst of innovation, may then be explainable, at least in part, by the low level of investment.[1]

It clearly does not follow from this that innovation is unimportant. Surely, innovation *does* count very much. Indeed, it is hardly plausible that anything else played as crucial a role in the Industrial Revolution and the explosion in living standards in the two centuries that followed. But historically it seems, as least sometimes, to count less in the intermediate run, compared to rates of investment.

1.3   The U.S. Productivity Performance in Historical Perspective

There are three phenomena that underlie recent concerns about U.S. economic performance in terms of productivity growth. First, there is the clear slowdown that the productivity growth rate underwent during the period, roughly, between 1965 and 1980. Second, there is the dramatic rise in the share of the U.S. labor force and gross national product that is associated with the service sector of the economy rather than manufacturing. Third, as we have already noted, there is the fact that the growth rate of American labor productivity since World War II was substantially below that of Japan, France, West Germany, Italy, Sweden, and a number of other indus-trialized countries. All of these manifestations are real, and are legitimate

causes of concern, both for the absolute prosperity of the American economy, and for its relative position. But in evaluating the seriousness of the
dangers they signal, it is important to determine whether these phenomena
are merely transitory or herald a long-run change in the underlying relationships. No one doubts that the United States is still among the world's
economic leaders, and that, on the average, its population still enjoys a very
high standard of living. A temporary decline in productivity growth or a
brief period in which the productivity of other countries rises more rapidly
than its own are surely no reason for great worry. Only if the developments
in question are long-run events do they matter seriously. For that reason,
we shall seek to examine with considerable care the evidence indicating
whether the long run or only the the short run is what is involved.

The bulk of the book is devoted to examination of this evidence, and it
would be redundant to review the material in any detail at this point.
However, it is easy to characterize its implications in a general way, and
such a preview may well prove helpful to the reader in evaluating the
details of the argument as it proceeds. The overall conclusion that follows
from the (far from perfect) evidence that we have been able to assemble is
that there is no basis for either of the extreme interpretations that can be
given to postwar developments in productivity growth. On the one side,
the data offer no clear basis for a conclusion that the long-run growth rate
of productivity in the United States has fallen below its historical level, or
that it is about to do so. The available statistics also are not inconsistent
with the possibility that the recent superiority in growth rates of other
industrialized countries will turn out to have been a temporary affair,
representing a period of catch-up during which the others were learning
industrial techniques from us. Thus, the longer-run data constitute no
grounds for hysteria or recourse to ill-considered measures that are grasped
at in a mood of desperation.

While our conclusions on these subjects will probably prove surprising
(and, we hope, gratifying) to the nonspecialist audience, we should make it
clear that a number of careful analysts have in recent years reached results
that are consistent with ours and, in some cases, anticipate them (see, for
example, Singh [1987], Darby [1984], Helliwell, Sturm, and Salou [1985],
Lawrence [1984], Fuchs [1981], Branson [1981], Summers [1983], and Norton
[1986]).

On the other hand, the data equally fail to provide guarantees that all is
well and will continue to be so. Obviously, the only certain thing about the
relatively distant future is our inability to predict it; and so one can never
proceed on the comfortable assumption that it will contain no nasty sur-

prises. But the grounds for concern are somewhat stronger than that. Some of the trends, even if extrapolated with a degree of conservatism, are less than reassuring. As will be shown in the last chapter of the book, unless American productivity growth performance improves somewhat, the trends suggest that the U.S. *can* lose its economic leadership and its *relatively* high standard of living, perhaps within a matter of a few decades. The calculations imply that the task that will have to be undertaken in order to avoid this will not be an easy one, but it is at the same time not so difficult as to make us despair of success in the undertaking.

Accordingly, the book will end with a set of policy proposals that, we hope, will prove sufficient to elicit an improvement in the American productivity performance consistent with the goal of retention of its current relatively felicitous position. We hope to go beyond mere listing and description of those proposals. In addition, we seek to muster whatever statistical and other evidence that is available to evaluate their promised effectiveness and, as it were, to determine the proper dosage of the measures that will suffice to produce the desired effects.

As will be discussed in some detail in chapter 2, failure to institute such a program, or to carry it out effectively, can have profound and disturbing implications for the general position of the United States in the world economy of the future, and for the welfare of American workers in particular. If the U.S. productivity level really were to fall substantially below that of its leading industrial rivals, the main consequence is clear. An apt way of describing it is via the observation that, in such circumstances, instead of, as in the past, the United States having grounds to fear the competition of cheap foreign labor, the shoe in the future would almost certainly be on the other foot. It would be the rest of the world that would be led to fear the deplorable and unfair competition of the underpaid labor of the United States. The prospect is unappetizing. But it is certainly not our manifest destiny, nor is it even strongly foreshadowed in the U.S. productivity record. Above all, the evidence offers no grounds for the conclusion that the country is powerless to deal with the perils in this arena that may be in prospect.

Note

1. All of this information is to be found in Jeffrey G. Williamson [1984]. Williamson provides the various sources from which the estimates reported here are derived.

2

Why Productivity Matters—and Why It Does Not

"No matter how refined and how elaborate the analysis, if it rests solely on the short view it will still be ... a structure built on shifting sands.
Jacob Viner [1958, pp. 112−113]

For real economic miracles one must look to productivity growth. And economic miracles it has indeed provided. Until at least the seventeenth century all of human history entailed an unending struggle with starvation. Except during periods of favorable climatic change, famines every 3−10 years were the normal state of affairs, and corpses could be expected to litter the roadsides. Yet, even this marginal existence typically required some 90% of the employed population to be engaged in agricultural pursuits. Even during the periods of surprisingly fertile invention and extensive practical application of the new ideas (and there were several such periods well before the onset of our Industrial Revolution), living standards were not drastically improved (unless the innovations were primarily agricultural) because other activities produced so small a share of society's output. Today, in contrast, the primary economic problem of agriculture is disposal of its vast outputs, which threaten to leave unmanageable surpluses. Yet, rather than occupying the bulk of the labor force, agriculture requires only some 3% of the population of an industrialized country to provide that abundance. Later, we shall provide a fuller description of the economic changes that make the past two centuries totally different economically from anything that occurred or could even have been imagined before. And this change, which certainly merits the term "miracle," is clearly ascribable to two centuries of productivity growth whose magnitude is without precedent.

The major theme of this chapter, then, is that productivity does matter. In terms of human welfare, there is nothing that matters as much *in the long run.* In chapter 1 we discussed the pertinence of the long run and the justification of the heavily historical viewpoint adopted in much of the next few chapters. In this chapter we also argue that, while insufficient attention may have been devoted by the mainstream of the economic literature to the long-run side of productivity growth, the short-run role of productivity may well, sometimes, have been exaggerated to some degree. We shall suggest that growth in productivity matters less for such important but transitory issues as inflation, international competitiveness of particular industries in an economy, and the associated availability of jobs. Ultimately, we shall maintain, productivity policy is not the ideal instrument to deal with these problems. Rather, what productivity policy does contribute to effectively is real wages and the economy's general standard of living.

The chapter begins with a review of the historical data showing just how much productivity growth has in fact accomplished in recent centuries. The data provide quantification of the magnitude of the truly remarkable transformation in living standards. Then, in the following chapter, we undertake to go beyond mere statistics—to provide to these dry numbers "a local habitation and a name."

2.1 The Extraordinary Contribution of Productivity Growth

Above all, productivity growth provides the most obvious benefit—it contributes to the general standard of living of a society. When each worker produces more with a given outlay of effort, that person's family can generally expect (albeit with some lag, as we shall see in chapter 8) to have more real income to spend on behalf of its members. This benefit of productivity growth is so self-evident and well-known that any fuller discussion of the relationship itself would be otiose. But what is not widely known is just *how much* productivity growth has contributed to living standards. Indeed, as we shall see next, even when the facts are described, the magnitude of the changes is so great that they resist comprehension.

Perhaps some sense of the immensity of the productivity achievement of the past 150 years is imparted by contrast with the preceding centuries. We obviously possess no reliable measure of productivity in the world of antiquity, but everything we know about standards of living in ancient Rome suggests that they were not lower, and in many respects may have been higher, than in eighteenth-century England. This is probably true even for the lower classes—certainly for the free urban "proletariat" and perhaps even for Roman slaves. As for the upper classes—a Roman household was served by sophisticated technical devices for heating and bathing not found in an eighteenth century home of similar socioeconomic position. Had a wealthy Roman been transported magically into an eighteenth century English home, he would probably have been puzzled technologically by only a very limited set of products. Few items other than the clocks, the window panes, the printed books and newspapers and the musket over the fireplace represented technological breakthroughs achieved anywhere in the intervening 15 or 16 centuries.

It is true that by the middle of the eighteenth century and even during the Middle Ages (see, e.g., Cipolla [1976]) there had been substantial technological changes in the workplace and elsewhere. Ship design had improved dramatically. Lenses and, with them, the telescope and microscope had been a major innovation in the sixteenth century and had generated a great demand for the specialized skills required to produce them (see, e.g., Wilson [1968]). Earlier, the stirrup, the harness, and the heavy plow had changed agriculture drastically and the water mill had relieved humans and animals not only of the tasks of grinding grain but also polishing metal, sawing lumber, hammering metal, and processing wool by beating it (see White [1962] and Gimpel [1976]). The eighteenth century yielded the ship's chronometer, which revolutionized water transportation by permitting longitude to be calculated. Yet none of this led to rates of productivity growth anywhere comparable to those of the nineteenth and twentieth centuries.

Nor has any of what has just been said been meant to imply that productivity growth came to a standstill for nearly two millennia. Probably from the fall of Rome to sometime near the Carolingian Renaissance of the eighth century, it declined substantially and then proceeded to increase in fits and starts until the eighteenth century. The early agricultural revolution brought by the heavy plow, the horse harness, and the three-field crop rotation system expanded and improved food output for several hundred years before the fourteenth century. There were apparently at least two early "industrial revolutions" in Europe, one in the twelfth and thirteenth centuries (see Carus-Wilson [1941], White [1962], and Gimpel [1976]), and one, according to Nef [1934] (other historians do suggest that Nef's views on this entail some exaggeration), roughly extending from about the end of the reign of Henry VIII, say, 1540, to about 1640 (the onset of the civil war of Charles I and Cromwell). Yet all the accompanying spurts in productivity could not have added up to a growth rate of more than negligible magnitude. A simple calculation indicates the grounds for this conclusion. Maddison [1982, p. 8] provides estimates of real GDP per capita in the United Kingdom and France in 1700 that translate into some $600 of 1980 purchasing power per year. This is somewhat below the Summers-Heston [1984] figure for India in that year (again, crudely translated from their 1975 "international dollar" figure into 1980 dollars). Now, if we arbitrarily take one-quarter of the 1980 Indian GDP per capita as the minimum required for sheer survival, in the year 700 real GDP per capita could not have been much lower than the equivalent of 200 1980 dollars. This is readily shown by a direct arithmetic calculation to have permitted an average annual growth rate no greater than 0.11% over the 10 centuries since 700 AD.[1] If there has been no secular decline in the number of labor hours per year over the period, the average growth rate of labor productivity could have not been materially larger than this.[2] This figure contrasts dramatically with an average growth rate well in excess of 2% per annum for the world's leading industrial countries according to Maddison's figures for the period 1870–1979.

By the last third of the eighteenth century the Industrial Revolution is generally taken to have been under way. But it is not usually recognized that initially it was a fairly minor affair so far as the economy as a whole was concerned. At first the bulk of the newly invented equipment was confined to textile production (though some progress in fields such as iron making had also occurred). Yet, as Landes [1969][3] indicates, an entrepreneur could undertake the new types of textile operations with a very small capital outlay, perhaps amounting only to a few hundred pounds, which by our calculations (using the Phelps Brown-Hopkins [1955] data) translates into something on the order of 100,000 1980 dollars. Jeffrey Williamson [1984, p. 688] reports that in England during, roughly, the first half-century of the Industrial Revolution, real per-capita income grew at a rate of only 0.33% per annum.[4] This contrasts with estimates of the corresponding growth rate for the Third World during the troubled decade of the 1970s, which came to nearly 3%—almost 10 times the early British figure.

Table 2.1 shows the remarkable contrast of developments from 1870 to 1979 with those of the earlier period. We see in (column 2) that, for the 16 countries for which figures are available, output per labor hour grew by multiples ranging from approximately 5 for Australia (i.e., Australian output per labor hour increased by almost 400%) all the way to 26 in the case of Japan. The twelvefold increase in labor productivity in the United States placed it somewhat below the middle of that range, and even the United Kingdom managed a sevenfold rise. Thus, after not manifesting any substantial long-period increase for at least *15 centuries*, in the course of *11 decades* the median increase in productivity among the 16 industrialized leaders in Maddisons's sample was about 1,150%! This rise in productivity

Table 2.1
Growth in productivity (GDP per capita), 1870–1979, for 16 industrialized countries

Country	Growth in real GDP[a] per capita (%)	Growth in real GDP[a] per person–hour (%)	Growth in volume of exports (%)
Australia	221.0	398.0	—
United Kingdom	325.0	585.0	930.0
Switzerland	472.0	830.0	4,400.0
Belgium	411.0	887.0	6,250.0
Netherlands	423.0	910.0	8,040.0
Canada	754.0	1,050.0	9,860.0
United States	691.0	1,080.0	9,240.0
Denmark	650.0	1,090.0	6,750.0
Italy	493.0	1,220.0	6,210.0
Austria	642.0	1,260.0	4,740.0
Germany	1,396.0	1,510.0	3,730.0
Norway	872.0	1,560.0	7,740.0
France	694.0	1,590.0	4,140.0
Finland	1,016.0	1,710.0	6,240.0
Sweden	1,084.0	2,060.0	5,070.0
Japan	1,653.0	2,480.0	293,060.0

Source: Maddison [1982, pp. 172–177, 182–187, 212, 248–253].
a. In 1970 U.S. dollars.

was sufficient to permit a rise in output per capita of more than 300% in the United Kingdom, almost 1,400% in West Germany, over 1,600% in Japan, and nearly 700% in France and the United States. The growth rates of other pertinent variables were also remarkable. One more example will suffice to show this. Table 2.1 shows the ratio of volume of exports in 1979 to the corresponding figure for 1870 for 15 countries. Here we see that the median increase is on the order of 6,300%!

2.2 Limitations of Productivity as a Short-Run Policy Instrument

While our primary purpose here is to emphasize the importance of productivity growth, it is also appropriate to try to clear up some misconceptions, largely in popular discussions, attributing to productivity policy more than should reasonably be expected of it. In recent decades productivity has often been invoked as a suitable instrument for dealing with problems such as inflation, unemployment, and deficits in the balance of

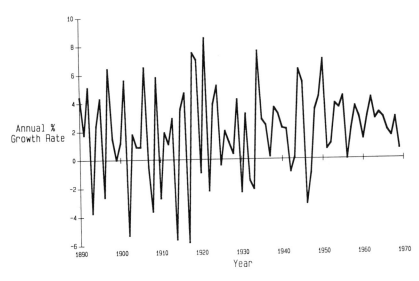

Figure 2.1
Annual growth rate, U.S. labor productivity, 1884–1969. Source: Kendrick [1973a, b].

payments. The basic shortcoming of all the suggestions for use of productivity measures as means to deal with such short-run problems is that productivity growth is not readily responsive to attempts to change its magnitude, and that nontransient changes may only come about rather slowly. Besides, for each of these problems there are policy instruments arguably better designed for the purpose.

Productivity growth rates are, actually, surprisingly volatile. Examination of year-by-year data on growth in either labor productivity or total factor productivity in the United States over some eleven decades suggests that something like a 3-year cycle may be present (see figure 2.1). We are not proposing this as a hypothesis to be taken seriously; we propose it merely as an easy way to suggest how unsteady a record this variable has accumulated. Yet that clearly does not mean that policy can quickly change the course of an economy's productivity trends. First, we are unfortunately unsure of the means that policy designers can employ with any degree of confidence to achieve such a goal. Economic literature offers much valuable discussion of the subject, but little of it can pretend to be definitive. Second, one can hardly carry out overnight the introduction of profoundly new productive techniques (much less the requisite research and development) or substantial expansion of plant and equipment. Such measures can often require as much as a decade and more for their execution. The short-run problem at issue may well have disappeared, or at least have changed its character drastically, before one can hope to bring substantial productivity changes to bear upon it.

It is true that, other things being equal, a jump in productivity can reduce the rise in price level that an inflationary process would otherwise have brought. In an economy in which prices are rising, a leap in the annual growth rate of productivity from, say, 2% to 3% can slow the pace of inflation commensurately: by about 1 percentage point. But such a spectacular rise in the productivity growth rate is no mean accomplishment, and we certainly know no policy programs that can be depended upon to bring it about very quickly. The conclusion that follows is that one must continue to depend on such standbys as monetary or fiscal policy for effective means to deal with inflationary problems. Productivity policy simply is not a major contender for that role.

2.3   Productivity, Unemployment, and "Deindustrialization"

In popular discourse there is a closely related set of misunderstandings about productivity. Besides considering it as a contender for a substantial role in short-run policy, productivity growth is often mistakenly taken as a major long-run source of problems such as unemployment and balance of payments deficits. The long-term data again permit us to dispose of some of these imagined perils. First, we are warned that rapid increases in labor productivity (the adoption of labor-saving methods) will destroy jobs, even in the long run. Second, and perhaps somewhat inconsistently, it is argued that if an economy's productivity growth lags behind that of other countries, it will lose jobs to foreign workers, its industry will suffer, and its balance of payments will be subject to chronic deficits (these last alleged consequences of lagging productivity are sometimes referred to as "deindustrialization"). As we shall show next, the data do not support any of these conclusions.[5]

If the specter of long-run unemployment were a reality, one would expect that the twelvefold increase in output per labor hour in the United States since 1870, its sevenfold increase in the United Kingdom, and its sixteenfold rise in Germany would have had a devastating effect on the demand for labor in those countries. Even with an approximately 50% fall in working hours per year, output per capita in the United States during the last century could have been kept about constant if the employed labor force were cut to one-sixth of its initial size relative to population. Figure 2.2 shows that nothing of the sort has actually occurred. The graph reports

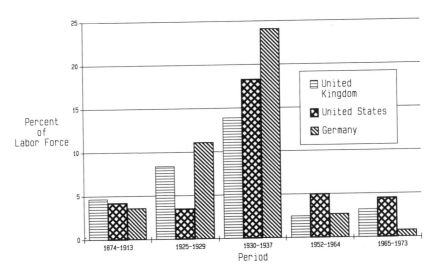

Figure 2.2
Unemployment rates, 1874–1973, United Kingdom, United States, and Germany. Source: Matthews, Feinstein, and Odling-Smee [1982, p. 94].

unemployment rates for the United Kingdom, the United States, and Germany from 1874 to 1973. It is evident that, aside from the period between the two world wars with the Great Depression, there has been no upsurge in unemployment, and the trend, if anything, has been somewhat in the downward direction. This is so, moreover, despite the fact that the ratio of number of persons in the labor force to total population has, according to Angus Maddison's [1982] figures, risen substantially in all three of the countries (from an unweighted mean of 34% in 1870 to 45% in 1979). The same graph also undermines the (nearly) opposite apprehension—it shows that a country such as the United Kingdom, which is a laggard in productivity growth, need not be subject to greater unemployment problems than others. Indeed, comparing the graph's bars for 1874–1913 with those 1952–1964 and 1965–1973, we see that the United Kingdom has made out relatively well on that score. In sum, neither rapid absolute productivity growth nor a slow relative productivity growth rate need subject a country to secular increase in unemployment rates.

The reasons, of course, are clear to those familiar with the pertinent analytic writings. In the long run, comparative advantage and the equilibrating mechanisms of international exchange will create new jobs in other sectors of the economy to replace those that have been lost as a result of the economy's relative or absolute productivity performance—a theme to which we return in the following paragraphs. Moreover, as Keynesians and monetarists agree, the equilibrium or the "natural" rate of unemployment depends primarily on the macroeconomic influences. Productivity growth itself has always automatically expanded purchasing power and effective demand, thus in the long run offsetting the reduction in required labor time per unit of output that rising labor productivity automatically brings with it.

Much of this is related to the view widely held among noneconomists that a persistent lag in a nation's productivity growth will place it at an increasing competitive disadvantage in international trade, and that it will thereby be excluded increasingly from its export markets, with devastating effects upon its export industries, its balance of payments, and the economic welfare of the community. Economic analysis suggests that much of this will not happen—that, if nothing else, a falling exchange rate for the laggard country caused by low foreign demand for its products (and therefore its currency) must ultimately bring its balance of payments into equilibrium, whatever the nation's productivity performance. In addition, since export markets depend heavily on comparative rather than absolute advantage, a country whose lagging industry is no longer able to compete will find itself able instead to export the products of agriculture or mining or some other sector of its economy. We shall turn presently to an examination of the process through which the adjustment is achieved, which will show the true social cost of a productivity lag. But first it will be useful to pause and see how well the economists' conclusions that have just been described stand up under comparison with the facts. Actually, the history turns out to have been more complex.

Figure 2.3, based on data provided in Matthews, Feinstein, and Odling-Smee (we shall refer to that set of authors as MFO) [1982, p. 435], shows what has happened over the course of a century to the share of world trade of six leading industrialized countries. Three countries with good to outstanding records of productivity growth—Japan, Italy, and Germany—all increased their shares substantially.[6] Germany's share rose some 40%, and Italy's increased more than 300%, while Japan's share of world exports of manufactures went from essentially zero at the end of the nineteenth century to 13% of the world total a century later. The United States, with its mediocre productivity growth record, first increased its share significantly and then fell again (though in 1973 it was still about $2\frac{1}{2}$ times as large as it was in the 1880s). However, the United Kingdom's share has fallen steadily and spectacularly from 43% of the world's total all the way down to 9% of the total in 1973. France is the notable exception to the

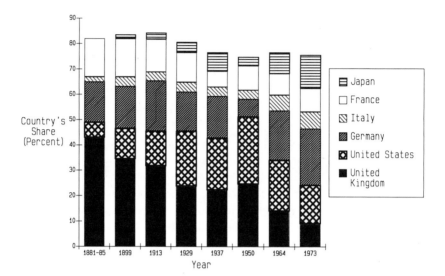

Figure 2.3
Share of world manufacturing exports, 1883–1973, 6 industrialized countries. Source:
Matthews, Feinstein, and Odling-Smee [1982, p. 435].

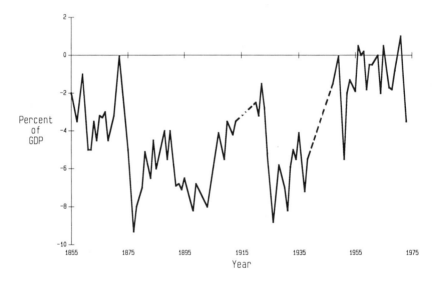

Figure 2.4
Ratio, for the United Kingdom, of balance of visible trade to gross domestic product
(GDP), 1855–1973. Source: Metthews, Feinstein, and Odling-Smee [1982, p. 443].

apparent link between productivity growth and the trend in manufacturing exports—despite its fine productivity record its share fell from 15% of the world's total to 9% during the century.[7] These data would seem to favor the popular view over that of the economists. The equilibrating forces and the law of comparative advantage apparently were unable to save the United Kingdom from the erosion of competitiveness resulting from the relative lag in its productivity growth.

But there is more to the story. First, though it may operate very slowly, the equilibrating mechanism has apparently not failed in the long run. Figure 2.4, adapted from MFO [1982, p. 443], shows that Britain's net exports of goods and services (the balance of visible trade) has certainly moved in its favor since the 1870s. True, part of the reason is that Great Britain lost a great deal of income that its foreign investments might have earned as a result of the two world wars, which could only be replaced by increased exports. But the figures certainly do not show a country increasingly unable to pay for its imports through its exports. Moreover, the *volume* of the United Kingdom's exports, despite their declining *share* of the world total, has risen spectacularly. As we see in table 2.1, between 1870 and 1979 the volume of British exports increased about tenfold, and from 1855 to 1973 U.K. exports of *goods* increased an astonishing 13 times (MFO [1982, p. 427]).

Nor has the United Kingdom been forced to deindustrialize internally. According to Maddison's [1982, p. 205] figures on the percent of the labor force employed in industry (defined as mining, construction, and manufacturing—as compared to agriculture and services), Britain declined from first place in the sample of 16 countries in 1870 to fourth place (behind Germany, Austria, and Switzerland) in 1979. But industry's share of employment in the United Kingdom was still 88% of that of the leader in this respect (Germany), and the United Kingdom continued ahead of such countries as Sweden, France, the United States, Belgium, and Japan.[8] If this is deindustrialization, it certainly is not very extreme.

Once again, we must come to the conclusion that there is a marked contrast between the relative and the absolute performance of the United Kingdom. In comparison with other countries its export record is miserable. However, in absolute terms it must be considered quite spectacular. These observations suggest that there is some truth both to the economists' view of the matter and the general public's interpretation. Yet, from figure 2.3, we see that there is, apparently, a significant (relative) sense in which lagging productivity *does* impede a nation's competitiveness in terms of *share* of world exports. Of course, Britain's long-run export handicap was not an absence of absolute productivity growth since, as we have seen, over the course of a century that growth has hardly been negligible. The problem for the United Kingdom was that productivity in other countries grew even faster.

There remains the question whether the decrease in *share* of world exports was actually severely damaging to the economic welfare of the British population. That is, if Germany, Japan, and Italy had not outpaced U.K. productivity growth and had consequently not increased their share of world trade at the United Kingdom's expense,[9] would an average British subject have been far better off economically? The easy conclusion that it would is disputed strongly by D. N. McCloskey [1981, p. 173−83] (at least for the period 1870−1913) in a thoughtful and well-reasoned paper. There are several considerations that underlie his conclusions. First, since British employment and output have certainly not fallen in the long run, whatever British production did not end up as exports must have become available for domestic consumption and investment. The *net* loss on this score may well have been negligible. To this we must add the fact that growing productivity in Japan, Germany, and elsewhere means that a British subject can import cameras, TV sets, and any other items far more cheaply in real terms than if the productivity of those countries had stagnated. Moreover, there must have been an upward shift in the demand for British goods by those countries because of their rising incomes. McCloskey concludes that for this period (and it seems equally plausible for later periods as well) the detrimental effect on the British standard of living of the productivity record of its industrialized rivals has been greatly exaggerated.[10]

2.4 The Mechanism of Equilibration and the True Cost of Productivity Lag

At first glance the economists' conclusions that have just been described seem too good to be true. There would appear to be no real penalty for the productivity laggard. In the long run such an economy will suffer no unemployment that it would have avoided otherwise. Despite its relative inefficiency in the use of its inputs it will be able to compete successfully on the international marketplace, and consequently, any initial deficit in its balance of payments will not long persist. With such apparently optimistic conclusions, why need anyone ever worry about a nation's failure to keep up in its productivity growth? That is hardly the sort of conclusion one would expect from the dismal science, and predictably, therefore, it is only the beginning of the story. As in all matters in economics, nothing ever turns out to be free; and here, indeed, the cost of the cure turns out to be very high even in comparison with the dangers of the disease. As we shall see now, a nation pays for its poor productivity performance by transforming itself into a supplier of *cheap labor*, that is, by offering low living standards as its chief attraction as a place to do business, and as the primary reason for the competitiveness of its exports.

To see how this comes about we must quickly review the pertinent elements of the equilibration process in international trade. While international trade theory has shown that the process involves far more options and more subtleties, the following simplified summary entails no basic misrepresentations. When a country persistently lags behind others in terms of productivity growth, the prices of inputs such as fuel, raw materials, and capital that are purchased by all economies on the international marketplace will continue to be more or less the same for everyone. Only the prices of inputs that do not readily move from one country to another can change their relative levels materially. Suppose, however, that wages and the other prices of internationally immobile inputs in the laggard country at first resist reduction. Then the exports of the productivity laggard will inevitably become more expensive in comparison with the economies that are consistently more successful in reducing the quantities of input they use per unit of output, i.e., in increasing their productivity. The principles of supply and demand will then take their toll. The quantities of the laggard's goods sold on foreign markets will fall, and that country's own residents will buy a larger share of their total purchases from abroad.

Inevitably, the next step will be a decline in foreign demand for the laggard's currency, as foreigners find that they no longer have to make payments to that country as large as before. As always, declining demand for any item (and a nation's currency is no exception) means that the price of the item will fall. That is another way of saying that the exchange rate of the productivity laggard must ultimately but automatically decline, and it must decline sufficiently to restore competitiveness to the laggard's exports. That is the surface layer of the story—the one that is relatively familiar. It does suffice to show how the international monetary mechanism, acting on the market's valuation of the money of the productivity laggard, will eventually ensure that its exports will be competitive, that its foreign trade balance does balance out, and that its labor force will not be beset by chronic unemployment.

But there are (at least) two other layers to this story, and those parts of the story are considerably less comforting than the first. The second layer of the story is the real wages portion. Here it is only necessary to recognize that a fall in a nation's exchange rate is correctly interpretable as a disguised means to cut the real wages of its labor force. For example, a 50% cut of the exchange rate of the dollar relative, say, to the Swiss franc means that an American worker must work twice as long as before to pay for a pound of Swiss cheese. The same must be true of all other commodities imported from countries against whose currency the dollar has fallen. Looked at the other way, what that amounts to is a fire sale of all American products, *including labor,* that are exported, directly or indirectly. That is the true secret of the exchange rate "cure" of the symptoms of productivity lag. If the laggard's workers can no longer compete, as they used to by producing twice as much per hour as a foreign worker, they can only continue to compete by accepting a cut in their relative wages. A fall in the country's exchange rate only softens the blow by concealing the fact that a fall in the purchasing power of wages has in fact occurred.[11] Of course, the secret will emerge eventually, as it has in England, where every worker is aware that wages are now below those on the continent of Europe. But by then the damage is done.[12]

The third layer of this unhappy tale is not much better. Once a productivity laggard country finds itself reduced to the status of purveyor of cheap labor, it must find that its comparative advantage pattern has also been modified. That is to say, it will no longer specialize in the same industries as before. Instead of being able to compete most effectively in technologically advanced industries with a high capital-labor ratio (in which an economy with highly productive labor and high wages does best), it will find itself best fitted to hold its own in industries that make heavy use of large quantities of cheap labor and relatively little capital. The reason is obvious, but the nature of the true social cost is not. Here the primary social cost is the transition, the process by which the labor force is moved out of the industries that have lost their comparative advantage into the industries that now replace them. For some, the resulting unemployment will be temporary, if nevertheless sometimes very painful. But for older workers, and for those with highly specialized skills that are rendered useless and unrecoverable by the shifting of the nation's industries, the loss is incalculable, and it may never be made up.

Of course, the main implication of what has just been said is that productivity growth *is* beneficial. For one thing, if its pace is sufficient, it prevents many of the problems that have just been described.[13] That is the other side—the sanguine obverse of the preceding discussion. But productivity growth does much more than this. For one thing, it provides the resources, and smooths the political process, for the activities undertaken to improve the status of society generally. Education, environmental protection, widespread public health care, income redistribution programs, and a variety of other activities that will readily occur to the reader are most easily financed out of the yields of productivity growth. This is particularly so because, in an economy whose productivity is growing, an increase in outlays on such social services can be paid for entirely out of the annual increment in national output that productivity contributes, hence entailing no offsetting reduction in private disposable incomes and expenditures. It is precisely for this reason that widespread public expenditures on universal education, on the environment, for redistribution, etc., are a product of the modern era, and why the world's poorer countries still are far behind in those arenas.

2.5 Productivity Growth: Absolute and Relative and the Position of the Leader

Success in productivity growth can be judged in either absolute or relative terms, sometimes with very different results. The case of the United Kingdom again dramatizes the point. As we know, Great Britain is generally taken to be the outstanding example of failure in productivity performance among industrialized free-market economies. Yet, taken either in historical term or evaluated absolutely, so far as one can, its performance must surely be judged to have been exemplary. The last 11 decades coincide roughly with the period since Britain began to lose its economic leadership.[14] Yet during that interval it managed to increase its exports by more than 900%, its output (GDP) per work hour nearly 600%, and its per-capita output by over 300%—surely an accomplishment that would have been envied profoundly, indeed scarcely believed, in any earlier century. A fourfold rise in living standards and a 45% cut in annual working hours is no mean absolute feat, and undoubtedly constitutes a demanding standard for the future to live up to. The fact that the world nevertheless judges the British performance of the past century to have been a failure indicates that envy and the relative standards that go with it remain powerful motivations, even in societies of unprecedented abundance.

However, an important third element also enters the matter. The emphasis that has widely been given to England's loss of the world's economic *leadership* implies more than just a relative standard of evaluation. The world contains many competitive economic activities in which only a single contestant is awarded the status of victor, and even if the performance of the runner-up is very close to the winner's, that offers little consolation to the second-best country. Put another way, in such an undertaking, a participant may prefer to turn in a performance that is rather mediocre, if that of every rival is even more so, than to perform exceedingly well absolutely but nevertheless be beaten by a hair by some competitor. The fact that since the 1830s Belgium's per-capita GDP seems usually to have been only negligibly below that of the succession of world economic leaders gave Belgium not even the slightest claim on the leadership position. As in competitive games or military victory, world economic leadership goes to the country that is second to none in performance. In the West, undisputed leadership was held by northern Italy in the thirteenth to sixteenth centuries, by the Dutch republic in the seventeenth and part of the eighteenth, by Britain during the end of the eighteenth and most of the nineteenth, and since then by the United States.

The advantages of leadership to the general public are not entirely clear. Perhaps first among them is its stimulus to national pride. It also undoubtedly makes some contribution to military strength, though in the case of Italy it did not suffice to prevent French invasions and Hapsburg domination, while for the Netherlands it did not permit clear naval victory over England. Often, economic leadership has served as a temptation into imperialist adventures that are now widely judged often to have constituted a net drain upon the economy. However, our purpose here is not to judge the value of any or all of the three goals—absolute prosperity, relative prosperity, and economic leadership. Here we want only to distinguish among them and to note that while productivity growth is an essential requirement for successful pursuit of any of the three, the pattern of growth that is called for does differ distinctly from one objective to another. Later, in chapter 8, we shall return to the records of the former world leaders to see what we can infer from them. For now, we need merely note again that loss of leadership and a fall in relative productivity standing is by no means incompatible with sharp growth in living standards and rapidly rising absolute prosperity.

2.6 Concluding Comment

The central implication of this chapter's discussion is that in the long run productivity growth can make an enormous contribution to living standards, and that there is no substitute for productivity growth in this respect. There are many other economic problems for which productivity policy offers no promising solutions. But what productivity growth has accomplished for conditions of living since the beginning of the Industrial Revolution makes it a matter of highest priority in terms of human welfare.

The next chapter undertakes to impart substance to the bare statistics that have been presented here to describe the spectacular accomplishments of the preceding century.

Notes

1. A growth rate of 0.2% per year between 700 and 1700 would mean that real GDP per capita at the earlier date must have been about one-tenth of the figure for India today.

2. Isolated bits of evidence permit us to go somewhat further, confirming that productivity did in fact grow, at least in particular fields of endeavor. For example, according to Hodges [1982, p. 99], archaeologists have found enough medieval ships to estimate their evolution in size and rowing arrangements. The evidence suggests that between 700 and 1000 AD their typical cargo capacity rose from 10 to 30 tons, while the number of rowers per ship declined rather steadily from a little more than 30 to something below 10. This amounts to a rate of growth in direct labor productivity of about 0.8% per year.

3. "The early machines, complicated though they were to contemporaries, were nevertheless modest, rudimentary, wooden contrivances which could be built for surprisingly small sums. A forty-spindle jenny cost perhaps £6 in 1772; scrubbing and carding machines cost £1 for each inch of roller width; a clubbing billy with thirty spindles cost £10.10s" (Landes [1969, pp. 64–65]). This suggests at least the possibility (pointed out by Landes) that part of the reason investment was low is that not very much capital may have been required.

4. This observation does not quite seem to square with Feinstein's [1972, pp. 82–94] estimates, which indicate that while output per worker in the United Kingdom increased 0.2% per year between 1761 and 1800, between 1801 and 1830 the growth rate leaped up to 1.4% per annum. He estimates that total factor productivity behaved similarly. However, between 1801 and 1810 total annual investment fell to 10% of GDP, in comparison with its 14% rate in the immediately preceding and succeeding periods.

5. For a systematic study that rejects the deindustrialization thesis for postwar America, see Lawrence [1984].

6. Perhaps the common thread is found in the old joke that the way for a country to solve its economic problems is to wage war against the United States—and lose.

7. We should note here that a number of capable observers take the view, associated with Kaldor and Verdoorn, that the direction of causation runs the other way from that under discussion here—that lagging exports impeded productivity

growth rather than the reverse. There is a substantial literature suggesting that lagging exports reduce the opportunity to turn over capital stock and reduce pressures upon capacity that stimulate productivity advance. The other side of the coin is the fact that growing exports lead to an expanding market, new investment, and the introduction of new technology. For a brief summary discussion, see MFO [1982, pp. 533–534].

8. Here, too, there has been a considerable narrowing of range. Among member countries of the Organization for Economic Cooperation and Development (OECD) in 1870 (with data for four countries missing), the share of workers in industry extended from 9.7% (Finland) to 42.3 (United Kingdom), with several countries near 20% and several in the high 30s. By 1979 that range ran only from a low of 28.7% (Canada) to high of 44% (Germany).

9. If the gains of those three countries and that of the United States were eliminated and instead reverted to the United Kingdom, the United Kingdom share of 1973 world manufactures exports would, *ceteris paribus*, have been almost as large as it was a century earlier.

10. "For reasonable values (of the parameters of the estimation model) the result is the same: The gain of income (in the U.K.) from deindustrializing the rest of the world in 1913 would have been remarkably small ... Britain's income 'depended' not on the great changes in the international economy of the 19th century, but on the race of technological change and enterprise at home" (McCloskey [1981, pp. 181–182]). However, one reader asks, "Has McCloskey drawn the right counterfactual in this analysis? Could British growth have been fast enough to support income growth and capital formation elsewhere, avoiding the backwash effect of 'deindustrialization' of the rest of the world?"

11. It is, unfortunately, easy to confirm from recent U.S. experience that cheapening of (American) labor can indeed be forced upon the country when it undergoes a significant decline in the exchange rate of its currency,—i.e., it is no mere theoretical possibility. The approximately 50% fall in the exchange rate of the dollar that has occurred since 1985 has been greeted with considerable satisfaction by some politicians and journalists, who hail it as the salvation of U.S. competitiveness and as the prospective rectifier of the huge American trade deficit. But at what a price this has been achieved. It means that Japan and Germany can now acquire U.S. labor time or its products at about half the price it paid for them in 1984. That is, indeed, a cheapening of American labor to those countries. Nor has it failed to have a detrimental effect on real U.S. earnings. Since imports constitute about 15% of this country's GNP, it follows that, other things remaining equal, the 50% fall in the value of the dollar is sufficient to cut an average American's real income by some 7% or more. Incidentally, it is at least plausible that no major role in this matter has been played by U.S. productivity performance at all. It has been argued, for example, that the main underlying cause is the enormous government deficit incurred during the Reagan administration. Thus, the fact that real wages at the end of the 1980s are hardly higher than they were in the 1960s does not necessarily mean that they have embarked on a course of long-term stagnancy or decline.

12. Of course, English workers may now shift their consumption patterns away from the more expensive foreign goods to the cheaper domestic goods. Yet this is tantamount to a reduction in their real wage, since they are now forced to accept a less desirable basket of consumer goods.

13. It does not, unfortunately, eliminate all of those problems. Extraordinarily rapid productivity growth, like its opposite, is also likely to modify considerably a nation's pattern of comparative advantage, once again leading to a shift in labor force and investments among industries, thereby leading to all the painful transition problems that have just been noted.

14. The entire matter is a subject of spirited dispute both among the economic historians themselves and between the historians and cliometricians (who define themselves as students of economic history with a training in formal economic analysis). Not only are there considerable differences about the date at which "it" occurred, but there is not even agreement about what it was that took place at whatever date it may have been. However, a consensus seems to be emerging to the effect that "the climacteric" entailed no actual decline in GNP, GDP, GNP per capita, productivity, or whatever the relevant measures may have been, but that there was only a decline in some or all of their growth rates. While some observers (e.g., Coppock [1956], Aldcroft [1964], and MFO [1982]) place it in the 1870s, Phelps Brown and Handfield-Jones [1952] take it to have occurred in the 1890s, and McCloskey [1981, pp.94–110] believes that (if it occurred at all) it was later still. There is even more debate about the role of entrepreneurship in the matter.

3

A Century of Productivity Improvement: Revolution in American Living Standards

... the frontier has often been described as one big rural slum saved only by the fact that the open spaces were not far away....
Furnas [1969, p. 261]

3.1 Introduction

In the last 100 years American economic growth and productivity gains have been so great that they elude intuitive grasp. The average American's scale of living has risen to a level undreamed of a century ago. In the mid-1800s U.S. per-capita output has been estimated to have been similar to that in such present-day less developed countries as Honduras and the Philippines, and slightly below that in China, Bolivia, and Egypt. Since then the real value of the goods and services available to an average American is calculated to have risen by an astonishing 700%.[1] These developments helped an extraordinarily high percentage of Americans to achieve what in the nineteenth century would have been considered an incredible standard of living. The amenities of life that almost all of us take for granted today—including electricity, indoor plumbing, safe public water and sewage systems, instant mass communications, access to technologically sophisticated medical care, a remarkable variety of fresh and ingeniously packaged foods from around the nation and the world, free public education, low infant mortality, and long life expectancy—were all virtually absent a century ago.[2]

In this chapter we seek to describe in some detail how economic growth transformed American life.[3] By comparing today's living conditions with those that prevailed in the nineteenth century (and earlier), we hope to bring to life the striking but abstract statistics on productivity and output gains discussed in this book. We shall touch on a broad range of activities and conditions—including housing, diet, working conditions, incomes and family budgets, public health, longevity and physical stature, transportation, education, leisure time, and consumer goods—and draw upon a wide variety of sources of evidence—vital statistics in U.S. Census reports, personal oral histories, hypothetical "typical" budgets produced by newspapers and magazines, genealogical records and mail-order catalogues, diaries and journals of foreign visitors, and broad-ranging sociological and historical studies.

Of course, most readers are aware, as we were when we embarked on this research, that the American standard of living has improved greatly since the 1800s. Still, the enormous magnitude of the change may come as a surprise. Nineteenth-century America of popular literature and film is often shown in a romantic light, peopled by robust, hardworking, but ultimately prosperous pioneers, or members of polite Victorian society in the established towns and cities of the East, the picture marred only occasionally by glimpses of poverty in the backwoods and tenements. But for much of the nineteenth century the reality of life for the great majority of the population was unrelieved drudgery and deprivation. Average incomes were abysmally low (far below any modern standard of poverty), providing only the bare necessities of life. The state of medical care and public health was appalling—great epidemics of deadly disease were commonplace and infant mortality cruelly high—and the average life expectancy of a person born midcentury was only 40 years. Cities were unsanitary, crowded places where smokestack industries were beginning to foul the air. In the countryside people lived and worked in conditions that would not have been unfamiliar in the Middle Ages. Most families were housed in places affording no privacy or any of the most basic amenities. Men, women, and, often, children worked long hours to secure this scale of life, and vacations or retirement for the elderly were unheard of. As we shall see, the reality of the change in American life in the last century is even more startling than the statistics on economic growth suggest.

3.2 Life in the Nineteenth Century: Overview

In the mid-1800s the United States, with a total residential population of about 32 million, was predominantly a rural, agricultural nation. Fully half the workforce was involved in the most basic task of feeding the population (Beniger [1986]). Only one-eighth of the population lived in "cities" of 8,000 or more; 44% of the country's citizens lived on farms, and perhaps half of those dwelt in log cabins of one or two rooms (Martin [1942,

p. 106]). Today, in contrast, less than 4% of the labor force is employed in agriculture and nearly three-quarters of the population live in areas classified as urban (U.S. Department of Commerce, Bureau of the Census [1982, pp. 21, 375]).

There seems no better way to get a sense of the pace and scale of life in the 1800s than to read some first-hand accounts from that time. In this chapter, we present a few such descriptions of nineteenth-century American life. In the account that follows, living conditions of a rural "mechanic's"[4] family in Pennsylvania during the latter quarter of the nineteenth century through the early part of the twentieth are described by a daughter, Nettie, in an oral history compiled by Peggy Heim [1985]:

[The family] lived far out in the country [where] the nearest villages were 7 and 10 miles away in opposite directions [and] neighbors lived far apart. They built their house by hand and made most of their own tools [and had to dig their well by hand, using pick and shovel].... The father made his livelihood as a skilled laborer, and the family had 16 acres for a garden, a field each of wheat and corn, and some fruit trees. They had no horse, no carriage, no wagon; there was no public transportation.... The children walked 5 miles each way ... to the one-room school house. The father walked 7 miles each way to pay his taxes.... They raised pigs and chickens [and] shot rabbits, squirrels, game birds, and deer to increase their meat supply.... They had to borrow a horse to plow the field; the rest of the [farm] work they did by hand—with such hand-made tools as spade, hoe, clod-hopper, hand-pushed tiller, hand-pulled sled, and wheelbarrow. Their house had no indoor plumbing. Water had to be pumped, carried by bucket to where they used it, and carried out again after use for disposal. They dipped their hot water from a bucket on the stove. They washed their hands under the pump, and washed themselves in a basin of water. A more thorough basin-washing was their bath. The house had no closets. Clothes lay in hand-made chests or hung on wooden pegs from doors and walls. Since they had only a few changes of clothes, a few pegs each sufficed. They warmed the house with a wood stove, which also provided the heat for cooking. Except for the room with the stove, the rooms were cold in winter. They sat, cooked, ate and worked in one room; and the five of them slept in another. For their firewood, they had to chop down a tree in the near-by forest, drag it in on a hand-pulled sled, chop it into stove lengths, stack it, and then carry the wood into the house when they wanted to use it. They had to grow or raise almost all their own food or find it in the wild. They raised many root crops, like potatoes, turnips, and beets, or other vegetables, like cabbage, which kept well in a root cellar over the winter. To have additional food for winter, they spent many hours preserving fruits and vegetables. They dried grapes and sliced apples for pies, peas and beans for stews and soups.... In the late winter and early spring they dug dandelion roots and crowns, gathered their tender leaves, and cooked greens of wintercress, pokeweed and wild mustard. They made their tea from the dried leaves of wild plants—mint, comfrey, and pennyroyal. They ground dandelion roots, which when boiled made a passable native coffee. The daughters had

Table 3.1
Average income for 397 Massachusetts families of wage earners in 15 cities and 21 towns, 1874–1875

Average money income ($)	763
Average family size	5.1
Average expenditures for goods and services ($)	
Subsistence (food)[a]	427
Clothing	106
Rent	117
Fuel	44
Sundry expenses[b]	44

Source: U.S. Department of Commerce, Bureau of the Census [1975, pp. 320, 322], which cites Massachusetts Bureau of Statistics of Labor, *Sixth Annual Report*, March 1875, Public Document No. 31, pp. 221–354, 372, 373, 441. Figures are in current dollars.
a. Includes kerosene.
b. Some specified sundries included furniture, carpets, books and papers, societies and religion, charity, sickness, care of parents, care of house, recreation, housegirl, travel to work, and life insurance.

to stop school after 8th grade; the family couldn't pay the board and public school fees in town. They could read and comprehend quite well—though they had little around to read.

Rural life in the 1800s, then, was not easy. Nevertheless, life in urban America was often even worse. As Heim writes in her account of Nettie's life [1985, p.11], "They worked hard, and their life was far from easy. But compared with factory workers and day laborers of that era, their level of living and comfort was noticeably higher than their urban counterparts, for they had outdoor space, healthful environment, a varied and sufficient diet, diverse activities, and some control over their use of time and the way they expended effort. If they had had no land, had been unable to raise pigs and chickens, and had only a miniature garden, their life would have been far less satisfactory."

3.3   Family Budgets: Subsistence in the Nineteenth Century

In the mid-nineteenth century most American families spent nearly every dollar on the basic requirements of life: food, clothing, and shelter, obviously leaving little for medical care, education, entertainment, and so on. For example, a survey in 1874–1875 of wage-earners' families in urban Massachusetts (table 3.1) found that an average family of five spent fully

Table 3.2
Workingman's budget, Philadelphia, 1851

Item of expenditure	Amount ($)
Butcher's meat (2 lb. a day)	72.80
Flour ($6\frac{1}{2}$ bbl. a year)	32.50
Butter (2 lb. a week)	32.50
Potatoes (2 pk. a week)	26.00
Sugar (4 lb. a week)	16.64
Coffee and tea	13.00
Milk	7.28
Salt, pepper, vinegar, starch, soap, soda, yeast, cheese, eggs	20.80
Total expenditures for food	221.52
Rent	156.00
Coal (3 tons a year)	15.00
Charcoal, chips, matches	5.00
Candles and oil	7.28
Household articles (wear, tear, and breakage)	13.00
Bedclothes and bedding	10.40
Wearing apparel	104.00
Newspapers	6.24
Total annual expenditures	538.44

Source: Martin [1942, p. 394], who cites *New York Daily Tribune*, May 27, 1851. Figures are in current dollars.

91% of its income on these needs. In another budget from 1851, reproduced by Edgar Martin [1942], the "typical" Philadelphia workingman's family spent 41% of its budget on food alone, and 97% on food, clothing, and shelter (see table 3.2). A "Standard Workingman's Budget" for New York City in 1853 (table 3.3) devoted 46% to food and 92% to the combined needs of food, clothing, and shelter.

In contrast, as early as 1950 an average urban family of 3.4 persons was spending 31% of its after-tax income on food, and only 68% on food, clothing, and shelter (table 3.4). The Bureau of Labor Statistics' hypothetical average budgets for lower-, intermediate-, and higher-income families in 1978 devoted, respectively, 58%, 54%, and 51% of family income to food, clothing, and shelter (see table 3.5), and as table 3.6 shows, between 1888 and 1961 average family expenditures on food and drink fell from 44% to 27%.

Table 3.3
Standard workingman's budget, New York City, 1853

Item of expenditure	Amount ($)
Groceries	273
Rent	100
Clothing, bedding, etc.	132
Furnishings	20
Fuel	18
Lights	10
Taxes, water, commutation	5
Physicians' and druggists' charges	10
Traveling	12
Newspapers, postage, library fees	10
Church, charity, etc.	10
Total annual expenditures	600

Source: Martin [1942, p. 395], who cites *The New York Times*, November 8, 1853. Figures are in current dollars. Martin writes that even these minimal budgets "represent a scale of living which must have been out of reach of the great majority of working-class families" [p. 396].

In New York City in the mid-1800s not even 1% of the population earned as much as $850 (roughly the equivalent of $7,000 1980 dollars). In most parts of the country the average laborer earned only $250–400 a year (or about $2,000–3,500 in 1980 dollars), while skilled workmen did very well to make $700 a year (less than $6,000 in 1980 dollars).[5] Even the highest of these incomes is below the U.S. government's official 1980 poverty line of $8,400 (for a family of four persons), not taking account of all the noncash benefits such as food stamps, Medicaid, and public housing that most low-income persons receive today, all of which were absent in the 1800s.[6]

3.4   Food Consumption

These days, not only do Americans spend a much smaller proportion of their incomes on food, but they have a vast cornucopia of food products from which to choose. Today's supermarket, with its 8,000 items (Lebergott [1984, p. 68]), includes fresh fruits and vegetables transported across the country year-round, frozen, canned, and freeze-dried produce, and other items packaged to assure safety and wholesomeness.

Table 3.4
Consumption expenditures of 7,007 city wage- and clerical-worker families of 2 or more persons, 1950

Average annual income after taxes ($)	3,923
Average family size	3.4
Average expenditures for current consumption ($)	
Food	1,205
Alcoholic beverages	70
Tobacco	79
Housing	415
Fuel, light and refrigeration	163
Household operation	155
Furnishing and equipment	278
Clothing	453
Transportation	
Automobile	472
Other	69
Medical care	200
Personal care	91
Recreation	177
Reading	34
Education	17
Miscellaneous	47

Source: U.S. Department of Commerce, Bureau of the Census [1975, p. 320]. Figures are in current dollars.

In the mid-nineteenth century low incomes, local weather conditions, crop cycles, an almost complete lack of refrigeration, and very limited transport of goods bound a very large part of the population to a minimal and nutritionally inferior variety of foods—potatoes, lard,[7] cornmeal, and salt pork were consumed in large quantities, particularly outside the population centers. Most travelers' accounts of meals in nineteenth-century America lament the ubiquity of some kind of one-pot stew. Ruth Schwartz Cowan [1983, page 38] writes, in a historical study of household practices,

That meal, the stew, symbolizes the very simple standard of living that most Americans (and, indeed, most Europeans) maintained in the centuries prior to industrialization. Everyday meals were uncomplicated and monotonous; much of the food that people ate was served without preparatory effort or with minimal cooking. Diets lacked variety, and standards of cleanliness were not what they are

Table 3.5
Annual budgets for urban families of 4, at three levels of living, autumn 1978

	Lower	Intermediate	Higher
Total budget ($)	11,546	18,622	27,420
Total family consumption ($)	9,391	14,000	19,225
Food	3,574	4,609	5,806
Housing	2,233	4,182	6,345
Transportation	856	1,572	2,043
Clothing	847	1,209	1,768
Personal care	301	403	570
Medical care	1,065	1,070	1,116
Other family consumption[a]	515	956	1,578
Other items[b]	502	810	1,365
Taxes and deductions	1,654	3,811	6,830
Social security and disability	719	1,073	1,091
Personal income taxes	935	2,738	5,739

Source: U.S. Bureau of Labor Statistics [1980, p. 44]. Figures are in current dollars.
a. Includes average costs for reading, recreation, tobacco products, alcoholic beverages, costs for education, and miscellaneous expenditures.
b. Includes allowances for gifts and contributions, life insurance and occupational expenses.

today.... There were, of course, a few people who knew what it was to ... eat a meal that consisted of more than one course; but there were very, very few such people, and they were all very rich. The poor, and even the middling comfortable, could not aspire to such creature comforts.... Cleanliness of body and variety of foodstuffs were perquisites only of the very rich in ages past.

Still, when compared with other countries and earlier ages, nineteenth-century Americans were fortunate in the foods they consumed. Cowan lists the foods that ordinary Americans ate before the twentieth century: "Bread, cheese, butter, porridge, eggs, raw fruits and vegetables in season, preserved fruits and vegetables out of season ... all of it washed down by beer, cider, milk, or coffee (rarely water as that was often undrinkable)" (p. 21).

Moreover, by the mid-1870s things were beginning to change, at least for the upper-middle class. The noted Philadelphia Centennial Exposition of 1876 publicized a variety of new food processing techniques: canning, mechanical refrigeration, machines for popping corn, condensing milk, making ice cream, and peeling apples, all of which, according to the Smithsonian Institution [1986], "caused sensations." The commentary goes on to add that "the simple and unvaried American diet based on seasonally and

Table 3.6
Consumption expenditures of city wage- and clerical-worker families of 2 and more persons, 1888–1891 to 1960–1961

	1960–1961	1950	1934–1936	1917–1919	1901	1888–1991
Families covered (number)	19,455[a]	5,994	14,469	12,096	11,156	2,562
Average family size (persons)	3.6	3.3	3.6	4.9	4.0	3.9
Average money income before taxes (current dollars)	6,763	4,299	1,518	1,505	651	573
Money income after personal taxes (in constant 1950 dollars[b])	4,877	4,005	2,659	2,408	1,914	1,793
Average outlays (1950 dollars[b]) Current outlays for goods and services, total	4,604	4,076	2,564	2,163	1,817	1,671
Food and drink	1,297	1,335	1,030	854	952	797
Clothing	541	473	309	343	—	—
Shelter (current expense)	539	448	356	252	—	—
Fuel, light, refrigeration, and water	207	153	158	126	—	—
Housefurnishings and equipment	297	281	119	109	—	—
Household operation	225	167	80	479[c]	—	—
Automobile purchase and operation	635	457	150		—	—
Other transportation	50	81	57		—	—
Medical care	243	213	88		—	—
Personal care	130	93	55		—	—
Recreation	194	191	67		—	—

Table 3.6 (continued)

	1960–1961	1950	1934–1936	1917–1919	1901	1888–1991
Reading	34	36	27		—	—
Education	42	19	11		—	—
Tobacco	88	80	46		—	—
Miscellaneous goods and services	82	49	11		—	—

Source: U.S. Department of Commerce, Bureau of the Census [1975, p. 322].

a. Estimated number of families, in thousands, represented by sample.

b. The cost of living index developed by Paul Douglas [1926, p. 22] was used to convert the 1888–1891 and 1901 expenditures into 1950 dollars. The Consumer Price Index of the Bureau of Labor Statistics was used for the surveys thereafter.

c. Total average outlays for last 10 categories in 1917–1919.

locally available foods was revolutionized almost overnight as people at the exposition were introduced to unusual foods from far away places that could be preserved and shipped economically, with little risk of spoilage, to local market."

Even before the Exposition most Americans undoubtedly had reason to feel that they lived in a land of unprecedented abundance, since that one-pot stew was quite sure to be there every day.[8] For many centuries in Europe most of the population spent nearly half the food budget on breadstuffs (for example, in 1790 in France, according to Robert Palmer [1964, p. 49], "The price of bread, even in normal times, in the amount needed for a man with a wife and three children, was half as much as the daily wage of common labor"), and for most of them the bread was of what was considered a very inferior variety. Still more commonly, it took the form of gruel (in good years)—what we could think of today as a thin, cooked breakfast cereal. Gruel was consumed in life-sustaining quantities, but there were many years when even gruel was unavailable. Indeed, famine continued to threaten Europe until the beginning of the nineteenth century, and earlier had constituted a normal fact of existence. Fernand Braudel [1979, volume I, pp. 73–75, footnotes omitted, Braudel's emphasis] writes,

A few overfed rich do not alter the rule.... Cereal yields were poor; two consecutive bad harvests spelt disaster.... Any national calculation shows a sad story. France, by any standards a privileged country, is reckoned to have experienced 10 *general* famines during the tenth century; 26 in the eleventh; 2 in the twelfth; 4 in the fourteenth; 7 in the fifteenth; 13 in the sixteenth; 11 in the seventeenth and 16 in the eighteenth. While one cannot guarantee the accuracy of this eighteenth-century calculation, the only risk it runs is of over-optimism, because it omits the hundreds and hundreds of *local* famines.... They did not always coincide with more widespread disasters.

The same could be said of any country in Europe. In Germany, famine was a persistent visitor to the towns and the flatlands. Even when the easier times came, in the eighteenth and nineteenth centuries, catastrophes could still happen.... famine struck Bavaria, and moved beyond its frontiers in 1816–17: on 5 August 1817, the city of Ulm celebrated with thanksgiving the return to normal with the new harvest....

It would be rash to conclude that the towns, habitual grumblers, were the sole victims of these acts of God. They had warehouses, reserves, corn exchanges, purchases from abroad—in fact, a whole policy directed towards future contingencies. Paradoxically the countryside sometimes experienced far greater suffering. The peasants lived in a state of dependence on merchants, towns and nobles, and had scarcely any reserves of their own. They had no solution in case of famine except to turn to the town where they crowded together, begging in the streets and often dying in public squares, as in Venice and Amiens in the sixteenth century.

The towns soon had to protect themselves against these regular invasions, which were not purely by beggars from the surrounding areas but by positive armies of the poor, sometimes from very far afield. Beggars from distant provinces appeared in the fields and streets of the town(s) ... starving, clothed in rags and covered with fleas and vermin.

In sum, the American's monotonous one-pot stew, while a far cry from today's widespread variety, was an incredible improvement over what had almost always been available to the bulk of the population before.

3.5   Housing

The housing story is similar to that of food. The end of the nineteenth century was a midpoint, far worse than today, but far better than that in earlier Europe. Thus, for example, in the seventeenth century (Braudel [1979, pp. 284−286]),

... in Paris, in the suburbs of Saint-Marcel and even Saint-Antoine, only a few craftsmen-joiners were comfortably off; in Le Mans and Beauvais the weavers lived in penury. But in Pescara on the Adriatic, a small town with about a thousand inhabitants, an inquiry in 1564 revealed that three-quarters of the families in the town, who had come from the nearby mountains or from the Balkans, were virtually homeless, living in makeshift shelters (what we should call shanty-towns). And yet this was in a town which, although small, had its fortress, garrison, fairs, harbour, salt works and was, after all, situated in Italy in the second half of the sixteenth century when it was linked with the Atlantic and the wealth of Spain. In the very rich town of Genoa, the homeless poor sold themselves as galley slaves every winter....

The poor in the towns and countryside of [Europe] lived in a state of almost complete deprivation. Their furniture consisted of next to nothing, at least before the eighteenth century, when a rudimentary luxury began to spread.... Inventories made after death, which are reliable documents, testify almost invariably to the general destitution. Apart from a very small number of well-to-do peasants, the furniture of the day laborer and the small farmer in Burgundy even in the eighteenth century was identical in its poverty.... But before the eighteenth century, the same inventories mention only a few old clothes, a stool, a table, a bench, the planks of a bed, sacks filled with straw. Official reports for Burgundy between the sixteenth and the eighteenth centuries are full of "references to people [sleeping] on straw... with no bed or furniture" who were only separated "from the pigs by a screen."

In the United States in the second half of the nineteenth century things were better, but still quite primitive. The amenities of life in rural Illinois, Michigan and Minnesota in 1850 were described in one Midwesterner's reminiscences (Martin [1942, pp. 136−138]):

In the ruder cabins floors were made of [rough planks], in the better ones of evenly sawed oak boards (which in time shrank and left cracks which let in the cold air).... The clapboard roof of the cabin let snow sift in. The stone fireplace and hearth occupied a large part of one end of the cabin.... The one window contained six panes of glass, six by six inches, and the door was swung on wooden hinges and was fastened with a wooden latch and a leather string. The furniture included a little table with a Bible and an almanac on it, two beds, each with a huge feather tick and sheets and blankets and a prized counterpane and perhaps a trundle bed.... A large chest contained more bedclothing and some of the better wearing apparel. Meals were cooked on the stone hearth and over the fireplace.... The chief cooking utensil was a "spider"—a skillet with legs and with a heavy iron cover which held hot coals; other skillets were also used, placed directly on the fire.... Candles were made at home, in molds, and coarse cloth and carpets were woven at home on a loom. Outhouses were built with several rooms—a smoke-house, a room for rendering lard, rooms for soap-making, washing, and so on. People in that part of the country seldom took baths; when a bath was necessary they used a wooden tub.... In some cabins and houses there was furniture brought from the East; but usually split-bottomed chairs and homemade walnut or maple chests and bedsteads were the best the prairie could afford. In the more remote communities, at least, settlers were dependent for light upon "grease dips"—twisted woolen rags fastened to a button sunk in a saucer of melted grease.

Most of the homes that Frederick Olmstead saw on his travels in rural America in the mid-1800s "... were small houses of logs or loosely boarded frame construction, usually without glass windows. Some were built on stilts, and many of them were built with roofs projecting eight or ten feet beyond the wall; a part of the space thus formed could be enclosed to make a sort of room. The fireplace was usually at one end, of sticks and mud. Other travelers described the farmers' houses in much the same terms—no glass, no lighting except for the fireplace, the doors hung on gudgeons and fastened with wooden latches and strings of green hide, outside chimneys of the crudest construction. Furniture was scanty and homemade" (Martin [1942, p. 131]).

Living conditions in the tenements (that is, the slums) of urban America during the 1800s were truly abysmal. In New York City in the 1860s an average of six persons living in a single 10-by-12 room was common. In 1890 Jacob Riis wrote, of the lower Manhattan tenements, "It is said that nowhere in the world are so many people crowded together on a square mile as here. In [one seven-story tenement building] there were 58 babies and 38 children that were over five years of age.... In Essex Street two small rooms in a six-story tenement were made to hold a 'family' of father and mother, twelve children, and six boarders.... These are samples of the packing of the population" (Riis [1890, p. 77, 1957 edition]). The worst evils of these overcrowded slums were insufficient light and air, with narrow airshafts that conveyed foul air and disease and served as inflammatory flues when fire broke out; there were no private water closets or washing facilities in these buildings, and cellars and courtyards were foul.

For the better-off in towns and cities (a very small proportion of the population) life was, of course, much easier and the level of housing far superior.[9] By modern standards, however, it was still very crude. For example, even in the cities baths were rare. Obviously, no homes had electricity and few had gas. Fewer still had hot running water, and not even 2% had indoor toilets and cold running water. Boston, with a population of nearly 200,000 in 1860 had only 31,000 sinks, 4,000 baths, and 10,000 water closets (about half of which were extremely primitive affairs). New York City, population 630,000 in 1855, had only 1,400 baths and 10,000 water closets. Albany (population 62,000 in 1860) had in 1859 only 19 private baths and 160 water closets. Outdoor privies were the norm and baths, for the great majority, a luxury. Kerosene for lamps was just catching on, with most lamps lighted by lard oil, whale oil, and some coal oil (while most of the country was still lighted by homemade candles).[10]

Again, for contrast, we note that in 1980 the U.S. Census of Housing found that only 2.2% of American housing units (including private, single-family homes, apartments, trailers, and so on) lacked complete plumbing (defined officially as hot and cold piped water, a flush toilet, and a bathtub or shower, for the exclusive use of that housing unit), and only 4.5% were occupied by more than 1.01 persons per room (U.S. Department of Commerce, Bureau of the Census [1982, pp. 754–755]). Of the new, privately-owned, one-family houses built in 1981, fully 60% had three bedrooms, 46% had two bathrooms, and 65% central air conditioning (p. 748). And 99.9% of all American households owned an electric vacuum cleaner, toaster, radio, iron, coffeemaker, and television (89.8% owned a color television). 99.8% were equipped with electric refrigerators, 92.8% had electric mixers, 77% had electric washing machines, 68% had electric frypans, 63.6% had electric can openers, and 64% had electric blankets! (p. 758; figures are for 1979).

3.6 Clothing and Hygiene

As late as the mid-1800s almost all the clothing that Americans wore was handmade, though only in fairly remote regions and the poorest rural backwaters was cloth still handspun and handwoven. Over the course of the century factory production of cloth increased rapidly, and (spurred by the Civil War's demand for large quantities of uniforms in standard sizes and patterns) the production of factory-made clothing for men also expanded. Men's suits and overcoats were almost all factory-made by the late century, with women's and children's clothing still almost all handmade (except for women's heavy winter coats).

Of course, the wealthy few were outfitted in professionally hand-tailored clothing, and, indeed, well-to-to American women were sharply criticized abroad for their "extravagance" of dress. But the typical farmer made do with "... a pair of jeans or perhaps denim pantaloons [trousers], probably factory-made because they were so cheap, and a rough work shirt, possibly made by his wife or daughter. With these he probably wore a suit of flannel underwear, cotton or woolen hose, stout brogans, and a ... wool hat." His changes of clothing consisted of "... perhaps two or three shirts and as many pairs of socks, rarely an extra pair of pantaloons. In a day when cleanliness was not taken too seriously he didn't need to worry about what to wear when his shirt or drawers became soiled" (Martin [1942, p. 197]). A "poor white" girl glimpsed by a traveler in the South wore "a soiled, greasy, graying linsey-woolsey gown which was apparently her only garment" (Gilmore [1862, pp. 166, 170]). And the clothing of the children of the slaves in the South "... was like the annals of the poor, short and simple, merely a shirt which reached to the knees. Shoes and hats were useless encumbrances for [black children] in winter as well as in summer. Older Negroes received a new suit of clothes, two pairs of shoes, and a cheap hat each year...." (Martin [1942, pp. 201–202]).

In 1850 commercial laundries hardly existed; 40,000 women gave their occupation as laundresses in the 1860 census (Martin [1942, p. 215]). The latest in washday technology consisted of a revolving barrel turned by a handcrank, but most people still used a washboard to scrub their clothes, and ironed with heavy flatirons heated up on a stove. Most also made their own soap at home, and many recipes were available in the cookbooks of the time. In the mid-1800s any commercial manufacturing of soap was carried out by meatpacking enterprises, since a by-product of that industry was the fat necessary to make soap. In any event, as we have already noted, personal cleanliness was certainly not the obsession that it is among Americans today. The lack of indoor plumbing, unheated rooms in winter, few changes of clothing (and no easy way to clean them), plus the general poverty were all obstacles to the level of personal hygiene to which we are accustomed.[11] Even the relatively well-off readers of *Godey's Lady's Book* were admonished to beware of too many baths; the May 1860 issue summarized with approval an article from *Hall's Journal of Health*: Bathing in the evening was discouraged, but to bathe in the morning, briefly, and not oftener than once a week, was all right [volume 60, p. 464].

3.7   Nineteenth-Century Consumer Goods

As incomes rose over the course of the century Americans were able to purchase an ever-increasing variety of household conveniences and other consumer goods, including such items as the hand-driven washing machines just mentioned, water taps for indoor cisterns, egg beaters, pulley-driven butter churns, apple parers, double boilers, and so on. By the late 1800s mail-order department stores had begun to thrive; the Sears Roebuck and Montgomery Ward catalogues made it possible for Americans to order just about any of these household items.

Above all, these catalogues illustrate how much better off at least middle-class Americans were toward the end of the nineteenth century than anything that had been known in Europe in earlier centuries. They also offer a fascinating glimpse into the way of life then, showing what (at least a large portion of) the populace wore, how it traveled, what it read, how it spent leisure time and what amenities were available. For instance, in the 1895 Montgomery Ward catalogue only 4 pages are devoted to ready-made suits for ladies and children while 31 pages are packed with all manner of fabrics to be sewn by the housewife into the family's clothing, bed linens, and other household items. The 39-page book department advertises 3,000 titles, ranging from best sellers of the time to "How to Make and Use a Telephone" and "The Physical Life of Women." The optical goods department features a test-yourself chart to be held a certain distance from the eyes to determine which eyeglasses to order. There are "scientific" instruments such as the "Portable Electro-Medical Battery" to cure "paralysis, rheumatism, neuralgia, and all nervous diseases." Twenty-nine pages are devoted to saddlery and harnesses, and the largest department of the catalogue is Guns and Sporting Goods, with 30 of the 59 pages devoted to firearms and ammunition. Labor-saving devices for the household include hand-powered clothes wringers, self-adjusting carpet sweepers, ice boxes for refrigeration, and many hand- and animal-powered farm implements, including a sheep or dog-powered treadmill that powers a milk separator.

In tables 3.7A and 3.7B we present an unscientific, but illuminating, sampling of goods listed in the Sears Roebuck catalogues of 1908 and 1985. This small sample is sufficient to portray dramatically the differences

Table 3.7A
Items offered in the 1908 Sears Roebuck catalogue: a sample

Traveling trunks	Boil remedy
Hatmaking goods, trims, etc.	Blackberry cordial[b]
Games (checkers, ouija boards, dominoes, chess sets)	Quinine pills
Jokester articles	Methylene blue compound pills for gonorrhea
Dolls and toys	"Quick Death" bug killer
Chamber pots	Bed bug exterminator
Cuspidors	Hot water bottle
Butter ladles	Bust forms
Men's dogskin coats	Ladies', men's and children's shoes
Buffalo fur coats	Rubber footwear
Made-to-order men's suits	Leggings
Imported palm plants	Cobbler outfits
"Teddy" bears	Yardgoods
Wood, coal or corncob-burning stoves	Long underwear
Woodburning steel ranges	Men's furnishings
Pot-bellied stoves	Hand-cranked coffee mills
Laundry stoves	Galvanized, odorless commodes and slop buckets
Gas ranges	
Box and folding cameras	Clothes pins and lines
Photograph developing outfits	Irons
Draftsmen sets	Egg beaters
Kerosene-powered "Magic Lantern" outfits for slideshows	Tinware
	Brass beds
Lawn tennis goods	Oil-base house paint
Boxing equipment	Velocipedes (three-wheeled)
Carpet sweepers	Surveyor's instruments
Firearms	Hearing horns
Animal traps	Musical instruments
Hunting knives	Battery-operated telephones
Cowboy's waterproof wool-lined bed sheet[a]	Telegraph outfits
	Gas light fixtures
Gospel tents	Kerosene Lamps
Circus tents	Clocks
White duck emigrant wagon covers	Fountain pens and ink pencils
Razors	Pocket watches
Castor oil	Home tooth forceps for extracting teeth
Carbolic arnica salve	Toilet preparations
Cod liver oil	

Table 3.7A (continued)

Hair tonics	Moliograph motion picture machines (kerosene-operated)
Rouge	Windmills and towers
Toothbrushes and sundries	Clothes wringers
Hand-cranked cream separators	Bathroom equipment (toilets, sinks, tubs)
Treadle-operated sewing machines	Carpets
Books (Bibles, cookbooks, family doctor manuals, how-to-do books such as black-smithing and beekeeping)	Rubber buggy tires
	Paddles
Six-month correspondence course in bookkeeping	Hand-cranked sheep-shearing machines
	Lap robes
Stationery	Railroad attachments for bicycles
Buggies, surreys, phaetons, cabriolets	Stereoscopic views
Commercial and farm wagons	Talking machines (gramaphones and graphaphones with wax cylinder records)
Horse harnesses	Furniture (parlor suites, washstands, wardrobes, chifforobes, Morris chairs, china cabinets, sideboards)
Lariats and other ranch gear	
Buggy whips	
Tombstones	Stock food
Bicycles	Beehives and beekeeper supplies
Spectacles and eyeglasses[c]	Poultry brooders
Electric medical battery	Hand-operated washing machines
Groceries (in separate catalogue)	Home-building plans
Ice chests	Cavalry riding pants
Tools	Wigs
Rotary lawn mowers	Wallpaper
Horse-drawn plows	Cowboy saddles

a. "... for herders, prospectors, explorers who are compelled to sleep in a tent or on the ground."
b. "... formerly known as blackberry brandy... used and prescribed by many physicians as one of the simplest and most effective remedies for all derangements of the stomach and bowels... tones up and invigorates the system."
c. With "test-yourself" chart included in catalogue.

Table 3.7B
Items offered in the 1985 Sears Roebuck catalogue: a sample

Electronic, stereo televisions

Electronic sewing machines

Fluorescent light fixtures

Video cassette recorders

Electronic speech synthesis telephones

Exercise equipment

Electric weed trimmers

Digital automobile engine analyzers

Electronic blood pressure monitors

Power-propelled lawn mowers

Electric water pumps

Stainless steel sinks

Electronic clothes washers and dryers

Citizen band radios

Personal computers and software

Gas furnaces

Audio cassette players

Electronic bathroom scales

Backyard storage buildings

Electric irons, skillets, coffeemakers, woks, toasters, waffle irons, vacuum cleaners, etc.

Microwave ovens

Frostless refrigerator/freezers with automatic ice/water dispensers

Fitted, no-iron sheets

Electric razors

Men's, women's, children's clothing (about half the catalogue)

Plastic house shutters

Convection electric heaters

Electronic dishwashers

Video movie cameras

Electronic typewriters

Automatic-dial telephones

Electric air conditioners

Portable radios

Plastic indoor/outdoor carpeting

Latex house paint

Farm and Ranch catalogue, which includes
  Beekeeping outfits
  Bees
  Poultry and supplies
  Electric grain mills
  Electric milk pasteurizers
  Electric winches
  Electric sheep-shearers
  25-mile solar-powered electric fencing
  Gas or electric chain saws
  Gas-powered tractor mowers

Plus 19 other special catalogues, including
  Big and tall men's clothing
  Women's and half-size clothing
  Uniforms
  Work clothes
  Home health care products
  Mother-to-be and baby products
  Carpeting
  Power and hand tools
  Office equipment and supplies
  Heating and cooling supplies
  Recreational boating equipment
  Cameras and photo/video supplies
  Stitch, latch and other crafts
  Recreational vehicle and camping equipment
  Toys
  Motorcycle accessories

in the kinds of consumer goods that have become widely available since the turn of the century: for example, a "Speech Synthesis" electronic telephone in 1985 versus one year's supply of stationery in 1905; a "Shapemaster 1000" exercise machine in 1985 versus a state-of-the-art, handpowered sheep-shearing machine in 1905; a digital automobile engine analyzer versus a side-sprung runabout buggy. And, in table 3.8 we reproduce Stanley Lebergott's [1984] wrap-up of some of the dramatic changes in American consumption and living conditions since 1900—among them the sharp drop in consumption of inferior foods, the decrease in the percent of families taking in boarders and lodgers, and the number of families today with running water, flush toilets, and refrigerators (virtually 100%).

3.8 Working Conditions and Leisure Time

In 1850 the typical workday in factories, shipyards, and shops was a little over 11 hours (6 days a week), and even by 1900 workweeks continued to average about 57 hours.[12] Farm workers, who constituted half of the labor force, put in the traditional "first light to dark" workday, and employees worked even longer hours in some occupations (for instance, dry goods and grocery clerks in New York and Chicago in the midcentury worked 14 hours a day, 6 days a week) (Martin [1942, pp. 344–345]). Maddison [1982] reports that average annual hours worked per person in 1870 amounted to 2,964 compared to 1,607 in 1979 (p. 211). Clearly, the modern preoccupation with recreation and leisure activities such as sports, cultural events, vacationing and vacation travel, television viewing, and the like is a vast change from life in the nineteenth century. Vacations were certainly unknown except for the very rich; for nearly all of the population there was little time (or money) for recreation;[13] almost all time and energy were taken up with long hours of hard work. What little leisure time did exist was often devoted to religious activities or the celebration of rare general holidays (such as the Fourth of July).[14]

It was also virtually unknown in the nineteenth century for members of the laboring population to enjoy a period of retirement in their later years; people literally worked themselves into the grave. It was common for children to work. As late as 1890, 150,000 children were employed in factories. Today, adult wages have risen enough that children no longer must contribute income to ensure most families' economic survival. Mandatory school laws and child labor laws have also contributed to this change (Wells [1982]).

Working conditions, too, were far from idyllic, as is illustrated by the

Table 3.8
Consumption changes, 1900–1979

	1900	1979
Food: percent families consuming		
Lard	95	9
Salt pork	83	4
Molasses	69	2
Corn meal	90	22
Food: per capita consumption (pounds)		
"Inferior" foods		
Flour and meal	300	140
Potatoes	212	83
Milk	274	187
Preferred foods		
Sugar	86	132
Meat	148	222
Food preparation		
Flour: percent baked at home	92	22
Expenditures on raw vegetables as precent of all food	96	30
Expenditures on food at home as percent of all food	99	82
Housing: value of average dwelling (1958 dollars)	$4,727	$7,000
Housing: percent of families		
With boarders and lodgers	25	2
Over 1 person per room	49	8
Over $3\frac{1}{2}$ persons per sleeping room	23	7
Without		
Running water	76	2
Flush toilets	87	4
Central heat	99+	22
Gas or electric light	88	0
Heating with		
Wood	50	1
Coal	50	3
Owing		
Refrigerator	18	99
Washing machine	5[a]	70
Vacuum cleaner	0	92
Tobacco: cigarettes produced (millions)	5	673

Table 3.8 (continued)

	1900	1979
Transport: percent of urban families		
Owning a horse	20	
Owing a car		80
Recreation: percent of families with		
Radio	0	96
TV	0	99
Telephone	5	91
Health: death rate (per 1,000) from		
Pneumonia	153	33
Diarrhea	116	0
Typhoid	31	0
Physicians per 1,000 population	1.72	1.86
Service expenditures per capita (1972 dollars) (rent, health, transport, recreation, personal care, education, etc.)	37	340

Source: Lebergott [1984, pp. 492–493].
a. Rough approximation.

following recollections of Pauline Newman, who in 1911 was a child laborer in a garment factory (Morrison and Zabusky [1980, pp. 10–13]):

We started work at seven-thirty in the morning, and during the busy season we worked until nine in the evening. They didn't pay you any overtime and they didn't given you anything for supper money. Sometimes they'd give you a little apple pie if you had to work very late. That was all. Very generous. . . .

We had a corner on the floor that resembled a kindergarten—we were given little scissors to cut the threads off. It wasn't heavy work, but it was monotonous.

Well, of course, there were laws on the books, but no one bothered to enforce them. The employers were always tipped off if there was going to be an inspection. "Quick," they'd say, "into the boxes!" And we children would climb into the big boxes the finished shirts were stored in. Then some shirts were piled on top of us, and when the inspector came—no children. The factory always got an okay from the inspector, and I suppose someone at City Hall got a little something, too.

The employers didn't recognize anyone working for them as a human being. You were not allowed to sing. . . . We weren't allowed to talk to each other. . . . If you went to the toilet and you were there longer than the floor lady thought you should be, you would be laid off for half a day and sent home. And, of course, that meant no pay. You were not allowed to have your lunch on the fire escape in the summertime. The door was locked to keep us in. . . .

The employers had a sign in the elevator that said: "If you don't come in on Sunday, don't come in on Monday." You were expected to work every day if they needed you and the pay was the same whether you worked extra or not.

Conditions were dreadful in those days. We didn't have anything. . . . There was no welfare, no pension, no unemployment insurance. There was nothing. . . . There was so much feeling against unions then. The judges, when one of our girls came before him, said to her: "You're not striking against your employer, you know, young lady. You're striking against God," and sentenced her to two weeks.

3.9   Education

By one estimate, in 1860 each person in the United States received during his or her lifetime, on average, only 434 days of schooling (or 21 school months plus 14 days), a decided improvement over the average of 82 days in 1800, but still little more than the most rudimentary formal education (Martin [1942, p. 297]). In 1870 20% of the population was illiterate, compared to about 4% in 1930 and only 1% in 1969. Only 2% of the 17-year-olds in 1870 graduated from high school; 100 years later close to 76% did (U.S. Department of Commerce, Bureau of the Census [1975, p. 379]). Urban schools, though free, were not well attended (in 1858 the number of children registered for school in New York City was 139,441 but the average attendance was only 51,430). Rural schools were often hardly better than none. Teachers were usually poorly trained and paid, and the average annual school expenditure per pupil was only $4.50 in 1858 (Martin [1942, p. 299]).

3.10   Travel

By the mid-1800s the isolation of the population was starting to give way, as the railways spread and roads were improved (though, even by 1900, only 20% of all urban families owned a horse). But travel was still very difficult and time-consuming. Railroads served only large cities and some towns that happened to be on the trunk routes. Stagecoach travel was still very important; in many of the frontier states it was the only means of travel, and a very arduous means of transport it was, not to be undertaken casually. Most roads were very bad, obviously unpaved, often unpassable, with almost no bridges outside of the cities.

Furnas [1969, pp. 278–279] writes of one traveler in the 1830s, who commented,

"As no attention has been paid to forming or draining roadbeds, . . . it is only for a few months during summer that they . . . are tolerable." He was aghast at the corduroy roads made in backward areas by juxtaposing 12-foot logs across the road, which kept wheels from sinking into soft ground but also forced them to progress "by . . . leaps and starts, particularly trying to those accustomed to the comforts of European travelling." Less temperate comments were frequent from testier travelers. The Reverend Mr. Read of the Congregational Union of Great Britain, touring Ohio in 1834 on the Lord's business, thought the road between Sandusky and Columbus more like a stony ditch than a road; a stagecoach with him as sole passenger took seven hours to go 23 miles. He was even worse off when, below Cincinnati, he was one of three passengers in a fast mail coach the horses of which trotted, keeping him so "jarred and jolted, as to threaten serious mischief ... my hat was many times thrown from my head, and all my bruises bruised over again. It was really an amusement to see us laboring to keep our places." It was, after all, an American stage driver in Illinois who said that the mud was often so deep on his run that though he had driven a team of mules for months, he did not yet know what color they were—he never saw anything of them but their ears.

And, after completing an arduous trip by camel through the Middle Eastern desert, George Perkins March wrote, "Any forty days of *stage* travelling in the United States would involve more of fatigue, danger and discomfort of all sorts" (Furnas [1969, p. 279]). Today, one can get some feel for this kind of travel in places like the jeep trails of the Rocky Mountains, where just an hour in a modern, well-sprung, four-wheel-drive vehicle can leave the passenger tired, sore, and nauseated.

An average of 5 miles per hour between Cumberland, Maryland, and Wheeling, West Virginia, was typical of the rate of speed possible. Boston to New York in the 1800s was about 6 miles per hour. Even city streets were poorly, if at all, paved, obstructed and filthy—overrun with animal scavengers. In cities as large as New York goats, geese, chickens, sheep, and pigs wandered the streets.

3.11   Life Expectancy, Physical Stature, and the Public Health

American children born in the 1980s can expect to live an average of almost 75 years. By 1984 infant mortality had fallen to only 10.6 deaths per 1,000 births.[15] In stark contrast, a century ago infant mortality hovered around 170 deaths per 1,000 births;[16] and a female born in 1855 could expect to live an average of a little less than 41 years, while a male could expect an average life span of less than 39 years (Martin [1942, p. 220]). The increase in life expectancy is truly one of the extraordinary accomplishments of modern society, and one in which productivity improvements and the resulting rise in living standards have played an important role. Recent studies have suggested that, along with improvements in medical technology and the expansion of hospital services, nutritional status has played a major part in the trends in average life span (accounting for perhaps as much as 40% of the drop in mortality rate). In a study of the trends in both

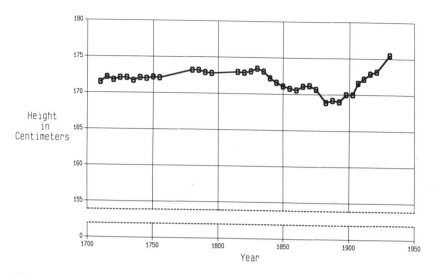

Figure 3.1A
Trend in mean final height of native-born American white males, 1710–1931. Source:
Fogel [1986b, p. 511].

life expectancy and physical stature[17] between 1720 and 1980, Fogel et al.
[1986b] found that the middle of the nineteenth century probably represented a low point for both of these measures of living conditions. According to their preliminary analysis of recently tabulated genealogical records,
the trends in American life expectancy and height have not risen in a
continuous, smooth curve toward modern levels. In fact, modern levels of
life expectancy and height were reached in the mid- to late 1700s, during a
time when America was sparsely settled, population density was too low
to support major epidemics, and rural colonialists were relatively well-fed
(particularly compared to their European counterparts). Then, starting in
the 1790s average life span began to decline and continued to decline for
more than half a century. Average heights started to fall at the end of the
1700s and then declined sharply after about 1830; heights did not begin to
rise again until the end of the nineteenth century. Figures 3.1A and 3.1B
portray the rather similar histories of height and life expectancy.[18]

The reasons for the declines of the 1800s are the subject of continuing
debate, but they do coincide with a number of changes in American life
that are plausible explanations. Certainly living conditions for much of the
laboring population deteriorated in the nineteenth century; a huge influx of
poor immigrants, most of whom settled in the cities, together with the
general move of the population from the relatively wholesome and healthy

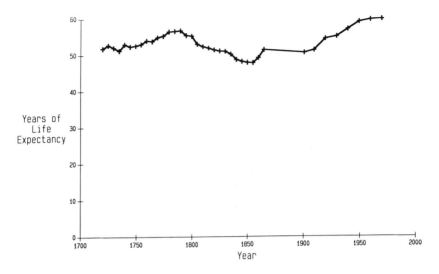

Figure 3.1B
Trend in life expectancy of native-born Americans at age 10, 1710–1970. Source: Fogel
[1986b, p. 511].

countryside to urban areas (as factories sprang up and offered employment) produced extreme overcrowding. Housing conditions were wretched, and the crowded tenements with their primitive sanitary provisions were perfect breeding grounds for disease. Increasing urbanization also probably contributed to the pollution and increase in disease in adjacent rural areas, for example, by polluting rivers and streams. Despite the evidence that real wages and per-capita food intake were generally rising throughout the nineteenth century, it is also clear that these improvements were not only sporadic but very unevenly divided among the population.

Thus, public health in the 1800s (particularly in the cities, but also in towns and rural areas) was at best precarious. Great epidemics of diseases, now essentially unheard of, periodically ravaged the population. The most dreaded diseases were cholera and yellow fever. Particularly severe country-wide epidemics occurred in 1849 and 1854. In New Orleans alone there were 30,000 cases of yellow fever in 1853, and as late as 1879 yellow fever killed 4,000 in Memphis in a single epidemic. In the early 1860s in New York City there were as many as 12,000 cases of typhoid fever a year. Smallpox was still widely prevalent, particularly in the seaports, and in the South and West was so common that it was taken for granted. Diphtheria was not believed to be communicable so no precautions against its spread were taken. Scarlet fever, dysentery, and tuberculosis also levied a heavy toll.[19]

It was only in the late 1800s that scientists started to identify disease microbes and discover causes and cures. Up until then, medical practice was very crude; doctors could do almost nothing to cure disease, and their main functions, besides setting broken bones, sewing up wounds, and other purely mechanical tasks, were to comfort and console.[20] Medicine had made only a few advances in diagnosis, treatment and operative techniques (for example, the use of general anesthesia in 1844). Even these few advances had little effect in improving the general medical practice of the country, which was characterized by poorly trained and scientifically ignorant physicians[21] and a scattered population, the great mass of which tended to rely on family remedies and fads of all sorts: cure-all patent medicines (which were mostly alcohol), mechanical, magnetic, and electrical devices supposed to be useful in treating diseases, phrenology, spiritualism, muscle manipulation, and so on. Scott and Wishy [1982] write that often the threats of disease were "... increased by supposed preventatives or palliatives like closed windows or increased warmth to treat fevers. Too many medicines were eventually found to be dangerous drugs or poisons" [p. 393]. As late as the 1830s Samuel Clemens would describe the ministrations of local Missouri doctors: "Castor oil ... half a dipperful ... the next standby was calomel.... Then they bled the patient and put mustard plasters on him...." (Furnas [1969, p. 333]). In 1860 Oliver Wendell Holmes declared, "If the whole materia medica, *as now used*, could be sunk to the bottom of the sea, it would be all the better for mankind,—and all the worse for the fishes" (Martin [1942, p. 231, Holmes's emphasis]).

There were very few hospitals. In 1873 there were only 149 hospitals and allied institutions in the country (and one-third of them were for the mentally ill). Most were charitable institutions for the poor, and operated under very crude, unsanitary conditions with frequent epidemics among the unsegregated patients. Anyone who could afford it was treated at home or in a doctor's office.

There was little knowledge in the 1800s about the means for prevention of the spread of epidemic disease. Absence of municipal cleanliness was a major public health problem, and facilities for disposal of human wastes, animal manure, garbage, and other household refuse were grossly inadequate. Garbage was thrown into the streets and alleys, and pigs and dogs, in cities as large as New York, served as scavengers (in some cities the scavengers were geese, and in many Southern cities buzzards cleaned up the garbage). Slaughterhouses, livery stables, rendering plants, junk and manure heaps were unregulated; animals had the freedom of the streets in all but a few cities. The absence of regulation of food markets also made for extremely unsanitary conditions.

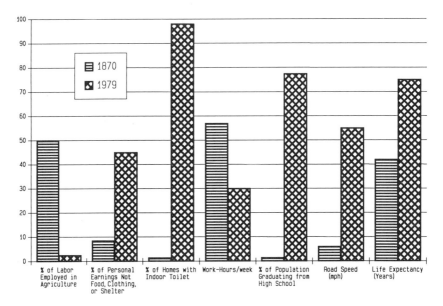

Figure 3.2
Some life-style changes, 1870 and 1979. Source: Compiled by authors.

Hardly an American city had an adequate sewage system. Even Boston, New York, and Philadelphia had only partial systems whose conditions and operations were so poor that the stench from the inlets and outlets was almost intolerable. Streets were filthy more often than not, with street-cleaning inadequate or completely absent. Everywhere, ordinary sanitary precautions were neglected, and mosquitoes, flies, and other germ-harboring pests were regarded with equanimity.

3.12   Conclusions

The preceding account of the American standard of living in the nineteenth century reads remarkably like a description of a contemporary, less developed country, and recalls the comparison made early in the chapter: American per-capita GNP in the mid-nineteenth century just about matched that in present-day countries, the majority of whose citizens struggle through a rude, hand-to-mouth existence in many ways medieval in its primitiveness. We have touched on a number of the components of the standard of living in this chapter, and have tried to show how economic growth has profoundly altered American lives. Figure 3.2 dramatically portrays a number of those changes, including share of the labor force in agriculture, percentage of personal income devoted to the basic requirements of food, clothing and shelter, and work-hours per week. Rising incomes and the fruits of the technological revolution have filled our lives with goods and services unavailable, and even unimaginable, 100 years ago and, perhaps most important, the revolution has produced its most dramatic changes in the lives of the millions of ordinary working people. Today, virtually no American family is without electricity, or hot and cold running water, or an indoor toilet, or household amenities such as stoves, refrigerators, and vacuum cleaners. Televisions, automobiles, educated and healthy children, reasonably nutritious diets, freedom from the dreaded diseases of the past, the luxury of vacations and retirement years, and long life expectancy have all become part of the American standard of living. Indeed, the continual rise of real incomes and the constant parade of new consumer products have become commonplace phenomena. Among the items that have reached mass markets during the lifetimes of many of us are video recorders, personal computers, microwave ovens, and jet airplanes. Yet few people regard any of these with the wonderment that early in this century greeted the advent of electric lighting, the radio, and the automobile. Change has become so commonplace that we all have become blasé about it. That is a striking departure from virtually anything that humanity has experienced before.

Postscript: Which Income Groups Gained Most from the Revolution in Living Standards?

Though benefits as spectacular as those that have been described in this chapter can hardly have left any income group in the American population untouched, they probably have not been distributed perfectly evenly. The evidence on their distribution is far from clear, and we can offer only a few suggestive observations on the subject.

Some observers have suggested that the very wealthy were those who gained the least from the increase in living standards. Rosenberg and Birdzell [1986] write, "... Western economic growth ... benefited the life-style of the very rich much less than it benefited the life-style of the less well-off.... The very rich were as well-housed, clothed, and adorned in 1885 as in 1985.... In fact, the innovations of positive value to the rich are relatively few: advances in medical care, air conditioning, and improvements in transportation and preservation of food" [p. 27]. A primary consequence of mass production was to reduce the real cost of items previously beyond the means of any but the most affluent. As we have seen, variety in foods was once available only to the very rich. And only the very rich once possessed more than one or two changes of clothing, lived in comfortable homes, or traveled for pleasure. Today all these things are widely enjoyed by members of even the lower middle classes. The homes of the wealthy today are not notably more elegant than those of 1870; nor is their clothing more luxurious. This is in sharp contrast to what has happened to the median American income group whose living conditions have undergone an improvement of revolutionary proportions. In terms of assistance in household tasks, the middle and lower classes now have at their disposal a great variety of equipment—washing machines, vacuum cleaners, refrigerators, and so on. The upper income groups, in contrast, may even be held to have lost out somewhat through the reduction in number of household servants, even in the wealthiest of homes.

There is probably much truth to this evaluation, but it surely requires some additions and amendments. The first relates to the very poor, the miserable stratum of society that inhabits the most dreadful slums or is altogether homeless. Descriptions of nineteenth-century tenements are indisputably horrifying, but who is to say whether they are matched by reports of vermin-infested slums of today, in which cracked walls cannot exclude the cold and legal heating requirements are regularly flouted. The inhabitants of those slums, it is true, are offered various forms of public assistance today; their children are entitled to schooling and medical treatment that would have been beyond anything their predecessors could have aspired to a century earlier. Yet one can hardly muster confidence in an assertion that these most underprivileged members of our society are really better off today. The very increase in the relative standards attained by other income groups must surely increase the frustration and despair of those to whom the American dream is hardly even worth dreaming about.

The story, however, is even more complex than this reservation suggests. While it may be true that the very poorest, like the most wealthy, have gained *relatively* less over the course of a century, comparison with their status in the sixteenth and seventeenth centuries suggests that both these groups have gained a great deal indeed, at least over this *longer* period. To recognize what the poor have gained we need merely recall section 3.4 on food consumption. Even welfare recipients today are hardly expected to subsist on the one bowl of gruel, which, with rare exceptions (usually on holidays), was the universal food of much of the population in earlier centuries. Far more than that, the perpetual threat of famine, which was likely to recur and cause widespread death by starvation, has disappeared in this country and other industrialized lands. The end of that

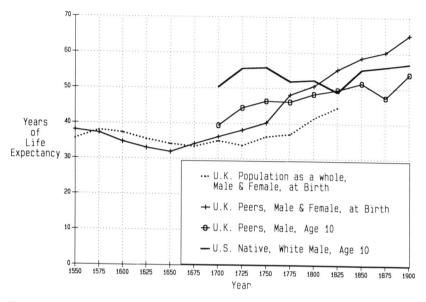

Figure 3.3
Life expectancy for four British and American groups (at birth or age 10), 1550–1900.
Source: Fogel [1986b, pp. 445–467].

specter is economic progress indeed, even for the poorest members of the community.

Not only the poor but the very rich have also gained much in terms of health and personal comfort in the course of two or three centuries. The evidence of genealogical records is remarkable in this regard. In the first quarter of the twentieth century the average expected longevity at birth of a member of the British peerage (nobility), male and female, had reached 65 years. But in the two centuries following 1550 (in the middle of the reign of the Tudors) that figure was a mere 35 years. More remarkable, for that period the average longevity figure for peers was almost identical with that of the general male and female population of England and Wales, despite the miserable living conditions of the bulk of the nation. It is also noteworthy that as late as the first quarter of the eighteenth century, when the life expectancy of a British male peer at age 10 was a bit more than 39 years, that of an American male of age 10 was a bit more than 50 years (the full time series are depicted in figure 3.3). Clearly, the health of a British nobleman several centuries ago still had a long way to go.[22]

In terms of comfort the improvements in the circumstances of the rich over a longer time period is equally dramatic. We illustrate the change in terms of one development: home heating technology. Before the early decades of the eighteenth century the role of the draft in fireplace construction had not been discovered. As a result, the huge fireplaces in the homes of the nobles, though beautiful, were extremely ineffective as heating devices, roasting nearby persons on one side while they froze on the other side. As a result, as Braudel [1979] reports, "Cold weather, at that period, could be a public disaster, freezing rivers, halting mills (with little or no flour having been stored because preservation methods were largely unknown), bringing packs of dangerous wolves out into the countryside, multiplying epidemics" [p. 299]. This affected the nobility as well. On this subject, historians like to cite the Princess Palatine (the German sister-in-law of Louis XIV, living in Paris and Versailles), who reported in one cold January that "... all entertainments have ceased as well as lawsuits." More remarkable is her report in February of 1695 that "[in the Hall of Mirrors at Versailles] At the King's table the wine and water froze in the glasses." One may note that matters began to improve for the wealthy in France during the period of regency (1717–1723) of the Princess Palatine's son, Philip of Orleans (Braudel [1979, p. 299]).

Figure 3.3 suggests that for the British aristocracy improvements in health and longevity began perhaps a few decades earlier and that since then the longevity of peers increased almost uninterruptedly at least until the beginning of the twentieth century. Improvement for the bulk of the population of England and Wales waited about another century for its inauguration; and the rate of ascent of their life span seems not to have attained that of the peers during the period for which data are reported by Fogel [1986a, b]. At least in that sense, then, the Industrial Revolution may have benefited "the upper crust" even more than it did the population generally.

Notes

1. See table 2.1.

2. Cowan [1983, p. 194, citing Patterson [1981]:

The minimum subsistence budget that was used to determine welfare payments in New York City in 1960 specified a set of material conditions for family life that would have been regarded as fairly luxurious in 1910 [much less 1860].... A four-person family was permitted to rent a five-room flat, so that each member of the family who wanted to could "be alone in a room"—a luxury inconceivable to most poor families earlier in the century. The flat was to be outfitted with a complete bathroom (hot and cold running water, toilet, bath or shower, and a sink), a complete kitchen (sink with a drain, hot and cold water, refrigerator, and a gas or electric range), and central heat. Plain but adequate furnishings were allowed (each person was to have a bed and a complete set of eating utensils) as well as annual replacement clothing for the children (shoes that fit, dresses that were new and not made over from hand-me-downs). The diet for such a family was not to contain luxurious foods such as steak, but did allow meat, milk, fresh fruits and vegetables to be served at least once a day. The family was also allowed an iron and a vacuum cleaner (although not a washing machine or a dryer) and linoleum (although not carpeting) to cover all the floors. That set of material conditions ... regarded as deprivation in terms of the general standard applying throughout the country in 1960 ... was luxurious (compared to how people lived in the nineteenth century, and even early in the twentieth).

3. Here we offer two words of caution: First, in this chapter, we present evidence on the vast improvements in material welfare since the nineteenth century. We do not make any judgments, however, about whether Americans are better off than their nineteenth-century counterparts in other, less tangible ways. Who can say, for example, whether the mass exodus from farms to cities benefited society's psychic state? And what price have Americans had to pay for their increased prosperity—emotionally, culturally, and environmentally? Second, it is clear that the improvements in material welfare have not accrued evenly among all income groups. Wealthy nineteenth-century Americans already lived a life of luxury, and while they certainly participated in many of the gains of the twentieth century (including improved life expectancy and better medical care, plus all the technological wonders such as air conditioning and jet airplane travel), they also lost some of the amenities that they enjoyed (for example, large staffs of personal servants; indeed, even middle-class nineteenth-century families routinely employed a number of servants, such as laundresses, scrubwomen, gardeners, and seamstresses). At the other extreme, the very poorest in America today have also benefited from the increase in prosperity (for example, in medical care and some other basic amenities like electricity and plumbing), but certainly have not participated fully in the huge improvements in material conditions that have accrued to the millions of middle- and lower-middle-class Americans. We explore this issue further in the postscript to this chapter.

4. A mechanic was a semiskilled day laborer. Nettie's father made the family's living by subsistence farming, living off the land, trading his services for other goods like milk and the use of a neighbor's horse to plow his field, and selling his services or handmade tools for money.

5. In 1860 the *New York Tribune* wrote that it was rather above the mark to place annual earnings of skilled workers in New York City (such as journeymen mechanics and manufactures) at $400 (or about $3,500 1980 dollars) (Martin [1942, p. 410]).

6. Income figures for 1860 are from Martin [1942, p. 393]. To convert nineteenth-century incomes into 1980 dollars, we spliced together two GNP implicit price deflator series: one series (U.S. Department of Commerce, Bureau of the Census [1975, p. 224]) runs from 1869 to 1970 (1958 = 100); the second series (*Economic Report of the President* [1984, p. 224]) runs from 1929 to 1983 (1972 = 100). To make the two series comparable, we converted the second series to a 1958 baseline (by dividing each number by the 1958 number). Then, in order to express incomes

in 1980 dollars, we divided the numbers in both series by the 1980 deflator figure. The official U.S. poverty level for 1980 is taken from U.S. Department of Commerce, Bureau of the Census [1982, p. 417].

7. In 1899 per capita consumption of lard (animal fat) was 12.8 pounds, compared to 4.6 pounds per person in 1970 (U.S. Department of Commerce, Bureau of the Census [1975, pp. 329–330]).

8. American abundance relative to European standards was not new in the second half of the nineteenth century. As we shall see later in the chapter, there is evidence suggesting that Americans were also better fed and healthier in earlier periods.

9. The homes of well-to-do Americans were described by one British traveler as "tasteful and elegant" (Reid [1861]), and included such amenities as weighted sash windows, rainwater cisterns, lever-operated water closets, copper-lined bathtubs and showers, hot and cold running water, furnace heating, gas lighting, and elaborate Victorian furniture. Many of the residences of St. Louis were "costly and beautiful" (Dana [1857]), and in Westchester, New York, "Miles and miles of unmitigated prosperity weary the eye. Lawns and park-gates, groves and verandahs, ornamental woods and neat walls, trim hedges and well-placed shrubberies, fine houses and large stables, neat gravel-walks, and nobody on them" were to be seen (Willis [1853]).

10. The statistics in the paragraph are taken from Martin [1942].

11. In an entertaining review of Corbin [1986], Gewen writes [1986, p. 12],

It is no exaggeration to say the past stank. The smells of refuse, stagnant water, cesspools, offal, even corpses, were facts of daily life. Breaking wind in public was an approved practice. In the cities, people emptied their chamber pots in the streets, in the country they lived alongside their animals. Infants padded about unswathed, free to urinate and defecate at will.
  Personal cleanliness was almost nonexistent—bathing and the brushing of teeth were rare, shampooing unknown. As recently as the end of the nineteenth century, it was said that most Frenchwomen died without ever having taken a bath. Underwear was infrequently changed. In the Middle Ages, both castle and hovel were so immersed in muck that, as Emmanuel Le Roy Ladurie points out, "villagers carried around with them a whole fauna of fleas and lice: people not only scratched themselves, but friends and relations from all levels in the social scale deloused one another."
  Filth was not merely accepted, it was esteemed. No one, for example, had to explain to farmers the worth of human excrement as fertilizer, while sewage and waste products were widely believed to *prevent* disease. Grandmothers passed on to mothers the folk wisdom that "the dirtier children are, the healthier they are." It was bathing that was considered unhygienic, causing infertility and diminishing beauty. No less than the filth itself, the stench of filth was valued for its medicinal qualities, and also as a sexual stimulant. Victims of tuberculosis were advised to inhale animal vapors. The ardor of romantic suitors was awakened by the aroma of their loved ones' underarms. Goethe stole the bodice of a ladyfriend so that he could sniff it in private. The historian Michelet sought inspiration for his writing in a woman's menstrual odors, as well as through the scents of latrines.

12. Baydo [1982, p. 6] and Martin [1942, p. 432].

13. Transatlantic travel was certainly out of the question for all but the few wealthiest. An 1858 *Harper's Weekly* advertised a pleasure voyage on the Mediterranean aboard the steamer *Ericsson* for $750 per person (or close to the annual income of the average urban Massachusetts family of five described in section 3.3).

14. It may be of interest to note that, despite the advent of all the modern-day, worksaving household amenities, such as indoor plumbing, electric washing and drying machines, vacuum cleaners, canned goods, and ready-made clothing, some recent historical studies of housework conclude that the time women spend on household chores has not decreased. Modern amenities have dramatically reduced the back-breaking drudgery of many household tasks, but have also created different sorts of housework. For example, Cowan [1983] points out that when gas stoves replaced woodburning stoves, no longer did wood have to be chopped, split, and carried in (tasks often performed by men and children), but the task of cooking remained the same or became even more difficult (since meals no longer were limited by the vagaries of woodstoves). In fact, the amount of time spent on cooking increased as women produced meals much more complicated and nutritious than the one-pot stew dictated by primitive stoves. Similarly, Caroline Davidson [1982], in her history of housework in the British Isles from 1650 to 1950, concludes [p. 192],

... the spread of utilities and time- and labour-saving appliances did not have any discernible long-term effect on the average housewife's working hours. Time saved on one task was simply put to new use and the scope of housework redefined. A woman who saved an extra 45 minutes a day through the introduction of piped water into her house would use them to do more cleaning and washing. Similarly, a woman whose coal range was replaced with a gas stove would cook more elaborate meals than she had previously, because it was so much easier. In this way, housework remained a full-time occupation for most women in 1950, just as it had been in 1650 [or 1750 or 1850].

Cowan writes [1983, p. 201],

... there is more work for a mother to do in a modern home because there is no one left to help her with it. Almost all the work that once stereotypically fell to men has been mechanized. Families tend to live a considerable distance from the place where the male head of the household is employed; hence, men leave home early in the morning and return, frequently exhausted, late at night. Children spend long hours in school and, when school is over, have "after school activities," which someone must supervise and from which they must be transported. Older children move away from home as soon as they reasonably can, going off to college or to work. No one delivers anything ... to the door any longer, or at least not at prices that most people can afford; and domestic workers now earn salaries that have priced them out of the reach of all but the most affluent households. The advent of washing machines and dishwashers has eliminated the chores that men and children used to do as well as the accessory workers who once were willing and able to assist with the [other] work. The end result is that, although [house]work is more productive (more services are performed and more goods are produced, for every hour of work) and less laborious than it used to be, for most housewives it is just as time consuming and just as demanding.

15. The *New York Times* [1986, p. A19].

16. Figures for Massachusetts in 1870–1874, from U.S. Department of Commerce, Bureau of the Census [1975, p. 57].

17. Physical stature (height) is also a good measure of gains in the standard of living (and in fact may be a better measure than real wages or per-capita food consumption). Average height is apparently a nearly foolproof measure of the nutritional status of a population, particularly the nutritional status of the infant and child population.

18. For dramatic evidence on the decline of mortality and the contribution of scientific development, see Coale [1987].

19. As Scott and Wishy [1982] point out, "... even today, despite the use of vaccines, our annual 'flu' epidemics remind us mildly of the low odds against disease with which American families lived...." [p. 393].

20. Well into the twentieth century hospital wards were filled with cases of tuberculosis, pneumonia, syphilitic heart disease, pneumococcal and streptococcal meningitis, typhoid fever, and other acute, and at that time incurable, microbial diseases. As late as the 1930s, "... the physician more commonly 'shared' in the agonizing process of waiting for 'nature to take its course' or in helping patients cope with illness that could not be modified medically [as is, unhappily, true of AIDS in 1989]" (Rogers [1986, pp. 11–15]).

21. Legal requirements for practicing medicine were *very* unexacting: usually three years of study with a practicing physician and two courses of lectures at a medical college. Dentistry was a branch of doctoring, consisting largely of extractions, with ingested alcohol the only anesthetic available.

22. The data are reported and analyzed in Fogel [1986a, b]. Fogel offers some conjectures about the explanation of what he calls "the peerage paradox"—the approximately equal life expectancy of peers and commoners in the period noted. He suggests that many of the killer diseases of the time such as plague, malaria, smallpox, and typhus are affected minimally by nutrition, that cleanliness was not fashionable, and that upper-class diets of the period contained extraordinarily high quantities of substances (notably alcohol) toxic to the unborn or to the nursing child. Moreover, the aristocratic diet shunned healthful root vegetables and cereal products that economic circumstances often forced peasants to eat (Fogel [1986a, pp. 64–70]).

4

Long-Run Growth in U.S. Productivity: Is There a Slowdown?

This country's productivity growth in recent years is extremely disquieting. But the troubling trend is only symptomatic of much more serious productivity problems.
Baumol and McLennan [1985, p. 3]

Very preliminary inspection of the evidence initially convinced us that the United States had indeed experienced a sharp and sustained decline in its productivity growth, and that this represented a marked departure from its long-term performance, threatening grave consequences for the nation's future. Closer study of the facts has, however, forced us to acknowledge that this widely accepted judgment is simply incorrect. Not that the opposite is true. There clearly has been a short-term slowdown; but the evidence suggests that it is merely the end of an extraordinary period of postwar growth—a return toward normal growth rates—that was experienced in *all* industrial countries.

More than that. Much of the popular disquiet over U.S. productivity performance has centered on the manufacturing sector of the economy. We have all seen statements deploring the loss by our manufactures of their ability to hold their own against the incursions of foreign competition both in the domestic market and abroad. "Deindustrialization" has been inscribed on the banners of those who believe that the U.S. economy faces a profound long-term crisis. This will be studied in some detail in chapter 6. But here we shall already see that growth in productivity of our manufacturing continues high, and is, perhaps, even somewhat above the historical rate of expansion.

This chapter examines the pertinent evidence on productivity growth both for the economy as a whole, and (for the period after World War II) for each of 11 subsectors into which the available statistics subdivide the economy. While it is true that some of these sectors have shown signs of a slowdown, that by itself should hardly be considered to constitute a shocking observation, especially in light of what we know of the particular sectors in question. In short, the chapter offers a guardedly optimistic view of the economy's productivity trends, at least as matched against the country's own historical performance, leaving international comparisons to the chapter that follows.

None of this is, of course, meant to advocate complacency and inattention to the productivity issue, which will continue to be of critical importance for the nation's prosperity. But it does suggest that the way in which we think about the issue merits a calmer stance than some observers seem to have considered appropriate.

4.1 Cyclical Behavior in Productivity Growth and Proper Evaluation of the Evidence

As we know, the serious concern about the recent U.S. productivity record is over its *long-term* implications. A very transitory downturn, distressing though it may legitimately be, represents no threat to the continued leadership of our industry or to the prospects for the living standards enjoyed by our population. Chapters 1 and 2 have already emphasized the fact that productivity growth is of importance primarily in the long run, and have argued that in the long run there simply is no influence of greater importance for the welfare of the economy. That is the main reason why it is necessary here to focus almost exclusively on statistics of long duration—on historical data spanning as long a period as possible.

However, there is a second reason for our preoccupation with the long run. As we noted in chapter 2, productivity growth data are peculiarly responsive to cyclical influence. In particular, it is well known that labor productivity—output per unit of labor input—generally rises markedly whenever the economy emerges from a recsssion, and usually falls sharply when the economy turns down after a period of prosperity. This is important for our purposes because it means that the statistics can be expected to exhibit a fall in the growth rate of productivity whenever a recession strikes. When this happens, observers may be tempted to foresee the onset of an enduring malaise, when in fact all that is entailed is a very normal (though hardly a welcome) cyclical phenomenon. Thus, while in *any* statistical data series it is dangerous to attempt to draw inferences about long-run behavior from data spanning a relatively brief period, in the case of productivity growth the peril is particularly acute.

The reason for the cyclical behavior of labor productivity growth is easy to describe. During a downturn, as purchases fall, employers are reluctant to reduce their labor force commensurately. In part, this may be attributable to sentiment and good will, but there are also pressing economic grounds for this behavior pattern. The building of an effective and loyal labor force is far from costless. It entails training outlays, which can be substantial; new workers in the firm often must undergo a learning period during which they acquire experience and adapt themselves to the ways of the company before their contribution can reach its maximum. All this is lost, along with good will and loyalty, when workers are dismissed. Consequently, straight-forward profit considerations call for management to hold back in firing workers if a fall in company sales is expected to be fairly brief. Even if the duration of the decline is difficult to estimate, moderation in reduction of the labor force makes good sense in terms of longer-period company profits.

But if output falls more quickly than the size of the labor force, then labor productivity *must* be affected adversely (since labor productivity is simply the ratio of output to labor input). More generally, even if techno-logical progress continues to contribute to productivity growth, the cycli-cal pattern under discussion will act as a drag upon this expansion, and the rate of productivity growth will generally be pulled below its previous level. Add to this such influences as the decline in business investment outlays that generally accompanies a recession, as well as a greater reluc-tance to undertake the risks of innovation, and it is easy to see why declining growth of labor productivity is a normal accompaniment of the initial stages of recession. Exactly the opposite reasons account for the rise in labor productivity that typically goes along with a return to prosperity.

The statistical record suggests that the volatility of productivity growth is even greater than that of the business cycle. That is, rises and declines in productivity growth seem to be even more frequent than those in GNP, making it all the more inappropriate to attempt to draw inferences about long-term trends in productivity growth from statistics covering only short periods of time. John W. Kendrick [1961, 1973a, b], one of the most eminent analysts of productivity data, has carefully compiled, under the sponsorship of the National Bureau of Economic Research, a very rare set of year-by-year productivity figures for the United States, spanning a very long period. Figure 4.1 shows the annual growth figures for total factor productivity that emerge from these estimates for the period 1884–1969.[1] (Figure 2.1 depicted the very similar oscillations of growth rates of labor productivity.)

The main lesson that seems to emerge from these two graphs is the propensity of productivity growth to rise and fall with considerable fre-

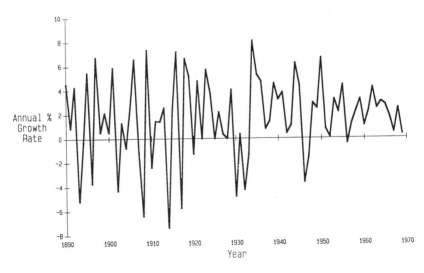

Figure 4.1
Annual growth rate, United States, total factor productivity, 1884–1969. Source: Kendrick [1973b].

quency. The graphs indicate that these oscillations lasted only about 3 years on the average during the period covered. We have very little to go by in order to explain the high frequency of these oscillations,[2] but they clearly serve to make it more urgent for us to focus our attention on long-period data.

4.2 Implications of the Long-Period Productivity Statistics

We have been able to find only two sources of productivity growth estimates encompassing any considerable period beginning well before World War II. The first is the Kendrick-NBER series already summarized in figure 4.1 (and figure 2.1). The second series is to be found primarily in Angus Maddison's deservedly noted work [1982], whose estimates end in 1979, but which can be extended with the aid of an article more recently published by Maddison [1987]. Unfortunately, the figures in the two sources are not comparable without some manipulation, a requirement that may raise some question about the legitimacy of the marriage of the two sets of statistics.

Let us begin by reexamining figure 4.1. What is perhaps most striking about this graph, aside from its highly oscillatory character, is the fact that it exhibits virtually no trend. There is no sign of the slightest uphill or

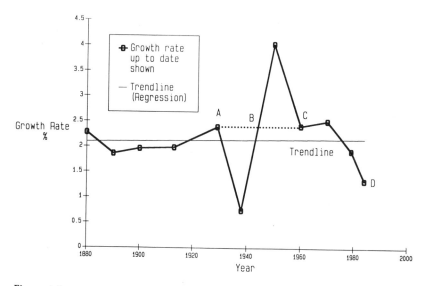

Figure 4.2
Growth rates, United States, GDP per work-hour, 1870–1984. Sources: Maddison [1982, 1987].

downhill movement over the course of the 85 years examined. It is true that if one covers up the portion of the graph that pertains to the period before 1960, the data for the subsequent 8 years do exhibit a downward trend. This is consistent with the conclusion, generally agreed upon, that the 1960s (together with the 1970s) constituted a period of falling productivity growth. But examination of the entire graph indicates that U.S. productivity growth in some 12 *earlier* years had been well below any of the figures experienced in the most recent of the years for which data are provided. Surely, in this graph there is nothing supporting a conclusion that the American economy had entered a period of long-term productivity slowdown. Still, since many observers place the heart of the slowdown period in the decade of the 1970s, with its oil shocks, recessions, and other serious disturbances, it can rightly be objected that the data in the figure under discussion are simply insufficiently recent to be very helpful in a study of the long-term slowdown hypothesis.

The Maddison figures, as has been noted, extend to a far more recent date. While the figures are given only (roughly) by decade and, for the reasons already discussed, are no doubt somewhat distorted by the fortuitous relation between the dates reported and the timing of business fluctuations, Maddison's estimates are widely relied upon by those who specialize in the field. Maddison's data on growth in labor productivity (GDP per work-hour) for the period 1870 to 1984 are shown in figure 4.2 (the most recent data point, i.e., the one furthest to the right, is based on our own calculations using Maddison's more recent figures). In contrast with figure 4.1, the data in figure 4.2 constitute a striking pattern. There is virtual constancy from 1870 to 1929, with productivity growth staying remarkably close to about 2% per year, compounded. Then, with the onset of the Great Depression of the 1930s, productivity growth plummeted, according to Maddison's figures, to well under 1% per year. During World War II and immediately after, productivity soared to a peak growth figure of 4%, thereafter returning roughly to its historic 2% level until 1979, falling further, to about 1.3% in 1984.

A persuasive interpretation of these figures suggests itself. The low point shown for 1940 can be taken as the expectable result of the Great Depression. Similarly, we can attribute the great jump in productivity growth during World War II and the early postwar period to America's immunity to war damage and the shortage of labor due to military demands (whose inevitable consequence was a low labor/output ratio, i.e., a move to an extraordinarily high level of labor productivity). After the war the U.S. economy shared in a worldwide explosion of productivity growth, which probably represented a catch-up in the utilization of accumulated technological ideas—inventions whose utilization was held up by the Depression and war, as well as a backlog of savings that had previously gone uninvested in productive capacity. Here, it is perhaps suggestive to note that there is a striking symmetry between the prewar shortfall in growth reported in the graph and the extraordinary postwar achievement. In figure 4.2, if one draws an imaginary line between 1929 (point A) and 1950 (point C), it can be seen that the earlier shortfall triangle (below line segment AB) is virtually identical in height and length to the overrun triangle above line segment BC. This means that the shortfall and the overrun period were, apparently, just about equal, both in duration and in the amount by which they deviated from the productivity growth rate that may be considered "normal" for the period, as indicated by the height of line AC. The postwar period of "overachievement" thus seems to be interpretable as a time interval in which U.S. productivity growth made up, almost exactly, for its underaccomplishment in the 1930s.

The pertinence of all this for the long-term slowdown hypothesis is clear. Viewed in the light of history, there may be little that can be considered unusual in the productivity growth record of the United States that Maddison reports for 1960 to 1979. Rather, it is the high productivity growth figures just before then that may well constitute an (easily explainable) historical aberration. Naturally, a return to a normal level of performance, from one whose height was an unprecedented historical freak, must have entailed an intermediate period of sharp decline. Such a slowdown, *which also occurred in virtually every industrialized country in the 1970s*, surely constitutes no conclusive portent of a long-term fall in growth levels below their historical magnitude.[3]

This might be the end of the story, were it not for the very low 1984 productivity growth figure, represented by point D in figure 4.2. More on the implications of recent performance will emerge when we examine the detailed postwar figures that will be discussed in later sections of this chapter. However, several pertinent observations can be made already. First, we have already noted the fact that the 1984 figure is not taken directly from Maddison. This, together with the short interval of time between it and the 1979 date of the previous growth figure, as well as the high volatility of productivity growth statistics displayed in figure 4.1, suggests that relatively little reliance can be placed on that one observation as an indicator of a long-period trend. Second, more recent data about U.S. productivity growth indicate that, at least in manufacturing, the mid-1980s have brought a significant upturn in productivity, though, of course, these few years alone also have little standing as reliable indicators of long-term developments.[4] Finally, and perhaps most significant, we employed the statisticians' standard procedure (called regression analysis) to calculate the trend exhibited by the Maddison figures, giving to the relatively low 1984 growth statistic equal weight with that of any of the other figures. The trend line that was derived from this calculation is the apparently horizontal line in figure 4.2. As a matter of fact, though not visible to the naked eye, the trend line is not horizontal, but turns out, rather, to have a (very slight) upward slope. Thus, the Maddison data themselves, analyzed by standard statistical procedures, display no sign of any long-term decline.[5]

4.3   The U.S. Postwar Growth Record: In Aggregate and in Manufacturing

Much of the earlier work analyzing the slowdown of productivity growth in the 1970s showed that during that period most industries in the economy experienced a slowdown, and in many cases a substantial one (see, for example, Baily [1986]). The investigators concluded from this observation that the explanation of this economy-wide slowdown need not concern itself with changes in the *share* in GNP constituted by the various industries, since the deceleration in aggregate productivity would have occurred whether or not the economy's output composition had been shifting toward slow-growth sectors. As we shall see, in the 1980s this has changed drastically: Some sectors of the economy not only have increased their rates of productivity growth, but actually have made up for the losses of the previous decade. In the next few sections we shall focus on the annual labor productivity data provided by the national income accounts tables of the U.S. Bureau of Economic Analysis. Labor productivity growth rates have been calculated both for the economy as a whole (TOT) and for the economy divided into 11 sectors. The statistics span 39 years, 1947–1986. The sectors are (1) agriculture, forestry, and fisheries; (2) mining; (3) construction; (4) durable manufacturing (DurMfg); (5) nondurable manufacturing (NDurMfg); (6) transportation and public utilities (TransPubUtil); (7) wholesale trade (Wholsl); (8) retail trade (Retl); (9) finance, insurance, and real estate (FinInREst); (10) other services; and (11) government and government enterprises. Two different productivity series were calculated for each sector, one for the change in gross national product per full-time equivalent employee (GNP/FTE) and the other for the change in gross national product per person engaged in production (GNP/PEIP).

It should be noted before getting to the story told by the data that these official U.S. Department of Commerce figures for both the manufacturing and the service sectors have recently been subjected to criticism. Lawrence Mishel and Edward F. Denison (see Mishel [1988] and Uchitelle [1988]) have argued that errors in the construction of the statistics make the performance of the manufacturing sector appear better than it was. A number of other commentators have suggested that the service sector data undervalue its productivity growth (see, for example, Baily and Gordon [1988]).[6] The matter is far from settled, but it should not seriously modify our main results. This is obviously true of our conclusions for the economy as a whole. And data such as those in figure 5.8, showing the indisputably rising share of the United States in industrial employment among the leading free-market industrial economies, indicate that our conclusions about the manufacturing sector are not unfounded.

Figure 4.3 shows what those data report about the performance of productivity growth for the entire period 1947–1986, both for the economy as a whole and for the manufacturing sector. To bring out the intertemporal patterns more clearly (that is, to eliminate the sharp oscillations that, as we have seen, characterize year-by-year productivity growth statistics), the graph depicts 5-year averages rather than the data for individual years.[7] We see that since about 1963 productivity growth for the economy as a whole has, indeed, generally been falling, at least until 1980. But since 1980 the average growth rate has been climbing each year, though it has

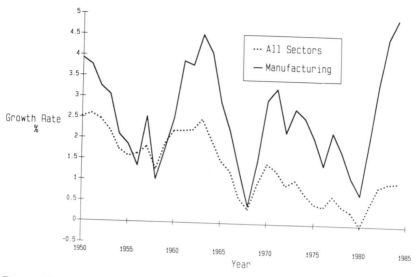

Figure 4.3
Sectoral productivity growth rates, 5-year moving averages, 1947–1986. Source: National Income and Product Accounts, *Survey of Current Business*, various issues, tables 6.2 and 6.8.

by no means come anywhere close to reattainment of its level in the 1960s. Specifically, the average growth rate for the 5 years ending in 1960 reached a peak of about 2.2% per year, while the corresponding figure for the 5 years ending in 1986 was 1.05%. (The actual growth rate for the year 1985–1986 was 1.2%.)

The same graph also shows the 5-year average growth rates for productivity in manufacturing. Here, clearly, the pattern is very different. While there have been, perhaps, three intervals of decline, at least two of them (1950–1956 and 1963–1968) very sharp, and one of them (1971–1980) rather protracted, the general time pattern is neither markedly downhill nor markedly uphill. At least that was so until the 1980s, when a spectacular rise began, bringing rates of growth higher than any previously experienced in postwar American history. The conclusion is that whether the *aggregate* figures are or are not taken to be on the brink of heralding a long-term slowdown in U.S. productivity growth, that certainly cannot be said for manufacturing on the basis of the data available so far. The statistics simply do not provide any grounds for pessimism about the prospects for productivity growth in U.S. manufacturing relative to its historical performance. Our saying this, however, does not constitute a sanguine forecast for the future. We intend absolutely no prediction here, since we believe strongly that past and current trends are at best highly fallible presages of the future. The only sure conclusion is that the data up to this point clearly do not imply the opposite.

Two significant observations follow from the preceding evidence on the performance of manufacturing. First, the U.S. manufacturing sector has been the central focus of those who have expressed profound fears about the consequences of the U.S. productivity performance. The deindustrialization thesis stresses the danger that the "competitiveness" of American manufacturing is about to be lost, meaning that a slowdown in the productivity growth of the nation's industrial sector will make its products vulnerable to displacement, both at home and abroad, by the manufactures supplied by the Far East and Europe. If, as we have seen to be true, there is in fact no sign of such a slowdown in manufacturing productivity, one leg of the deindustrialization argument is obviously undermined. The other leg, the relative growth rates of productivity in the industrialized countries that are main competitors of the United States, will be left for discussion in the next chapter. Only one preview remark on the subject is appropriate here—whatever our intercountry growth rate comparisons turn up, they will surely not resuscitate the role of the slowdown in the United States. The United States did indeed experience such a slowdown in the 1970s, but, as will be verified, in that respect we were hardly alone. Throughout the free enterprise, industrialized economies of the world a similar slowdown occurred during roughly the same period, for reasons that are far from certain. But whatever the causes, the United States was not alone in suffering from the slowdown malaise.

The second crucial implication of the facts summarized in figure 4.3 is that, with overall productivity continuing to decline, while manufacturing exhibited no such trend, the performance of some other sectors of the economy must have been responsible for the disappointing aggregate performance of the economy. The question that follows, then, is which sectors these were. This is the subject to which we turn next.

4.4 U.S. Postwar Growth Performance in the Other (Nonmanufacturing) Sectors of the Economy

Figure 4.4, which is identical in layout to the graph that has just been discussed, describes the postwar productivity growth record of four of the eleven sectors into which the available statistics divide the economy. These are four sectors which seem of particular interest: (1) agriculture; (2) finance, insurance, and real estate; (3) other services; and (once again, for ease of comparison) (4) manufacturing. Two of the four sectors represented—

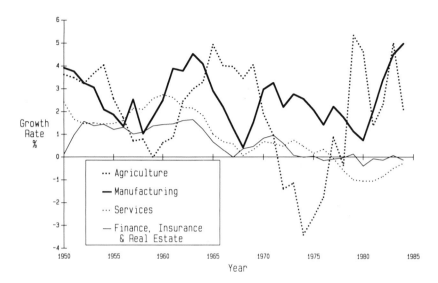

Figure 4.4
Sectoral productivity growth rates, 5-year moving averages, 1947–1986. Source: National Income and Product Accounts, *Survey of Current Business*, various issues, tables 6.2 and 6.8.

finance, insurance and real estate, and services—are among those whose growth, on balance, declined over the postwar period. On the other hand, agriculture and manufacturing are shown by further calculations to have manifested some minor increase in growth rate over the period as a whole. The two service sectors did not merely slow down. Their rates of productivity growth actually fell to negative levels (that is, output per worker actually began to decline) toward the end of the period, and those growth rates have only reattained positive magnitudes in the last year or two for which data are available. Agriculture's record is characterized by particularly great volatility, with pronounced peaks and valleys, and even an interval of sharply negative growth in the 1970s. But no clear story on long-term trends seems to emerge from figure 4.4. A coherent picture requires us to turn to a slightly different graphic approach, one that also enables us to compare the record of all 11 sectors at once.

This is undertaken in figure 4.5, a bar graph that depicts two productivity performance attributes for each of the 11 sectors—the sector's average productivity growth rate over the entire period and an indicator of the degree to which that growth rate was rising or declining. The latter was measured by constructing for each sector a trend (regression) line for productivity growth over the entire period, using the standard statistical

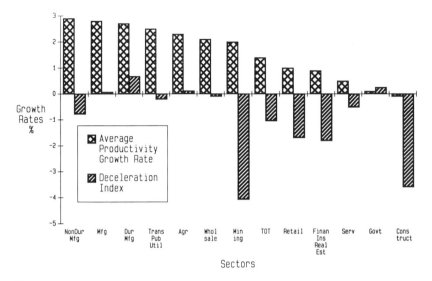

Figure 4.5
Sectoral productivity growth rates and slowdown indices, 1947–1986. Source: National
Income and Product Accounts, *Survey of Current Business*, various issues, tables 6.2 and 6.8.

technique for trend line calculation that was mentioned earlier. The slope
of that trend line, that is, the steepness with which it was rising or falling,
then served as the basis for our index of the degree of rise or decline in
productivity of each sector.

The first bar for each sector shows the sector's average growth rate over
the entire period of some four decades. The sectors have been placed, from
left to right, in order of descending average growth rate, and we see that 6
of the 11 sectors achieved growth rates for the entire period that exceeded
2% per annum. These were (1) durable manufacturing; (2) nondurable
manufacturing; (3) transportation and public utilities; (4) agriculture; (5)
wholesale trade; and (6) mining. The slow-growth sectors were construction and four service sectors: retail trade; finance, insurance, and real estate;
other services; and government. The second bar for each sector shows
whether and by how much the growth rate for the sector was increasing (a
bar above the zero baseline) or decreasing (a bar below the baseline) over
the period as a whole. The graph shows that for only one sector, durable
manufacturing, was there a substantial rise in growth rate. Four sectors
more or less remained unchanged in growth rate. These were public utilities and transportation; agriculture; wholesale trade; and government. Four
sectors showed very large drops in growth rate—mining; retail trade;

finance, insurance, and real estate; and construction—with the remaining sectors registering modest declines. The really serious losers in this process were mining and construction.

The graph immediately yields one suggestive observation: The significant losers in terms of decline in productivity growth rate were generally sectors whose growth was slow to begin with. Only one of them, mining, had an average growth rate greater than 2%, and that sector was the highest in this group. All of the others were the substantial growth laggards of the economy. In other words, the sectors of the economy to which the United States has traditionally looked for productivity growth have all continued to perform reasonably well through the period as a whole. There is no sign of a long-term slowdown in any of them, with the exception of mining. It is only those sectors that generally hold back the growth of any developed economy that seem to have slipped even further. (One plausible conjecture for several of these sectors is that they had undergone a one-shot jump in productivity growth through the contribution of computerization, but then once again new sources of growth became difficult to find.) The one clear conclusion from the sectoral breakdown of the data is that there is absolutely no evidence of a long-term slowdown in the sectors of the economy that are most progressive in terms of productivity growth.

4.5 Plotting the Time Path of Productivity Growth—Preliminary Notes on Our Statistical Tests

In the underlying postwar scenario suggested by our earlier discussion of the Maddison data, a great upward leap in productivity growth is followed by a sharp decline in the mid-1960s or early 1970s (representing, at least in part, a return to its normal level), which is followed by a revival of increased growth in the 1980s. Thus, it looks like the four decades under discussion were dominated by a long-period cycle, with one period of protracted decline and two periods of sustained rise. Our next task is to find out whether the facts support this conjectured description of the course of events. In particular, if the story has substance, one may well expect it to hold for at least a considerable proportion of the sectors of the economy. While the technical details of our statistical tests of this hypothesis can only be described fully to specialists (and so are left to the appendix to this chapter), we offer a short, non-technical summary here.[8]

In essence, a statistical test of a hypothesis such as ours is carried out by adopting a flexible mathematical equation with several numerical parameters, the shape of whose graph (called a regression curve) depends on the values assigned to those parameters—in our case, the statistical data describing the actual course of productivity growth for each sector of the economy for the period 1947–1986. The parameters of the equation are calculated by means of special statistical techniques that are designed, in effect, to make the regression curve come as close as possible to yielding the numbers given by the actual statistics, i.e., to make the shape of the curve correspond to the actual sequence of events. This procedure permits one to test a hypothesis such as ours by empirical means, letting the data themselves determine whether the regression curve has the shape our hypothesis predicts, or whether the facts call for a curve of very different shape.[9]

This is not the end of the story. For even if the regression curve turns out to have the "right" shape, it may or may not correspond to the data points very well. In real life statistical data rarely form a perfectly clear and simple pattern. Some of the data points, usually, are scattered far from the others, so that no simple curve can come close to them all. In extreme cases, the data points are so randomly scattered that statisticians would say that "the correlation is poor," and conclude that the calculated parameter values are "not statistically significant," meaning, roughly, that one cannot place much faith in the likelihood that they represent a true and reliable underlying relationship. There are standard techniques used to determine whether a parameter value is or is not "statistically significant" and there is a standard indicator called R^2 (R squared) which serves as a measure of how good the calculation actually is. R^2 is measured on a scale from 0 to 1.0. When R^2 equals 1.0 the correlation is said to be perfect, and then each and every one of the data points given by the actual statistics must lie precisely on the regression curve. At the other extreme, when R^2 equals 0, the data points generally constitute a shapeless blob, so that the regression curve really describes none of the observed data with any accuracy. In reality, R^2 figures generally lie between these extreme values, and the closer the calculated R^2 number is to 1.0, the better the correlation is said to be.

Armed with these fundamental statistical concepts, we can now turn to the statistical analysis of our sectoral productivity growth figures for the postwar American economy.

4.6 Results: Statistical Study of Sectoral Productivity Growth Patterns

The statistical calculations, in sum, confirm no universal and simple scenario. In particular, while they do not totally reject our hypothesis (that there was a postwar productivity boom, perhaps making up for the previous depression lag, then a decline back to the normal growth rate, followed by an upturn in growth rate in the 1980s), the hypothesis is shown to hold in only a few sectors at most, and even for those in a manner that has by no means been uniform. There are only four sectors for which the regression analysis supports the validity of the hypothesis, and even there the support is hardly emphatic. In no case, for example, is the R^2 value as great as 0.5, though in one case (mining) it comes close to that figure. The four sectors are mining; transportation and public utilities; wholesale trade; and other services. With the exception of transportation and public utilities and wholesale trade, these exclude the economy's productivity growth leaders, notably the two manufacturing sectors and agriculture. It is also noteworthy that the timing of the cycles differs among these four sectors. The peak is calculated statistically to have occurred in 1956 in mining, but not until 1962 in transportation and public utilities, with the other two sectors falling in between. Similarly, the subsequent bottom point of the curve occurred in 1976 in wholesale trade and mining, in 1979 in other services, and not until 1983 in transportation and public utilities. The downturn in mining and the upturn in wholesale trade and mining probably occur a bit too early to fit in very comfortably with the hypothesis.

As for the remaining sectors, three of them (construction, durable manufacturing, and retail trade) show a simple U-shaped pattern, with a downhill movement in productivity growth lasting until 1969 (durables) or even to 1973 (retail trade) followed by upward movement since then. None of these three shows an R^2 value that is impressively high. Two sectors, agriculture and nondurable manufacturing, show absolutely no simple time pattern that is statistically significant. The government sector shows a steady (linear) upward trend in productivity growth. However, little weight can be given to the statistical result for this sector, since productivity growth in government is difficult even to define, much less measure reliably. Matters are quite different for the remaining sector, finance, insurance, and real estate, which is the only sector showing a pronounced and statistically significant downward trend in productivity growth throughout the period ($R^2 = 0.48$). It is widely agreed that this is the "sick" sector of the economy in terms of productivity growth,[10] and its importance cannot be denied, even though it is hardly key in terms of the productivity status of American *industry*. Our statistical study, then, leaves us with no clear and universal pattern for developments in sectoral productivity. But, except for finance, insurance, and real estate and two sectors (agriculture and nondurable manufactures) which underwent no pronounced and protracted downturn, it is noteworthy that *every* sector seems to exhibit a pronounced pattern of rising productivity growth in recent years, all but one of them at least since 1979.

4.7   Subsector Productivity Trends

The same considerations that called for an examination of the postwar productivity record for each of the 11 sectors into which the Bureau of Economic Analysis divides the economy also led us to look further, into a finer subdivision, which breaks seven of the 11 sectors into smaller subsectors. Data are available for 65 such subsectors, of which 21 are in manufacturing, 12 are in transportation and public utilities, 7 are in finance, insurance, and real estate, and 13 are in other services. For each of these, calculations identical with those conducted for the 11 sectors were carried out. A more detailed description is provided in the appendix, but we summarize the main results here.

First, we should observe that of the 75 sectors and subsectors (3 aggregate sectors, 11 major sectors, and 61 subsectors) only 19 show any systematic pattern related to the passage of time that is statistically significant. That is, roughly speaking, about three-quarters of the sectors and subsectors do not display any significant time trend. This implies that for the preponderance of sectors long-run productivity growth was not changing in any particular direction. On the other hand, for the remaining 19 sectors and subsectors for which growth *did* manifest a significant trend, 17 exhibited a declining rate of growth over the postwar period as a whole. This is noteworthy, though to us it is only surprising that such a pattern was not even more common, given the admittedly extraordinary level of productivity growth achieved by the economy in the early postwar period. For if every sector thereafter had merely returned to its historical rate of growth, each of them obviously would have undergone a declining trend. Yet, that, as we have just seen, was true of only 17, that is, of 25%, of the sectors and subsectors.

Next, we matched up each subsector to one of our multiplicity of trial regression calculations to see which calculation fit the data for that subsector most closely (that is, the regression-curve shape—linear, hill-shaped, valley-shaped, or one with a single major hill and a single major valley— that yielded the largest value of R^2). Only 6 of the 75 sectors and subsectors showed a trend that was consistently declining and statistically significant throughout the period. This interesting group includes (1) printing and publishing; (2) air transportation; (3) pipelines (except natural gas);

(4) electrical, gas, and sanitary services; (5) personal services; and (6) auto repair. The only real surprise in the list is air transportation.

The valley-shaped subsectors include agricultural services, forestry and fisheries, real estate, amusement and recreation services, and private household services. That is, these 5 subsectors all display a period of decline in productivity growth followed by a period of recovery. The most common pattern, aside from the large number of sectors and subsectors displaying no pattern at all, is a hill followed by a valley. There are 7 such sectors and subsectors altogether, thus constituting some 9% of the total. These include two manufacturing subsectors—nonelectrical machinery and petroleum and coal products. The others in the group are transportation and public utilities as a whole, railroad transportation, finance, insurance, and real estate, and its insurance agents and brokers subsector, other services and its two subsectors, health services, and legal services.

The conclusion from all this is no different from that we have reached before. For the entire postwar period there simply is no common pattern in the growth performance of the individual sectors and subsectors of the American economy. Or, rather, if there was one predominating pattern, it was the absence of any pattern at all, which encompassed by far the greatest proportion of the group.

4.8   Concluding Comments

The available data leave us with no clear and uniform productivity growth trends for the U.S. economy. This observation goes well beyond the usual warning that discovery of a trend is not tantamount to a forecast. For in this case, even the trends themselves are not clearly discernible. What this does tell us definitively is that none of the data offer rational grounds for the fears that the economy has suffered a slowdown in its long-term growth rate. True, this may be happening in one major sector, finance, insurance and real estate, but the opposite seems to be true in other sectors, notably manufacturing and agriculture. That *some* sectors are slowing while others are advancing should, at least in itself, neither be surprising nor be taken as grounds for alarm. Aside from that, the fact that U.S. manufacturing is alive and well in terms of its current performance relative to its historical productivity growth record provides reassurance in just that arena that has been the focus of the strongest concerns.

Of course, that is not the end of the story. Even if the United States is suffering no slowdown relative to its past, other economies may be doing even better than that, and the competitiveness of this economy may thereby indeed be threatened. It is true that recent figures from the U.S. Bureau of Labor Statistics indicate that between 1979 and 1986 manufacturing productivity in the United States grew faster than that in West Germany, France, or Canada, somewhat more slowly than that of Italy and the United Kingdom, and had substantially narrowed the growth rate gap with Japan, thus remaining behind, in terms of manufacturing growth rate, only one of America's industrial competitor economies. Still, as an indicator of long-run developments, one can no more rely on the (so far) brief recovery of the 1980s than upon the decline of the 1970s (which was nearly universal among the industrialized nations). The following chapter, therefore, turns to the international comparisons required for an evaluation of this remaining issue.

Notes

1. Roughly, total factor productivity is based on an index of the increased efficiency of *all* inputs used by the firm (e.g., labor, capital, fuel, raw materials) rather than just the quantity of labor that is employed as the denominator in a labor productivity calculation. The purpose of a TFP index is to evaluate whether technological progress and associated ancillary influences have expanded the capacity of the full range of inputs of the economy to produce outputs. For a fuller discussion of the concept of total factor productivity, see chapter 11.

2. The explanation of these oscillations may conceivably have some connection with chaos processes that have recently been analyzed in the economics literature. Such models are designed to explain oscillatory behavior in economic variables.

3. There are at least two excellent papers that have also reached this conclusion: one by Michael Darby [1984] and one by Helliwell, Sturm, and Salou [1985]. Others who have disputed the contention that the role of U.S. industry in the world economy is in decline include Branson [1981], Lawrence [1984], Summers [1983], Norton [1986], and Bergsten [1983].

4. Labor productivity in manufacturing, measured as GNP originating per full-time-equivalent employee, grew at an annual average rate of 5.2% between 1983 and 1986.

5. It will come as no surprise to the specialist that the statistical fit is unimpressive, given the small number of observations and the considerable deviation of the outlier points. The calculated least squares line is given by the following equation: growth rate $= 0.986 + (0.00059)$ (calendar year), where the standard errors of the constant term and the time coefficient are, respectively, 0.86 and 0.0075, thus making both variables statistically insignificant. The R^2 value is 0.00069.

6. The most obvious reason is the difficulty of measuring the outputs of services such as government. As a result some of these are measured by quantity of input (!), so that, by definition, their productivity (output/input) remains constant.

7. That is, we have plotted what are called "5-year moving averages." Thus, the first dot in the graph reports the average of the growth figures for the five years 1947–1951, while the second dot shows the average for 1948–1952, the third dot shows the average for 1949–1953, and so on.

8. The remainder of this section provides an intuitive introduction to regression analysis concepts; economists will no doubt prefer to skip it.

9. A linear (straight-line) pattern would mean an uninterrupted downward or upward trend in productivity growth throughout the entire period; a hill-shaped pattern would mean that productivity growth first rose and then began to fall; a valley-shaped graph would mean that productivity growth first fell and later began to rise; and a hill-shape followed by a valley would mean that productivity growth rose early in the postwar period, subsequently fell, and then began to recover (our hypothesized sequence of events).

10. This sector is also the service industry most severely plagued by measurement problems. So even for this one, the finding of a downward trend in productivity growth may be due to measurement bias.

5

International
Convergence: The
Comparative U.S.
Productivity Lag

... an alternative to the scenario of other industrial countries rapidly surpassing America in technological and economic leadership is that of a number of countries drifting, within a narrowing range, toward some asymptotic level of economic performance, a level first attained by America.
Rosenberg [1982, p. 282]

In the last chapter we concluded that, in absolute terms, the productivity growth record of the United States offers no grounds for alarm. Its productivity growth performance *relative to other countries*, however, may appear to be quite another matter. Not only has U.S. productivity growth been significantly slower than that of a number of industrialized countries, but the shortfall has persisted for a very considerable period of time—in several cases more than half a century—certainly no temporary aberration. Indeed, the magnitude and persistence of this lag constitute real grounds for concern that over the long run the United States will lose out in terms of its relative position in the productivity growth race and in terms of its status as the world's economic leader, both of which, as we have seen, are legitimate yardsticks for evaluating productivity performance. There is no doubt that in the past few decades the United States *has* lost out in relative terms, while a number of other economies have all but caught up to this country's absolute productivity level and per capita output.

Yet, there is another way of looking at the matter that makes these developments seem much less threatening. This alternative interpretation of the record is called "the convergence hypothesis," which asserts that economic forces are enabling other countries to catch up toward the United States, but not (necessarily) to surpass it. Through the constant transfer of new technology, leader countries and those most closely in their van learn the latest productive techniques from one another, but virtually by definition the follower countries have more to learn from the leaders than the leaders have to learn from them (the so-called "advantages of backwardness"). This mechanism, which this chapter will examine in some detail, has two implications: First, it means that those countries that lag somewhat behind the leaders can be expected systematically to move toward the level of achievement of the leaders. Second, the mechanism undermines itself automatically as follower countries gradually eliminate the difference between their own performance and that of the countries that were ahead of them; i.e., the very fact of convergence means that the differential learning opportunities that are the source of these advantages of (slight) backwardness will exhaust themselves. This is a fundamentally optimistic view of the economic prospects for at least those countries that share in the convergence process (though, as we shall see, the bulk of the world's nations do not). For the more fortunate economies (a group we have dubbed the "convergence club") the convergence process offers the prospect of shared prosperity, in which similarity in achievement all but eliminates the special significance of the role of leader.

In this chapter, we examine both the logic of and the evidence relating to the convergence hypothesis. We find that, while convergence has exerted a strong influence on the ordering of nations in the productivity race, its workings are not overwhelmingly powerful, swamping all other pertinent influences. Moreover, while there is clearly a group of nations that participates in the convergence process, it is neither an unchanging group nor one whose membership requirements can be explained trivially. From all of this, we can draw some comfort about the general prospects for U.S. productivity performance and about its apparently inferior record in the recent past. (Some others who have considered this interpretation of the relative U.S. productivity growth performance include Abramovitz [1986] and Rosenberg [1982].) But, for several reasons aside from the slightly mixed picture that emerges, the convergence hypothesis does not offer reasonable grounds for complacency. First, as we shall see, the fact that a nation has achieved membership in the "convergence club" is no guarantee against subsequent ejection from that select group; and we know relatively little about why or when this is apt to occur. Second, the sources of convergence are obviously not the only variables affecting the course of an economy's productivity, and an effective productivity policy for any country must take many other influences into account. Third, one cannot ignore the nations that have not succeeded in entering the club, particularly because this group of have-not nations includes some of the world's poorest countries, and because some of them appear to be falling even further behind. Finally, we cannot rely on convergence necessarily to continue largely unchanged or to continue indefinitely. As a matter of fact, we shall see that there has been a considerable period in the not very distant past when *divergence* in productivity growth was probably the predominating tendency. What has happened before cannot be ruled out for the future. We shall see, then, that while the convergence phenomenon does remove any grounds for panic about the U.S. record of relative productivity growth, it does not by any means eliminate all reasons for careful consideration of productivity policy.

5.1   The Record of Relative U.S. Productivity Growth

We begin by reviewing some of the data describing the record of U.S. productivity growth. Table 5.1, based on Angus Maddison's [1982, p. 212] estimates of real absolute gross domestic product (GDP) per work-hour, shows the growth rate of GDP per work-hour for 16 industrial countries between 1870 and 1979.[1] The last two lines in the table show how the U.S. growth rate for the period compares with the average growth rate for all 16 countries in that period, and (last line of table) how many of the countries among Maddison's 16 achieved growth rates superior to that of the United States. First, looking at the most recent data, we see that almost every other country's labor productivity growth rate seems to have been superior to that of the United States. In both the decades of the 1950s and the 1960s 14 countries outperformed the United States. The United Kingdom was the only exception in the first half of this period and Australia in the second. In the decade of the 1970s Canada and Switzerland were the only countries that fell behind the United States. In the two most recent decades the American growth rate was only a bit more than half of the average for the other countries in Maddison's group.

The earlier figures in the table show that since 1880 the United States has *never* been in the vanguard in terms of its productivity growth rate. In fact, according to Maddison's calculations, in no peacetime period since 1880 has the United States been outperformed by less than 5 countries, often including such major economies as France and Germany. While between 1890 and 1929 the American growth rate was some 15% higher than the average for the other countries, by the 1930s the ratio of the U.S. figure to the average for the others had fallen to its century-long low. Only in the decade of World War II did relative U.S. achievement reattain a high

Table 5.1
Growth rates of GDP per work-hour, for 16 industrial countries, 1870–1979

Country	1870–1880	1880–1890	1890–1900	1900–1913	1913–1929	1929–1938	1938–1950	1950–1960	1960–1970	1970–1979
Australia	1.82	0.37	−0.80	1.01	1.49	0.88	2.20	2.76	2.22	2.83
Austria	1.50	1.98	1.93	1.50	0.72	0.21	1.61	5.69	5.90	4.32
Belgium	1.84	1.36	0.93	0.90	1.79	1.01	1.14	3.14	4.88	4.88
Canada	2.19	1.23	1.70	2.70	1.21	0.0	5.36	3.09	2.72	1.83
Denmark	1.47	1.95	1.90	2.21	2.57	0.43	1.23	2.97	4.90	3.06
Finland	1.29[a]	1.14[a]	3.36[a]	2.42[a]	1.95	1.89	2.10	3.96	6.37	2.60
France	2.32	0.90	2.02	1.82	2.34	2.83	0.75	4.39	5.38	4.09
Germany	1.50	2.15	2.42	1.41	1.40	2.34	−0.40	6.64	5.29	4.50
Italy	0.22	0.43	1.20	2.35	1.92	2.96	0.56	4.27	6.69	3.91
Japan	1.87[a]	1.72	2.11[a]	1.88	3.42	3.41	−3.20	5.57	9.96	5.03
Netherlands	1.44[a]	1.26[a]	0.98	1.07	2.44	−0.10	1.93	3.33	4.93	4.06
Norway	1.39	1.96	1.17	2.02	2.78	2.61	1.88	4.03	4.52	3.66
Sweden	1.76	1.95	2.70	2.62	2.40	2.66	3.43	3.43	4.79	2.55
Switzerland	1.59[a]	1.37[a]	1.47[a]	1.26[a]	3.18	1.01	1.52	2.98	3.69	1.91
U.K.	1.61	1.20	1.24	0.90	1.44	0.87	2.21	2.19	3.56	2.77
U.S.	2.28	1.86	1.96	1.98	2.39	0.74	4.03	2.41	2.51	1.92
Ratio: U.S./average	1.39	1.30	1.19	1.12	1.14	0.50	2.44	0.63	0.51	0.57
Number superior to U.S.	1	5	5	6	6	11	1	14	14	13

Source: Maddison [1982, p. 212]. We would like to thank Jeffrey G. Williamson for pointing out some errors in this table in the hardcover edition.
a. Figure estimated by interpolation.

level (in that wartime period the U.S. growth rate exceeded that of all but 1 country in the group, and its growth rate figure was some $2\frac{1}{2}$ times the average—about twice the ratio for the period 1870–1929).

We conclude from the preceding figures that the lag in the U.S. productivity growth rate behind those of other leading industrial countries is a long-standing phenomenon, one whose magnitude has, at least in some time periods, been substantial, and that the set of countries that have outperformed the United States even before very recent decades has not been negligible in number. Recent experience, then, is no mere aberration and represents no sudden collapse in relative American performance. It does, however, represent some considerable worsening relative to what that economy was able to achieve in earlier periods. All of this obviously calls for some explanation, as does the near-paradoxical fact that the United States has been able to retain its *absolute* productivity lead for so long a period despite the frequent inferiority of its *growth* performance. Yet, while explanation is clearly desirable, we shall not attempt anything so ambitious. Rather than aspiring to disentangle the many influences that undoubtedly went into the underlying process, we shall focus on only one element that we consider to be particularly significant: the convergence phenomenon. We shall see that it can shed some light on the long duration of the lag in U.S. performance, though it will offer less enlightenment on the sources of its postwar deterioration.

5.2   The Logic of the Convergence Model: A First Look and Some Implications for Productivity Policy

Before we lay out the evidence for the convergence hypothesis, we first consider very briefly what can give rise to the phenomenon and what it implies for the issue before us here. We save a more detailed discussion of convergence until later in the chapter, when we shall have the benefit of some pertinent historical background.

Convergence is an idea that is familiar to economic historians, and goes back to the work of such eminent writers as Alexander Gerschenkron, Simon Kuznets, and Moses Abramovitz. The hypothesis asserts that when the productivity level of one (or several) country(ies) is substantially superior to that of a number of other economies, largely as a result of differences in their productive techniques, then those laggard countries that are not too far behind the leaders will be in a position to embark upon a catch-up process, and many of these lagging countries actually will do so. This catch-up process will continue so long as the economies that are approaching the leader's performance continue to have a lot to learn from the leader. However, as the distance between the two groups narrows, the stock of knowledge unabsorbed by the laggards will grow smaller and approach exhaustion. The catch-up process will then tend to terminate unless some supplementary and unrelated influence fortuitously comes into play. Meanwhile, those countries that are so far behind the leaders that it is impractical for them to profit substantially from the leaders' knowledge will generally not be able to participate in the convergence process at all, and many such economies will find themselves falling even further behind.

The most important influence underlying this hypothesis is the transfer of technology that constantly takes place among many of the world's economies. There is indisputable evidence that every advanced industrial country constantly adopts technical ideas from the others. Competitive pressures in the international marketplace and the vigilant activities of entrepreneurs (who do not care from which country they get their ideas or in which countries they operate) guarantee effective and rapid dissemination of superior productive techniques from one country to another. However, in the process of reciprocal exchange of ideas, clearly it is the laggard economies that have more to learn from the leaders than the reverse. That is the heart of the explanation of a convergence process.

How does convergence affect our evaluation of the U.S. productivity record? If there really is a convergence process that dominates the productivity performance of a significant set of industrialized countries, then a lag in the productivity growth of those countries that are in the vanguard, rather than constituting a manifestation of failure, must be a normal and, indeed, unavoidable part of the process. In a catch-up process those who were initially behind *must* advance more rapidly than those who were ahead. Otherwise, the distance between them could not possibly narrow. Consequently, if it turns out that the evidence for the convergence hypothesis is persuasive, we must modify our evaluation of the U.S. productivity performance correspondingly. We shall see, in fact, that at least over the longer run, growth of productivity in the United States has been substantially faster than would have been expected in a hypothetical, perfect convergence process. In other words, on this view of the matter, U.S. relative performance over the course of about a century, rather than falling short, has instead been better than might have been expected. The record since World War II is not quite as outstanding, but it still constitutes no basis for the conclusion that the country has entered a period of serious relative productivity decline.

5.3   The Empirical Evidence on the Convergence Phenomenon: Part I

To test empirically whether a convergence process is in fact underway it is necessary to deal with data that span a substantial period of time. Over shorter periods such as a decade or two matters are too likely to be affected preponderantly by transitory influences that can give spurious indications of convergence or the reverse. For example, data for the period immediately following World War II for the leading industrial countries seem unambiguously to show a strong convergence process, when in fact they may merely reflect the recovery of the economies most heavily damaged by the war. To escape the problems caused by figures pertaining only to short intervals, one must usually turn to historical data whose earlier components are apt to be incomplete and less reliable. Fortunately, there do exist productivity estimates spanning more than a century, which have been assembled with care and insight by Maddison [1982, 1987], and which will serve as the basis for the initial portion of our analysis. These are the data that were used in table 5.1. We shall also make use of some valuable estimates provided by R. C. O. Matthews, C. H. Feinstein, and J. C. Odling-Smee [1982], henceforth referred to as MFO, in their illuminating treatise.

Maddison's data for 16 countries[1] over the course of more than a century (1870–1979) show labor productivity (gross domestic product per work-hour) in the industrialized countries to have tended to approach ever closer to that of the leader.[2] This closing of ranks is obvious from figure 5.1, which shows the history of absolute productivity levels in seven of the countries (the graph is based on Maddison's data and patterned after a graph in MFO). The strong convergence toward the vanguard (led in the first decades by Australia and the United Kingdom and, approximately since World War I, by the United States) is even more evident when we examine the underlying statistics closely.[3] In 1870 the ratio of output per labor hour in the country with the highest productivity level (of Maddison's sample of 16 nations) to the same figure for the least productive country was approximately 8 : 1. That is, an hour of Japanese labor in 1870 produced only 1/8th the contribution to GDP of that of an hour of Australian labor (and about 1/5th of that of an hour of U.K. labor). By 1979 that ratio for the leader (the United States) to the laggard (still Japan) had fallen to about 2 : 1. Figure 5.2 gives the details for intermediate dates for both productivity growth and GDP per capita. It plots for each year for which Maddison supplies data the coefficient of variation (the ratio of the standard

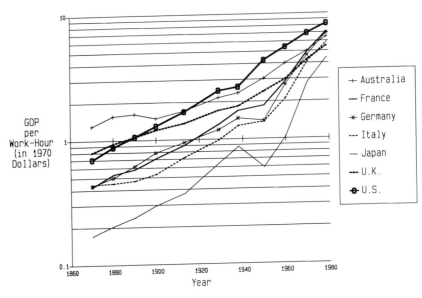

Figure 5.1
Labor productivity (GDP/work-hour), 7 leading industrial countries, 1870–1979. Source:
Maddison [1982, p. 212].

deviation to the mean) of GDP per work-hour and GDP per capita for all
16 countries. The *coefficient of variation* is a standard statistical measure of
the similarity or dissimilarity of a group of numbers; that is, if the coefficient
of variation turns out to be high, it means that the numbers in question are
relatively far apart, while if the coefficient is low, it means the numbers are
comparatively close to one another. Figure 5.2 uses this coefficient to show
that the narrowing of the range of levels of productivity and GDP per
capita among the countries has proceeded steadily, with the exception of a
brief but sharp fallback during and after World War II. Certainly, the
downward trend in this dispersion measure is strong and steady in each of
the two periods separated by World War II, with the post-1970 figures
apparently rejoining the prewar trend.

We undertook a similar analysis using Maddison's data on movements
of total factor productivity (TFP) over time. TFP is a measure of the
productivity of the aggregation of the inputs used rather than just the
productivity of labor alone. It is defined as the share of gross domestic product growth not attributable just to expanded amounts of capital and labor
used and so, rather, to rises in their productivity. Scarcity of capital stock

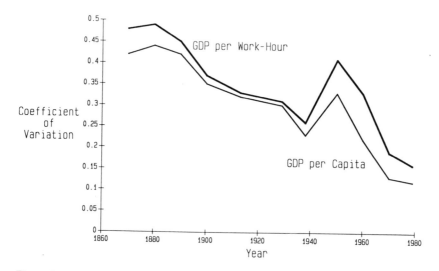

Figure 5.2
Coefficients of variation, GDP per work-hour and GDP per capita, 16 Maddison countries, 1870–1979. Source: Maddison [1982, p. 212].

data restricted our computations to 7 countries: Canada, France, Germany, Italy, Japan, the United Kingdom, and the United States. The data indicate that for this sample of countries there has also been a steady convegence of TFP levels from 1880 to 1979. This result held up among a wide variety of alternative definitions and measures of TFP levels and growth rates, and convergence was more rapid after World War II than before it. The coefficient of variation of TFP levels among these 7 countries declined from 0.4 in 1950 to 0.1 in 1979. (See Wolff [1987b] for more details.)

The strength of the convergence can also be examined in another way. Convergence means, tautologically, that countries that start out behind must grow more rapidly than those that begin ahead of the average, and that the further ahead a country starts, the slower its subsequent growth must be. Figure 5.3 confirms that this is indeed what happened in GDP per work-hour (labor productivity) in the time period 1870–1979. The graph shows the growth rate of labor productivity for Maddison's 16 countries (on the vertical axis) plotted against the initial (1870) level of labor productivity on the horizontal axis. The strong inverse relation between growth rate of labor productivity or GDP per capita and initial level of each measure is clear from the diagram.[4] An analogous graph (not reproduced here) for GDP per capita displays exactly the same pattern.

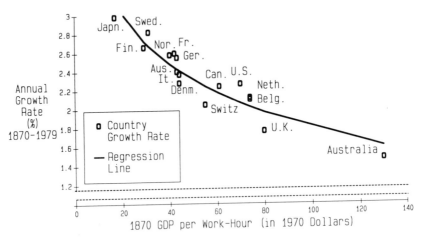

Figure 5.3
Labor productivity since 1870 (GDP per work-hour), growth rate vs. 1870 level, 16 industrialized countries. Source: Maddison [1982, p. 212].

5.4   The Empirical Evidence, Part II: Expanding the Database

The preceding interpretation of the historical data has recently been subjected to some very cogent criticisms (see, e.g., Romer [1986] and De Long [1988]). Perhaps most important, it has been pointed out that the data encompass a very limited number of countries (for example, only 16 countries in Maddison's rich body of figures) and that, in the nature of the case, these are the *ex post* success stories; i.e., the countries studied were chosen on the basis of their current level of economic prosperity, rather than on the basis of their economic status in 1870. They include Japan, which no one would have listed among the industrial nations a century ago, and exclude Argentina, which might well have seemed then to be among the world's most promising economies. An *ex post* sample of successes is, almost by definition, likely to display greater convergence than a sample selected *ex ante* (before the fact), in which a number of the participants may turn out to be relative failures. The question, then, is whether the convergence result of the preceding statistial calculations can be attributed largely, or even entirely, to use of our *ex post* sample of successful industrial nations.[5] Without adding data on countries other than those in the Maddison and MFO samples, we cannot reject this possibility. We therefore shall report the results of some tests of this issue using rather extensive recent data. First, however, we shall examine some additional estimates for earlier time periods.

a. *Bairoch's Data on 19 European Countries, 1830–1913*. Bradford De Long has called our attention to some estimates of GNP per capita going back before 1870, notably those provided by Bairoch [1976].[6] While such early figures obviously raise questions of reliability, we know of no reason to distrust Bairoch's painstaking estimates more than other estimates for the period. Bairoch provides data for 19 European countries,[7] essentially by decade, for the period 1830–1913. To test our convergence hypothesis using Bairoch's data, we arranged the 19 countries in descending order of their per capita GNPs in 1870, an intermediate date in the data. (We also did the same thing using an 1830 classification, with roughly similar results.) We then constructed a sample of countries consisting of the top 8 economies (that is, the set of 8 countries at the top of the list). Then we successively constructed samples of the top 9, the top 10, and so on, until we got to the top 14 (beyond that number of countries, too many data points were missing to permit an illuminating calculation). For each sample size we calculated a time series of the coefficients of variation (again using it to measure the degree of similarity or dissimilarity of the economic performance of the countries studied) for each year for which estimates were provided.

The results showed a straightforward pattern. Up until a bit after the middle of the nineteenth century there seems to have been a universal pattern of *divergence*: That is these countries drew ever further apart from one another. However, convergence in the top group (8 countries) appears to begin perhaps as early as 1860, and certainly by 1880 (figure 5.4). By 1880 convergence had also begun to characterize somewhat larger groups of countries—the sets of the top 9 and top 10 countries. But for larger country groups divergence persisted right up to World War I.

To the extent one can give credence to these calculations, the general conclusions are clear. Much of the nineteenth century was a period of divergence in standards of living of the leading European economies. Then, some time between the middle and the end of the century, this process began to erode, and was replaced by convergence among the initially (or later) more affluent of the countries. As Moses Abramovitz has pointed out to us in conversation, this is precisely what one should have expected. Before the Industrial Revolution the countries of Europe were relatively homogeneous in their general poverty. Then Great Britain pulled ahead of the others, inaugurating a growth in heterogeneity that was intensified as a small set of European leaders, including Belgium, Switzerland, the Netherlands, France, and Germany, also jumped ahead of the others. Only toward the end of the century was the leaders' example able to

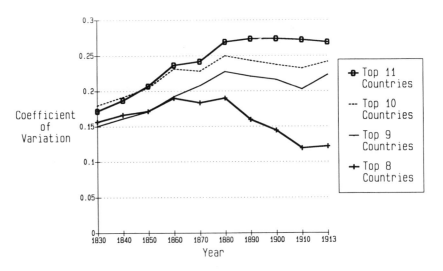

Figure 5.4
Coefficient of variation, GNP per capita, 1830–1913, Bairoch countries, 1870 ranking.
Source: Bairoch [1976].

spread, so that convergence could extend to a group of any considerable size.

This discussion of Bairoch's figures is not meant as a serious contribution to the basic issue that concerns us here—the reality of the apparent convergence process. Bairoch's figures largely precede the period that is at issue, and his sample of countries is still far too small to permit any convincing test based on an *ex ante* classification. Rather, his numbers are examined here primarily to provide some interesting background on the subject. They do suggest that somewhere in the last quarter of the nineteenth century a group of more prosperous countries did begin to converge. However, for a fuller test of the convergence hypothesis one must turn to a more extensive data set.[8]

b. *Summers and Heston's Data for 72 Countries, 1950–1980.* Fortunately, for the period 1950–1980 (and a few years after that) Summers and Heston [1984] have provided excellent data on per-capita GDP for 72 countries (data for additional countries are provided for a somewhat briefer period). The figures for different countries are rendered comparable by a sophisticated adjustment in terms of relative purchasing power rather than currency exchange rates. They are expressed in units that Summers and Heston call "1975 international dollars," and the statistics are referred to as real per-capita GDP (RGDP). These figures permit a comparison of the performance

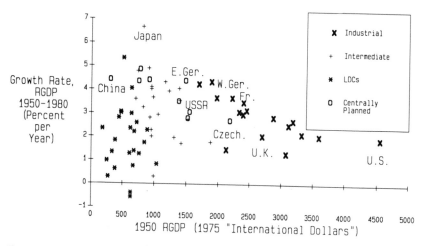

Figure 5.5
Growth rates of real gross domestic product (RGDP), 1950–1980, versus 1950 RGDP, for 72 countries classified by 1960 RGDP (in 1975 "international dollars"). Source: Summers and Heston [1984].

of the less developed countries, the Soviet countries, and other groupings with that of the leading industrial countries (see note 9 for a listing of the 72 countries). But more important for our purposes, they permit the selection of an *ex ante* (or, alternatively, a midpoint) sample of countries, and thus an *ex ante* test of our convergence hypothesis. Most of our tests which will be described here are based on an *ex ante* (1950) ranking of the countries, though many of them were repeated with a midpoint (1960) ranking, with rather similar results.

The Summers-Heston data are summarized in figure 5.5, which extends the construction of figure 5.3 to their 72 countries. Figure 5.5 plots the average annual growth rate of each country's RGDP (1950–1980) against the 1950 value of this variable for that country. The countries have been divided into 18 industrialized countries, 21 "intermediate countries," 9 centrally planned economies, and 23 less developed countries.[9] Examination of the data points indicates that, with the noteworthy exception of the LDCs, each of the country groups exhibits the characteristic negative slope of figure 5.3, that is, the pattern in which the initially poorest countries are those that subsequently grow fastest, as is required if they are to begin to catch up with the initially wealthier countries. This statistical evidence suggests that the LDCs alone have failed to meet this necessary condition for intragroup convergence—the poorest country in the group approaching closer to the wealthiest.

The important point is that, with the exception of the LDCs, real GDP per capita (RGDP) in each of the other country groups approached closer to that of the industrialized economies. For the set of all other countries the ratio of RGDP of the richest to the poorest country fell over 50%, from 15.2 in 1950 to 7.4 in 1980. For the planned economies the coefficient of variation fell from 0.44 to 0.33 between 1950 and 1980. Even more to the point, average RGDP among the intermediate countries rose 24% closer to that of the industrial nations, and in the centrally planned economies it moved 32% closer to that of the industrialized economies. The coefficient of variation for RGDP for all three groups together fell from 0.55 in 1950 to 0.42 in 1980. These country groups, then, seem to be made up of members of the convergence club (even if some of them are only second- or third-class members.)

Matters are quite different for the less developed countries. It is clear from inspection of figure 5.5 that the data points for the LDCs constitute no clear-cut pattern and certainly show no sign of the negative slope characteristic of the points for each of the other groups. The ratio of the highest to lowest RGDP for countries in the LDC group *rose* more than 45%, from 5.8 in 1950 to 8.5 in 1980, and the coefficient of variation rose from 0.36 to 0.53. All of this indicates that, on the average, rather than converging, the poorer LDCs are in fact growing poorer and the relatively rich LDCs are getting richer. Even more important, average RGDP in the LDCs relative to that of the industrial countries was actually 17% lower in 1980 than in 1950.

The failure of the less developed countries to achieve convergence is probably explained in good part by the likelihood that in very poor countries lack of education, impeding social arrangements and other such influences tend to swamp the advantages of backwardness—the fact that less developed countries have more to learn from the leaders than the leaders have to learn from them. Only in a country with a sufficient head start is the balance between these forces of convergence and its ab- sence reversed. We shall have more to say about the prospects for the LDCs in chapter 9 on the role of education in productivity growth.

Let us see, next, how the preceding statistical observations stand up under an *ex ante* classification of countries.

c. *The Summers–Heston Data and the Convergence Hypothesis: Summary of Some Statistical Tests.* In an effort to avoid overstating the case for conver- gence, we subjected the Summers–Heston data to literally every statistical test we could devise. For the interested reader, the details of our five tests (which include a moving average approach, nonlinear and piecewise regressions, ratios of coefficients of variation for country samples of different size, year-by-year coefficients of variation, and year-by-year Gini coefficients and regressions) are found in the the appendix to this chapter, but in general the results seem to add up to the following story: For perhaps the top 15 countries convergence has been marked and unambiguous between 1950 and 1981, though there has been something of a retreat in the last few years. Taking all non-LDC countries together (48 in all), there has also been some overall convergence. However, the complete sample of 72 countries contains a number of fairly extreme deviants. Some of these are countries like Uganda and Nigeria, desperately poor nations that have fallen far behind the top group. On the other hand, countries like Japan and Taiwan, with relatively low initial economic levels and subsequent outstanding performances, are deviants in the other direction. Thus, the data are not inconsistent with the view that a convergence club of countries does indeed exist, at least in the postwar period. Use of *ex ante* samples does not undermine this conclusion. Besides that, there are some other countries that are knocking insistently at the doors of the club or have even achieved membership. But this movement is still far from universal.[10]

5.5　The Convergence Process: Its Logic and Operation

Having examined the pertinent facts, and having concluded that the convergence hypothesis survives, we can now return once more to its explanation. What is there in the growth process that can lead to the formation of a select and relatively fortunate group of countries that simultaneously lead the world in productivity levels and whose growth rates enable the followers to come rather steadily closer to the position of the leader? Without an explanation there is relatively little that one can hope to learn from mere examination of the facts or even from the outcome of statistical tests of significance, and one can have little confidence that the observed behavioral trends are more than fortuitous developments, in large part an illusion engendered by our deliberately loose definition of what constitutes membership of the convergence club. If members are defined simply to be those economies that have in fact converged upon the leaders, then in a random world in which some economies end up closer to the leaders while others do not, the existence of a statistically determined convergence club would be attributable simply to the way in which we have chosen to define it. We believe, however, that the theoretical analysis to which we turn next, no matter how informal it unavoidably is gives us good reason for more confidence in the substance of the statistical results.

We follow standard analysis by taking technological innovation and the accumulation of capital to be the two primary sources of productivity growth. The role of the dissemination of innovation in general and of technology transfer in particular in a convergence process has already been suggested. We begin our discussion here by pointing out some of the implications of this phenomenon. We shall turn to the connection with international differentials in capital accumulation and its role in the convergence process in chapter 8, which examines the role of saving and investment in productivity growth.

As usual, the role of the entrepreneur is associated with the innovation process. However, here, in distinction from Joseph Schumpeter's [1911] classic discussion of the entrepreneur whose primary role is the initial innovation, the entrepreneur on whom we are driven to focus our attention is the *imitator*, the one who recognizes previously unexploited opportunities for profitable transfer of productive knowledge that is already in use elsewhere. Though in Schumpeter the imitator plays a role that is entirely subordinate to the innovator's, here we reverse the hierarchy. Before discussing the reason, we may pause to note that the concept of "imitative entrepreneurship" is not mere abuse of language. The decision to invest time, effort, and capital in the transfer of a new process or a new product to an area not previously considered promising for the purpose requires imagination, alertness toward unexploited opportunities, leadership, organizational ability, and a considerable willingness to bear risk. In short, the imitative entrepreneur who does not simply repeat what has been done a thousand times before, but creatively seeks out new locations in which to carry out activities fairly recently introduced elsewhere, requires all the personal qualities that characterize the successful innovator.

Why, then, does imitative rather than innovative entrepreneurship play the main role in our explanation of the convergence process? The answer lies in the orientation of our analysis toward the long run. We shall argue now that, while the presence of an initial innovation within a particular nation's geographic boundaries may confer some transitory advantage to that economy, the *transfer* of technology tends rapidly to wipe out further differential gains. We are all generally aware how swift the technology transfer process has become in recent years. The evidence confirms this view. For example, Edwin Mansfield et al. [1982], in a study based on a sample of chemical, semiconductor, and pharmaceutical innovations, found that, "technology is being transferred across national boundaries more rapidly than in the past" (p. 209); Mansfield's [1985, p. 221] study of 10 industries found the median rate of diffusion to be 6 to 18 months; and a study by John Tilton [1971] of the semiconductor industry found that the average diffusion time for innovations was only about $2\frac{1}{2}$ years. These examples are not atypical. In the industrial world's higher-tech industries, product specifications and production techniques have an astonishing degree of similarity. There is little doubt that a General Motors auto plant of 1988 bears less resemblance technically to itself as it was 15 years earlier than to corresponding 1988 plants in France, Germany, or Japan.

What is less widely recognized, however, is how rapid technology transfer sometimes was in earlier periods. Railroads provide a prime example. Stephenson's *Rocket* is generally considered to have been the first successful passenger locomotive, and it had its inaugural prize run in 1829. In that very same year two locomotives were exported from Britain to the United States. The following year witnessed the successful run on the Baltimore and Ohio tracks of the first U.S.-built locomotive, the *Peter Cooper*, whose traction power was three times that of Stephenson's engine. A very similar story can be told of the steamship. Robert Fulton's *Claremont* was conceived in Paris, built with the aid of British engine technology, constructed and run in the United States, and imitated in England within about a year. This last example also shows that leader nations also learn from the laggards—the traffic in technical knowledge does not move only one way. Here we have a case of the clear leader, England, learning from the still primitive U.S. economy. As a matter of fact, that same example carried forward in time makes a related point rather dramatically. Between 1870 and World War II, when other economies making heavy use of British inventions had caught up with and overtaken the United Kingdom, the latter continued to retain predominance primarily in one industry—shipbuilding, whose technology was initially so heavily American.

We conclude from this discussion that over longer periods priority in invention may matter less to the relative productivity growth of an economy than does the effectiveness of the activities of the imitative entrepreneurs who operate within its boundaries. Here it is important to note that no reference was made to *native* entrepreneurs. This is because the evidence seems to indicate that imitative entrepreneurship is among the most internationally mobile of inputs. Eric J. Hobsbawm [1969, p. 137] recounts how in the first half of the nineteenth century British entrepreneurs traveled to many foreign lands seeking and finding opportunities to exploit the introduction of English productive techniques and local manufacture of new British products, illegally smuggled before 1825, and openly after that date. The opening of Japanese firms in the United States and Great Britain represents just the same sort of export of imitative entrepreneurship today.

5.6 The Convergence Evidence and U.S. Productivity Performance: Some Quantitative Comments

Before concluding this chapter, we can now see very briefly in more quantitative terms what our statistical convergence evidence implies about the U.S. productivity growth record (for a good parallel discussion of the general subject, see Nelson [1988]). Convergence, as we have several times noted, implies that it is perfectly "normal" for the leader nation to exhibit a productivity growth rate that is usually lower than that of the economies that are moving closer to it. But a leader's growth performance can conceivably be worse than that; that is, it may be even slower than that called for by the convergence process and the record of achievement of the other participant countries. One way to impart substance to this notion is offered by the statistical (regression) curve depicted in figure 5.3. This is a standard statistical representation of the overall pattern shown by a set of data points like that in the figure. There, if the data point that represents U.S. performance were to lie precisely on the line of the regression curve, we could interpret that to mean that American productivity performance was exactly as predicted by a hypothetical, perfect convergence process. If that data point were to fall below the curve, it would mean that U.S. productivity growth had been worse than could have been expected and a reason for special concern. The interpretation of a data point above the curve is clearly analogous.

What do we find to have occurred in fact? In figure 5.3, we find the U.S. data point clearly to lie well above the regression curve. Roughly speaking, the U.S. growth rate was some 20% higher than the figure that the regression curve called for. That is, for other countries to have caught up to us at the same rate as they were catching up to still other countries previously ahead of them, productivity in the U.S. would have had to grow some 20% more slowly than it did in fact. Thus, rather than simply achieving consistency with the requirements of convergence, the *long-term* U.S. growth record has clearly been a superior one on that standard. This conclusion is supported by a slightly different way of looking at the matter. While in 1870 U.S. GDP per work-hour ranked 5th from the top among Maddison's 16 countries, its subsequent productivity growth was 7th, not 5th, from the bottom. Thus, over longer periods at least, the relative American growth

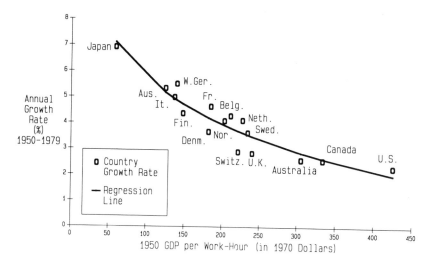

Figure 5.6
Postwar labor productivity (GDP per work-hour), growth rate vs. 1950 level, 16 industrialized countries. Source: Maddison [1982, p. 212].

performance does not in itself seem to constitute legitimate grounds for concern.

The natural question, particularly in light of the data already presented in table 5.1, is whether all this has changed since World War II. To test this we calculated a regression equation from Maddison's data for the time period 1950–1979. Figure 5.6 shows the graph of this equation, together with the GDP per work-hour growth rates and 1950 values for the 16 Maddison countries. Since the United States was the clear productivity leader in 1950 it is represented by the rightmost point in the graph. We see that it clearly lies above the regression curve. Indeed, the calculation can be shown directly to imply that for the entire postwar period the U.S. productivity performance was some 15% superior to that predicted by a hypothetical convergence relationship. All in all, that is still not too bad a record.

But all of these arguments may strike the reader as more than a bit abstract. One may reasonably ask what the bottom line shows. Does all this mean that the United States, despite all the misgivings that fill the popular press, is holding its own in the struggle for competitiveness on the international marketplace, or is it being displaced, either rapidly or gradually? In particular, in manufacturing and in "high-tech" exports, which have been the focus of concern of the proponents of the deindustrialization thesis, how has the American economy fared? The answer may be as surprising to the reader as it was to the authors of this book.

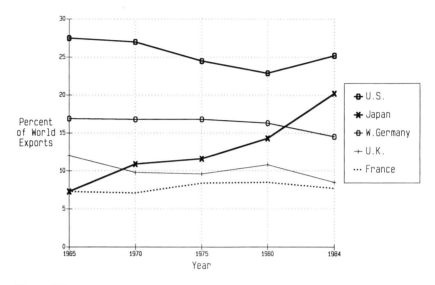

Figure 5.7
Shares of the world's technology-intensive exports, 5 industrialized countries, 1965–1984.
Sources: National Science Foundation [1986, p. 58] and McCulloch [1988, p. 39].

Figure 5.7, based on data provided by the National Science Foundation (see McCulloch [1988]) shows what has happened since 1965 to the share of the world's high-tech exports originating in 5 leading industrial countries, including the United States. It will hardly be unexpected to find that Japan's share of world high-tech exports has been rising dramatically, from some 7% of the total in 1965 to more than 20% in 1984. But at least recent U.S. performance is arguably 2nd of the 5 (in terms of growth in its share of these exports), having risen since 1980, and having for all practical purposes held its own over the two decades reported. While Germany, France, and the United Kingdom also have suffered no significant losses, their share of the world's high-tech exports has in every case been falling since 1980, while, as we have just seen, that of the United States has been rising.

More remarkable evidence is depicted in figure 5.8, which shows for the same 5 countries their shares of the world's total employment in industrial occupations (more accurately, the data refer to industrial employment in the 24 countries that constitute the Organization for Economic Cooperation and Development [OECD], which includes the world's most industrialized free-market economies, including both Japan and the United States). Once again, the graph depicts the remarkably steady rise of Japan's share of industrial employment. But, as we see, the U.S. record is virtually parallel to

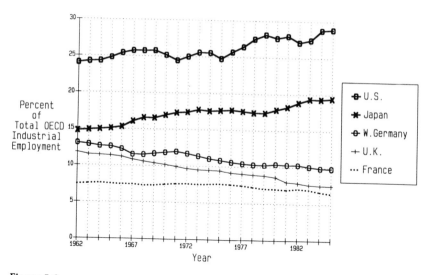

Figure 5.8
Shares of total OECD industrial employment, 5 countries, 1962–1985. Sources: OECD, *Indicators of Industrial Activity*, various issues, and *Labor Force Statistics* [1965–1985].

that of Japan, having risen from some 24% of the total in 1962 to about 28% in 1985—about a 20% increase. This is hardly what one would expect of a country undergoing deindustrialization. It is noteworthy that this pattern of increase persists throughout most of the nearly quarter-century reported, and persists through administrations both Republican and Democratic, so that little political capital seems to be provided by the record. As is indicated in table 5.2, the U.S. share of OECD manufacturing *output* (and not just employment) also rose, at least throughout the briefer period for which we have data. In contrast to the U.S. and Japanese performance, as the graph shows, the shares of OECD industrial employment in the United Kingdom, France, and Germany have all indisputably been falling.

Yet we cannot leave the subject without noting that there is another side to the story. Populations in Britain, France, and Germany have all been nearly stationary in the period in question. In contrast, those of the United States and Japan have risen far more rapidly. The result is that, despite the United States and Japan's rising shares of the world's industrial employment, these shares have not enabled them to achieve nearly so spectacular a record in terms of share of population employed in industry. In figure 5.9 each country's graph from the previous figure has been adjusted to indicate growth of its share of total OECD employment *relative to the growth in the*

Table 5.2
Indicators of U.S. competitiveness in manufacturing, 1973–1985 (percent)

Year	U.S. share of OECD manufacturing output (%)	U.S. share of OECD industrial employment (%)	U.S. industrial employment (× 1,000)	OECD total industrial employment (× 1,000)
1962	—	24.1	23,219	96,433
1963	—	24.3	23,775	98,010
1964	—	24.3	24,291	99,799
1965	—	24.8	25,211	101,598
1966	—	25.4	26,278	103,334
1967	—	25.7	26,653	103,566
1968	—	25.7	26,896	104,498
1969	—	25.8	27,533	106,812
1970	—	25.2	27,029	107,398
1971	—	24.5	26,092	106,705
1972	—	25.0	26,766	107,066
1973	36	25.6	28,225	110,387
1974	36	25.5	28,194	110,383
1975	35	24.8	26,288	106,179
1976	36	25.7	27,354	106,553
1977	37	26.4	28,402	107,495
1978	37	27.5	29,889	108,719
1979	37	28.1	30,918	110,027
1980	36	27.6	30,313	109,663
1981	37	27.9	30,191	108,060
1982	36	27.1	28,256	104,308
1983	37.5	27.4	28,253	102,992
1984	39.2	28.8	29,892	103,911
1985	38.8	28.9	30,047	104,049
1986	38.7	—	—	—

Sources: For first column, Organization for Economic Cooperation and Development *Indicators of Industrial Activity*, various issues; for third and fourth columns, OECD, *Labor Force Statistics, 1965–1985*, [1987, pp. 36–37].

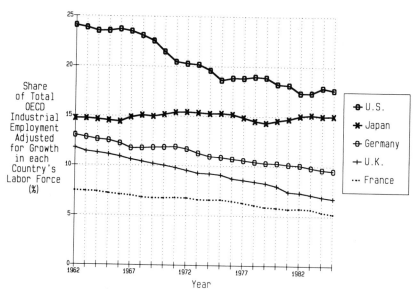

Figure 5.9
Shares of OECD industrial employment for 5 countries, relative to each country's total labor force, 1962–1985. Sources: OECD, *Indicators of Industrial Activity*, various issues, and *Labor Force Statistics* [1965–1985].

size of its own labor force. We see from the figure that the graphs for the United Kingdom, France, and Germany continue to fall, roughly as before the adjustment for population size. The graph for Japan does continue to grow, but its rise becomes virtually insignificant. That is, the rise in Japan's share of industrial employment has barely surpassed the increase in the size of its labor force. The graph of the United States, however, is transformed from one showing a sharp and sustained upward trend to one whose trend is distinctly downward. What this means is that while the world's appetite for the products of U.S. industrial labor has been growing sharply and rather steadily, its population and, hence, its total labor force has grown even more rapidly, forcing more of the U.S. labor force to seek employment *outside of industrial fields*. Does this mean that the U.S. labor force, more than that of other industrialized economies, has been driven into the services, to make the United States, as is often implied, the prime case of evolution into a service economy? The surprising answer, as will be documented in the next chapter, is emphatically—no. Rather, it will be shown that the U.S. economy is among the industrialized world's laggards in the rate of movement of its labor force toward the services.

5.7   Concluding Comments

The long-term growth trends examined in this chapter seem to uphold our hypothesis that the convergence club is a reality. We have hardly begun, however, to explain what determines its membership. While in this book we shall undertake to offer a few pertinent ideas, we do not pretend to offer a systematic analysis of this issue that is so important for productivity policy, particularly for the less developed countries. There are many mysteries such an analysis will be required to explain—among them the curious consistency with which recent candidates for convergence have been drawn from the Far East, while those countries that seem to have lost their membership have all been in Latin America.

The evidence of convergence suggests that the U.S. is not about to lose its economic leadership or its prosperity. But while convergence may explain the long-standing lag in relative U.S. productivity performance, it hardly guarantees the harmlessness of the postwar deterioration. It has been suggested here that this is attributable more to a marked improvement in the productivity growth of other countries than to any fall-off in absolute U.S. achievement, but the sobering side of that explanation is that it is not so different from the British experience before World War I, when that country embarked on its long period of decline toward the status of one of the most impoverished of Europe's industrial countries. It is clear that productivity policy remains a critically important matter for the long-run economic welfare of the United States, as well as that of the world.

Notes

1. Maddison's 16 countries are Australia, Austria, Belgium, Canada, Denmark, Finland, France, Germany, Italy, Japan, the Netherlands, Norway, Sweden, Switzerland, the United Kingdom, and the United States.

2. Maddison's data are, with a few exceptions, by decade, and report output per work-hour. It should also be noted that the MFO figures have one highly desirable feature that Maddison's do not. MFO report productivity statistics only for years that can be considered to contain peaks of the business cycles, so that the calculations are not distorted by the well-known effects of the business cycle on labor productivity. Yet over the long period in question here no remarkable differences in patterns seem to emerge from the two sets of figures. Thus, as we have seen, the use of cycle peaks (or failure to do so) does not affect the basic conclusion that labor productivity in each of the industrialized countries seems to be approaching that of the leader.

3. The convergence is, in fact, much more striking in the MFO graph (MFO [1982, p. 32]), which is not reproduced here because the Maddison figures are somewhat

more up-to-date. There is, in fact, a substantial difference in degree between the two graphs, though for reasons explained in the next paragraph, the figures are quite consistent, and they do exhibit the same general patterns. The following figures indicate the magnitude of the difference. In 1870 the United Kingdom-Japanese ratio was about 5 in MFO and slightly less than that in Maddison. By 1970 the ratio of leader to laggard (United States to Japan) had fallen to 1.75 in MFO but only to 2.5 in Maddison.

One reason convergence in the MFO data occurs more rapidly than in Maddison's data is that, while Maddison reports GDP per work-*hour*, MFO give GDP per work-*year*. Now, it is at least plausible that the higher a typical worker's income, the greater will be the income effect of further wage increases relative to their substitution effect, so that the number of hours of labor expended per year by an average worker will fall more rapidly with growth in productivity the greater the productivity level a country has already achieved. Thus, in relative terms, output per year can be expected to grow more slowly than output per hour in a high-productivity country than in one that is low, and such a pattern can account for much of the observed difference in convergence rates of the MFO and the Maddison productivity graphs.

This is certainly true, according to Maddison's data, for Australia, the United Kingdom, and the United States, the three productivity leaders at various points in the period, vis-à-vis Japan, the persistently low-productivity country. Thus, while in 1870 in the four countries the annual labor hours worked per person ranged from 2,945 to 2,984, by 1979 it ranged from 1,607 to 1,619 for the three current or former leaders but was still over 2,100 in Japan (Maddison [1982, p. 211]).

4. If convergence were perfect, we would have $z_{it} = z_{jt} = z_t$ for all i, j (letting z_{i0} represent the initial value of the pertinent variable for country i, and z_{it} its later value). Then the average growth rate from time zero to t for each and every country i must exactly satisfy the (semi) log-linear relationship

$$r = (\ln z_t - \ln z_{i0})/t = a - b \ln z_{i0}, \qquad a, b \text{ constants.} \qquad (1)$$

It is clear from (1) that as we go from country to country, proceeding from initially poorer to initially richer countries, so z_{i0} increases steadily, that r must fall steadily and approach zero as z_{i0} approaches z_t from below. (Of course, in a world in which every country grew to some degree we must have $z_t > z_{i0}$.)

To test the strength of the convergence process we therefore carried out regressions corresponding to (1) and obtained for GDP per work-hour,

growth rate (1870–1979) = 5.25 − 0.75 ln (GDP per work-hour, 1870),
[10.0]

$$R^2 = 0.88 \qquad (2)$$

(where the t-ratio is shown in brackets under the coefficient, here and in subsequent equations), while for GDP per capita we obtain

growth rate (1870–1979) = 7.68 − 0.91 ln (GDP per capita, 1870),
[12.4]

$$R^2 = 0.92. \qquad (3)$$

The dissemination of technology and the role of the imitative entrepreneur may help to explain the dramatic inverse correlation between the 1870 productivity levels of Maddison's 16 nations and their subsequent productivity growth record shown in the two preceding equations. This seems to imply that only one variable —the GDP per work-hour in 1870 (or, rather, the relationship of a country's GDP per work-hour to that of the productivity leader)—had any influence on that country's productivity standing 110 years later; and that other variables (cultural patterns, forms of government, savings rates, even economic policies) mattered little. Indeed, had an otherwise uninformed observer in 1870 been provided with our (highly significant) statistical relationship plus the data on GDP per work-hour for each of the 16 countries, *and absolutely no other information about each country,* that observer could have predicted each country's GDP per-work hour 110 years later with an average absolute error smaller than 15%.

But even if all data were to support the statistical relationship unambiguously, such a conclusion would undoubtedly be quite incorrect and would not really be implied by the facts. Rather, the preceding statistical results are perfectly consistent with a scenario in which national behavior patterns and policies *do* substantially affect productivity growth. But in that model, if country A's extraordinary investment level and superior record of innovation enhances its own productivity, it will almost automatically do the same in the long run for industrialized country B, though perhaps to a somewhat more limited extent. In other words, no industrialized country is an island, and a contribution to productivity, so far as such nations are concerned, is in the long run in the nature of a public good. That is, the absolute benefits of such a productivity advance are not depleted as they flow to additional countries, and no industrialized country is in the long run excluded from their enjoyment. Hence, each country's productivity enhancement efforts are ultimately shared by others, and that is how each country remains in what appears to be its predestined *relative* place along the regression curve of figure 5.3.

5. In addition, the apparently strong regression results that were just reported in the preceding note have been subjected to a number of other criticisms. First, the 1870 figures were calculated by Maddison using backward extrapolation of growth rates, and hence their high correlation is hardly surprising. Second, since growth rate, r, is calculated by solving $z_t = e^{rt} z_0$ for r, to obtain $r = (\ln z_t - \ln z_0)/t$, we have a regression equation, $r = f(z_0)$, that contains the same variable, z_0, on both sides of the equation, thus tending to produce a spurious appearance of a close relationship.

In addition, if the 1870 figures, z_{i0}, are measured with considerable error, this must result in some significant downward bias in the regression coefficient on $\ln z_{i0}$. This is a point distinct from the one concerning the size of the correlation coefficient, although the latter is affected by the fact that relatively large measurement errors in the 1870 levels enter as inversely correlated measurement errors in the 1870–1979 growth rate.

One of the authors of this paper has devised a way to correct or to make allowance for some of these distortions (Wolff [1987b]). A spurious correlation between two terms may be introduced if the two are linearly related. Suppose for two random variables Z and W that

$$Y = Z - bW,$$

where b is a constant. It can be shown that if Z and W are perfectly correlated, then the correlation coefficient $COR(Y, W) = +1$. On the other hand, if Z and W are independent, then it can be shown that

$$COR(Y, W) = -1/[1 + VAR(Z)/b^2 VAR(W)]^{1/2},$$

where VAR is the variance. In other words, even if Y and W were completely unrelated, the correlation between Y and W would indicate that there is a negative relationship between them. We refer to this as the "spurious correlation." In the case here, a spurious correlation can be induced between r and $\ln z_{io}$, even if beginning and ending productivity levels are unrelated by country.

In order to correct for the spurious correlation bias, it is necessary to add one other condition. In particular, the null hypothesis that is of interest here is not only that initial and ending TFP levels are independent but that there is no convergence in productivity levels. This can be captured by assuming that the relative dispersion in productivity levels remains constant over time. In this case, it is possible to use the log-variance of TFP levels as a measure of relative dispersion. Thus, under the null hypothesis, $\ln(z_{i0})$ and $\ln(z_{it})$ are independent and $VAR(\ln(z_{i0})) = VAR(\ln(z_{it}))$. Then, $COR[\ln(z_{it}), r] = -1/2^{.5}$, or -0.7071. To show convergence, it is thus necessary to show that the correlation lies in the range from -1.0 to -0.7071. If the correlation coefficient is negative but less than 0.7071 in absolute value, then the calculation cannot be interpreted to support the convergence hypothesis, since spurious correlation alone could have accounted for the negative relation. The preceding results and the results on the convergence of total factor productivity (TFP) growth among a sample of 7 countries over the period 1870–1979 indicate that the adjusted correlation coefficients differ very little from the standard correlation coefficients. Thus, the spurious correlation problem does not appear to be very important.

6. In much of the remainder of the chapter we will rely on statistics on national output (GNP or GDP) *per capita* rather than labor productivity (output per work-hour). Output per capita is a measure of standard of living rather than productivity, but the two are highly if imperfectly correlated. We make the change only where we are forced to do so by unavailability of productivity figures.

7. The Bairoch countries are the United Kingdom, Belgium, Switzerland, the Netherlands, France, Germany, Norway, Denmark, Spain, Finland, Italy, Austria-Hungary, Portugal, Russia, Greece, Sweden, Serbia, Bulgaria, and Romania.

8. Maddison provides another set of estimates for real per-capita GDP for a set of 22 countries for 1913 and 1965 (and two intermediate years) in his 1969 study. Though for Maddison's purpose, the study of developing economies, the sample of countries seems entirely appropriate, its small and rather special set of developed countries makes its usefulness for our purposes more questionable. The terminal date for the estimates, dictated by the date of publication of the source, also affects the results of an analysis of the figures in a way that is illuminating, but that for our purposes can be misleading. This is shown in table 5.3, which reports both Maddison's figures and the ratio (for each of the 2 years and for each of the countries) of the country's real GDP per capita to that of the United States. We see

Table 5.3
GDP per capita at factor cost, 1913 and 1965 (1965 dollars at U.S. relative prices)

Country	1913 ($)	1965 ($)	Ratio to U.S. 1913	1965
U.S.	1,239	3,179	1.0	1.0
U.K.	1,037	1,985	0.84	0.62
Germany	811	2,109	0.65	0.66
Argentina	788	1,272	0.64	0.40
France	774	1,990	0.63	0.63
Chile	545	863	0.44	0.27
Italy	521	1,345	0.42	0.42
Spain	419	975	0.34	0.31
Japan	366	1,466	0.30	0.46
USSR	339	1,495	0.27	0.47
Greece	315	676	0.25	0.21
Malaya	221	528	0.18	0.17
Yugoslavia	217	736	0.18	0.23
Taiwan	206	573	0.17	0.18
Philippines	201	269	0.16	0.08
Colombia	182	375	0.15	0.12
Mexico	178	423	0.14	0.13
Egypt	176	295	0.14	0.09
Peru	147	397	0.12	0.12
India	138	182	0.11	0.06
Ghana	117	230	0.09	0.07
Pakistan	117	152	0.09	0.05

Source: Maddison [1969, p. 18].

from the last column that by 1965 the effects of World War II had just begun to wear off for most European countries. France, Germany, and Italy had only just about reattained their 1913 status, relative to the United States. Only Japan had made any real relative progress. Add to this the marked lag of Argentina and Chile, 2 of the 10 or so countries in the group that can be considered to have been developed at any time during the pertinent period, and it becomes clear why every calculation we have carried out with the figures quite appropriately shows divergence to have prevailed between 1913 and 1965.

9. Our classification into industrial, intermediate and LDC groups was carried out more or less objectively, in terms of rank in 1960 RGDP. This was selected as a fairly *ex ante* classification basis, but used a year in which abnormalities in ranking as a result of World War II had at least partly evaporated. The break points between the groups correspond to relatively large jumps in the RGDP figures. In our classification, the industrial countries are the United States, Switzerland, Luxembourg, Sweden, Canada, Australia, Denmark, the Federal Republic of Germany, New Zealand, the United Kingdom, France, Norway, Iceland, Belgium, Finland, Venezuela, and Austria; the intermediate countries are Uruguay, Italy, Trinidad, Argentina, Israel, Ireland, Spain, Japan, Chile, South Africa, Mexico, Greece, Barbados, Cyprus, Peru, Costa Rica, Portugal, Panama, Colombia, Guyana, and Turkey; the centrally planned economies are Bulgaria, China, Czechoslovakia, the German Democratic Republic, Hungary, Poland, Rumania, the USSR and Yugoslavia; and the less developed countries are Sri Lanka, the Dominican Republic, Guatemala, Brazil, Nicaragua, Mauritius, Nigeria, Paraguay, Ecuador, El Salvador, Honduras, Taiwan, Bolivia, the Philippines, Morocco, Uganda, Egypt, Thailand, India, Pakistan, Kenya, Zaire, Ethiopia, and Burma.

10. Another data source that we investigated was the World Bank's *World Development Report* for various years. This source covers an even wider range of countries than the Summers-Heston data. Figures on real GDP per capita are readily available for the late 1970s and the 1980s, and the World Bank kindly supplied 1960 data. In general, but with some substantial exceptions, these data show slightly less convergence than the Summers-Heston data. Using a graph similar to figure 5.5 for the two data sets, one obtains strikingly similar patterns once the sample exceeds some fairly small number of countries.

Three other studies that we know of also have yielded statistical evidence of convergence (with *ex ante* selection in effect): Kormendi and Meguire [1985] for 47 countries over the period 1950–1977, Barro [1984] for 9 countries between 1950 and 1980 (using Summers-Heston data), and Landau [1983] for a sample of 96 countries for various time periods between 1961 and 1976.

6

The Service-Economy Prognosis: Cost-Disease Illusions

Daniel Bell suggests that when over 50% of all employees are in service industries, the economy is entering a period of softening and servicing. Right after the oil crisis, Japan entered this stage.
Ishinomori, *Japan Inc., The Comic Book* [1988, p. 144]

A near flood of writings tell the American public that the United States teeters on the brink of economic mediocrity, its competitive leadership about to be lost to Japan, to the other miracle economies of the Far East, and even to the venerable economies of Europe. We have already seen in the two preceding chapters that the foundations for this gloomy prophesy are rather less firm than they appear to be on first examination of the pertinent facts. Here, we shall not consider this central scenario further, but shall turn, rather, to one of its purported corollaries, the "deindustrialization thesis." This hypothesis conjectures that, largely as a result of the poor productivity performance of our manufacturing sector, the American labor force is being driven inexorably into service-sector jobs at low pay, thus transforming the nation into a "service economy," in which people earn their livings by flipping one another's hamburgers and washing up the dishes.

Part of this deindustrialization thesis rests on dramatic evidence showing indisputably that the service sector of the U.S. economy has indeed been swallowing up an ever-growing share of the labor force, and that the services have also constituted a sharply growing share of U.S. gross national product. These figures (which will be reported presently) would appear to confirm unambiguously and dramatically the contention of those who maintain that the United States is rapidly evolving into a service economy, if it has not become one already.

In this chapter we shall show that the conclusion is, nevertheless, funda-mentally illusory, i.e., that there has been virtually no change in the share of *real* national output constituted by the services. How can that possibly be? How can the relative output of the services remain constant despite the explosion in their part of gross national product? We shall see with the aid of our analysis, which has been referred to as the "unbalanced growth" or the "cost-disease" model, that differences in the rates of productivity growth in the pertinent sectors of the economy explain nearly all of the expansion of the services as a share of both the labor force and GNP, the latter being accounted for by a rise in the relative prices of the services at issue rather than by any expansion of their *real* outputs.

Similar conclusions also hold true for the international sphere, where *there is no sign that the United States is shifting into services any more rapidly than other industrialized economies*, and where the sort of illusion just noted yields the false impression that the services' share of a nation's output is higher the richer that country is in terms of its per-capita income. (Some other analysts have questioned whether the United States is in some important sense different from most other industrialized countries in its transformation into a service economy. See Fuchs [1968], Summers [1985], and Gerschuny [1978].)

Finally, our discussion will turn from those service industries whose productivity growth, at least in the past, has been relatively stagnant, and focus our attention on the opposite end of the services spectrum, where activities such as electronic computation (data processing) and television broadcasting have achieved some of the economy's most outstanding records of productivity growth. We shall use a simple extension of the cost-disease model to show that some of these brilliant productivity performers may actually be condemned by their spectacular technological achievements to "burn themselves out," ending up as stagnant services. Thus, we shall refer to such lines of activity as "asymptotically stagnant."

Aside from the importance of dispelling the service-economy illusion—the idea that it is lack of U.S. competitiveness in manufactured products, along with changing demand patterns, that is shifting the nation's output from industry toward the services—the analysis of this chapter will prove important in a companion volume (Baumol and Wolff [forthcoming]) because of its implications for the role of research and development in the productivity growth process. There, we shall provide evidence suggesting that R&D activity is itself subject to the cost disease because it contains elements that are not amenable to rapid increases in productivity. The consequence may be an impediment to adequate funding of R&D activity, that is, to a level of funding consistent with the requirements of economic efficiency and the general economic welfare.

6.1   The Services: What Are They, How Do They Differ, and How Do We Measure Them?

Before we enter the substance of our discussion, let us first dispose of several preliminary, definitional issues. Generally, a service is defined as an economic activity that yields a product that is not a physical object. Transmission of a telephone call, the defense efforts of an attorney, and the teaching of a course in automobile repair all have their market prices and are clearly valued by consumers. Each purchaser of such a service may have a good deal to show for the expenditure, but it is not incorporated in a tangible product.

Intangibility of product, however, is probably the *only* attribute common to all services. In particular, there is one way in which they differ from one another that is crucial from the point of view of our analysis, and that is their extreme differences in amenability to productivity growth. Some services, like data processing and telecommunications, are impersonal and electronic and, as we shall see later in the chapter, have achieved unequaled productivity growth records. We shall refer to these services with a propensity to rapid productivity growth as *progressive*, meaning thereby no value judgment on their virtues, but merely a dispassionate description of one of their technological attributes. Those services for which productivity change is most difficult to achieve will be called *stagnant*. Such productivity stagnancy may be virtually endemic to the product (consider, for example, how much labor time is required for the performance of a half-hour Bartok string quartet). Or such a service may be so unstandardized that it is incompatible with mass production methods (for example, the diagnosis of a rare disease, or the untangling of a legal problem). Or it may simply result from the fact or belief that acceptable product quality requires some specifiable minimum input (labor) content (for example, direct attention by a skilled physician or a teacher). Of course, in reality there are all sorts of gradations in between the extreme cases of the progressive and the stagnant services, but our exposition here is facilitated by focusing on these polar cases.

Despite their intangibility, it is not true that all service outputs are difficult to measure directly. For example, the number of attendances of movie and stage performances is not inherently difficult to observe, and in fact such data are collected regularly. It is no more difficult in principle to measure the number of students graduating from high schools than to measure the output of wines from California vineyards. Of course, the quality of the educational product may vary from student to student or from year to year, but similar problems clearly beset the measurement of wine output. (More will be said in chapter 11 about product quality issues in productivity measurement.) There are, nevertheless, some services that defy direct measurement. For example, many activities of governments, though widely recognized to be highly useful, yield no discrete flow of products. As a result, statisticians measure the output of government activity in terms of the inputs that go into it, saying in effect that the output of government is equal to the amount it spends on labor, materials, energy, and so on. Whatever the virtues or deficiencies of such an approach for other purposes, it obviously does not serve our needs, since our central objective here is to distinguish what has happened to the *outputs* of the services from developments in the quantities of their *inputs*.

Where direct measurement of service outputs is not possible, an indirect procedure can often be used. This consists, in essence, of the determination of a price index for the service in question, with subsequent use of that index to deflate the more readily available index of money expenditures on that service. For example, if statistics indicate that over some specified period national expenditures on medical care have doubled, but that "the average price of medical care" has simultaneously risen, say, 75%, we may conclude that only 25 percentage points of the 100% rise in expenditure represents a real rise in the output of medical services.[1]

6.2   Deindustrialization: The Evidence

As has already been noted, on first examination the facts do indeed appear to provide firm and dramatic evidence for the deindustrialization thesis. The share of the U.S. labor force employed in the services has been rising sharply and now accounts for some two-thirds of the country's jobs. The share of the services in the nation's gross national product has increased correspondingly. Between 1950 and 1986 the proportion of total U.S. employment (as measured by persons engaged in production) accounted for by the service industries grew from 49% to 69%, and the services' share of GNP rose during that same period from 48% to 65%. Virtually all of the vast increase in the size of the U.S. labor force that has occurred since World War II, a total of some 46.3 million jobs between 1948 and 1986, is accounted for by the rise in service-sector employment.

These facts are well-documented and seem to constitute unambiguous confirmation of the deindustrialization thesis. Two complementary explanations are generally offered for the developments that have just been described. The first, as already suggested, is the failure of the United States, like that of England before it, to keep abreast of its foreign rivals in the world's markets for industrial products, as a consequence of its own lagging productivity. As a result, it is said, those competitors from abroad have succeeded increasingly in capturing for themselves the world's customers for manufactured goods, luring them away from American industry. In addition, it is suggested that as countries grow wealthier, their consumers become relatively sated with manufactures, and so domestic market demands turn ever more strongly to the products of the service sector of the economy, dragging the composition of national output and employment ever further in that direction.

A closer look at the facts provides no support for any of this. The deindustrialization thesis implies that the United States is virtually alone (except, perhaps, for a few other productivity laggards) in the shift of its labor force from manufacturing to the services. If the source of the problem is American inability to compete in the international marketplace that enables other countries to steal the customers for U.S. manufactured products away, then as the American economy becomes more service oriented some other leading economies should be interchanging roles with the United States, moving increasingly into industry and out of services. On this view we should expect other industrial countries to be decreasing the share of their labor force in the services, as more of their workers go into the production of the manufactures that displace the products formerly supplied by the United States.

Now, we have already seen other evidence (figure 5.8) showing that U.S. industrial employment is actually *rising* relative to that of other industrial countries as a group, so it should come as no surprise that in reality *all* industrial countries are experiencing a marked rise in the share of the services in their total employment. This is shown in table 6.1, which provides the figures for all the countries for which the statistics are reported by the OECD, and for which we were consequently able to obtain data. The table shows (column 3) that of the 19 industrial countries represented, the share of the labor force in manufacturing rose in only 3 cases—Spain, Japan, and Ireland—in the period 1965–1980. However, *in all but two of the 19 countries, by 1980 the service sector provided more than half of the nation's total employment* (column 5). This group of "service economies" clearly includes Japan as well as the leading European industrial countries.

More than that. In the 15-year period reported, *in every one of the 19 countries* the share of the labor force devoted to the services has risen

Table 6.1
Share of labor force in industry and services, 19 OECD countries, 1965–1980

	Percentage of labor force in					
	Industry		Percentage change	Services		Percentage change
Country	1965 (1)	1980 (2)	(3)	1965 (4)	1980 (5)	(6)
Spain	35	37	6.0	32	46	43.8
Italy	42	41	− 2.4	34	48	41.2
Austria	45	41	− 8.9	36	50	38.9
Sweden	43	33	− 23.3	46	62	34.8
Switzerland	50	39	− 22.0	41	55	34.1
Japan	32	34	6.3	42	55	31.0
France	39	35	− 10.3	43	56	30.2
Finland	36	35	− 2.8	41	53	29.3
Norway	37	29	− 21.6	48	62	29.2
Belgium	46	36	− 21.7	48	61	27.1
Netherlands	41	32	− 22.0	50	63	26.0
Denmark	37	32	− 13.5	49	61	24.5
Germany	48	44	− 8.3	42	50	19.0
United Kingdom	47	38	− 19.1	50	59	18.0
Australia	38	32	− 15.8	52	61	17.3
Ireland	28	34	21.4	41	48	17.1
Canada	33	29	− 12.1	57	65	14.0
United States	35	31	− 11.4	60	66	10.0
New Zealand	36	33	− 8.3	51	56	9.8

Source: World Bank [1987, p. 239].

substantially. Which country is it then that, by taking away the American market for manufacturing exports, has become less service oriented?

There is still more to the matter. While the United States is somewhat ahead of the others in terms of the 1980 proportion of service employees (column 5), about a half-dozen countries are very close behind it. But *in terms of the percentage growth of the share of its service employment, the United States is second from the bottom of the list* (column 6). If America's 10% rise in the share of its labor force employed in the services constitutes a move toward a "service economy," what is one to make of the 19% rise in Germany, the 30% increase in France, and the 31% expansion in Japan? It would seem that we are *all* becoming service economies. Certainly, the facts just cited are completely incompatible with the first explanatory scenario of the deindustrialization hypothesis, the conjecture that it is a matter of other countries shifting from services into manufactures and doing so by capturing our markets for the latter.

The facts are equally unkind to the second explanatory conjecture of the proponents of the deindustrialization view—the notion that as countries grow richer the public's tastes shift toward the services. The evidence that will be cited next serves also to dispel the illusion that our national output, along with that of other industrialized countries, is being composed increasingly of products of the service sector.

It is, indeed, true (as has already been reported in this chapter) that the share of American GNP constituted by the total market value of the outputs of the service sector has been rising sharply. But that is merely an illusion created by the relative rates of inflation in the service and manufacturing sectors, and bears no resemblance to the behavior of their *real* outputs. As will be shown later, there is clear evidence that, on the average, the prices of the services have been rising far more rapidly than those of manufactured goods. If one deflates the output figures for these two sectors, adjusting each with its own price index to construct estimates of their real outputs, one finds that, at least in the United States, *the share of the real outputs of the services relative to that of manufacturing simply has not been rising.* An example will bring out the point. Suppose that over some period of time the *money value* of the total output of manufactured goods had risen $1\frac{1}{2}$ times while that of the services had tripled. But if it were to turn out that over the same time the prices of services had increased on the average twice as quickly as those of manufactures, it is obvious that their actual output quantities would have increased precisely in lockstep, maintaining an unchanging proportion with one another.

This is roughly what has happened in fact in the past three or four decades in the United States. The combined output of services such as product repair and household help as well as education, health care, and telecommunications has, of course, gone up as the nation became wealthier. But the outputs of industrial products, if anything, rose even a bit faster. The data confirming this will be reported later in this chapter. The main point here is that this record of real output composition hardly comports with the allegation that the preferences of American consumers are turning sharply toward the services and dragging the economy's output proportions along.

There is a second body of evidence, which uses comparisons of the outputs of wealthier and poorer countries, that pertains directly to the conjecture that rising wealth drives consumer preferences away from manufactured goods and toward the services. International price data indicate that other industrialized countries are also paying high relative prices for their services, so that those services also constitute a fairly large proportion of their gross domestic product (GDP), calculated at (nominal, i.e., unadjusted) market prices, even though the actual volume of such service outputs consumed in those countries is not unusually large. For reasons that will be made clear presently, the opposite price pattern has been characteristic of poorer and less productive countries. In general, then, we should anticipate a systematic pattern that gives the impression that the richer and more productive an economy is, the higher is the share of the services in its GDP, that is, the closer that country will have approached becoming a service economy. We should also find that the apparent relationship becomes considerably weaker or disappears altogether once one corrects for the price illusion introduced by the differences in price behavior of manufactures and services in the poorer and richer countries. That is, after correcting for the false perception of high service output in richer countries (which stems from the higher relative price of services in such economies), we should not be surprised that the services' *real* share of output does not have any clear relationship to the level of prosperity of a country. The true relationship may even be the reverse of what it appears to be, with low-wage/cheap services countries devoting larger real shares of their incomes to the services than do the rich countries where high wages make service outputs relatively costly to buy.

The empirical evidence is provided by excellent cross-sectional international data for 1975 contributed by Robert Summers [1985]. Real (inflation-adjusted) gross domestic product per capita, the services' proportion of total real GDP expenditures, and their proportion of total nominal (*un*-adjusted for inflation) GDP expenditures were collected for a sample of 34 countries, ranging from very poor countries, such as Malawi and India, to highly industrialized states, like Germany and the United States. Our price observations imply, as we have seen, that if the real share of GDP devoted to services remains roughly constant among countries, the nominal share devoted to services will rise with real GDP per capita because the relative prices of services are higher in wealthier than in poorer countries.[2] Figures 6.1 and 6.2 show patterns completely consistent with these predictions: In real terms, the share of GDP devoted to services remained roughly constant as real income per capita increased, whereas, in nominal terms, the share of total expenditures in the services grew markedly with income. This result (which is also confirmed in a later paper by Summers and Heston [1988]) obviously is completely consistent with our conclusion that it is largely an

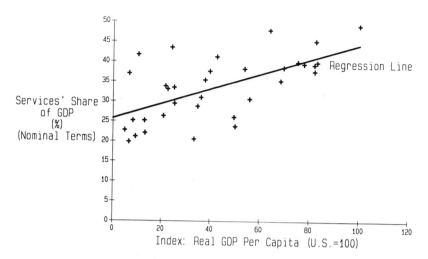

Figure 6.1
Nominal (unadjusted for inflation) share of services vs. per-capita income, 39 countries,
1975. Source: Summers [1985].

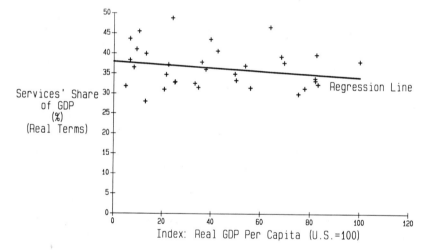

Figure 6.2
Real (inflation-adjusted) share of services vs. per-capita income, 39 countries, 1975. Source:
Summers [1985].

illusion that the United States and other prosperous countries are becoming "service economies."[3]

6.3 Accounting for Labor's Increasing Share: The Cost Disease of the Personal Services

If deindustrialization is not the answer, how can one explain why the relative output of the services can have remained roughly constant while their shares of gross national product and the labor force have both risen sharply? The cost-disease model (Baumol [1967]) will provide the framework for our empirical analysis, and also offer us some ancillary conclusions that will prove important in the sequel. We shall show that the expansion in the share of GNP constituted by services is not composed of services generally, but is accounted for largely by the *stagnant services*—those that have experienced relatively little productivity growth. We shall also show that such stagnant services have an inherent tendency to rise in cost and price, persistently and cumulatively, relative to the costs and prices of the economy's other outputs. That is to say, the stagnant services have an inherent tendency to rise in price at a (compounded) rate faster than the economy's overall rate of inflation. Technological necessity also requires these stagnant activities to use a share of the economy's labor inputs that grows at a rate disproportionately larger than the growth in the share of the economy's output.

Formal proofs of these conclusions are shown in section A of the appendix to chapter 6. However, their logic is easily summarized. For this purpose, let us focus on two activities: one highly progressive, say, the manufacture of watches, and one extremely stagnant, say, harpsichord performance. We have data indicating that before the introduction of the revolutionary quartz watch, labor productivity in watchmaking had risen almost exactly a hundredfold since the time that Domenico Scarlatti was composing his harpsichord works (circa 1700). But, of course, neither the labor time nor the amount of equipment required to play one of those pieces has fallen one iota since the day they were written.

With the aid of these two examples it is easy to show the logic of the first of our conclusions—that the persistently more stagnant of two activities must also rise persistently in cost and price. The reason is that the more progressive activity constantly uses less and less input per unit of its output. The stagnant output does not, or at best does so to a far lesser degree. If, then, both activities must pay the same wage rate[4] and the same prices for other inputs, it follows that the relative cost and price of the progressive output must fall, or put the other way, that those of the stagnant output must rise. If, in the year 1700, one watch required as much labor as 100 harpsichord performances, the watch would have been correspondingly more expensive than a performance. But by, say 1960, when watch productivity had risen a hundredfold, the cost of a watch and a concert would been about the same. This means that in these 260 years the price of concert tickets must have risen about a hundred times as fast as the price of a watch, if both their costs were to be covered.

It should also now be equally obvious why, if over those years the output of concert performances and that of watches had maintained an absolutely unchanging proportion, the share of the economy's GNP accounted for by concert performances must have risen about a hundred times. With relative outputs unchanged, but with the market value of a concert having gone up a hundred times as fast as that of a watch, this must necessarily be so, since GNP is defined, in essence, as the sum of the *market values* of the economy's outputs.

We can now see directly why, if output proportions between the stagnant and the progressive services happen to remain constant, an ever-growing share of the economy's labor force must be devoted to the stagnant services. The point is that the growing productivity of the progressive activities means that less and less labor (as well as declining quantities of the other inputs) will be needed to produce a unit of their outputs. If the outputs of progressive and stagnant activities are indeed to increase in lockstep, more and more input must be shifted from the progressive to the stagnant activities. In terms of our watch/harpsichord example, if in Scarlatti's time there had been a hundred times as many watchmakers as performers, and output of the two products had remained proportionate (and if labor had been the only input), simple arithmetic proves absolutely that by now the number of watchmakers and performers must have reached equality. This must be so, since the productivity of watchmakers has gone up a hundredfold, while the performers' remained completely unchanged.

We may note, incidentally, that the cost-disease model helps to explain a widely noted (and deplored) phenomenon. This is the fact that, despite the rapidly rising real cost of a number of the stagnant services, their quality has deteriorated markedly. For instance, streetcleaning in the cities has become poorer and the streets have grown dirtier. Postal deliveries have become less frequent (the 12-times-daily delivery schedule in central London in the mid-nineteenth century is hardly imaginable now!). Home visits by doctors are virtually a thing of the past. Expensive restaurants offer simplified menus that provide only the appearance of haute cuisine, and many surreptitiously provide only frozen dinners. And the list goes on and on. Every reader no doubt has a number of (un)favorite examples.

This is hardly the place for a full discussion of such developments, but the cost disease provides a partial explanation. To retain quality, other things being equal, the price of a stagnant service must rise every year at the overall inflation rate *plus* an amount corresponding to its lag in productivity growth. If the price of that service does indeed rise faster than the general price level but is nevertheless insufficient to satisfy this criterion, then the phenomenon we are seeking to explain must follow: the double blow of steadily rising real prices *and* deterioration of product quality. For example, if the economy's current rate of inflation is 4% per year and productivity stagnancy in streetcleaning requires its budget to rise by an additional 3% annually, then a 5% growth in the budget of sanitation services, which political pressures can well yield, will be sufficient to elicit both sources of irritation—declining streetcleaning quality and a budget whose growth is consistently greater than the rate of increase in costs and prices in the economy generally.

6.4   Empirical Evidence on the Services' Share of Outputs, GNP, and the Labor Force: Unbalanced Economic Growth

We turn now to the empirical evidence relating to unbalanced growth between economic sectors. We shall show that (a) In real (inflation-adjusted) terms, there has been almost *no* shift in the relative shares of economic output from the manufacturing sector to the service sector, not only with the passage of time but also with increasing wealth as one goes from less developed to industrialized countries; (b) just as unbalanced growth calls for, both the relative prices of the services and the services' share of total expenditures in the economy have markedly increased with the passage of time and with increased industrialization; (c) the service sector contains some of the economy's most progressive activities, as well as its most stagnant; and (d) the U.S. labor force has been absorbed increasingly not just by the services generally, but predominantly by their stagnant subsector.

To investigate these developments statistically it was necessary first to classify the actual sectors of the economy into our progressive and stagnant categories, a division whose boundary line was inevitably somewhat arbitrary. We based the classification on input and output data for the U.S. economy for 1947–1976, since consistent national account data and input-output tables are available for those years. A variety of measures of productivity growth rates were used to test the robustness of our classification scheme.

In table 6.2, the first column shows calculations of annual (compounded) rates of labor productivity growth using official National Income and Product Account (NIPA) figures. [The sectoral productivity concept is gross product originating in the sector (GPO) per person employed, and that of aggregate productivity is the ratio of gross domestic product (GDP) to total persons employed.[5]] The average annual rate of aggregate productivity growth was 2.16% over the period. Sectoral rates of productivity growth ranged from a high of 5.42% in communications and broadcasting (a service sector), to a low of −0.51% in government enterprises. Though there is a fairly wide spread in sectoral rates of productivity growth, there also appears to be a sharp break between the construction sector at 1.66% and the narrowly defined "general services" sector, at 0.93%. Using this criterion and these data, four sectors are classed as stagnant: general services (0.93%), finance and insurance (0.50%), government industry (0.31%), and government enterprises (−0.51%). Productivity growth in the remaining sectors was fairly rapid, putting them in the progressive group. It is noteworthy that this progressive group includes three service sectors—communications, trade, and real estate.[6]

The second column of table 6.2 uses gross domestic output (GDO) in constant dollars as its sectoral output and number of persons employed as its labor input. (GDO in constant dollars, an input-output concept, equals gross value of a sector's output or sales deflated by the *sectoral* price deflator.) These new estimated rates of sectoral productivity growth differ somewhat from those in column 1, though the rank orders are quite close. The major exception is the construction sector, whose 1.19% rate now places it in the stagnant category. The input-output data also permit disaggregation of general services into 6 subsectors, as shown in table 6.2, and evaluation of their degrees of stagnancy. The range of sectoral productivity growth rates of these subsectors is fairly wide, though they all lie below the economy's 2.18% rate. The last 3 subsectors in this group all seem clearly to be stagnant. The first 3 are more marginal, though we shall, somewhat arbitrarily, draw the line between business and professional services (1.70%) on the one hand, and hotels, personal and repair services (1.37%) and auto services (1.45%) on the other, placing only the former in the progressive group. (Columns 3−7 in tables 6.2 and 6.3 correspond to other measures of output and productivity growth, which are described in appendix B.)

Table 6.2
Average annual rates of productivity growth by sector, 1947–1976[a]

		Productivity growth measures						
		GPO[a] per worker (%) (1)	GDO[a] per worker (%) (2)	ρ (%) (3)	λ (%) (4)	λ_m (%) (5)	$\tilde{\rho}$ (%) (6)	$p/\bar{p}$ (7)
1.	Agriculture	3.59	4.47	1.56	3.95	3.66	2.05	1.64
2.	Mining	2.70	2.76	0.08	1.38	1.09	−0.51	−1.60
3.	Construction	1.66	1.19	−0.34	1.49	1.42	0.64	−0.72
4.	Manufacturing—durables	2.52	2.80	0.58	3.08	2.87	1.77	0.89
5.	Manufacturing—nondurables	3.21	3.23	0.41	2.56	2.43	1.34	0.20
6.	Transportation and warehousing	1.74	2.74	0.68	2.42	2.45	1.33	0.39
7.	Communications and broadcasting	5.42	5.50	3.99	5.21	4.62	2.76	1.38
8.	Utilities	4.96	4.77	1.53	2.96	2.62	1.05	0.09
9.	Trade		2.17	1.09	2.19	2.09	1.47	0.58
	a. Wholesale trade	2.37						
	b. Retail trade	1.99						
10.	Finance and insurance	0.50	0.31	−0.27	0.57	0.50	−0.26	−1.18
11.	Real estate	2.72	3.10	2.87	4.86	4.81	3.21	0.51
12.	General services	0.93						
	a. Hotels, personal, and repair (except auto)		1.37	−0.31	1.35	1.36	0.65	−0.40
	b. Business and professional services		1.70	0.83	2.30	2.09	1.60	−1.10
	c. Auto repair and services		1.45	−0.84	1.04	−0.09	−0.18	−0.60

	(1)	(2)	(3)	(4)	(5)	(6)	(7)
d. Movies and amusements		0.99	−0.56	0.64	0.57	−1.08	−1.05
e. Medical, educational, and nonprofit		−0.46	−1.14	−0.19	0.03	−0.86	−1.63
f. Household workers		−0.21	−0.21	−0.21	−0.21	−0.21	−0.87
13. Government enterprises	−0.51	1.10	−0.52	0.99	0.96	0.56	−1.08
14. Government industry	0.31	−0.18	0.08	−0.18	−0.18	0.31	−2.44
Overall:							
GDP	2.16						
GNP		2.18	1.17	2.18	1.17	1.17	0.0

Sources: column (1): Department of Commerce, Bureau of Economic Analysis, [1981, tables 6.2 and 6.11]; column (2): GDO for 1947 was obtained from the standard 87-order Bureau of Economic Analysis input-output table for 1947, and GDO for 1976 was obtained from the Department of Labor, Bureau of Labor Statistics, [1979]; columns (3)–(7): U.S. input-output data (see note 14 of this chapter for details).
a. Key: GPO-gross product originating in the sector, GDO-gross domestic output, GDP-gross domestic product, GNP-gross national product.

6.5   Statistical Tests of the Unbalanced Growth Premise

The data in table 6.3, which show estimates of the growth in employment and share of gross national product (or the analogous concepts indicated) of the various stagnant and progressive sectors of the economy, will play the key role in testing our two hypotheses about the real and nominal outputs of the sectors of the economy and their shares of the labor force and, above all, about the reality of the "service economy." We first examine the evidence for our basic contention—the view that, in real (inflation-adjusted) terms, the output share of the stagnant services has remained constant over time. We used two definitions of output for this purpose: final output (panel D in table 6.3) and gross domestic output (panel F). Our first classification scheme (column 1) tells us that real (in constant 1958 dollars) output shares remained constant over the time period in terms of both final output (21.4% in 1947 compared with 21.2% in 1976) and GDO (16.8% in both years). Column 2, using our other classification scheme, indicates that there might even have been a slight decline in the stagnant sector's real share of final and gross output (falling from 31.2% to 29.2%, and from 21.9% to 19.8%, respectively). Thus the data do indeed show that in terms of real outputs the United States is, at least so far, emphatically not evolving into a (stagnant) service economy.

We are now also in a position to test the main implications of the cost disease. The first of these is the prediction that the relative prices of the stagnant sectors' outputs will rise at about the same rate as the shortfall in their rates of productivity growth. This is, indeed, confirmed by the data. By the first two measures of table 6.3, the rate of productivity growth of the stagnant sectors is from about $2\frac{1}{4}$ to $2\frac{1}{2}$ percentage points below that of the progressive sector. As indicated in the last column of table 6.3, the price of stagnant output relative to progressive output increased at 1.85% per year.

The second implication of unbalanced growth is that, since the stagnant sector's output share has been fairly constant, its share of *employment* must rise over time. By all seven definitions, the share of employment in the stagnant sector rose by over 10 percentage points between 1947 and 1976 and, by the first definition, by almost 14 percentage points (panel C, table 6.3). The third prediction is that, with output shares of the stagnant and progressive sectors roughly constant in real terms, the share of output produced by the stagnant sector will rise in *nominal* (inflation-*un*adjusted) terms with the passage of time. This is confirmed in panels E and G of table 6.3, which exhibit increases that range from 6% to 12%.[7]

One other issue can readily be examined with the aid of our data—the comparative performance of the progressive services and goods production. As has been shown, the service sector includes both progressive and stagnant activities. In panel B of table 6.3, we have calculated separately the rate of productivity growth for progressive services. We find that the progressive services experienced slightly lower rates of growth of labor productivity than progressive goods producers but higher rates of total factor productivity growth. Moreover (panel H), we find that while employment in progressive services increased over the period 1947–1976, it rose very modestly, as our analysis might lead us to expect. Thus, progressive services behaved very differently from stagnant services over the postwar period and behaved very much like progressive goods sectors, and while it is true that the nation's labor force moved toward services, both stagnant and progressive, it was the stagnant services whose labor force increased most substantially. While the labor force of the progressive services rose somewhere between 5% and 14%, that of the stagnant services rose between 32% and 50%.

6.6   Television Broadcasting and Data Processing: Asymptotically Stagnant Services

Earlier in the chapter we used the example of harpsichord performance to illustrate the workings of the cost disease and the resistance of the stagnant services to productivity growth. But, it has been objected that this sort of example ignores the contribution of the mass media to the productivity of the performer's efforts. The criticism is entirely correct—in the short run. There can be no doubt that the advent of broadcasting has multiplied many times the size of the audience served by a musical performance, and that it has done so with very little increase in expenditure on labor per performance. The result has been a spectacular, but basically once-and-for-all, productivity leap. We shall show now why the resulting "remission" from the cost disease is only temporary, and why one can confidently expect the problem gradually to set in again, approaching ever closer to its previous virulence. Indeed, we shall see why the same problem affects most of broadcasting as well as a number of other activities that are initially highly progressive (data processing is another clear example). In the next section, we shall provide statistical evidence that what has just been described is actually happening in broadcasting and in electronic computation.

This type of behavior—outstandingly rapid productivity growth followed by a gradual onset of the cost disease, until the cost behavior and the low productivity growth of the overall activity begins to approximate

Table 6.3
Share of employment and output in stagnant sectors,[a] 1947 and 1976

	Productivity growth measures						
	GPO/ worker (1)	GDO/ worker (2)	ρ (3)	λ (4)	λ_m (5)	$\tilde{\rho}$ (6)	$p/\bar{p}$ (7)
A. Stagnant sectors[b]							
2. Mining	X		X	X	X	X	X
3. Construction		X	X	X	X	X	X
10. Finance and insurance	X	X	X	X	X	X	X
12. General services							
a. Hotels, personal, and repair (except auto)	X	X	X	X	X	X	
b. Business and professional	X						X
c. Auto repair and service	X	X	X	X	X	X	X
d. Movies and amusements	X	X	X	X	X	X	X
e. Medical, educational and nonprofit	X	X	X	X	X	X	X
f. Household workers	X	X	X	X	X	X	X
13. Government enterprises	X	X	X	X	X	X	X
14. Government industry	X	X	X	X	X	X	X
B. Annual productivity growth rate, 1947–1976 (%)							
a. Progressive sectors (all)	2.94	3.04	1.09	2.92	2.73	1.95	0.59
b. Stagnant sectors	0.64	0.56	−0.84	0.73	0.61	−0.57	−1.26
c. Progressive service sectors[c]	2.71	2.79	1.63	2.79	2.64	2.12	0.67
d. Overall	2.16	2.18	1.17	2.18	1.99	1.17	0.0

C. Percent of employed persons in stagnant sectors

a. 1947	27.6	30.7	32.4	32.4	32.4	32.4	34.6
b. 1976	41.2	42.0	43.0	43.0	43.0	43.0	47.2

D. Stagnant sector share of final output (1958 $)

a. 1947	21.4	31.2	31.5	31.5	31.5	31.5	32.1
b. 1976	21.2	29.2	28.9	28.9	28.9	28.9	29.9

E. Stagnant sector share of final output (nominal $)

a. 1947	17.9	26.8	27.0	27.0	27.0	27.0	27.6
b. 1976	29.9	38.6	38.1	38.1	38.1	38.1	39.3

F. Stagnant sector share of GDO (1958 $)

a. 1947	16.8	21.9	24.2	24.2	24.2	24.2	26.4
b. 1976	16.8	19.8	21.3	21.3	21.3	21.3	24.9

G. Stagnant sector share of GDO (nominal $)

a. 1947	13.7	18.3	20.4	20.4	20.4	20.4	22.2
b. 1976	22.9	24.5	26.7	26.7	26.7	26.7	31.1

H. Percent of employed persons in progressive services[c]

a. 1947	21.3	23.5	23.5	23.5	23.5	23.5	21.3
b. 1976	22.5	26.7	26.7	26.7	26.7	26.7	22.5

a. Panels B–H results are shown in percent.

b. In panel A, an × indicates that a sector is classified as stagnant by the corresponding measure of productivity growth.

c. In column 1, progressive services are defined as communications and broadcasting, trade, and real estate. In columns 2–6, they include the same three sectors and, in addition, business and professional services.

that of a stagnant service—is what we label (with apologies) *asymptotic stagnancy*. We shall also see that the faster the initial productivity growth of such an activity, the sooner it must exhaust itself and the sooner it must approximate the behavior of a stagnant service. How can this occur? All that is needed for an activity to be condemned to such a history is that it be composed of two subactivities—one highly stagnant and one very progressive—of fairly fixed proportions. For example, the live television broadcast of a 1-hour soap opera episode requires two components whose proportions cannot be changed: 1 hour of live performance, and 1 hour of simultaneous electronic transmission of the images. Now, as has recently been true of electronics everywhere, the technical activities encompassed in broadcasting have benefited from continuing and substantial productivity increases. In contrast, the performance of the actors has for all practical purposes undergone no rise in productivity. It should be obvious that this implies that the relative costs of the electronic component of broadcasting must grow ever smaller while, by the same token, the comparative cost of the live component must grow constantly larger. Moreover, it is obvious that the more progressive the electronic part of the overall activity, the faster must be the course of these cost developments.

The rest of the story is now simple. The progressive component's share of the overall broadcasting budget must grow smaller and smaller as a consequence of the unavoidable cost developments that have just been described. Ultimately, that share must become a negligible part of the whole. If in year Y electronics accounted for, say, 70% of the total broadcasting budget, a drop of 10% per year in electronics costs would reduce the overall broadcasting budget by some 7 percentage points per year below what it would otherwise be as a result of the rising relative cost of the stagnant component. But if by some later date the share of the electronic component has fallen to only 5% of the overall budget, even though its cost continues to decline at the same rate as before, its ability to pull down the overall budget will decline to negligibility, along with its share in the budget.

A numerical example (with costs unadjusted for inflation) will nail down the point. Imagine an industry with two component activities, A, which is highly progressive, and another, B, which is very stagnant, and that their relative quantities are fixed, just as the asymptotic stagnancy scenario requires. Assume that the cost of A falls 25% per year as a result of its productivity growth, while the cost of B rises 6% per year for the corresponding reason. Finally, suppose that expenditure on activity A at first constitutes 80% of the total expenditure of the industry. A little direct computation using these numbers shows that *initially* the industry's overall costs per unit of output will fall sharply with the passage of time, because the component that constitutes 80% of its total budget (progressive activity A) is the one whose cost declines rapidly. On the other hand, the arithmetic also shows that 10 years of compoundedly falling relative costs of A and rising costs of B will have reduced A's share of the overall industry budget to a mere 20% and, as a result, the rising cost of B will now start to dominate developments, forcing the cost per unit of the industry's product to take an *upward* course thereafter. As we shall see next, the illustrative numbers that we just used are not entirely imaginary; they correspond roughly to the correct figures for the hardware (component A) and software (component B) inputs of electronic computation.

6.7 Empirical Data on Television Broadcasting and Electronic Computation

We turn now to empirical evidence on two asymptotically stagnant activities, television broadcasting and data processing (alternatively called information processing, computer services, or electronic computation). We shall see that in both activities the progressive component's share of total costs diminished continually, while the stagnant component increased both in real terms and as a share of total cost. We shall also see that the time path of broadcasting cost per unit of output now behaves like that of stagnant product.

a. *Electronic Computation.* In the last 20-odd years the cost of computer hardware apparently fell some 25% per year (per unit of processing power), the like of which has probably never occurred before in any other industry (see, for example, W. J. Kubitz [1980], S. Triebwasser [1978], R. N. Noyce [1977], and C. Burns [1977]; a recent systematic study by Robert Gordon [1987] estimates the average annual rate of decline to have been 19% between 1954, when the first commercial computer was delivered, and 1984[8]). Meanwhile, the cost of (labor-intensive) computer software assumed an ever-greater share of the total cost of computation. Software was once a relatively minor element in computing cost—indeed, IBM once gave software away with its machines. Now it is computer hardware that is becoming almost incidental in total computation cost (see, for example, T. J. Gordon and T. R. Munson [1980]). By some estimates software represented only 5% of system costs in 1973, had increased to 80% by 1978, and had exceeded 90% by 1980 (see Kubitz [1980] and M. Schindler [1979]). One observer predicted that soon "it will probably pay to substitute one hour of computer time for six minutes of staff time" (Paul Grabscheid

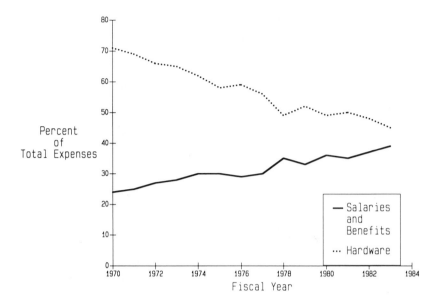

Figure 6.3
Electronic computation costs: labor and hardware as percent of total, Princeton University
Computer Center, 1970–1983. Source: Princeton University Computer Center, James
Poage, Director [1983].

[1982]). Software development remains essentially a handicraft activity and
is, so far, a stagnant service.

Some operating data from the Princeton University Computer Center
(figure 6.3) substantiate dramatically the growing importance of labor costs
in total computation expenditures and the accompanying sharp drop in the
dominance of the hardware component.[9] Figures 6.4A and 6.4B show the
actual costs of the center's computer hardware and personnel, which again
show the pattern of rising relative labor costs and decreasing equipment
costs. Between 1970 and 1983 total real labor costs at the center rose at a
compound rate of 2.6% per year, while total real equipment costs fell at an
annual rate of 4.6%.[10] Since the volume of computations at the center has
risen rapidly, equipment costs per unit of output have fallen far more
rapidly (and per unit labor costs have risen more slowly).[11]

b. *Television Broadcasting.* Television broadcasting, as we have noted, also
has progressive and stagnant components: transmission, which includes
circuit costs, and programming, dominated by human labor. Here, too, the
evidence on trends in costs is striking. TV broadcasting costs have increased dramatically. H. J. Levin's [1980] figures show that the cost of a
half-hour episode of a new prime-time program, when deflated by the

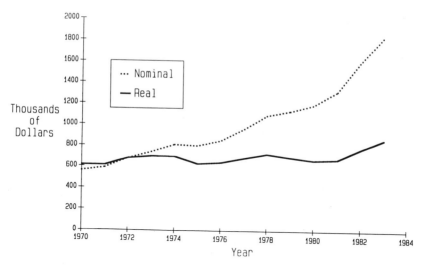

Figure 6.4A
Salaries and benefits expenses, Princeton University Computer Center, 1970–1983. Source: Princeton University Computer Center Financial Data, James Poage, Director [1983]. Source for GNP Implicit Price Deflator: Department of Commerce, Bureau of Economic Analysis, *Survey of Current Business*, various issues.

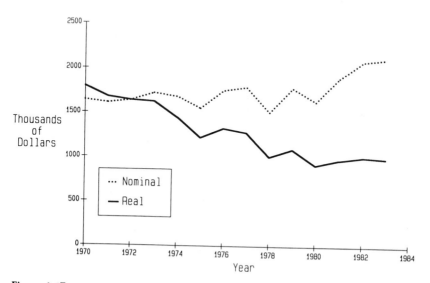

Figure 6.4B
Hardware costs, Princeton University Computer Center, 1970–1983. Source: Princeton University Computer Center Financial Data, James Poage, Director [1983]. Source for GNP Implicit Price Deflator: Department of Commerce, Bureau of Economic Analysis, *Survey of Current Business*, various issues. See note 9 for a further explanation of hardware costs.

wholesale price index, was $90,759 in 1976, compared with $51,633 in 1960, an increase of over 75% (an average real rise of 3.5% per annum). Over a longer period, and again adjusting for inflation, a typical half-hour film cost $14,466 in 1952 and $73,079 in 1974 (both figures are expressed in 1967 dollars), a rise of 405%, or 7.4% per year (Levin [1980, p. 28]). Total network program expenditures (unseparated from technical and also in 1967 dollars) rose comparably—from $404,731,000 in 1960 to $1,273,241,000 in 1975, some 215%, or 7.6% per year!

The split between technical broadcasting expenses and program expenses has changed, like that between hardware and software costs. N. J. Paik, an independent TV producer, comments, "In a 'typical' educational TV show of the past, hardware costs took so much money that producers had no way of hiring good talent for appearances or research.... The result was talking head after talking head" (Paik [1979, p.23]). New hardware developments have reduced costs; thus, "A new 1-inch recorder ... is supposedly better than the 2-inch recorder.... The price reduction from $2,500 a day for 2-inch to about $500 a day for the 1-inch system will pay the new equipment off in 35 days, or roughly 10 TV shows" (pp. 23−24). Figure 6.5, using U.S. Federal Communications Commission data, shows

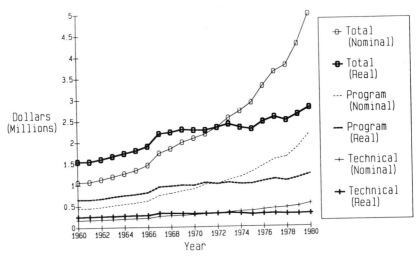

Figure 6.5
Broadcasting expenses, average television station, 1960−1980. Sources: U.S. Federal Communications Commission, *Annual Report*, various years, and "Television Financial Data 1980, FCC Financial Figures" [1981]. Source for price deflator: *Survey of Current Business*, various years.

Table 6.4
Technical and program expenses as a percentage of total television broadcasting expenses, 1960–80[a]

Year	Total broadcast expenses (all TV stations[b] in millions of dollars)	Technical expenses (millions of $)	Technical expenses as percent of total	Program expenses (millions of $)	Program expenses as percent of total
1960	563.3	92.9	16.5	239.1	42.4
1961	579.5	96.2	16.6	245.2	42.3
1962	626.6	101.3	16.1	265.4	42.3
1963	674.5	106.3	15.8	290.5	43.1
1964	725.4	113.8	15.7	315.1	43.4
1965	787.7	120.2	15.3	338.8	43.0
1966	885.0	131.1	14.8	380.1	43.0
1967	948.3	141.4	14.9	409.2	43.2
1968	1,040.1	151.5	14.6	449.2	43.2
1969	1,176.4	161.4	13.7	504.9	42.9
1970	1,245.2	170.6	13.7	534.7	43.0
1971	1,303.7	179.6	13.8	599.2	46.0
1972	1,457.6	196.5	13.5	628.6	43.0
1973	1,577.9	210.5	13.3	677.9	43.0
1974	1,706.7	228.3	13.4	733.7	43.0
1975	1,830.0	229.6	12.5	805.3	44.0
1976	2,108.1	256.7	12.2	912.3	43.3
1977	2,297.1	270.3	11.8	995.1	43.3
1978	2,705.4	318.4	11.8	1,162.5	43.0
1979	3,100.6	346.3	11.2	1,343.6	43.3
1980	3,614.6	390.0	10.8	1,588.3	43.9

Source: U.S. Federal Communications Commission, *Annual Report*, various years.
a. Technical expenses include payroll and other technical expenses such as circuit costs incurred in delivering programs to local stations. Program expenses include "talent" employees, other employees, rent and amortization of film and tape, records, and transcripts, outside news service costs, payment to talent, music license fees, other performance and program rights, and all other program expenses. Other categories not listed in the table are selling expenses and general and administrative expenses (which includes general and administrative payroll, depreciation and amortization, interest, allocated costs of management from home office of affiliate(s), and other general and administrative expenses). These descriptions are taken from "Television Financial Data 1980, FCC Financial Figures" [1981].
b. Does not include the three major television networks but does include network-owned and operated television stations.

average expenses of television stations between 1960 and 1980 (in both real and nominal dollars) and confirms the steep rise in broadcasting costs. It also depicts the trends in the two relevant components of broadcasting expenses—technical and program expenses—showing that real program costs have climbed steadily, while real technical expenses have remained about constant over the 20-year period. Table 6.4 shows that, as a percent of total expenditures, technical costs dropped continuously from 16.5% in 1960 to 10.8% in 1980. In real (inflation-adjusted) dollars, over the 20 years in question total technical expenses per station actually rose, but at the modest rate of 0.8% per year. However, the average rate of increase of real programming cost was 3.1%, and total (technical plus programming) real expenses increased at virtually the same annual rate, 2.9%. This is, in short, exactly the pattern that the asymptotic stagnancy analysis leads us to expect.

6.8 Concluding Comments

Our empirical data seem consistent with the hypotheses enunciated earlier in this chapter. Above all, at least in output terms, the "rising share of services" turns out to be deceptive. The output shares of the progressive and stagnant sectors of the economy have in fact remained fairly constant in the postwar period, so that, just as the cost disease leads us to expect, with rising relative prices, the share of total expenditures on the (stagnant) services and their share of the labor force have risen dramatically. Similar trends are also found internationally. There is only one sense in which some validity remains to the thesis that the United States (along with other prosperous countries) is becoming a service economy. As we have seen in this chapter, it is true that an increasing share of the labor force of such countries is being absorbed by the stagnant services. This in itself is not undesirable. It is only disturbing if this sector offers more poorly paid jobs with less opportunity for advancement, or if this shift of the labor force toward activities with low productivity growth serves to impede the overall productivity growth rate of the economy.

Notes

1. For a discussion of the difficult problems of the construction of defensible price indices for services, see Robert Summers [1985] and the pertinent bibliography in his paper.

2. Technically speaking, our model's prediction of nominal share of expenditures relates only to *stagnant* services. Though Summers did provide a breakdown of service expenditures by type of service, it was not possible to fit his data into the progressive and stagnant categories. Therefore, the calculation here refers to the entire service sector.

3. The regression results corresponding to figures 6.1 and 6.2 are

share of services in real GDP = 37.95* − 0.039 real GDP per capita,
$$(12.51) \quad (1.23)$$

$\qquad\qquad\qquad\qquad\qquad\qquad\qquad\qquad\qquad\qquad\qquad\qquad\qquad$ (i)

$R^2 = 0.04$,

share of services in nominal GDP = 25.77* + 0.184* real GDP per capita,
$$(12.85) \quad (4.62)$$

$\qquad\qquad\qquad\qquad\qquad\qquad\qquad\qquad\qquad\qquad\qquad\qquad\qquad$ (ii)

$R^2 = 0.40$

(* = significant at the 1% level; *t*-ratios are shown in parentheses). The coefficient of real GDP per capita in the first (real shares) regression is statistically insignificant and slightly negative, meaning that, if anything, in output terms the richer a country is, the (slightly) less likely it is to approximate a true service economy. In contrast, in the second equation, dealing with nominal shares of GDP, that coefficient is significant at the 1% level, and strongly positive, meaning that richer economies do *appear* to produce more services only if we do not correct for nominal price differences. Moreover, the R^2 of the second equation is 10 times larger than that of the first, thus showing the strength of the price illusion with respect to output.

4. Though wages in labor-inflexible industries have often lagged behind those in the rest of the economy, they have generally caught up over longer periods. For example, right after World War II salaries of college faculty members had fallen behind salaries and wages in industry, but by the end of the 1960s the gap had been closed. Economic pressures simply do not permit growing divergences in real wages in different economic activities, for, if growing disparities were to persist, labor would move into the increasingly better-paid occupations, and the resulting shortages would force wages up in the activities where they had lagged.

5. Here, as the total value of goods and services produced domestically, irrespective of ownership, gross domestic product (GDP) is actually the preferable concept. The level of industry disaggregation was determined by the available statistics for the period. The output variable is gross product originating (GPO) in constant (1972) dollars. GPO in constant dollars is defined as the difference between the deflated value of output and the deflated value of interindustry inputs. The input concept is "persons engaged in employment" (L), defined as the sum of the number of full-time-equivalent employees and self-employed workers. This is perhaps the best available measure of labor input.

6. The real estate data must be interpreted cautiously, since part of the "output" is the rent imputed to owner-occupied housing. However, where imputed rent enters official GNP and GDP statistics, the reported rate of productivity growth in the

real estate sector should include imputed rent to owner-occupied housing as part of output.

7. We also found that the share of total capital stock in the stagnant sector declined by about 5 percentage points, indicating that the capital-labor ratio grew faster in the progressive sector. This result is consistent with the spirit of our model, since the progressive sector is characterized by more rapid changes in technology, which can be expected to involve a more rapid displacement of labor by capital.

8. We summarize some of Gordon's [1987] results in section C of the appendix to chapter 6.

9. In the three years, 1976, 1979, and 1981, in which the downward trend was interrupted, the increased share of hardware cost is ascribable to major equipment purchases and changes in equipment financing, rather than to increases in hardware prices. The director of the center does caution that, although the bulk of the drop in center expenditures on hardware is attributable to actual hardware cost decreases, some part of it is the result of more favorable lease-purchase arrangements and an increase in the percent of equipment owned rather than rented. We should also note here that the category of expenses designated as "hardware" in figures 6.3, 6.4A, and 6.4B also includes some "other expenses" (for example, computer supplies). If hardware costs were completely separated from these other costs, the downward pattern would be even more pronounced.

10. Some industry figures produce results that are less clear-cut. For instance, the Diebold Group [1982] has studied computer operations of large U.S. corporations over the 10 year period 1971–1981. Their surveys showed that the average share of computer operations budgets devoted to hardware fell from 35% in 1971 to 27% in 1981; the share of expenditures on computer operations personnel (employees such as keypunchers, whose work is most susceptible to automation and productivity increases) fell from 29% in 1971 to 18% in 1981, while the share of the budget spent on systems development personnel (the "brainpower" employees) remained essentially the same over the 10 year period (25% in 1971 and 24% in 1981).

11. Although the number of computations performed at the center is not recorded, according to the director of the center, this number has clearly increased dramatically. In particular, as the computer programs handled at the center became ever more complex (i.e., as the "captured intelligence" in each program grew), each keystroke punched into the computer gave many more commands to the machine.

We should note here that another side of the phenomenon of increasing domination of labor costs in computer budgets is the leap in labor productivity some observers believe to have been brought about by computerization. New computer technology permits users to accomplish much more much faster. For example, a company that once paid a roomful of workers to tabulate year-end accounts can now computerize those operations and retrain the workers to analyze the data the computer puts out, accomplishing far more for the company. At the Princeton University Computer Center the budget for salaries used to be dominated by keypunch personnel; today the staff there is far more skilled and professional.

7

Is the United States Becoming an Information Economy?

By virtue of this concatenation of processes the modern industrial system at large bears the character of a comprehensive, balanced mechanical process.... The higher the degree of development reached by a given industrial community, the more comprehensive and urgent becomes the requirement of interstitial adjustment.
Veblen [1904, p. 16]

To say that the advanced industrial world is rapidly becoming an Information Society may already be a cliche. In the United States, Canada, Western Europe, and Japan, the bulk of the labor force now works primarily at informational tasks such as systems analysis and computer programming, while wealth comes increasingly from informational goods such as microprocessors and from informational services such as data processing.
Beniger [1986, p. v]

As we saw in chapter 6, the evidence does not support the popular view that the United States is rapidly becoming a service economy. Indeed, the facts conflict directly with the assertion that the services constitute an ever-growing share of the real output of the American economy. In this chapter we shall investigate another, parallel, premise about the United States—that it is evolving into an "information economy," i.e., that the increasing complexity and technical sophistication of our economic activities, coupled with the growth in the complexity of the interrelations among the country's business firms, makes it ever more necessary for them to engage in massive accumulation and processing of information, and that this constitutes a major upheaval in our way of doing business.[1] Since information gathering and processing (because they are themselves largely service activities) may be as vulnerable to the cost disease as are the services generally, this opens up the possibility that exactly the same illusion generated in the service sector is also applicable to the information sector. In other words, the spectacular growth of this sector of the economy may be due largely to the characteristic that the amount of labor it uses is not easily reduced. Exploration of this possibility for the nation's information activities is no mere idle exercise. If the cost disease, rather than a growing demand for information, does account for the bulk of the growth of the information sector, then the "information economy" view apparently must be deflated considerably by the results of our study of the pertinent statistics. This is, in fact, what the data suggest, as will be reported in this chapter.

7.1   Growth of the Information Economy: Our Classification Scheme

Before turning to the statistics about the nature of the information economy, we first describe the procedures we shall adopt. The central procedural problem of all studies of the size and growth of the information sector is the absence of any obvious boundary between the activities that should be included in that sector and those that should be interpreted to be outside it. Any such boundary must inevitably be somewhat arbitrary at best. Where, for example, should one classify banking, insurance, and even book publication (with its double purpose: entertainment and provision of information)? There is, of course, no one correct solution to this classification problem. We shall adopt an arbitrary classification scheme whose justification is that it is closely related to those used by previous writers on the subject. More to the point is evidence that our qualitative conclusions remain robust under substantial changes in the classification. This should not be very surprising, first because the growth in the proportion of information workers must be evaluated via a comparison of that share at two different dates (so whatever classification one adopts must remain the same at both dates) and second because the evidence indicates that the upsurge in information-related employment has been so large that it will show up in the data, no matter what taxonomy is adopted.

Our basic data are from the U.S. Decennial Censuses of 1960, 1970, and 1980. In our calculations, the row figures in the Census tables of occupations-by-industry were first aggregated, in conformity with an internally consistent classification scheme, into 267 occupations and 64 industries (see Wolff and Baumol [1989] for details). The occupations were aggregated once more into six categories:

i.   knowledge production,
ii. data processing,

iii. supply of services,

iv. goods production,

v. a hybrid class including both knowledge and data activities, and

vi. a second hybrid class including both data and service activities.

We then (somewhat arbitrarily) divided those that fell into the hybrid knowledge/data category, classing half of them as knowledge workers and half as data workers, and, in similar fashion, we have split the hybrid data/service category half into data and half into service workers. The resulting groups are referred to as the "total knowledge," "total data," and "total service" categories. Information workers were then defined as the sum of (total) knowledge and (total) data workers. The noninformation category is composed of the residual, including (total) service and goods workers.[2]

7.2   Growth of the Information Sector's Labor Force: The Empirical Data

The statistics that are usually presented to suggest the validity of the information economy hypothesis are similar to those cited by proponents of the service economy hypothesis. The standard evidence used for the purpose consists of figures indicating that there has been a striking increase in the share of the U.S. labor force that produces, acquires, or processes information. It may be noted that these figures are, if anything, considerably more shaky than the corresponding statistics pertaining to the services, since the boundaries of the service sector are at least tolerably well-defined, while, as has already been emphasized, no clear-cut boundaries for the economy's knowledge sector even seem possible, unless they are settled by arbitrary convention. Yet the data on the explosive growth of the information sector's share of the labor force are so striking that it seems reasonable to conjecture that the conclusion is highly robust—that any reasonable change in the boundary lines will not materially affect the conclusion.

Figure 7.1, derived from data reported by James R. Beniger [1986], is a good example of the sort of observations that emerge from such studies. The graph divides the American labor force into four sectors: agriculture, industry, (other) services, and information.[3] We see that the information sector's share of the labor force toward the beginning of the nineteenth century was so close to zero as not to be discernible on the graph (at least before 1830). By 1980, according to Beniger, employment in this sector had expanded so dramatically that it accounted for some 45% of the total

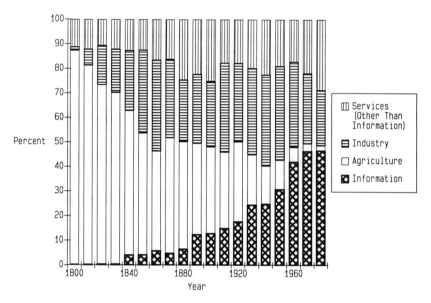

Figure 7.1
Sector shares, U.S. labor force, 1800–1980. Source: Beniger [1986, p. 24].

labor force and, in this respect, handily outdistanced any of the remaining three sectors. This is extraordinary growth indeed. One can easily understand why, from this observation alone, reasonable observers have been prepared to infer that there has been an explosion in the economy's information activity.

Our own data, taken from U.S. Census tables, permit us to provide similar supplementary statistics along with further details for the briefer period since the conclusion of World War II. Table 7.1 gives a breakdown of total employment by type of worker from 1960 to 1980 and the corresponding growth rates in each category, while table 7.2 reports the pertinent percentages. Over the two decades, knowledge workers were the fastest growing of the group, increasing 3.5% per year (line 8). They were followed by the data workers at 3.1% per year (line 9) and service workers (after inclusion of the allocated portion of the mixed data/service category), at 2.4% per year. In contrast, goods producers increased their number by only 0.4% per year (line 6). Altogether, employment of information workers grew 3.2% per year (about 1 percentage point above average), while noninformation workers increased 1.1% per year (a point below average). The developments can also be described by decade. Between 1960 and 1970, the total number of knowledge and data workers (line 10) increased

Table 7.1
Growth in U.S. employment: information workers and others, 1960–1980

Type of worker	Total employment (thousands)				Annual rate of growth (percent)		
	1960	1970	1980		1960–1970	1970–1980	1960–1980
1. Knowledge	1,951	3,294	4,821		5.24	3.81	4.52
2. Data	19,399	26,214	35,861		3.01	3.13	3.07
3. Knowledge/data	4,893	5,216	8,044		0.64	4.33	2.49
4. Data/services	1,950	2,735	4,796		3.38	5.62	4.50
5. Services	8,266	9,830	13,250		1.73	2.99	2.36
6. Goods	28,056	27,010	30,596		−0.38	1.25	0.43
7. Totals	64,515	74,299	97,369		1.41	2.70	2.06
8. Total knowledge[a]	4,398	5,902	8,843		2.94	4.04	3.49
9. Total data[a]	22,821	30,189	42,282		2.80	3.37	3.08
10. Total information[a]	27,218	36,091	51,125		2.82	3.48	3.15
11. Total noninformation[a]	37,297	38,208	46,244		0.24	1.91	1.08

a. The total for knowledge workers (line 8) is defined as the sum of line 1 and half of line 3. The total for data workers (line 9) is defined as the sum of line 2, half of line 3, and half of line 4. The total for information workers (line 10) is defined as the sum of line 8 and line 9. The total for noninformation workers (line 11) is the residual.

Table 7.2
Percentage composition of U.S. employment by type of worker, 1960–1980

Type of worker	Percent of total			Percentage change		
	1960	1970	1980	1960–1970	1970–1980	1960–1980
1. Total knowledge	6.8	7.9	9.1	16.5	14.3	33.2
2. Total data	35.4	40.6	43.4	14.9	6.9	22.8
3. Total services	14.3	15.1	16.1	5.2	6.6	12.2
4. Goods	43.5	36.4	31.4	−16.4	−13.6	−27.7
5. Totals	100.0	100.0	100.0	0.0	0.0	0.0
6. Total information[a]	42.2	48.6	52.5	15.1	8.1	24.5
7. Total noninformation[a]	57.8	51.4	47.5	−11.0	−7.6	−17.8

a. See note to table 7.1 for details.

by 2.8% per year, almost twice the overall rate of growth of employment, while the combined employment of service and goods employees remained almost unchanged in number. In the second decade, 1970 to 1980, total employment in the U.S. grew at 2.7% per year. Altogether information (knowledge and data) workers rose in number 3.5% per year, while the employment of noninformation workers increased by 1.9% per annum.

Table 7.2 provides another way of viewing the growth of the information sector. In 1960, 7% of total employment consisted of knowledge workers and 35% of data workers. Altogether, 42% of the employed labor force was made up of information workers and 58% of noninformation workers. By 1980, the proportion of information workers in total employment had increased to over half the total. The number of knowledge workers had risen to 9% and that of data workers to 43% of total employment.

7.3 Growth of the Information Economy: Breakdown by Industry and Sector

Since our subsequent analysis depends substantially on comparative shifts in the share of information workers among industries, we pause here to examine what the data show on this matter. Table 7.3 reports the percent of information workers in the labor force of each of the major industrial groups.[4] It is instructive, first, to consider the relative information-intensity of the various sectors. The finance, insurance, and real estate sector is the most information-intensive—about 90% of its employees are knowledge or data workers. The trade, services, and government sectors are next in line, with between 45% and 70% of their employees in information occupations. In mining, construction, manufacturing, and transportation, information workers comprise between 19% and 47% of total employment. Agriculture is the least information-intensive, with under 10% of its employees in information jobs.

What about trends? In most sectors, the relative growth in employment of knowledge workers was maintained over the two decades. Between 1960 and 1980, data workers increased relative to total employment in all industries except trade and the government sectors, where they declined slightly in percentage terms. However, the relative gains were greater in the 1960s than in the 1970s. All told, information workers increased in number relative to noninformation workers in all sectors except trade over the two decades. One obvious explanation for these trends is that the increasing sophistication and complexity of our productive mechanism requires ever more information for its "interstitial" adjustments, or that an

Table 7.3
Knowledge and data workers as a percent of U.S. employment by major industry, 1960–1980

	1960			1970			1980		
	Knowledge	Data	Information	Knowledge	Data	Information	Knowledge	Data	Information
1. Agriculture	0.8	1.4	2.3	2.2	4.1	6.3	3.2	6.4	9.6
2. Mining	6.4	18.4	24.8	8.7	24.8	33.4	10.6	28.3	38.9
3. Construction	6.9	12.6	19.4	7.0	17.3	24.3	7.1	20.3	27.4
4. Nondurable manufacturing	5.3	22.7	28.0	6.7	26.5	33.2	7.3	28.5	35.8
5. Durable manufacturing	7.2	24.8	32.0	9.9	27.0	36.8	10.1	28.0	38.2
6. Transportation	5.8	32.7	38.6	6.9	36.6	43.5	8.5	38.2	46.6
7. Trade	7.5	54.9	62.4	6.5	53.0	59.5	8.8	52.1	60.9
8. Finance, insurance, and real estate	8.7	81.0	89.6	8.5	82.4	90.9	8.4	83.0	91.4
9. Services	8.4	37.9	46.2	9.4	45.7	55.1	10.2	48.7	58.9
10. Government	8.7	57.2	65.9	10.7	56.1	66.8	11.7	55.0	66.7
Totals	6.8	35.4	42.2	7.9	40.6	48.6	9.1	43.4	52.5

increasingly educated population demands products with ever greater information content. However, an alternative line of explanation is possible. As we saw in the previous chapter, according to our unbalanced growth hypothesis, *with constant output proportions*, employment in activities with relatively slower rates of productivity growth must increase relative to employment in high-productivity growth activities. We saw also how the cost disease affects (asymptotically stagnant) industrial activities that use in fixed proportions some inputs whose production is progressive and some that are stagnant in terms of labor productivity growth. If the progressive and stagnant inputs are used in fixed proportions in real terms, then it follows that labor employed in producing the stagnant component will increase relative to the employment in the progressive component. Thus, there will be a relative increase of employment of workers engaged in relatively stagnant activities if output or input proportions stay relatively fixed.

Of the four classes of workers in our classification scheme, it seems plausible that the activity of knowledge workers is the most technologically stagnant, in the sense that the production of knowledge is itself an activity that is not readily amenable to technical change. The activity of data workers would seem to be more progressive, since part of their task involves the acquisition and transmission of information, activities that *do* benefit from technological advance (through computers, new telecommunications equipment, and the like). However, the portion of their activity that involves the analysis and comprehension of information (reading, for example) seems much more difficult to change technologically. The activity of service workers is, perhaps, a bit more progressive than that of data workers, since new equipment can often increase their productivity (as in telecommunications). Finally, the activity of goods workers, as a group, is the most progressive, since goods production would appear to be the most amenable to the substitution of capital for labor.

The relative decline in the number of goods workers over the period and the corresponding increase in knowledge, data, and service workers can, thus, conceivably be attributed, at least in part, to unbalanced growth. The increase in the number of knowledge workers relative to service and goods workers during the 1960s and relative to the other three categories of labor during the 1970s is also consistent with that phenomenon. However, the explanation offered by the unbalanced growth hypothesis is imperfect at best. For example, it does not account in any obvious way for the fact that the employment of knowledge workers and data workers both increased at about the same rate during the 1960s, while that of data and service workers grew proportionately during the 1970s. Obviously, the influence of unbalanced growth has to be tested with the aid of tools more powerful than just review of the statistics. This is a task to which we turn next.

7.4   Is the Information Explosion Real?: The Testing Procedure for Our Central Hypothesis

We now turn to the central issue of the chapter—whether the information explosion is a real phenomenon or is largely an illusion contributed by the cost disease. To examine this issue empirically we shall break down the changes in the information workers' share of the labor force into three parts:

i. the *input substitution* of information labor for labor of other types within the production process, i.e., the change in the proportion of information workers in each industry's labor force,

ii. the change in each industry's share of the economy's total *output*, and

iii. the change associated with relative variations in *labor productivity* of the different industries.

The first of these three components can be interpreted to indicate the extent to which the composition of the labor force in a typical industry has become more information-intensive (assuming all other things remain the same). If all output proportions had remained unchanged and all industries had experienced the same rate of productivity growth, we would ascribe to this input substitution element the entire observed rise in the share of information workers in the overall labor force. The second element in our breakdown, output composition, relates to different industries' shares of the economy's total output and is pertinent in determining the extent to which the expansion in information-related employment is attributable to an increase in the economy's *demand* for products with a high information content. Finally, the productivity-growth component in our breakdown plays the critical part in testing the role of unbalanced growth in the information explosion. If *it* were the only one of our three elements to undergo a nonzero change, that would imply that the entire information explosion of the labor force could be attributed to relatively higher productivity growth in industries using less information, driving the labor force toward the remaining industries, where slow productivity growth kept demand for information-related labor (along with that for other types of labor) relatively high. For brevity, it is convenient to refer to these three elements, respectively, as (i) the input-substitution component, (ii) the output-composition component, and (iii) the productivity-lag component. (The appendix provides details on this decomposition.)[5] Our analysis then proceeds by direct use of the available estimates of the input-output co-efficients and the statistics on information workers, total employment, and outputs by industry, simply substituting these data into a mathematical equation [identity (ii) in note 5] that encompasses the breakdown of in-formation employment growth into its three components. The propor-tions among the resulting terms, then, are taken to indicate the relative shares of the three components in the explosion of information employment in particular industries, in particular sectors, and in the economy as a whole.

The implication of two of these components about the source of the grow-ing share of information labor is unambiguous. If the output-composition component turns out to be large, it must imply that consumers (or industry) shifted their preferences toward heavy information-using goods and ser-vices, as the term "information revolution" implies. A large productivity-lag component has the reverse implication—that a correspondingly sub-stantial share of the shift in the labor force represents mere technical read-justment rather than a true rise in the share of information output. However, the remaining element, the input-substitution component, is rather am-biguous. True, it surely is, in part, a consequence of technical changes in the production processes, which require more information creation and use, and hence also constitute legitimate manifestations of an information revo-lution. However, there is also a second side to the substitution of inputs that is merely an unbalanced-growth response to uneven productivity growth in different processes. For example, consider an industry which engages in just two activities, A and B. Assume that A is much more information labor-intensive than B but that labor productivity in A grows far more slowly than that in B. Then even if the relative use of activities A and B by the industry is absolutely fixed, the share of the labor force devoted to A must grow as rising productivity reduces B's relative demand for labor. As a result, the use of labor by activity A must rise *in comparison with activity B* and so the share of information labor will also rise automa-tically, not because of an increase in sophistication of the total production process that requires more use of information labor, but because of the rela-tive lag of productivity of information-intensive process A. If information-intensive activities are generally those whose productivity grows most slowly, such a scenario will not be rare.

Unfortunately, unavailability of the requisite data prevents us from sub-dividing the input-substitution component into its information-demand

and the productivity-lag portions. In much of the following discussion we shall treat it as though it were made up entirely of the former. However, it must be recognized that this may substantially overestimate the share of the relative rise in information employment legitimately attributable to growing complexity and sophistication of the production process.

7.5 The Growth of the Information Economy: Overall Results of Our Statistical Study

Table 7.4 reports the results derived from our breakdown of information employment growth (whose formal equation is derived in the appendix). The table contains three panels:[6] The first shows the growth (in percentage points) of each type of employment and divides it into our three components; the second translates these figures for the components into percentages of the total growth of employment in each labor category; and the third panel shows what annual percentage growth rate of each occupational group would have resulted from each component if total employment had been fixed. To show how to interpret this table, let us consider as an example the change in the share of the knowledge workers (the *producers* of information) in total employment during the first subperiod of our study. According to the first line in the left-hand panel of table 7.4, this share increased by 1.13 percentage points in that 1960–1970 decade. Of this, the input-substitution component accounted for 0.78 percentage points (first panel), or 70% of the total change (second panel). If total employment had been fixed, knowledge workers would have grown at a rate of 1.09% per year over this period because of the input-substitution component alone (third panel).

Before discussing the details, let us see what overall results are shown by table 7.4. The last line summarizes what happened to the share of all information workers (i.e., knowledge plus data workers) over the entire 20-year period. We see that this share grew by 10.3 percentage points (panel 1). Some 53% of this change was made up of the input-substitution component, and 38% was due to the productivity-lag (unbalanced-growth) component (panel 2, last line), while the shift in the composition of final output contributed only 9%.

In sum, on the production side of the economy, a large contribution was made by technological change within each industry that substituted information labor for other types of labor (our input-substitution component). The interindustry productivity-lag component was also quite strong. The absorption of workers by industries whose productivity grew relatively slowly served to increase the share of information workers by a

Table 7.4
Decomposition of the change in U.S. employment composition into input-substitution, productivity-lag, and output-composition effects, 1960–1980[a]

Type of worker	Panel (1): Decomposition (in percentage points) of change in employment composition				Panel (2): Change in employment composition (as percent of total)				Panel (3): Annual rate of growth of employment in percent (assuming total employment fixed)			
	Input-substitution effect	Productivity-lag effect	Output-composition effect	Total change	Input-substitution effect	Productivity-lag effect	Output-composition effect	Total change	Input-substitution effect	Productivity-lag effect	Output-composition effect	Total change
1. 1960–1970 period												
1. Knowledge	0.78	0.36	−0.02	1.13	69.6	32.3	−1.9	100.0	1.09	0.42	0.02	1.53
2. Data	2.06	2.69	0.51	5.26	39.1	51.2	9.6	100.0	0.57	0.74	0.08	1.39
3. Services	0.06	0.73	−0.05	0.75	7.8	98.3	−6.1	100.0	0.04	0.48	−0.02	0.51
4. Goods	−2.94	−4.00	−0.19	−7.13	41.3	56.1	2.6	100.0	−0.70	−1.00	−0.09	−1.79
Information[b]	3.01	3.01	0.36	6.39	47.2	47.2	5.6	100.0	0.69	0.68	0.04	1.41
2. 1970–1980 period												
1. Knowledge	0.96	0.52	−0.34	1.14	84.1	45.3	−29.5	100.0	1.14	0.45	−0.25	1.34
2. Data	1.40	0.78	0.62	2.79	50.1	27.8	22.2	100.0	0.34	0.18	0.15	0.66
3. Services	−0.08	0.99	0.09	1.00	−7.8	99.2	8.7	100.0	−0.05	0.65	0.05	0.64
4. Goods	−2.42	−1.99	−0.52	−4.93	49.0	40.4	−10.6	100.0	−0.69	−0.61	−0.16	−1.46
Information[b]	2.40	1.04	0.49	3.93	61.0	26.6	12.4	100.0	0.48	0.19	0.11	0.78
3. 1960–1980 period												
1. Knowledge	1.74	0.67	−0.15	2.27	76.9	29.6	−6.5	100.0	1.14	0.18	0.12	1.43
2. Data	3.51	3.28	1.26	8.05	43.5	40.8	15.7	100.0	0.47	0.43	0.13	1.03
3. Services	0.02	1.65	−0.08	1.75	1.3	94.3	4.4	100.0	0.01	0.54	0.03	0.58
4. Goods	−5.41	−5.76	−0.90	−12.06	44.8	47.7	7.4	100.0	−0.66	−0.79	−0.17	−1.62
Information[b]	5.49	3.90	0.93	10.32	53.2	37.8	9.0	100.0	0.61	0.39	0.09	1.09

a. Average period weights are used in all cases. The input-substitution, productivity-lag, and output-composition components are derived from equation (3) in the appendix.
b. Sum of (1) and (2).

significant amount (our productivity-lag component). The magnitude of these two components together implies that the so-called "information explosion" is primarily a consequence of unbalanced growth, and that the substitution of information labor within production and uneven productivity growth among industries together may have raised the share of information labor in the labor force by over 9 percentage points in two decades (panel 1, last line). In contrast, the role of demand shifts toward heavily information-using products (our output-composition component) was very modest. By itself it might perhaps have raised the demand for information labor only 0.1% per year, compounded, had total employment in the economy remained constant over the two decades (last panel of the table). In conclusion, the data indicate that, like the so-called "shift to the services," the autonomous growth in demand for information labor was quite minimal.

7.6 Details of the Statistical Study: Conclusions by Decade, and by Knowledge and Data Worker Categories

Having examined the overall implications of the decomposition calculation, let us turn to some of its details. For this purpose we go back to our subclassification of information workers into knowledge workers (information producers) and data workers (knowledge users). We begin with the knowledge worker subgroup. As we saw in our introductory discussion of the top row of table 7.4, the most important component in the relative growth of knowledge workers over the 1960s and 1970s was the substitution of knowledge workers for other classes of workers within industries. This component accounted for 70% of their relative growth over the 1960s and 84% over the 1970s. Productivity growth in knowledge-intensive industries was relatively low over the two decades and served to increase the employment of knowledge workers. During the 1960s, the relatively low productivity growth in this sector accounted for a 0.36 percentage point increase in the employment of knowledge workers, while during the 1970s it accounted for a 0.52 percentage point rise. The productivity-lag component was about half as strong as the input-substitution component in each of the two decades. The shift in output demand toward knowledge-intensive products was of negligible importance during the 1960s, while during the 1970s it actually served to depress the demand for knowledge workers. Over the two decades, the input-substitution component accounted for about three-fourths of relative employment growth of the knowledge workers, and the interindustry productivity-lag component the other quarter.

Next, consider data workers (second row in each section of table 7.4). Almost 40% of the increase in their relative share during the 1960s is attributed by the calculation to the substitution of data workers for other workers within industries. As in the knowledge-intensive industries, productivity growth was slower than average in data-intensive industries, and about half of the growth in employment of data workers is attributable to the relatively slower productivity growth of these sectors. The shift in demand toward data-intensive output was of minor importance during this period. During the 1970s, the input-substitution component was the dominant element, accounting for half of the increase in the share of data workers, while the interindustry productivity-lag component accounted for 28%. During the 1970s, there was a significant shift in demand toward data-intensive output, and this accounted for 22% of the employment growth of this period.

Next, consider the share of service workers. For them, as shown in previous studies, the interindustry productivity-lag component was dominant, accounting for almost all of their employment growth during the two decades. The relatively slower productivity growth of service-intensive sectors served to increase service workers' employment share in the two decades by 1.7 percentage points. Both the substitution of industry employment away from service workers and shifts in final output composition had a negligible effect on their relative employment. Finally, turning to goods workers, the two unbalanced growth components together accounted for almost all of the relative decline in their employment share. During the 1960s, over 40% of the relative decline in the employment of goods workers was accounted for by the substitution of other workers for goods producers within industries and 56% by the relatively *higher* rate of productivity growth of the goods-producing sectors. During the 1970s, the combined magnitudes of the two components remained virtually unchanged. The shift in output demand was again of relatively minor importance in the two decades, accounting for only 3% of the relative decline in the employment of goods producers during the first decade and 11% during the second.

In summary, the two dominant elements in the composition of employment were the input-substitution and interindustry productivity-lag components. Shifts in the composition of output were a relatively minor element, though the output-composition component grew in importance over the two decades. For knowledge workers, the substitution of workers within industry production was twice as important as unbalanced growth between industries. For both data and goods workers, the two components were of almost equal magnitude. On the other hand, relative productivity movements between industries were by far the dominant element in explaining the relative growth of service workers.

Finally, the third panel of table 7.4 exhibits another relationship that seems consistent with the expectations that might have been stimulated by unbalanced growth. To the extent that the logic of unbalanced growth underlies the behavior of the input-substitution component, we should expect, in terms of that component alone, that employment of knowledge workers would grow fastest, that of data workers second fastest, service workers third, and goods workers slowest (since in terms of their productivity growth they would be ranked in reverse order). This turns out to have been true in both the 1960s and the 1970s. Moreover, the number of service workers grew faster than total employment during the two decades, while goods workers grew less slowly than total employment, as unbalanced growth calls for. We would also expect the productivity-lag component to lead to these same employment growth rankings, and, indeed, this occurred over the two decades, with the important exception of knowledge workers. Finally, the output-composition component was positive for knowledge, data, and service workers, and negative for goods workers. The relative magnitude of this component varied over the two decades. However, over the 20-year period, the output-composition component was largest for knowledge and data workers, ranked second (and almost zero) for service workers, and ranked last (and negative) for goods workers. These results indicate a slight shift in demand toward information-intensive output.

7.7   Conclusion

This chapter documents once again the rapid growth of information workers in the U.S. economy, in both absolute and relative terms, over the period from 1960 to 1980. In terms of our classification, over these years knowledge workers (those who produce information) grew from 6.8% to 9.1% of total employment, data workers (those whose job is to use information) grew from 36% to 43%, and information workers as a body from 42% to 53%. These results are consistent with those of other studies.

The novel result of the work reported here is the evidence that the rising share of the labor force in information-related occupations is the result of two distinct forces, both of which may be considered the ingredients of unbalanced growth, leaving relatively little to be attributed to an autonomous explosion in demand for information. The first, and more important, of these is the substitution of information workers, particularly knowledge producers, for noninformation workers within production. This accounted for over half of the increase in the share of information employees in total employment. The second is relative productivity growth movements among industries, which accounted for over a third of the relative growth of information workers and over 40% of the relative growth of data workers. The shift in demand toward information-intensive output, then, was of relatively minor importance, accounting for only 9% of the growth in information employment, though 16% of the growth in data workers.

The one apparent anomaly in our results is that, contrary to expectations, low productivity growth in knowledge-intensive sectors did not play a large role in the relative increase in knowledge workers over the two decades. Yet, on second thought, this result may not be too surprising, since productivity growth in a sector can be stimulated by the employment of a large number of knowledge workers. Indeed, research on the sources of productivity growth have consistently found a large positive effect of the number of knowledge workers on an industry's rate of technological progress. Thus, even though knowledge production may itself be a stagnant activity, it may nonetheless contribute strongly to productivity growth in sectors in which the activity is located.

Notes

1. A number of studies have documented the explosive expansion in the share of the labor force engaged in information-related activities: see, for example, Machlup [1962], Porat [1977], and Beniger [1986].

2. We also split these groups using other ratios. However, the major results concerning the growth of employment of knowledge and data workers and of the information sector are quite insensitive to the proportions into which we split the two hybrid groups.

A word should be said here about the classification criteria. Professional and technical workers have generally been classified as knowledge or data workers, depending on whether they are producers or users of knowledge. The line is perhaps more than a bit arbitrary at points, and judgment has been exercised rather loosely. Moreover, in some cases, professional workers have been classified as data-service workers. For example, doctors and nurses were treated in this way, since they use information and also perform a personal service. Management personnel have been taken to perform both data and knowledge tasks, since they produce new information for administrative decisions and also use and transmit this information. Clerical workers were classed as data workers for obvious reasons. We have classified as goods workers all labor that transforms or operates on materials or physical objects. These include craft workers, operatives (including transportation workers who move physical goods), and unskilled labor. The remaining group is made up of the service workers, who, primarily, perform personal services. See Wolff and Baumol [1989] for details on the classification scheme.

3. One striking and novel implication of the graph of figure 7.1 is that once the information sector is separated out from the remaining services, the share of the labor force encompassed in the latter displays relatively little sign of expansion. It would then appear from Beniger's figures that the bulk of the widely noted expansion in the service sector's share of the total labor force can be attributed to developments in information services, and that the remainder of the services have attracted little if any expanded proportion of that labor force.

4. See Wolff and Baumol [1989] for details on the 10-sector industry classification scheme.

5. The basic relationship that enables us to distinguish these three components is readily described. Here we offer a simplified preliminary version that is easier to grasp intuitively than the matrix relationships that were actually used and will be described later. We require some simple notation:

M_j = the number of information workers in industry j,

L_j = total employment in industry j, and

Y_j = total output in industry j.

Then

$$M_j/\sum L_k = (M_j/L_j) \cdot [(L_j/Y_j)/(\sum L_k/\sum Y_k)] \cdot (Y_j/\sum Y_k), \qquad \text{(i)}$$

or, considering changes between time t and $t + 1$ and letting, e.g., $(L_j/Y_j)_t$ represent the value of the fraction in parentheses at time t, we obtain

$$\Delta(M_j/\sum L_k) = \Delta(M_j/L_j) \cdot \{[(L_j/Y_j)/(\sum L_k/\sum Y_k)]_{t+1} \cdot (Y_j/\sum Y_k)_t\}$$
$$+ (M_j/L_j)_{t+1} \cdot \Delta[L_j/Y_j)/(\sum K_k/\sum Y_k)] \cdot (Y_j/\sum Y_k)_t \qquad \text{(ii)}$$
$$+ (M_j/L_j)_t \cdot [(\ell_j/Y_j)/(\sum L_k/\sum Y_k))]_{t+1} \cdot \Delta(Y_j/\sum Y_k)$$

Here, we can obviously associate $\Delta(M_j/L_j)$ with the input-substitution component, $\Delta[(L_j/Y_j)/(\sum L_k/\sum Y_k)]$ with the (inverse of) the relative productivity-lag component (since it reflects productivity gains in sector j relative to overall productivity growth), and $\Delta(Y_j/\sum Y_k)$ with the output-composition component.

Identity (ii) relates only to a single industry, j. However, it is obvious that it can readily be summed over a number of industries or the economy as a whole with no change in the structure of the equations. Thus, it can be used to extend our analysis to an entire sector or to the economy as a whole. This identity, then, along with several variants derived by various degrees of aggregation or disaggregation, is the basic relationship of our empirical analysis.

6. The basic data come from the 1960, 1970, and 1980 U.S. Decennial Censuses. The employment tables by occupation and industry for each year were first aggregated in conformity with a relatively consistent classification scheme into

267 occupations and 64 industries. See Wolff and Howell (forthcoming) for a description of the construction of the occupational matrices and Wolff and Baumol [1989] for details of the classification. The sectoral output (in 1972 dollars) and hours worked by employed persons for 1960, 1970, and 1980 are based on 155-sector figures obtained on tape from the U.S. Bureau of Labor Statistics (BLS). The BLS data were aggregated into a 64-sector industry classification scheme, and the occupation-by-industry matrices were aligned to the BLS total hours figures. Standard 87-order Bureau of Economic Analysis input-output tables for 1958, 1963, 1967, 1972, and 1977 were used for the interindustry analysis. (See Wolff [1985] for details on sources and methods for the input-output data.) The occupation-by-industry matrices were merged with the input-output tables on a 47-industry level. See Wolff and Baumol [1989] for the concordance between the 87-sector Bureau of Economic Analysis (BEA) industry classification scheme for the input-output data and the 64-industry classification scheme used for the occupation-by-industry matrices. Since the occupation-by-industry matrices were for different years than the input-output data, geometric interpolation of industry employment for the census years was used to align industry employment to the input-output data.

Estimates of the decomposition shown in equation (3) in the appendix were based on three sets of weights: beginning of the period, end of the period, and average period shares. The results were quite insensitive to the choice of weights, and only results based on average period weights are shown.

8   Savings, Investment, and Productivity Growth

... the [Japanese] saving ratio began to rise with renewed vigor in the mid-1960s. A possible explanation of this resurgence is that consumers, facing a rapid increase in income during the rapid growth period, failed to make swift adjustment in their consumption level, which lagged behind income. ...
Sato [1987, p. 150]

It seems generally agreed that there are two prime ingredients in the growth of labor productivity: technological innovation and the accumulation of capital through saving (and the subsequent investment of those savings). So far in this book, we have implicitly emphasized the former. For example, in chapter 5 innovation and the international transfer of its products played a prime role in our discussion of the converging productivity levels of a number of relatively successful industrialized economies. But even if technological innovation is the undisputed star in the scenario (which is by no means certain), substantial capital accumulation very likely would have been required to put the inventions into practice and to effect their widespread employment. If, moreover, saving and investment plays a primary role of its own, it becomes all the more important to explore the nature of that role. That is the task this chapter undertakes, recognizing that because of unavoidable interactions between the rates of innovation and investment, any attempt to separate the two may prove to be artificial, if not ultimately unworkable.

This chapter will end, like a number of others in this book, with a discussion of the implications of the evidence for an evaluation of the savings-investment performance of the U.S. in comparison with that of other industrial countries. Consistent with our general theme, we shall suggest that while the relatively low American savings figures are disquieting, taken at face value they make matters appear far more serious than they probably really are. For example, if, as the data seem to imply, the spectacular savings rates of the late-blooming economies are largely a manifestation of the recentness of their takeoff and, consequently, constitute a transitory phenomenon, much of the implied long-term threat to U.S. economic leadership clearly evaporates. We shall even present calculations, provided by a group of careful and sophisticated observers, suggesting that the bulk of the widely reported differential between the rates of capital formation of the United States and its industrial competitors is illusory—an artifact of poor methods of measurement. If the recalculations of this group of economists are accepted, it will follow that there is much less ground for concern about the recent savings-investment record of the United States than has often been supposed.

Of course, others have studied the investment-productivity relationship, both empirically and theoretically (see Moses Abramovitz and Paul A. David [1973] for an extremely illuminating analysis of the data and the theoretical issues, as well as some references to other discussions by economic historians). In particular, the many studies of the sources of the productivity growth decline that beset most industrialized countries during the 1970s have tried to determine what part savings and investment played during this productivity slowdown, and in doing so they necessarily have dealt with the more fundamental issue of the role of capital formation in the mechanics of productivity growth. Those discussions encompass a considerable range of analytical approaches as well as a variety of hypotheses. Thus, we can hardly hope to provide any completely novel results in this much-studied area. What we do undertake in this chapter is an exploration of what a long-run point of view can suggest.

The chapter will begin with an investigation of the savings-investment record of three countries—Italy, the Netherlands, and the United Kingdom —each of which was once, in its turn, the economic leader of the Western world. We shall see that the decline of each of these countries (or the time period that immediately preceded the decline) was characterized by massive lending to other countries. What is not clear is whether this export of capital was a result of the decline or one of its causes. We shall suggest that, while such historical questions can never be settled definitively, some element of the former relationship—declining domestic investment opportunities as a possible consequence of loss of economic leadership—must have borne some degree of responsibility for the transfer of savings to other lands. This already indicates that investment was probably not the whole story, or even most of it, in the explanation of past prosperity or productivity growth.

We then turn to some empirical evidence that is more direct and more systematic by reviewing the available statistics on the course of total factor productivity and its relation to labor productivity for a number of countries and for relatively lengthy time periods. The concept of total factor productivity (TFP) will be defined more accurately at the appropriate point in the chapter. However, for now, we may describe TFP growth, very roughly, as the enhanced production attributable to improvements in the efficiency of all inputs together and not just labor alone. It is measured as the part of the growth of a country's output that is *not* attributable to mere increases in the quantities of its inputs such as labor and capital. TFP represents the share of output attributable to innovation and other influences that enhance the productive efficiency of those inputs. Since labor productivity growth probably depends primarily on two influences—innovation and investment per worker—information on TFP growth, as an indicator of that portion of labor productivity growth attributable to innovation, also indicates, residually, how much of the labor productivity growth can be ascribed to investment. We shall see that total factor productivity growth has generally been significant and, except during wars and depressions, rather persistent during at least the past 11 decades. Yet, it has generally been quite a bit smaller than the overall rate of labor productivity growth. This suggests, once again, that capital accumulation does matter, but that other things, notably innovation, matter a great deal too.

That result will hardly come as a surprise to anyone. But rather less obvious results will emerge in the second half of the chapter, which, somewhat superficially, discourses upon the determinants of the savings and investment that were entailed in the accumulation process. What has just been said should make it clear that the actual amount that ends up having been saved depends not only upon a nation's propensity to save but also upon the attractiveness of available investment opportunities. In our discussion of the savings propensity, we shall consider the part played by cultural influences. While not seeking to deny the importance of such things as tradition and religion in helping to explain phenomena such as the very high savings rates of the Japanese and the Taiwanese in the period after World War II, we shall offer evidence suggesting that the importance of this element in the story may have been exaggerated to some degree. Earlier figures, for example, indicate that Japan has not always been characterized by extraordinary rates of saving. Other data will be used to show (for the few countries for which longer-term estimates are available) that growth in a nation's capital stock has a distinctly inverse relationship with that country's productivity level at the beginning of the time period involved in the calculation. Since all the countries for which we have such estimates are members of our "convergence club," we interpret this statistical observation to mean that the countries with relatively high savings-investment rates are those whose economic takeoffs occurred relatively late, and are those that convergence required to grow most rapidly. Our explanatory hypothesis is that increases in consumption characteristically lag behind when a nation experiences a sharp growth in per-capita output, so that, by default, savings then typically rise. This is, however, to some degree a transitory affair, as the next generation rapidly learns to participate in "the good life" and consumption expenditures begin to soak up more of the national output formerly devoted to savings and investment. If that conjecture is valid, then the future savings rates of the "miracle economies" of the Orient may not be quite as spectacular as they were in the past. Some Chinese historical information on the declines in the fortunes of leading families in the Ming and Ch'ing eras will suggest that Eastern culture does not preclude such a course of events.

The chapter will then turn to a discussion raising questions about the international mobility of capital. If capital is truly mobile, and sharp differences in savings rates among countries are not attributable entirely to superior domestic investment opportunities, one might have expected to see a systematic pattern of shipment of capital from high-savings to low-savings countries, with investment rates considerably more equalized than rates of saving. Yet that is apparently not true of at least the postwar period. While we shall propose no definitive explanation for the high correlation between the savings and investment rates of the different countries, we shall suggest that if this secret is unlocked it will also offer us substantial insights into the growth process and the policies that may be effective in encouraging it.

8.1   Preliminary: The Well-Known Correlation between Output and Capital Stock, and Its Ambiguous Interpretation

Common sense suggests that the size of a nation's output should be related to the size of its capital stock—the amount of its investment in factories, warehouses, machines, transportation facilities, and the like. Similarly, we have good reason to expect that countries with larger amounts of output per person will tend to be those with relatively large amounts of capital per person. The statistics show that this is true to a remarkable degree. Graphs that have appeared elsewhere (Maddison [1982, p. 55]) indicate (for the 5 countries—Germany, Italy, Japan, the United Kingdom, and the United

States—for which estimates of the size of the capital stock are available for close to a century in the past) that there has been a dramatically close association in each country between level of output (GDP) and quantity of capital (gross fixed nonresidential capital stock). Correspondingly, Robert Lipsey and Irving Kravis [1987b, pp. 58–59] report, for 50 countries in 1970 and 34 countries in 1975, the striking correlation between per capita real nonresidential capital stock and real per capita income from one country to another. The association was so close in the latter case, for example, that "... capital by itself explained more than 95% of the differences in real income levels [among the countries]." That is, if one were to attempt to use this correlation to deduce the income level of a particular country knowing nothing about that country other than the size of its capital stock, one could, roughly speaking, expect to come out with an answer that was about 95% accurate.

Though the association between capital and output of an economy is, then, remarkably close, the significance of this observation is far from clear. The reason is that a two-way relationship may well be involved. A nation with an abundant supply of plant and equipment can be expected as a consequence to be in a position to produce a relatively large output. But the other side of the story is the observation that an economy with a larger output is in a better position to build plant and equipment. Which of these two relationships plays the preponderant role in the observed close relationship between capital and output is a subject of debate in the literature, with some observers favoring the one, some the other. So far, statistical tests of the matter have been inconclusive, and we ourselves conjecture that both of the two-way relationships are of some importance in reality. The issue is important for policy because if capital accumulation were to prove not to contribute significantly to output and productivity growth, then the stimulation of saving and investment would not be a promising means to improve a nation's productivity performance. The large capital stock of the wealthier countries would then be the consequence of their wealth rather than a significant part of its cause, and therefore not a promising policy instrument for the poorer countries.

Unfortunately, we cannot pretend to have strong evidence on the issue, one way or the other. Yet much of the discussion of this chapter may offer some illumination on the nature of the relationships in question, and some of the material will suggest, though hardly prove, that matters do indeed go both ways—that investment contributes to productivity growth, and that the latter, in turn, contributes to investment.

8.2 The Savings and Investment Patterns of Past Economic Leaders

Since long-run productivity growth is the central focus of this book, the main concern of this chapter is the role of investment in the pertinent process. Saving, as we have noted, is the source of the inputs—the labor, the raw materials, and the other such ingredients—that can be used to produce plant, equipment, and the other components of a nation's capital stock. When an economy consumes all of what it produces, none of that income is left over to serve as the source of investable inputs. All of the labor and raw material used will have gone into the production of consumers' goods rather than producers' goods. But if the community saves a substantial proportion of its output, then the resources that have not been used to supply consumers can instead be used for productive investment.

However, that is not quite the end of the story. Suppose a country has supplied itself with a considerable amount of saving. It can, indeed, use the resulting investable resources for the construction of domestic plant and equipment. But, alternatively, those resources can be exported to foreign countries, where they can be used instead for the construction of plant and equipment for those nations. Many economies, including the United States in the nineteenth century, have industrialized with the aid of the import of just such investable resources from abroad.

But this section does not concern itself with the effect on the country that borrows the investable resources, but rather with the consequences for the lender country. Would that country generally have been better off investing those resources at home, or does it lose nothing for its citizens by exporting them abroad? One's instantaneous commonsense reaction is apt to be that exportation is usually not the better option because it strengthens the exporting nation's potential competitors at the expense of its own economy's plant and equipment and, hence, its future productivity. Economists have generally disputed this view, arguing that if foreigners are prepared to pay higher amounts to the lenders than the resources can earn (produce) at home, then the exporting country must be a net gainer from the export process. Rather than devoting attention to the various theoretical issues involved here,[1] we shall look at some historical evidence that seems to lend support to the commonsense view that the export of investment resources is not always a good idea for the exporter. In this discussion we shall focus our attention upon a succession of former world economic leaders and their investment export behavior at the time they were losing their leadership.

Since the Middle Ages the Western economies have been led, in turn, by four countries—Italy, the Netherlands, the United Kingdom, and the United States.[2] Italy's economy was the model for the Western world perhaps from the middle of the thirteenth century until the beginning of the sixteenth (though such datings are always in dispute among historians). The Netherlands achieved clear primacy in trade and industry toward the end of the sixteenth century, and (depending on whose views one accepts) held on to it at least through the first half of the seventeenth century and perhaps even well into the eighteenth. (On this and the discussion of the following paragraphs, see De Vries [1984].) We all are aware of Britain's economic rise at the end of the eighteenth century and the loss of its leadership somewhere between 1870 and 1913 (virtually any date in this period has its partisans among historians).

Now, we have no systematic macroeconomic statistics for the northern Italian cities in the sixteenth century or for the Netherlands in the seventeenth, but figures on particular industries, some of them spotty, have led historians to conclude that they suffered from an absolute decline. It is reported, for example, that in Venice production of woolen fabric fell from 22,000 "cloths" in 1589–1600 to less than 3,000 in 1690–1699, and that Florentine output fell from 15,000 cloths in the earlier period to 100 (!) in the latter. The Lombard countryside apparently managed a substantial recovery, but well before 1700 the urban portion of the economy "... had become a backward and depressed area; here manufacturing industry had collapsed, there were too many people for the available resources ..." (Cipolla [1970, pp. 196–201]; see also the sections by Sella, Cipolla, and Molho in Krantz and Hohenberg [1975]). A decline in manufacturing apparently also occurred in the eighteenth century Dutch republic, where according to Wilson [1968], there was an "absolute decline of former great centers of industry. By the mid-eighteenth century, Leyden was a desolate town, its once flourishing cloth industry reduced to a fraction of its former size. The Haarlem linen industry was similarly shrunken" (p. 235).

For our purposes the more pertinent observation is that all three of the former leader countries became heavy lenders to foreign nations either during their period of decline or some time before the decline had begun. The United Kingdom, according to data provided by Feinstein [1972], was sending abroad some 30% of its savings in the decade 1870–1879, and by 1905–1914 this figure had reached 50%. Similarly, Holland, even in the seventeenth century, provided significant amounts of investment abroad, and by the eighteenth century there was "... an extraordinary growth of foreign investment...." Funding was provided to Scandinavia, Germany,

France, Spain, Poland, Russia and, above all, to England (Wilson [1969, pp. 35−36]. According to Palmer [1959], "the Dutch ... in 1771 ... owned 40 percent of the British national debt, and by 1796 the entire foreign-held debt of the United States was in their hands" (Vol. I, p. 324). We need hardly be reminded of the role of the Italian bankers in the high Middle Ages and the Renaissance. In the thirteenth and fourteenth centuries Florence financed the wars of the three English Edwards in Wales, Scotland and France (Braudel [1982, Vol. II, p. 393]). For example, "... in the early fourteenth century the English king owed the Bardi company [600,000 florins] according to English documents, which probably underestimated the debt, or 900,000 florins according to Villani, who may have overestimated it. In addition, the English king owed the Peruzzi company a sum two thirds as large" (Lopez [1969, p. 106]). To evaluate the magnitude of these figures, we note that, "... within a generation [after 1303], [the Florentine communal debt] had increased to the grand total of 450,000 florins, and this was in excess of the amount that the city could hope to raise from all revenue sources over a sixteen-month period" (Becker [1969, p. 124]). We also know that the debts of the Spanish monarchs in the sixteenth century (owed largely to the Genoese) were enormous by contemporary standards. Thus, according to Atkinson [1960, p. 155], "In 1560 [Philip II of Spain] himself estimated the royal indebtedness at some seven times the national revenue; by 1574 he was paying interest to his German and Genoese bankers in excess of his total incomings."[3]

The basic question remains: Did extraordinary amounts of lending by nations about to cede their leadership constitute a prime cause of their decline? Or was it merely a rational response to the decline and to the resulting contraction in profitable investment opportunities at home, which was ascribable largely to other sources? There is evidence that the latter played at least a substantial role. In all three cases domestic investment had become less rewarding than investment abroad. This is indicated by interest rate figures. Perhaps the most striking are the statistics provided by Braudel [1984, Vol. III, p. 167] for the case of Genoa, shown in figure 8.1. Based on calculations by Cipolla [1952], it indicates that real interest rates fell from about 5% at the beginning of the sixteenth century to about 1% in the seventeenth. Similarly, for the case of the Netherlands, "Against a local yield of $2\frac{1}{2}$ percent a Dutch investor willing to lend abroad could be sure of 5 percent or 6 percent and many did" (Wilson [1969, pp. 35−36]). Rather similar observations apply to England on the eve of her loss of leadership. According to Floud and McCloskey [1981], for the period 1870−1913, (geometric) mean rates of return on domestic British invest-

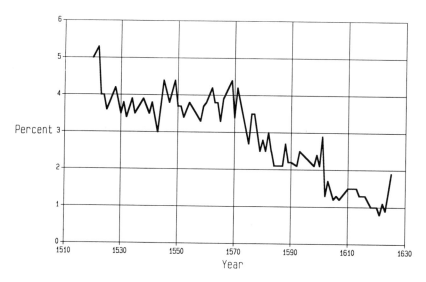

Figure 8.1
Real interest rates, Genoa, 1510–1625. Source: Braudel [1984, Vol. III, p. 167].

ment were 6.4% on equity and 3.2% on debenture, while on investment abroad those rates of return were 8.3% and 4.9%, respectively (Vol. II pp. 78–79). All of this suggests, at least for the case of the three fallen leaders, that decline in investment in their own economies was at least in part merely a reaction to whatever forces were responsible for a decline that was already under way, whether or not it had already been noticed; in other words, that the decline in domestic investment was to that degree a consequence, not a cause, of the overall state of the economy.

8.3 The Importance of Savings and Investment: Comparing Labor Productivity Growth and Total Factor Productivity Growth

As we noted earlier, comparison of the historical records of growth in labor productivity and that in total factor productivity can shed some light on the relative roles of innovation and savings and investment in productivity growth. Before turning to the underlying logic, we must pause to emphasize that this is a task beset by booby traps, and that any answers that pretend to be simple and categorical are almost certain to be either simplistic or simply incorrect. The need for such a warning is surely confirmed by the exemplary caution of Abramovitz and David [1973]: their reiterated citation of Voltaire's aphorism that "history is a fable which has been agreed upon," and their own guarded analysis that follows, is caveat enough. But having warned the reader, we think it best to avoid constant repetition of the perils that beset the discussion, and for the sake of exposition shall occasionally write in a manner that suggests that there is no danger.

What does seem clear is that the relative role of savings and investment has varied from one time to another as well as from place to place. This is demonstrated even by our rather naive procedure, in which we simply compare the magnitudes of two growth rates, that of labor productivity and that of total factor productivity. Total factor productivity is, in essence, an aggregative measure of the growth of national output (as measured, for example, by gross domestic product) per unit of some index of the combined quantities of inputs used for the purpose. Normally, it is interpreted to be whatever is left over after the subtraction of that part of output growth that is ascribable to any ordinary enhancement in the quantities of labor, capital and other inputs (sometimes additional adjustments, for such things as education of the labor force are also deducted from the residual). The implied inference is that, as far as is possible, this calculation will have eliminated from the statistics on output growth everything except for the contribution of technological change or innovation (in the broadest sense) to the economy's productive capability.[4] It follows from the implication that total factor productivity growth largely measures the contribution of innovation alone and the premise that growth in labor productivity is to be attributed largely to innovation and capital accumulation, that comparison between the growth rates of labor productivity and total factor productivity should indicate, at least roughly, the share of productivity growth that can be ascribed to savings and investment.[5]

This, then, is the statistical approach to the subject that we shall use. Table 8.1 summarizes the relatively long-term total factor productivity and labor productivity estimates available from a number of sources, including several estimates of total factor productivity that we have calculated ourselves on the basis of figures on its components that are provided by Maddison [1982]. Among them, the estimates span the period 1800–1980, and some refer to as many as seven leading industrial countries. The last column in table 8.1, the ratio of growth rates of total factor productivity to labor productivity, may be interpreted as a rough indicator of the proportion of labor productivity growth that can be attributed to innovation.

The first conclusion suggested by the comparisons in the table is that the contribution of savings and investment relative to that of innovation varies considerably from country to country and from period to period. Thus, we

Table 8.1
Growth rates, total factor productivity versus labor productivity, for seven industrial countries, several time periods since 1880

Country	Labor Productivity (%)	TFP Crude (%)	TFP Divisia (%)	TFP as % of labor productivity Crude	Divisia
I. 1880–1979					
Germany	2.63	1.88	1.56	71.48	59.32
Italy	2.56	1.99	1.36	77.73	53.13
Japan	3.06	2.6	1.62	84.97	52.94
U.K.	1.76	1.3	1.09	78.86	61.93
U.S.	2.24	1.55	1.37	69.20	61.16
Mean				75.45	61.16
Standard deviation				5.53	3.90
II. 1950–1979					
Canada	2.49	1.3	1.44	52.21	57.83
France	4.49	3.1	3.04	69.04	67.71
Germany	5.33	3.39	3.33	63.60	62.48
Italy	4.83	3.51	3.09	72.67	63.98
Japan	6.69	5.45	4.17	81.46	62.33
U.K.	2.75	1.68	1.48	61.09	53.82
U.S.	2.22	1.15	1.36	51.80	61.26
Mean				64.55	61.34
Standard deviation				10.00	4.12

Table 8.1 (continued)

III. U.S. (Abramovitz-David) estimates

Period	Labor productivity (%)		Total conventional factor productivity (%)		TFP as % of labor productivity	
	"Crude"	"Refined"	"Crude"	"Refined"	"Crude"	"Refined"
1800–1855	0.6		0.4		0.67	
1855–1905	1.1		0.5		0.45	
1905–1927	2.0		1.5		0.75	
1927–1967	2.7	1.6	1.9	1.3	0.70	0.81
Mean					0.64	

IV. U.S. TFP growth rates between major cycle peaks based on Kendrick-NBER estimates, 1874–1969

Period	Output/labor input	TFP (%)	TFP as % of output/labor input
1874–1892	1.7	1.55	91.2
1892–1907	1.21	1.01	83.5
1907–1913	0.76	0.57	75.0
1913–1920	1.3	0.88	67.7
1920–1929	2.28	2.09	91.7
1929–1937	1.14	0.99	86.8
1937–1948	1.95	1.91	97.9
1948–1957	2.71	2.07	76.4
1957–1969	2.42	2.03	83.9
Mean			83.8
Standard deviation			8.9

Sources: for I and II, Maddison [1982, p. 212] and Wolff [1987b, table 5]; for III, Abramovitz and David [1973, p. 430] and David [1977, p. 186]; for IV, business cycles selected from Moore [1983, p. 454] and productivity data from Kendrick [1973b].

see that over the century between 1880 and 1979, using the Divisia total factor productivity measure, the United Kingdom and the United States had relatively high ratios of total factor productivity to labor productivity, implying rather greater dependence on innovation and less on investment for productivity growth than was true for Italy and Japan. (It is worth noting that the data for the period after World War II and the crude total factor productivity data suggest rather different orderings.) Similar differences occur with the passage of time. These have been studied with considerable care by Abramovitz and David. Thus, David [1977] tells us, "... between the antebellum era (1800–1855) and the following half century (1855–1905) there occurred a decline in the *relative* contribution made by total factor productivity growth to the growth rate of real product per man hour—a fall from 54 percent to 42 percent, with a corresponding rise in the relative contribution being made by the growth of reproducible and nonreproducible capital in relation to labor inputs. During the transitional period, c. 1835 to c. 1890, the average growth rate of labor productivity was maintained at 0.83 percent per annum, of which three fourths ... must be ascribed to the growth of capital inputs per man hour of labor employed.... In the twentieth century, by contrast [TFP] ... represents more than two-thirds of the average rate of increase in real output per man-hour" (pp. 185–187, order of some passages inverted).

Unfortunately, this is not the end of the story. Innovation can, of course, increase the demand for new plant and equipment and so, by raising the prevailing interest rate, may induce a rise in saving, thereby accounting for at least part of the growth in nineteenth-century capital accumulation. In that case it may be that, after all, it is innovation, and not an independent rise in savings and investment, that ultimately lies behind most of the expanded growth of labor productivity of the nineteenth century. David does not clearly reject such an interpretation and offers additional speculation that raises a still deeper set of possibilities. Nonetheless, the immediate implications of the total factor productivity/labor productivity comparisons reported in table 8.1 do indeed display the patterns summarized in the preceding quotation.

Overall, table 8.1 shows that the total factor productivity/labor productivity ratio hovered at about 0.6. This implies (at our superficial level of interpretation) that, generally, about 60% of the growth of labor productivity in the periods and places covered in the table can be ascribed to innovation. The remaining 40% can perhaps be considered attributable to capital accumulation, including investment in human capital. Given the interdependence of investment and capital accumulation, the imperfection of both the data and the methods of calculation and a host of other reservations, such numbers, are hardly to be taken seriously. At best, they can be taken to confirm something that no one might in any event have doubted—that the growth of labor productivity (which can be taken as a reasonable measure of the expansion of the economy's ability to generate economic welfare) is ascribable, at least during the past century or so, both to innovation and to capital accumulation. Both seem to have made substantial contributions, with technical change probably being responsible for a somewhat larger share.

Here intuition and general impressions, which seem to support the same conclusions, may perhaps in this case deserve greater weight than the statistical calculations. After all, it is hardly plausible that the completely unprecedented explosion of outputs and living standards that followed in the wake of the Industrial Revolution could have occurred without the equally unprecedented spate of invention that has emerged steadily ever since. As T. S. Ashton [1948] put the matter in his classic essay on the Industrial Revolution, "'About 1760 a wave of gadgets swept over England.' So, not inaptly, a schoolboy began his answer to a question on the industrial revolution" (chapter 3, p. 48). It is equally implausible that this "wave of gadgets" could have accomplished what it did without the capital accumulation that allowed it to be embodied in railroads, steel mills, ships and shipyards, and the myriad other mighty instruments of production.

8.4 A Nation's Propensity to Save: Cultural and Economic Influences

We turn next to the determinants of saving, the source of the accumulation of capital. There is a vast empirical literature on this subject, and there is no point in our plowing once again over this heavily worked territory. Among the extensive list of variables that have been suggested as determinants of an economy's savings relative to its total income are the country's previously accumulated wealth, its current income, the age distribution of the population (on the hypothesis that younger people put money away for the education of their children, their retirement, etc., while older people live from their savings to a greater degree), the degree of inequality in income distribution (on the hypothesis that wealthy people save a larger proportion of their incomes), the ratio of current to past national incomes (on the hypothesis that savings habits were formed by past incomes), and the nation's religious, cultural, and ethnic attributes. Most of the variables listed so far are not easily influenced by government policy, but there are others that are more readily modified. Among these are the country's expenditure on education, the levels of interest rates (which affect the financial reward of saving), tax rates (which influence the amount of income the public has available for saving), and the rates at which savings are taxed, relative to the severity of taxation of consumption expenditure. (For a recent survey of the literature, see King [1985].)

We shall confine ourselves here to some rather unsystematic observations on the relative role of cultural and social influences, as distinguished from the influence of economic developments and the other variables in the preceding list (we shall return to some of the others in chapter 12). While not seeking to deny the role of culture and tradition, we shall suggest that their importance may have been somewhat exaggerated. We shall also suggest a particular avenue along which economic events may have affected savings rates, conjecturing that when there is a burst of economic growth in a society, consumption seems to lag behind per-capita outputs, and that perhaps one or two generations must pass before that society is transformed into one with a taste for goods and services that raises the average propensity to consume substantially. Until such a materialistic orientation takes over, that society will then tend to generate the large volume of savings needed to fuel the economic take-off process, and to establish the economy firmly on its new course. This consumption-lag hypothesis may, then, help to supplement the cultural explanations for the extraordinary savings rates that have, no doubt, served to fuel the growth process in places such as Japan and Taiwan.

Let us emphasize that in seeking other influences on the long-term behavior of an economy's rate of savings, we do not by any means intend to imply that culture and tradition have little if any role in the matter. On the contrary, we are convinced that cultural influences must play some key part in the growth process. If that were not so, how could one hope to explain why every brilliant economic success in the postwar era has occurred in the Far East, while almost every example of a profoundly disappointing economic performance has occurred in Latin America? Yet, if there *are* other influences, it is important to seek them out, even if they are less powerful than tradition and culture. For policymakers are virtually powerless to deal with cultural variables. No one knows any reliable and effective way to change a nation's culture, and probably many of us would consider such a step to be indefensibly invasive. Thus, if it is deemed important to raise a nation's long-term savings behavior, other means will undoubtedly have to be found.

Though we have agreed on their importance, it must also be emphasized that cultural influences can perhaps be more transitory than is sometimes assumed and that the direction of their influence may not always be quite what it seems. Today, it is easy to ascribe the economic troubles of the United Kingdom to the poor performance of its entrepreneurs and the absence of an instinct of workmanship in its labor force (see, for example, Martin J. Wiener [1981]). Similarly, it has become practically a cliche to ascribe the Japanese success to superior management and the dedication of its labor force to product quality and output quantity. But this was not always so. A very different view of English cultural influences was provided by J. B. Say in his nineteenth-century *Treatise on Political Economy* [1834]: "The enormous wealth of Britain is attributable [primarily] to ... the wonderful skill of her entrepreneurs ... and the superiority of her workmen in rapid and masterly execution.... The English laborer ... gives his work more care, attention and diligence, than the workmen of most other nations" (pp. 82–83).

Rather the opposite story can be told about Japan. In 1915 the Japanese government, concerned about the country's modest economic progress, employed an Australian engineer to investigate what could be done to improve matters. In a report that was widely noted in the local press at the time, and is still widely recalled today, it was asserted, "Japan commercially, I regret to say, does not bear the best reputation for executing business. Inferior goods, irregularity and indifferent shipments have caused no end of worry ... you are a very satisfied easy-going race ... the habits of national heritage" (as quoted by Jagdish Bhagwati in an unpublished paper [1983]). The evidence on earlier Japanese savings rates is consistent with the view that it was not unrelenting cultural pressures that imposed extraordinary thrift upon the nation. For example, Kazushi Ohkawa and Henry Rosovsky [1973] estimate Japanese savings rates (see table 8.2), and conclude, "Over time, and especially in this century, the savings ratio has risen sharply, *especially during expansion periods*. In 1908, for example, net savings were only 8 percent of net national product; by 1917 they had climbed to 22 percent; and in 1966 the ratio nearly reached 27 percent" (pp. 167–168, our italics). According to Lipsey and Kravis [1987a, pp. 1–2, table 1], in calculations based on the work of Kuznets, for the period 1887–1936 Japan's gross fixed capital formation averaged 12.9% of its GNP, while the comparable figure for the United States was about 19% (for the period 1950–1984 the American figure was about 18%). Clearly, though Japan's culture is old, its extraordinarily high savings and investment rates are rather new.

Table 8.2
Domestic savings in Japan, 1908–1966[a]

Year	Gross aggregate ratio[b]	Net ratio[c]
1908	15.6	7.9
1917	32.6	22.4
1924	15.6	5.3
1931	15.7	6.7
1937	24.5	16.3
1956	27.7	20.4
1962	33.9	25.6
1966	36.0	26.7

Source: Ohkawa and Rosovsky [1973, p. 167].
a. Smoothed series. Figures for 1908, 1956, 1962, and 1966 are 5-year moving averages; figures for 1917, 1924, and 1931 are 7-year averages; and figures for 1937 are 3-year averages.
b. National savings/gross national product.
c. Net savings/net national product.

Savings rates close to 30% have, until recently, continued more or less steadily in Japan. But they have been closely matched by savings rates in Taiwan (for example, according to the *Taiwan Statistical Data Book* [1980], net savings in 1978 were 29.6% of national income [p. 49]). The point is that the cultures of the two lands are very different. Taiwan, as we know, is very much subject to Chinese influence, tempered by the traditions of the considerable native population. Now, historical evidence suggests that the Chinese are not noteworthy for an extraordinarily high propensity to save. For example, this can be inferred from data derived from the vast body of formalized autobiographies customarily written by the scholar-officials who constituted the ruling bureaucracy at least since the Han dynasty (202 BC–220 AD). There have been several such studies for the periods of the Ming (1368–1644) and the Ch'ing dynasties (1644–1912) (see, for example, Ping-Ti Ho [1962] and Robert M. Marsh [1961]). These studies all show the systematic dissipation of family fortunes in the scholar-official class, which was at the apex of Chinese society in terms of power, prestige, wealth, and education. According to Ping-Ti, few of these families maintained their positions for more than two generations, and a five-generation history was truly extraordinary (pp. 165–166). In a calculation based on a sample of 454 such high-ranking families, Marsh finds that 51% of them retained their positions for only one generation, 37% retained their status for two generations, only 8% lasted for three generations, and only 4% for four generations (p. 159). Ping-Ti quotes another observer ("the prudent Chang T'ing-yu"), who commented, "Descendants who inherited ancestral wealth often could not manage it and were likely to indulge in music, women, or curios [notably paintings and libraries]. Those who indulged in music and women caused bankruptcy during their own lifetime. Almost none of those who indulged in curio collection could keep his collection for two generations" (p. 157; for extensive anecdotal evidence, see, especially, his chapter 4 and appendix). The similarity to the record of dissipation of family wealth in the West is striking (see, for example, W. D. Rubinstein [1980, pp. 27, 203–204]). Such evidence, while far from definitive, certainly casts doubts on the casual judgment that there exists an "oriental" tradition that pushes inexorably toward an extraordinarily high propensity to save. Surely, to say the least, there must be more to the matter.

8.5   Productivity Growth as a Stimulus to Saving

If culture and custom do not constitute the bulk of the mechanism that determines savings rates, one is impelled to look for other supplementary influences. We have already noted some of the other variables considered in the literature. Here, we intend no exhaustive survey of the possibilities, but will focus, rather, on an aspect of one of these influences that is suggested by some of our data analysis, and which seems not to have been emphasized before: the productivity growth rate itself. It is, of course, widely agreed that a rise in savings rate does contribute to growth in labor productivity. That was precisely the point that was central in the discussion with which this chapter began. But here we are proposing that there is a significant influence going in the *opposite* direction, and that has received much less attention.

The literature going back at least to James Mill and J. B. Say recognizes that output is the source out of which all saving is derived, and that enhanced output, such as that which productivity growth can permit, consequently expands the supply of resources available for saving. In this way, then, productivity has been recognized to contribute to *total* saving, but it is the *rate* of saving (as indicated perhaps by the ratio of saving to gross domestic product), rather than total amount saved, that is our concern here. A second way in which productivity growth has been recognized to affect saving is through its stimulus to investment demand. If increasing productivity raises the demand for new and better equipment, as it surely does, that can lead market forces to increase the rate of return to saving, in particular by raising the interest rate. That, in turn, can elicit a savings rate higher than it would otherwise have been. To these hypotheses, we propose to add a third, the notion that consumption patterns tend to be sticky, formed by earlier consumption habits that reflect the low income levels of the past, and that they take some time to respond to income growth. The implication is that during the early decades following a nation's productivity "take-off" (from a stage in which it was relatively stationary), per-capita output will tend to increase quickly, but consumption will lag well behind. In a sense, the hypothesis is a reversion to cultural influences, but in this tale culture plays the role of an inhibitor of change, rather than a force that is, at least for very long periods, immutable. Here, custom serves to slow consumption changes, but does not by any means bring them to a halt.

The evidence for this conjecture is largely anecdotal and is not unrelated to the reports of dissipation of family fortunes by later generations, discussed in the preceding section. History is replete with examples (the Medici are a prime illustration) of family fortunes whose founders were noted for the conservatism of their consumption patterns, but whose descendants competed for magnificence in their expenditures (for more recent reports, see Rubinstein [1980, pp. 203–204]). What has repeatedly been true of individual families may also hold for nations. Reports from Japan emphasize that living standards, measured in material terms, continue to be remarkably low for so wealthy a nation; however, other reports suggest that the consumption habits of the *next* generation are bringing substantial changes. Hamburgers and french fries are preferred to rice and raw fish, and along with this there is a rise in aspiration for material living standards closer to those of the Western industrialized societies. Similar stories appear in virtually every historical account seeking to explain the decline of the economies that had once held economic leadership: Italy, the Dutch republic, and the United Kingdom. In each case we are told of the rise of consumption standards, of a growing taste for luxury and for the lifestyle of the nobility among the families whose wealth derived from commerce and industry (see, for example, the discussions by the many noted economic historians in Krantz and Hohenberg [1975]).

All of this means that during the period of economic take-off, perhaps when it is most needed, there is a transitory mechanism that tends to provide the required saving of resources. However, as this influence diminishes, the result is yet another force making for a leveling-off of productivity growth. If the evidence supports these conjectures, it will help further in explaining the convergence process, and in accounting for the leveling-off

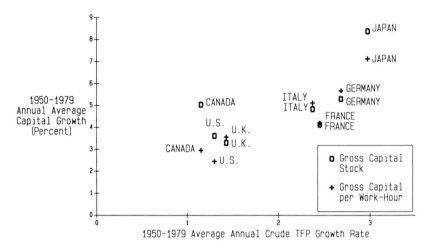

Figure 8.2
1950–1979 growth rates in capital and the capital-labor ratio, versus growth rate in TFP,
7 industrial countries. Source: Maddison [1982].

that seems to have been the fate of at least some of the countries in the economic vanguard.

The evidence so far does not seem to be able to distinguish between the different ways in which productivity growth may stimulate the savings rate, or even to distinguish any influence going in this direction, from one that goes the other way, with savings increases predictably stimulating productivity growth. What *is* clear from the evidence is that for the few countries for which the requisite data are available, there is a strong association between the rate of capital accumulation and the growth rate of productivity. This is shown in figures 8.2 and 8.3, both of which deal with annual rates of increase in the capital stock of the seven countries for which 1950–1980 data are available. They show the average annual percentage increase in the total capital (plant, equipment, etc.) for each of the countries. In addition, they show for each country the average annual rate of increase of capital per worker, that is, in the amount of plant and equipment available to the average worker to help expand that person's productivity.

Figure 8.2 shows the relation of these two growth rates to the rate of growth of the corresponding country's total factor productivity (see the appendix to this chapter for sources and further discussion). We see that the data points that lie relatively toward the right side of the graph are quite generally higher than those that lie toward the left. This positively sloping pattern clearly means that the higher a nation's total factor produc-

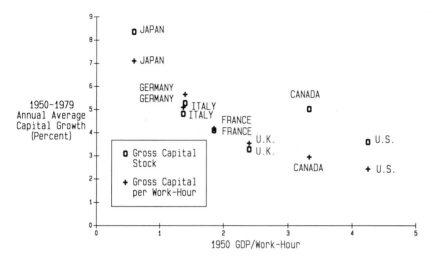

Figure 8.3

1950–1979 growth rates in capital and the capital-labor ratio, versus 1950 GDP per work-hour, 7 industrial countries. Source: Maddison [1982].

tivity growth has been, the more rapid, generally, has been the growth in its capital stock and the growth of its capital per worker, which is the relationship that has just been suggested. Figure 8.3 gets at the same relationship in a second way. It relates the rate of capital accumulation not to total factor productivity *growth*, but to the country's *level* of GDP per work-hour in 1950. Roughly speaking, this shows that in this narrow group of countries, those that were relatively worse off in 1950 in terms of productivity level expanded their capital stocks most rapidly, and that the better off the country was initially, the slower, generally, was the rate of growth of its capital. The two graphs do not really describe two independent phenomena, but are really two different ways of showing much the same thing. This is so since, as we know, because of convergence of productivities among these countries in the period in question, the lower the country's productivity level was initially, the more rapidly its productivity must have grown since. Hence, because we obtain an upward slope in a graph like figure 8.2 with productivity growth on the horizontal axis, we should expect the opposite slope in a graph like figure 8.3, in which a measure of the country's initial productivity level appears on the horizontal axis.

All of this statistical evidence, then, is consistent with our hypothesis that high savings rates are engendered by the onset of the take-off process,

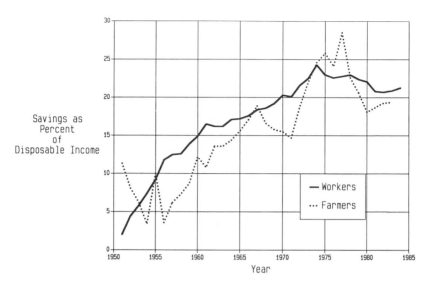

Figure 8.4
Japanese household savings ratio, 1951–1984. Source: Sato [1987, p. 149].

which means that when a country's productivity and per-capita income first begin to grow, its consumption, held back by old habits, does not initially keep pace. With incomes rising but consumption lagging, it means, by definition, that savings must rise. But, on this view, which is consistent with the evidence we have just seen, the high savings rates are transitory, subject to erosion by the higher consumption standards that an economy's upward mobility eventually engenders. As already noted, there is reason to conjecture that this is already happening in Japan. The statistics certainly do not reject this view. As is shown in figure 8.4, Japanese household savings rates have been falling sharply since at least the mid-1970s, though we do not pretend to know that the decline is ascribable to any one influence or that these rates will certainly not rise again.

8.6   The International Mobility of Capital

The mobility of capital (investment) from country to country is important for our analysis because if a shortage of investable resources in country A, resulting from low savings rates in that country, can easily be made up for by the lending of the required resources to A by other countries B, C, and D where such inputs are abundant, then the low levels of saving in A will be that much less a reason for concern as an impediment to productivity growth in that economy. In contrast, if there are substantial impediments to the transfer of investable resources to A from other countries, then A's low savings rates condemn it to low rates of growth of the plant and equipment available to its labor force, and that will probably constrain its productivity growth correspondingly. Capital has long been considered among the most mobile of resources, and certainly no one can doubt that it can and does move from country to country with considerable ease. As long ago as the High Middle Ages, when, despite the revival of trade, the movement of inputs and finished goods was still far from easy, international lending on a large scale was already occurring. Earlier in the chapter we alluded to the financing of thirteenth- and fourteenth-century English military ventures by the bankers of Florence. Later, foreign lending by the Dutch and the English attests to the same conclusion. Today, one is led to suspect that this state of affairs holds to an even greater degree, as a result of spectacular improvement in means of communication, together with the widespread acceptance of at least lip service to promotion of freedom of international exchange, whose desirability was by no means generally granted in the days of mercantilism (sixteenth–eighteenth centuries) and before. Yet we suspect that this picture may require two minor modifications. First (as we shall suggest in a companion volume; see Baumol [forthcoming]), *entrepreneurship* is an input characterized by mobility that may at least be comparable to that of capital. The second possible modification of the received views on the mobility of capital rests upon an empirical observation that is rather puzzling unless one accepts the conclusion that capital, so to speak, "prefers" to remain at home, and is therefore at least somewhat less movable than seems generally to be recognized.

The evidence suggesting that capitalists may be somewhat reluctant to send their resources out of their home countries is the striking correlation between the savings and investment rates of the countries for which such data are available. Figure 8.5 shows for 6 countries the uniform relationship between the two, with a country that has a higher rate of saving than another also having the higher rate of investment. This is a phenomenon that has previously been noted by others, and that has been subjected to systematic statistical study, beginning with the work of Feldstein and Horioka [1980]. Recently (see Frankel, Dooley, and Mathieson [1986]), this work has been summarized, the econometric objections against the earlier studies tested, and the sample extended to 14 industrialized and 50 developing countries. The study finds the relationship between saving and investment to be substantial, robust, and statistically significant, except for

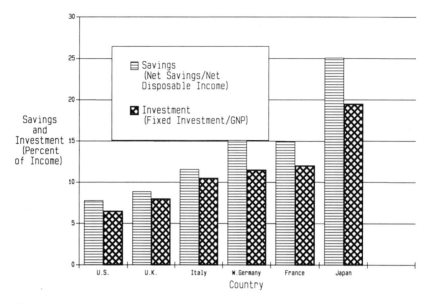

Figure 8.5
Savings and investment rates, for 6 industrialized countries, 1970–1980. Sources: for investment, *Economic Report of the President* [1983, p. 82]; for savings, Blades and Sturm [1982, p. 6].

those less developed countries whose investment programs are highly dependent on foreign aid.

The most important implication of these studies is that it is difficult to think of a general reason, other than the sources of the association between productivity growth and savings rates discussed in the preceding section, why those countries that happen in some period to have the highest savings rates should also be the countries in which investment happens to be most profitable. If one country is a rapid saver, but is also one in which the return to investment is low, one would expect (in the absence of impediments to capital movement) that country to export its capital to another country (or countries) in which the opposite is true. Thus, one would expect in a world of capital mobility to find little correlation between savings and investment rates. The high correlations that one finds in fact, then, suggest that there must be some impediments to the movement of capital that are either not widely recognized or are not given adequate weight. Perhaps it is a matter of avoiding the risks of exchange rate fluctuations, exchange controls, and the like. Or perhaps, as Adam Smith [1776] said on (nearly) the same matter, "The mercantile stock of every

country naturally courts ... the near and shuns the distant employment....
[It thereby saves] the trouble, risk and expense of exportation and ... will
upon that account be glad to [invest] at home not only for a much smaller
price, but with somewhat a smaller profit than [might be expected] abroad"
(p. 593, order of sentences reversed). The matter can perhaps be summed
up best by quoting the conclusion of Frankel, Dooley, and Mathieson
[1986]: "The evidence ... suggests that a close association between national
savings and national investment is a robust empirical regularity. This finding casts considerable doubt on the widely held view that international
markets for physical capital are highly integrated. The positive correlations
between levels and changes in national saving rates and investment rates,
which are apparent both for industrial countries and developing countries
and which are higher in recent years as compared to earlier time periods,
stand up to a variety of econometric objections. The only data set for
which the empirical regularity is not apparent includes developing countries
that depend primarily on aid to finance current account imbalances...."
(pp. 37–38).

8.7 Implications for the Performance of the U.S. Economy

Figure 8.5, which we have already used for other purposes, also can be
employed to suggest why those concerned about U.S. economic performance have devoted considerable attention to that country's record of
saving and investment. As the graph suggests, and as data for a more
extensive set of countries confirm, the share of American output devoted
to saving and investment is among the lowest of any of the industrialized
countries. The U.S. figures hover at about 8% of GNP, while Japan's are
above 20%, with those of other industrial countries generally in between.
This rightly raises fears that the equipment available to the typical worker
in a competitor country will become more extensive, sophisticated, and
up to date than that supplied to a member of the U.S. labor force.

Mobility of capital can, as we have noted, help the United States to
make up for its low savings rates. But we have seen that reasonable
questions have been raised about how mobile, internationally, investable
resources really are, and indeed, the figures for the U.S. domestic investment record over the period after World War II suggest that importation of
capital has not succeeded in raising our country's investment rates toward
those common in other industrialized countries. This story is rather reversed in recent years when foreign funds have flowed into the United
States to invest in the government bonds that were used to finance the

huge federal deficits. The government's need for funds has also driven up interest rates in the United States, thereby simultaneously making it attractive for foreigners to invest in private American enterprises, and raising fears that the country's economy was being bought up by foreigners. There seems to be little reason to expect that this vast influx of capital from abroad will continue indefinitely, and many observers expect it to decrease sharply as the U.S. federal deficit is brought under control.

However, that is not the main issue before us here. Rather, the central concern is whether the United States is condemning itself to economic mediocrity in the future by its low investment rates. We cannot offer firm reassurance that such worries are groundless. Yet there are at least two reasons why the situation may not be as ominous as it seems. The first is straightforward. If the fundamental pattern underlying the relative performance of the industrialized economies is the convergence trend discussed in chapter 5—the tendency of the less affluent of those countries to approach the prosperity and productivity of the United States (rather than threatening to leave the United States behind in their dust)—then those lagging economies must be expected to invest at a faster rate than the United States. For, otherwise, those other countries could never hope to approach America's overall leadership position in terms of plant and equipment per worker. Viewed in this way, higher investment rates abroad may just be a harmless component of a benign convergence process rather than a looming threat to American economic leadership.

The second reason why the low investment rate figures for the United States may not be as ominous as they seem is that those figures may be inaccurate, as a result of distortion from a number of sources. That is precisely the interpretation that emerges from the studies of Lipsey and Kravis [1988], widely regarded as leading authorities on the proper comparison of monetary data pertaining to different countries. These economists tell us that the standard data on savings and investment rates in the United States and its industrial competitors are seriously distorted, and that the corrected data show the U.S. performance in these areas to be very similar to that of its economic rivals (Lipsey and Kravis [1988, pp. 2–3]):

Conventionally measured, the share of U.S. output devoted to fixed capital formation *is* smaller than most other industrial countries.

The U.S. reputation for profligacy is undeserved, however. The conventional measures of investment omit many expenditures that meet the economic definition of investment, which is that they yield benefits beyond the immediate period of purchase. If the usual measures of saving and investment are adjusted: (1) to

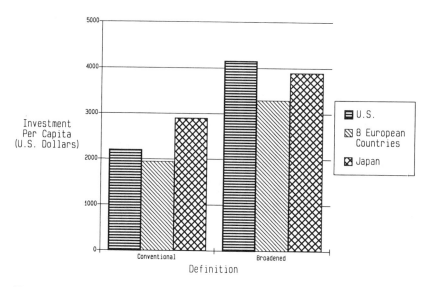

Figure 8.6
Per capita investment, 8 industrial countries, real gross fixed capital, 1980. Source: Lipsey and Kravis [1988, p. 3].

include expenditures for education (human capital), consumer durables, and research and development, and (2) to allow for the fact that capital goods are relatively cheap in the United States, U.S. investment ratios are close to those of other industrial countries. And when these investment levels are placed on a per capita basis, they show that real U.S. per capita expenditures for future-oriented purposes—the broadened definition of investment—are above those of all other advanced countries, as illustrated in Figure [8.6]. . . .

We are not able to calculate values for the stock of human capital and of R&D capital for many countries, but such additions would almost certainly place the United States even further ahead of the other developed countries. . . .

It is also appropriate to question the belief that the United States devotes an exceptional share of its capital investment to housing and consumer durables and, thus, too little to "more productive" business investment. The U.S. figures on housing are not out of line with other industrial countries. In consumer durables, however, the U.S. share is markedly higher, entirely because of personal automobiles. But in other countries, investment in transportation services is often made by the business or government sector in the form of buses and railroads. It is questionable whether these investments are "more productive" than those made by households—and some, at least, are in notoriously inefficient enterprises.

Of the two adjustments made in the standard savings-investment data by Lipsey and Kravis, that is, correction for differences in the prices of capital from one country to another, and differences in investment in education and consumer durables, one may well want to ask whether the latter is really germane to our purpose—study of the implications of the comparative investment records of the different countries for their productivity prospects. It is true, as will be argued in the next chapter, that the education of a nation's population may matter a great deal for its productivity performance. But one may well suspect in this connection that one of the things that matters here is the proportion of a country's educational expenditure devoted to such subjects as engineering and complementary technical training, fields in which the United States does not appear to be outstanding in terms of proportion of students specializing in those areas. More than that, whatever the benefits of investment in consumer durables, one may well question how much they contribute to a nation's productivity and its international competitiveness.

However, the first Lipsey-Kravis adjustment, that for differences in the prices of plant, equipment, and other forms of productive capital in the different countries, really is entirely to the point. If it were true, for example, that such items were priced 50% higher in other countries than in the United States, while the statistics showed per-capita investment in monetary terms in other countries to be 25% higher on average than that in the United States (all purely hypothetical numbers offered here merely for illustration), it would clearly follow, after correction for the price differences, that real U.S. investment per capita was actually substantially higher than that elsewhere. That is, because of lower capital prices in the United States, Americans would then be spending less money on investment goods, but acquiring more new plant and equipment than foreigners were. Since it is the amount of plant and equipment accumulated, and not the amount of money spent on it, that matters primarily for productivity growth, it is clear that the justification for this revision of the data by Lipsey and Kravis is difficult to dispute. And, indeed, those authors do conclude that if one employs the conventional definition of capital stock, but merely adjusts for differences in the prices of capital in the different countries, investment per capita in the United States turns out to have been 3% higher than the average for the other industrial countries in their sample in 1975 and 7% higher than that average in 1980, though, even in 1980, it still falls about 28% below Japan and about 13% below Germany (Lipsey and Kravis [1987a, appendix table 6, and 1987b, p. 37]). Thus, at the very least, their revised figures suggest persuasively that the published figures may significantly exaggerate any U.S. shortfall in saving and investment. Rather, their calculations suggest that the comparative position of the United States is not unlike its position in terms of absolute productivity level. "... every country [for which data are available] increased its capital stock relative to the U.S. [over the postwar period]... but it still left the major industrial countries [and particularly Japan] below the level of U.S. capital per person in 1980 [the most recent date for which the figures are available] (Lipsey and Kravis [1987a, pp. 25–26]). In other words, there appears to be convergence in capital stock per person among the industrial countries as well as in productivity and income per capita.

8.8 Concluding Comment

In this chapter we have presented a number of observations about capital formation, a component of growth in labor productivity whose importance is so widely recognized. The discussion has been relatively disorganized in comparison with the other chapters in this volume because here we have no central thesis to offer, though we believe that some of our observations may seem new to at least a number of readers, and may be stimulating to others. If there is one contention of this chapter that seems to fit most closely with the theses of the remainder of the book, it is the hypothesis that a take-off in productivity growth is apt to engender a transitory rise in the savings rate, which in turn starts to erode as consumption aspirations begin to catch up with rising incomes. If that is so, the low level of the U.S. savings rate relative to the savings rates of a number of other industrial countries may be part of a normal historical process, and may strengthen the prospects that productivity levels of other successful economies may simply be drawing abreast of ours, rather than being fated to surpass ours substantially. This, and the revised savings-investment data provided by Lipsey and Kravis, may serve to diffuse some of the aura of emergency engendered by the American record in accumulation of productive capital.

Notes

1. The point, for specialists in economic theory, is that in a world of universal perfect competition, absence of externalities, and (otherwise) complete freedom of trade, removal of a rule inhibiting export of capital from some country, A, will, on balance, clearly be beneficial to humanity as a whole. For transfer of capital to the location where its marginal (incremental) product is highest must add to the value of the world's output. However, the question is whether this must add to the economic welfare of the capital-exporting country, A. It must obviously benefit A's capitalists, but can it reduce the earnings of A's workers sufficiently to yield a net loss to that country?

Lars Svensson has shown us that in a standard neoclassical model of trade

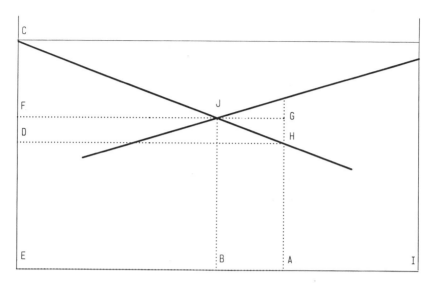

Figure 8.7
The classical model of intercountry capital transfers. Source: see note 1.

this can never occur. Country A *must* benefit. As he put the matter in a letter to us,

> ... let me make my point using a simple model and [a] diagram [figure 8.7]. (This analysis is from MacDougall's [1960] classic paper.) Suppose both England and India have a standard neoclassical one-sector production function. The diagram shows the marginal productivity of capital. England's is measured from the left and India's from the right. Suppose England's capital stock is EA and India's AI. In the absence of foreign investment England's GNP is ECHA, with profits EDHA and wages CHD. Suppose instead that England invests BA of capital in India. Then the rate of return is equal in the two countries and given by FE. England's GNP must be *greater* than before, namely ECJGA; the gain is GHJ. Wages, CJF, are lower, but profits, FGAE, are sufficiently larger.

In later correspondence, however, Svensson went on to point out (on the basis of an argument by J. I. Bulow and L. H. Summers [1986]) that where the neoclassical premises are violated it is no longer true that a country must gain by permitting freedom of export of capital. For example, if it has a dual labor market with some of its workers confined to the secondary market with its inferior (dead-end) jobs, then capital forced to remain at home and invested in the superior (primary) labor market may raise primary workers' earnings (rents) so much as to yield a net economic gain to the country because it restricts its capital exports.

2. Other possible candidates are Belgium (then called the Spanish Netherlands) in the thirteenth–sixteenth centuries, Spain in the sixteenth century, and France in the seventeenth. But, like Sweden, Spain and France were surely military, not economic leaders. The case for the Spanish Netherlands is more persuasive, but its sudden decline is probably attributable to destruction by Spanish troops, dispersal of its Protestant entrepreneurs, and restrictions on commerce imposed by the Dutch.

3. It is true that, unlike the Dutch, who were financing England (their chief economic rival), the Italians were providing funds to nations that dissipated them in military enterprises rather than using them to build up their industrial capital—nations that were not serious economic rivals. But, then, Edward III and Philip II both resorted to bankruptcy, the latter no less than six times, more than once bringing the lenders down with them.

4. An example may make this clearer: In an automobile assembly plant, the ordinary accumulation of capital may enhance labor's productivity by providing workers with additional state-of-the-art assembly equipment, or even more powerful versions of state-of-the-art equipment (or pay for workers to attend workshop training courses to improve their efficiency); on the other hand, a doubling of plant output brought about by the installation of a newly invented piece of assembly equipment would show up as part of the total factor productivity calculation.

Some of the "innovation" may conceivably include belated adoption of earlier inventions. It may also include increases in productivity attributable to sources largely independent of investment, for example, improvement in worker skills attributable to experience in working with new types of equipment or in other changed ways.

5. To enable such a crude two-way classification of the components of productivity growth to take account of the role of education on the output-producing ability of the labor force, we must interpret outlays on education as expenditures on *human* capital, i.e., as just another form of investment.

9

Education and the "Convergence Club": Lessons for Less Developed Countries

It is hardly a coincidence that, in the nineteenth and early twentieth centuries, the countries that were most successful in borrowing foreign technologies were those that had well-educated populations.
Rosenberg [1982, p. 247]

Urban minorities have been particularly vulnerable to [today's irreversible] structural economic changes. . . . job growth has been concentrated in industries that require higher levels of education.
Wilson [1987, p. 39]

In chapter 5 we presented evidence showing that, for a number of industrialized free-market economies, levels of productivity and per-capita output are converging toward one another; that is, the general productivity and living standards in these countries are approaching something like homogeneity. However, a rather large group of nations, notably the less developed countries (LDCs), have not managed to participate in this convergence process. In this chapter we hope to identify one of the major influences that has prevented the LDCs from full participation. The variable on which we shall focus is education.

We shall see that the statistical evidence is consistent with the hypothesis that the quantity of education provided by an economy to its inhabitants is one of the major influences determining whether per-capita income in that society is growing rapidly enough to narrow the gap with per-capita income in the more prosperous economies. This is important for policy because it suggests that a country can do a great deal to improve its performance in the convergence arena by increasing the resources it devotes to education. The moral, as we shall see, applies not only to the LDCs but also to some of the industrialized economies, at least to those that have within their populations a large number of persons who are impoverished and limited in their educational attainment, to a degree that makes them, in effect, an enclave of underdevelopment inside a highly developed nation.

The chapter begins with a brief survey of differences in educational attainment among the nations of the world. Our discussion will confirm that levels of education vary enormously from one economic group of nations to another, though these differences have been narrowing to a substantial degree, and have in many cases wiped out differences in the share of the pertinent age groups receiving an elementary education. It is at the secondary school level, and to an even greater degree in higher educa- tion, that large differences persist. After this brief international comparison we shall turn to statistical evidence on the magnitude of the role that education plays in determining the growth rate of an economy. We shall find evidence suggesting strongly that education does play a remarkably powerful role. If this result stands up under further investigation and criticism, it will contribute considerably to our understanding of the in- gredients of the growth process and help to confirm the promise of the associated avenue for growth policy. The chapter will end with a discus- sion of the implications for policy aimed at the underprivileged groups in wealthy economies. We shall focus on the limited educational attainments of average black and Hispanic Americans, and the disturbing implications for the future of the U.S. economy.

9.1   National Differences in Educational Attainment[1]

Universal education is a goal that is fairly recent even for industrialized countries. It has been estimated that at the birth of the Industrial Revolu- tion only some 30–40% of the adults in England were literate. As Eric J. Hobsbawm [1969] puts it, at that time, "English education was a joke in bad taste."[2] In the nineteenth century, school attendance became widespread in much of Western Europe and the United States. Compulsory schooling began to spread after 1870, and in England primary and secondary school attendance were required by law after the Acts of 1902 and 1944. Still, as late as 1975, according to one estimate, over two million British adults were considered illiterate or semiliterate.

The less developed countries, particularly those that achieved indepen- dence after World War II, in many cases found themselves in the late 1940s with an educated local elite and a small cadre of literate clerks. Even in Latin America, with its longer period of independence, schooling was apparently confined largely to better-off urban residents (Gillis et al. [1983, chapter 9]).

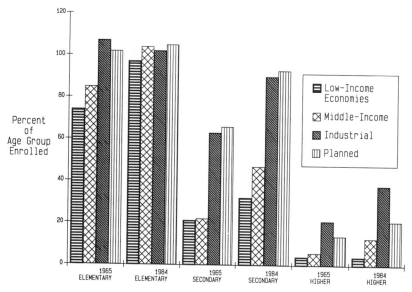

Figure 9.1
International comparisons of educational attendance (primary, secondary, and higher), percent of age group enrolled, 1965 and 1984. (For some countries with universal primary education, the gross enrollment ratios may exceed or fall below 100% because some pupils are above or below the country's standard primary-school age.) Source: World Bank [1987, pp. 262–263].

Early in the postwar era education became a pressing popular issue in the LDCs, and school attendance exploded. In the three decades after 1950 in Africa, Asia, and Latin America, primary school enrollment is reported to have increased some 300%, with the figure for Africa alone nearly twice as high as the average for the three. Secondary and higher education attendance levels rose even more rapidly, in percentage terms, but given the very small base with which some of the countries began, the relative growth figures can be somewhat misleading.

Figure 9.1, based on World Bank data, summarizes both the postwar changes and the current state of affairs. It shows that in 1965 the countries classified by the World Bank as low- and middle-income were already well on their way to achievement of parity with the developed nations in terms of the percent of children attending primary school. By 1984, the overall difference among these groups at the primary level was all but wiped out, although pockets of lack of education remained, and the quality of education was questionable in some of the poorest countries. Figure 9.1 also shows that there remains a very large gap between the LDCs and developed countries in terms of percentage of population of the pertinent ages receiving secondary and higher education. In 1984 90% of the population of the pertinent age group in the 18 industrial market economies (World Bank classification) was receiving secondary education and 38% was receiving higher education. For the 37 low-income countries, including China and India, the corresponding figures were 32% for secondary school and 4% for higher education. The conclusion from this very brief and superficial survey is that, while there has been a very substantial narrowing of the educational gaps separating the different economic groups of countries, there still remain enormous differences in attainment in terms of secondary and higher education. We turn, then, to a statistical inquiry into the apparent consequences of these differences.

9.2   Problems Besetting the Measurement of Education's Economic Benefits

Governments devote substantial outlays to education without having at their disposal any rational basis for deciding just how much to spend for the purpose. It is generally agreed that rational decisions in this area require some information on the social returns to education, that is, some evaluation of the benefits that society can expect in return for this expenditure. This has elicited a profusion of studies seeking to estimate the rate of return to educational outlays in industrialized economies, as well as a few studies for LDCs. Some of these studies have been carried out with considerable care by highly competent investigators. Yet, by and large, their results have elicited only very limited acceptance and are generally regarded, even by their authors, with considerable reservations.

The fundamental problem plaguing virtually all of these investigations lies in the distinction between *private* and *social* returns. Education, clearly, often yields substantial benefits directly to the student, in the form of higher income, a more interesting job, and better working conditions in that person's subsequent occupation. So far as these sorts of benefits are concerned, education can be considered as a personal investment, no different in principle from a carpenter's investment in woodworking tools, or a shopkeeper's investment in decoration of the premises. All of these are personal expenditures undertaken in the hope of a profitable payoff, and it is usually agreed that decisions on such outlays are best left to the individual whose interests are directly at stake. There are good reasons for the government to avoid telling the retailer how much to spend on decoration, inventory, lighting, or advertising: generally, no outsider is likely to have better information about the pertinent facts, and self-interest is apt to lead the individual to make decisions about these matters that are as rational and as close to optimality as can reasonably be expected.

The trouble is that if future income and job-benefit returns to the student were all that education had to offer, there would be little reason for governments to subsidize it as they do. Just as no one proposes that a prosperous department store should receive government subsidies for its investment in decoration, there would be no inherent reason for subsidy to an individual who proposes to invest in an expensive education, if it were true that the only benefit flowing from that outlay were a substantial enhancement of that person's private income. There *is* near-universal acceptance of government funding of education, but the rationale of that position rests on the belief that education yields something *more* than just increases in the private incomes of the recipients of the education. This is where the difficulties of measurement of the returns to education arise. Though it is agreed that the "something more" that education is believed to yield lies at the heart of all decision issues in the arena, we run into trouble in trying to identify and measure it. There is not even general agreement on the nature of this "something more"—on the precise social benefits of which it is composed. Moreover, those benefits that *are* widely accepted among analysts as items that belong on the list turn out to be difficult to observe empirically and to evaluate quantitatively.

Perhaps first on anyone's list of the social benefits of education is equalization of opportunity. This is so, presumably, because even if education constitutes a highly profitable private investment opportunity, there are those whose families simply cannot afford the requisite outlays and who, because of lack of previous education, are not even adequately informed about the private benefits it offers. These financially and culturally impoverished persons, then, are denied the opportunities that education offers, unless government or other entities provide financial assistance. But how does one measure the payoff? Just how much is opportunity equalized by the expenditure of an additional million dollars on education? Indeed, just what would such a number mean?

Matters become even worse when we turn to other social benefits that have been associated with education—that it produces better citizens, enriches the culture of society, and contributes to the creation and dissemination of knowledge. It is difficult to argue against the importance of any of these, but it is clear that the cause-effect relation between any of these and educational expenditure is difficult to describe, harder to observe, and is likely to resist numerical measurement altogether.

There is, however, one hypothesis about the yield of education to the community about whose measurement one can, perhaps, be more sanguine. This is the conjecture that education contributes to productivity growth amounts over and above the sum of its direct contribution to the incomes of the educated individuals themselves. That is, suppose that the education of a group of citizens at a cost of $1 billion were to increase their combined lifetime incomes by the equivalent of $1.5 billion relative to the incomes of those whose education had not been affected by the expenditure in question. So far, this is all private return to the students directly involved. But suppose, in addition, that this increment in educational outlay were also to result in increases in productivity that added to *everyone's* income by 2%, in addition to the private gains accruing to those whose education had been expanded. This is clearly a social productivity benefit going beyond the private returns to the recipients of the enhanced education. It is generally recognized among economists that such a social return, if evidence of its reality could be provided, could justify public outlays on education, and that information on the magnitude of the social benefit could help to determine what an optimal government budget for education may be.

This, then, indicates why there has been considerable interest in statistical evidence related to the hypothesized productivity contributions of education. It is clearly of some importance, and it offers some hope for statistical observation, which may be able to verify that this social benefit does in fact occur, and is substantial in its magnitude, even if it should transpire that estimation of that magnitude is not easy. It is just such evidence that the following sections of this chapter are intended to provide.

9.3   Verifying Education's Contribution to Productivity Growth

Typically, studies of the benefits of education focus on differences between the lifetime earnings of persons with more education and those with less. For example, many of these investigations have focused on the profitability of college attendance. But this, of course, considers only the portion of educational expenditure that can be left to take care of itself: its private payoff to the student. The issue of interest here—the *social* benefits to education, above and beyond those to the immediate subject of the schooling—is left out of such studies, usually with an apologetic remark by the author.

There have been some studies that examine directly the differences in the productivity performance of more and less educated individuals. These have focused on the less developed countries and have largely been carried out under the sponsorship of the World Bank. Estimates evaluating the social rate of return to education have now been accumulated for more than 50 countries. (For a discussion of this literature as well as some additional results, see Psacharopoulos and Woodhall [1985, chapter 3].) These studies linking productivity and education directly are exemplified by eight investigations providing data for Brazil, Colombia, Greece, Kenya, Malaysia, Nepal, and South Korea, which examined the association between 4 years of elementary education for a farmer and that individual's annual farm output. The average rate of return was calculated to be 6.3%, with the estimates ranging from approximately zero (in one of four studies for Colombia) to some 25% (Psacharopoulos and Woodhall [1985, p. 48]). Curiously, the studies showed no clear correlation between education and the prices the farmers paid for inputs or the prices they were able to obtain for their outputs. The implication is that the bulk of the advantage accruing to educated farmers was access to superior production techniques or superior use of those techniques.

The fact that the calculations in the studies pertained to measured differences in agricultural output, rather than just to changes in the incomes of the individuals who received the education, helps to avoid the key difficulty besetting evaluation of the economic contribution of education that was mentioned earlier—the difference between its private and social benefits. But there is a second difficulty that affects most such studies, including those we are now discussing: the possibility of confusing cause and effect. Merely correlating educational attainment of the population with the growth rate of per-capita output simply will not do, because there is a two-way relationship between the two. Richer countries spend more on education, at least in part because they can afford to do so. Thus, even if it were to transpire that education yields absolutely no economic returns, one should still expect to find a correlation between the two, with the richer countries devoting larger resources to the purpose, as a matter of enhanced consumption of this (hypothetically) unproductive luxury. Similarly, it is just possible that in less developed countries, farmers who are more successful (because for some reason their farms are more productive) are the very ones who are more likely to have been sent to school by their parents, who owned those same superior farms. It is plausible that this is only a secondary influence in the studies of farm production, but the two-way nature of the association between education and productivity should be kept in mind in interpreting the results. We shall return briefly to this problem later.

One result emerging from these agricultural studies that is worth noting for later discussion is the observation that the estimated yield of *primary* education is much higher than that of either secondary or higher education. Psacharopoulos and Woodhall [1985], aggregating the results for 22 African, Asian and Latin American countries, report that the rate of return on real resources expended was 27% for primary schooling, 16% for secondary, and 13% for higher education (p. 58). This seems to conflict with some of the observations of W. Arthur Lewis, a noted student of economic development. Professor Lewis has suggested to us (in personal conversation) that, from the viewpoint of economic development, it is the gap in *secondary* education that may be particularly serious. If a nation wants to enhance its use of modern technology, primary education is usually not enough to equip the populace to play an effective role in the process. Higher education is obviously more important here but, according to Professor Lewis, unless a country hopes to become involved in *extensive* research and development and innovation, only a relatively small group of persons with a university education is needed to permit the import and adoption of more sophisticated production techniques. It is the group of trained and skilled technicians that is absolutely required in large numbers, and for them secondary education is usually indispensable.

We believe, however, that there is no necessary conflict between Psacharopoulos and Woodhall's statistical results and Professor Lewis's observation. The apparent difference may mean only that use of improved *farming* techniques may not require a very extensive education and may, in any event, not require nearly the level of education needed for a skilled technician. That is, the Psacharopoulos-Woodhall observations appear to be directed primarily to agrarian economies, while the comment of Professor Lewis relates to an economy with more ambitious development goals that require substantial technical skills and considerably more than elementary education for their realization. The relative contribution of elementary and secondary education will recur briefly, later in the chapter.

In addition to the studies pertaining to the LDCs, there have been a number of statistical investigations of the association between productivity and education in industrial countries, notably the United States. (On this, see Dean [1984] and, particularly, chapter 1 by Haveman and Wolfe in that collection.) Studies by Denison and by Kendrick in the same volume indicate that, during the postwar period up to the mid-1970s, "... the contribution of education to output growth has always been positive and has accounted for about 15 to 25 percent of growth in national income per person employed" (p. 24). Jorgenson (chapter 3 in Dean [1984]) provides very sophisticated econometric estimates for the same period and concludes that "... the contribution of labor quality is a very important source of U.S. economic growth, accounting for 0.45 percent per year of a total contribution of labor input of 1.09 percent per year.... the contribution of education accounts for 0.67 percent per year of a total growth in the quality of labor input of 0.72 percent per year" (p. 97) In other words, education can be estimated to have been responsible for 38% [(0.67/0.72) × (0.45/1.09)] of labor's substantial contribution to the rapid growth of U.S. output during the period. All of these studies, then, imperfect though their authors emphasize them to be, are consistent in ascribing to education a very large contribution to an economy's productivity growth.

9.4   Convergence and Education: A Novel Statistical Test

We turn now to a very different test of education's influence on productivity growth. The calculation is based on our study of the convergence among industrialized nations in terms of their levels of productivity and real GDP per capita (reported in chapter 5) and the absence of such a convergence pattern for the LDCs.

J. Bradford De Long [1986], in an investigation of some of the convergence data provided by us in a previous publication (Baumol [1986]), sought to account for the failure of a number of countries to achieve membership in the convergence group. De Long tried as explanatory variables, first, whether the country in question was or was not democratic, and second, the identity of its dominant religion (this having been suggested by Max Weber's hypothesis that the "Protestant ethic" had a considerable role in accounting for the rise of capitalism). The statistical results he obtained with the aid of these variables were not exceedingly strong. That is, at least with the data he used, they do not seem to go very far in explaining the failure of laggard countries to converge toward the nations that achieved economic superiority. Here we shall find, in contrast, that education *does* go far toward providing the requisite explanation.

It will be recalled from chapter 5 that the accumulated evidence indicates strongly that there has been a rather dramatic pattern of convergence in levels of productivity and per-capita output, encompassing a growing set of countries since the last quarter of the nineteenth century. This has been true of both labor productivity and total factor productivity. However, the countries for which this has been true consist mainly of the members of the Organization for Economic Cooperation and Development (OECD) in Western Europe, North America, and Japan. Latin America, Africa, and much of Asia have been excluded from the "club" of converging economies almost completely. Although productivity in many (but not all) of these countries has grown, typically the rate has been so stately that they have fallen even further behind the leaders with the passage of time.[3] We shall make no attempt to pursue the elusive set of influences constituting "*the* reasons" for the relative growth lag of those countries. However, as suggested in chapter 5, there is reason to suspect as a prime villain the failure of the lagging countries to keep up with, absorb, and utilize new technological and product information, and to benefit from the international dissemination of technology. Countries only slightly behind the leaders, in contrast, have been eminently successful in doing so. Indeed, for these countries, having more to learn from the leaders than the leaders can learn from them has constituted a major element in what has been referred to as the "advantages of backwardness." But here, as elsewhere, there can be too much of a (not so) good thing. A bit of backwardness may contribute to a higher growth rate, but beyond some point it seems clearly to become pure handicap.

One of the elements that one may well expect to explain an economy's ability to absorb information and new technology is the education of its populace. As we have seen, particularly at the secondary and higher levels, the LDCs are well behind the industrialized countries in terms of share of the population receiving education; and it can be shown that per-capita expenditure on education displays a very similar pattern (although that can be explained in part by the fact that the money cost of such services—the cost of education per pupil-day—is quite uniformly higher in countries where real per-capita output is high, than in those countries where it is low [see chapter 6]).

To test the role of education in the convergence process we proceeded in the following manner. It will be recalled from our earlier discussion of the convergence phenomenon that our main statistical model was based on the observation that convergence (catch-up) requires countries that start out as laggards to grow rather consistently faster than those that start out as leaders. In other words, if that were the only factor in the relative progress of the economies in question, one would expect the initial level of a country's productivity or per-capita output to be completely responsible for the subsequent relative growth rate of that country. The poorer that country was initially, the faster its subsequent growth would be expected to be. That was precisely the pattern that chapter 5's statistics revealed for a fairly limited set of industrialized countries (selected mechanically as those with the highest levels of real per-capita gross domestic product [RGDP] in 1950). However, for the rest of the countries in the rather large sample we were able to obtain, no such neat statistical relationship emerged. Rather, the relation between initial RGDP level and subsequent growth rate seemed haphazard and fortuitous.

Now, this should not really be surprising. It is rare in economics to encounter a complex phenomenon that can be explained statistically (or logically) by any single variable. For example, any attempt to account statistically for the behavior of an economy's rate of inflation would normally employ a considerable number of explanatory variables such as the size of government deficits (as an indicator of net governmental demand), the foreign trade surplus (net demand from abroad), and the rate of increase in the money supply. Our way of testing statistically the role of education in the growth process was to undertake a very modest increase in our set of explanatory variables, seeing how far one progressed by adding only a single new variable (the share of a country's pertinent age group receiving formal education) to our other variable (the initial level of RGDP for the country in question). That is, of the host of variables that we might expect to influence a country's rate of growth of RGDP, we undertook to see just how much can be explained statistically using only two variables for each country: its RGDP level at the beginning of the period in question and the relative share of its population that was being educated.

The full set of our statistical experiments, along with data and results, is described in the appendix to this chapter. Here, only their most interesting features will be described. We calculated statistical regressions, that is, statistical estimates of the magnitude of the influence of each of our two variables on RGDP growth rates, when the two variables were considered in combination, each presumably having some effect on the growth rate. For our education variable we used three alternative statistics, one indicating proportion of the relevant age group receiving formal *primary* education, the next being the corresponding figures for secondary education, and the third statistics being those for higher education.

The results were dramatic. As we have seen, for the nonindustrialized world, with no education variable included, the pertinent statistical relationship degenerated into a pattern of confusion. However, with the educational variable added, orderly behavior was restored. That is, *in effect, countries with similar educational levels were shown quite consistently to be converging among themselves, in terms of RGDP, though not catching up with countries whose educational levels were higher.*[4] The obvious statistical tests were almost always passed uniformly; that is, they had the numerical values required for convergence (the initially lower RGDP countries grow-ing faster) and those numerical values almost always passed a reasonably demanding test of statistical significance (see chapter 4, section 4.5, for an intuitive explanation).[5]

Finally, the calculation's results turned out to be far stronger, consistent, and statistically significant when the education variable employed was that related to secondary education rather than to primary or higher education. In other words, the calculation firmly supported Professor Lewis's thesis, noted earlier, that education does matter a good deal for a nation's eco-nomic growth, and that what matters most is the share of the population with secondary education. And, at bottom, what the statistics suggest is that few if any nations have been excluded totally from the convergence process. For many of them it would appear to be a latent influence, waiting to emerge. Apparently, for many of them a high-priority step in any attempt to achieve this emergence is provision of secondary education to its population to a degree commensurate with that of the most prosperous nations. We are not suggesting here that increased education is a panacea, one that promises to be equally effective for all, and that requires no other supplementary measures. But our analysis surely adds to the accumulating evidence indicating that here is a policy instrument that governments dedicated to promotion of productivity and enhancement of living stan-dards can ill afford to ignore.

9.5 Implications for the United States: Education of Underprivileged Minority Groups[6]

While the discussion so far, by the nature of the subject, has been con-cerned primarily with less developed countries, it also has urgent implica-tions for an economy like that of the United States, which encompasses population subgroups with many of the earmarks of an LDC: ethnic minor-ity groups that are at a marked and persistent disadvantage in terms of educational opportunities and educational performance, and that constitute a growing share of the population. The existence of these minority en-claves may constitute a drag upon the growth rate of productivity of the nation as a whole that affects not only the living standard of the underpriv-ileged sector but also that of the remainder of the population. Thus, if education is one of the keys to redirection of the trends in question, the devotion of substantial effort and resources to improvement in this arena may recommend itself not only as a matter of social justice but as a critical step for the promotion of the interests of the other members of the economy as well.

The United States is not the only industrial country in which underprivileged minority groups threaten to constitute such a problem, but it is probably among those for which it is most acute, and given the information that has been assembled for the American case, it seems appropriate to focus on that country, both for its own intrinsic interest and as an example whose lessons are of wider applicability.

The minority groups in question—black, Hispanic, native American, and a substantial proportion of Americans of Asiatic origin or descent—already constitute a substantial part of the U.S. population.[7] According to a report issued in 1988 by a national commission of prominent persons in politics, education, and labor, and chaired by Presidents Ford and Carter (Commission on Minority Participation in Education and American Life [1988]), these minority groups now constitute 14% of the country's adults and 20% of persons under 17. In addition, the rate of growth of their numbers is significantly higher than that of other groups of Americans. Their high rates of birth (about 36% of the births in the United States were in minority groups in 1980) and immigration (legal and illegal) imply that they can easily be expected by the end of the century to constitute one-third of the additions to the country's labor force (the recent commission forecast). By 2020 these groups are expected to account for more than half the babies, according to L. Scott Miller of the Exxon Education Foundation. Obviously, they are not slated to be an insignificant portion of the work force or a minor influence on its productivity growth.

The minority groups in the United States are universally recognized to be disproportionately represented among the impoverished portion of the population. A study conducted in 1983 by the Congressional Research Service reported that about 50% of black children, 33.3% of Hispanic children, and 17% of white children were living in poverty. In 1986 31% of blacks and 27% of Hispanics had incomes lower than the poverty level, three times the rate of whites. And, while the median income of a black family rose from 54% of that for a white family in the 1950s to 61.5% in 1975, in 1985 the figure had retreated to 57.5%. Black and Hispanic children are also far more likely than white children to be born out of wedlock, and to be part of a family with only a single parent present.

All of this is reflected in differences in the educational performance of black and Hispanic students. In 1982, 84% of persons in the United States aged 20–24 had completed high school. This was true of 85% of whites, but for only 77% of blacks and 60% of Hispanics. There has been a recent improvement, at least for black students, with the percentage of black high school attendees who graduate rising from 61% in 1975 to 71% in 1985, according to the U.S. Bureau of the Census. But the proportion of these graduates who attended college has fallen, after an earlier increase, declining from 48% in 1975 to 44% in 1985. The corresponding figures for Hispanics were 49% and 47%, respectively, for the first and last years of that decade, also constituting a (small) decline.

There is also information suggesting the relative *quality* of the preparation of the students from different ethnic groups. Valerie Lee [1985] analyzed data on achievement test scores for 1980. As a standard of accomplishment, Lee used the number that a statistician would describe as "one half standard deviation above the average," where the standard deviation is the concept used by statisticians to calculate how much, typically, performances differ from the average. Of a representative sample of high school seniors, the students meeting or exceeding this standard constituted 46% of whites of high socioeconomic status (family incomes averaging $31,000 or more), 24% of whites of low socioeconomic status, and only 8% of blacks and Hispanics, including those of high socioeconomic status. Similar conclusions emerge from studies of scores on the well-known Scholastic Aptitude Test (SAT), administered by the Educational Testing Service. For the combined scores in the tests of verbal and mathematical achievement (1,600 was the maximum possible combined score and 400 the minimum) in 1985 the average score was 939 for whites, 922 for Asians, 808 for Mexican Americans, and 722 for blacks. It is also noteworthy that the test is voluntary and that it is taken predominantly by those hoping to go on to college. Thus, one can infer much from the fact that while 70% of the Asian students took the tests, this was done by only 30% of the whites, 18% of the blacks, and 11% of the Mexican Americans. Moreover, the disparities in performance become even more extreme when we turn to higher levels of performance. On the mathematics section of the SAT, for example, the proportion of black students scoring at least 750 out of 800 was only 2.7% as large as that of the whites! In contrast, that of the Asian students was more than 500% higher than that of the whites. More recent numbers suggest that the situation has not improved for black, Hispanic, and native American students.

The implications are clear. First, it is apparent that the United States does indeed maintain an enclave of ethnic minorities whose economic and educational characteristics are at least to a degree closer to those of an LDC than to those of a prosperous industrialized country. Second, the demographic data indicate that the size of the enclave is already substantial, and that it is certain to grow to a considerably larger share of the total. Third, the educational disadvantages to which the members of the enclave are subject are far from negligible, and at the highest levels of achievement have held the members of these economically handicapped groups to minute levels of participation. Fourth, trends in the educational levels and performance of the minority groups in question have been mixed. There have been some marked improvements, particularly in the middling achievement levels; but there have also been areas of retreat.

All of this adds up to a grim prospect for the individuals directly affected, but that is by no means all. While improvement in the circumstances of underprivileged minority groups is arguably the issue of highest priority, it is not the central focus of this book. For us, the most pertinent issue is the implication of our observations about the status of minority groups for long-run American productivity growth. The evidence provided by us earlier in the chapter supported the results of previous studies in indicating the importance of education for productivity growth. The likelihood that a markedly expanding proportion of the U.S. working population will be made up of persons drawn from groups whose amount of education and educational performance is significantly below that of the remainder of the nation presages a growing impediment to U.S. productivity performance. Thus, it may be that those of us who are affected only indirectly by the educational handicaps of underprivileged groups will nevertheless end up paying dearly if we do not provide the thought, the planning, the effort, and the resources needed to deal effectively with those educational problems.

Notes

1. We are grateful to our colleague, Michael Todaro, for help in assembling materials for this section.

2. This, and the historical material that follows, is taken from Fägerlind and Saha [1983, chapter 1].

3. Nevertheless, in historical terms the growth rate of the LDCs has been far from negligible, though rather unsteady. During the 1970s it is estimated that the growth rate of the LDCs averaged something close to 3% per year compounded. But, according to Williamson [1984], during the first half-century of the British Industrial Revolution growth of productivity in that economy was something like 0.3% per year, that is, about a tenth of that in the LDCs in the 1970s.

4. To check this further, the following rather crude calculation was carried out. The 124 countries in the sample were ranked in terms of educational level in 1965.

They were then divided into seven groups of 15 countries each, and one (lowest education) group of 19. The groups were selected to be composed of members with similar educational levels. Then each group was tested individually for intragroup convergence. Six of the eight groups now exhibited intergroup convergence, with only the two lowest-education groups failing to manifest such a pattern. However, these patterns tended to be rather "ragged," with a sufficient number of countries in each group (except the top one) exhibiting deviant behavior to yield relationships that did not pass tests of statistical significance.

5. These calculations avoided at least two of the pitfalls that have plagued other statistical investigations of the economic yield of education. First, by dealing with number of individuals educated in an age group, rather than with monetary outlays on education, the calculation escaped the distortions due to pricing patterns contributed by the cost disease—the fact that such services are relatively more expensive in wealthier countries and rise in cost more rapidly than an economy's rate of inflation.

Second, the calculation avoided the problem of cause and effect confusion arising from the possibility that wealth leads to more expenditure on education at the same time that education contributes to a nation's wealth. The problem of having to distinguish the two possible relationships statistically, and the danger of mistaking one for the other, was avoided by basing the calculations on levels of education early in the period under consideration and on *subsequent* growth in RGDP. A high rate of growth in RGDP between 1965 and 1980 may well affect levels of education in 1980 or 1985, but it can hardly influence the 1965 levels of education, at least not directly.

6. For a highly authoritative discussion of the U.S. record that emphasizes the role of education for the future of the country's productivity and also ascribes a substantial role to education in productivity growth more generally, see Nelson [1988].

7. The material that follows is taken from a variety of sources—reports of educational commissions, Census data, the Congressional Research Service, etc. We are particularly indebted to L. Scott Miller of the Exxon Education Foundation, who assembled and analyzed a considerable proportion of the information reported here.

10

Depletion of Natural Resources: Must Economic Growth Mortgage the Future?

Since Fuel is become so expensive and will of course grow scarcer and dearer; any new proposal for saving [fuel] may at least be thought worth Consideration.
Benjamin Franklin (1744)

Neither reduced demand nor expanded exploration can make our finite resources limitless.
Baumol and Oates [1979, p. 107]

In chapters 2 and 3 we described the unparalleled growth in living standards and economic output during the nineteenth and twentieth centuries. Our discussion emphasized the incredible magnitude of the break with all previous history—a history from which the threat of famine and near-universal poverty had rarely receded. While no one seems to dispute the magnitude of the accomplishment, there are observers who suggest that we have paid too high a price for it—that our current level of prosperity has been achieved at the expense of future generations, by depleting the earth's natural resources at an unprecedented rate.

The received wisdom of the environmental literature emphasizes the fact that the earth is a planet whose contents are finite and whose resources, if used continuously, must ultimately be exhausted. Taken in its most obvious sense, this observation is undeniable. However, as we shall show in this chapter, there is a sense far more significant for social welfare in which this need not be true. On the contrary, measured in terms of their prospective contribution to human welfare, the available quantity of our exhaustible and unreproducible natural resources may be able to rise unceasingly, year after year. Rather than approaching exhaustion with continued use, their effective inventories may actually be growing and may never come anywhere near disappearance. In short, our society's growing per capita output, rather than constituting a case of profligacy in which society "lives off its capital," may in fact involve what amounts to a net saving of finite natural resources, so that their *effective stocks* are constantly expanded by the same family of technological developments that underlie the growth in real per-capita income since the Industrial Revolution. Moreover, we shall provide evidence suggesting that this is no mere abstract possibility but is, at least to some degree, happening now.

The explanation of these paradoxes is quite straightforward. A technological innovation that increases the *productivity* of a natural resource (i.e., that increases the output of each unit utilized), either directly through increased efficiency and recycling of that resource, or by a decrease in waste (inefficiency) in the extraction or production process, obviously helps to cut down on the current usage of that resource. But, in addition, *it also increases the prospective output contribution of the as-yet-unused stock of those resources.* If a given year's technological change raises the effective quantity of the unused stocks by an amount greater than what is actually used up that year, then, in the only sense pertinent to economic welfare, the stock of that resource will be *larger* at the end of the year than it was at the beginning. And while it must remain true that with continued use the inventory of such a resource still remaining in its natural habitat must continually decline, we shall show that it need never be exhausted completely and its *effective quantity* may continue to rise, in effect, forever. It is true, however, that though the effective inventory of the resource need never decline, (annual) consumption of that resource *will* eventually have to decline and, indeed, eventually it must approach zero.[1]

10.1 Natural Resource Prospects: Some Suggestive Observations

Before going further into the analytic basis of our relatively sanguine contention, we must emphasize that it is not intended as a prophecy of a happy and certain future. On the contrary, there is no doubt that resource depletion can yet bring renewed misery to the human race, just as poisoning of our atmosphere and waters and depletion of the ozone layer can constitute disasters. What we are suggesting is that such a fate is not inevitable, that humanity itself may be able to prevent it, and that in fact, at least so far, we may not be headed in the direction of resource exhaustion. We shall begin by looking at some pertinent facts that, on preliminary examination, seem to offer little ground for optimism. Yet some anomalous observations will suggest that matters here may not be exactly as they seem.

The Industrial Revolution brought with it growing demand for power and raw materials such as the world had never seen; and the fantastic rate of expansion has continued through the twentieth century. It has been

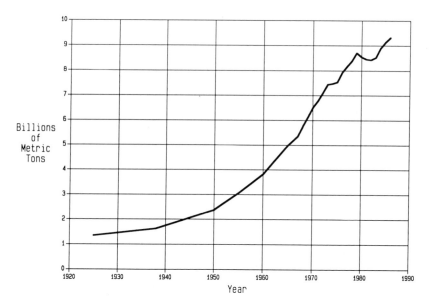

Figure 10.1
World energy consumption (coal equivalent), 1925–1986. Sources: 1925–1968 data, Darmstadter, Teitelbaum, and Polach [1971, p. 10]; 1968–1986 data, United Nations [1979, 1983, and 1986, table 1].

estimated, for example, that, in the first two decades of the twentieth century, mankind consumed more energy than it had used in all the previous centuries of its existence. During the following two decades, we again employed more power than in the totality of the past (including the part of the twentieth century that preceded it). Moreover, a similar statement has held for each 20-year period since then. Figure 10.1 depicts this dramatic increase in energy consumption over half a century, slowed down (apparently only temporarily) by the unprecedented high fuel prices of the late 1970s and early 1980s. Simple extrapolation of these trends suggests how enormous future demands for energy may be. Indeed, humanity has a long history of panicking about the imminent exhaustion of natural resources. For example, somewhere between the thirteenth and seventeenth centuries a large part of Europe's forests was cut down, primarily for use in metalworking (much of it for military purposes). Wood prices rose, and there was a good deal of talk about depletion of fuel stocks. People have been worried about resource depletion ever since, as table 10.1 illustrates. The table lists a number of rather gloomy prophecies about the available stocks of petroleum supplies at various times, prophecies that in fact proved to be far off the mark.

Table 10.1
Past petroleum prophecies (and realities)

Date	U.S. oil production rate (billions of barrels/year)	Prophecy	Reality
1866	0.005	Synthetics available if oil production should end (U.S. Revenue Commission)	In next 82 years the United States produced 37 billion barrels with no need for synthetics
1891	0.05	Little or no chance for oil in Kansas or Texas (U.S. Geological Survey)	14 billion barrels produced in these states since 1891
1914	0.27	Total future production only 5.7 billion barrels (official of U.S. Bureau of Mines)	34 billion barrels produced since 1914, or six times this prediction
1920	0.45	United States needs foreign oil and synthetics: peak domestic production almost reached (Director of U.S. Geological Survey)	1948 U.S. production in excess of U.S. consumption and more than four times 1920 output
1939	1.3	U.S. oil supplies will last only 13 years (radio broadcasts by Interior Department	New oil found since 1939 exceeds the 13 years' supply known at that time
1947	1.9	Sufficient oil cannot be found in United States (chief of Petroleum Division, State Department)	4.3 billion barrels found in 1948, the largest volume in history and twice our consumption
1949	2.0	End of U.S. oil supply almost in sight (Secretary of the Interior)	Recent industry shows ability to increase U.S. production by more than a million barrels daily in the next 5 years

Source: William M. Brown [1984, p. 362], who cites Presidential Energy Program, Hearings Before the Subcommittee on Energy and Power of the Committee on Interstate and Foreign Commerce, House of Representatives, First Session on the Implications of the President's Proposals in the Energy Independence Act of 1957, Serial No. 94–20, p. 643, 17, 18, 20, and 21 February 1975.

Table 10.2
World reserves and cumulative production of selected minerals: 1950–1980 (millions of metric tons of metal content)

Mineral	1950 reserves	Production 1950–1980	1980 reserves
Aluminum	1,400	1,346	5,200
Copper	100	156	494
Iron	19,000	11,040	93,466
Lead	40	85	127

Source: Repetto [1987, p. 23], who cites William Vogeley, "Nonfuel Minerals and the World Economy," in Repetto [1985].

Table 10.2, taken from Repetto [1987, p. 23], shows estimates of known world reserves of four important nonfuel minerals—aluminum, copper, iron, and lead. Reading this table we see that, even though extraction of these minerals between 1950 and 1980 all but exhausted known 1950 reserves, by 1980 the known supplies of these minerals were, nevertheless, much higher. The explanation of this apparent growth in the inventories of finite minerals lies in the nature of the data on natural resources. Each year the U.S. Bureau of Mines publishes estimates both of the U.S. and world demand for mineral resources and of the quantities of *identified* supplies of these resources. This has been interpreted as a measure of the adequacy of known supplies of resources relative to their anticipated demands—a kind of "reserve-demand" index (or, as Repetto [1987] puts it, a "working inventory"). It is figures of this sort that are shown in table 10.2. Of course, these figures do *not* mean that such nonrenewable resources can be made to grow. The figures represent what are called "proven reserves"—quantities of mineral that have actually been located and their amounts evaluated. But reserves are not "proven" by happenstance. Mineral exploration is expensive and is undertaken only when it is justified by prices, anticipated demands, and the levels of stock currently known. As a result, active exploration typically takes place only as previously discovered reserves are used up; frequently, new reserves are found as fast, or even faster, than previously proven reserves run out.

10.2   Resource Prices as a Test of Growing Scarcity

"Proven reserves" figures, then, do not really tell us whether a given resource threatens to run out in the foreseeable future. The proven reserves of a particular resource may have failed to grow, not because its supply is about to run out, but because market conditions did not make sufficient exploration worthwhile. Economists believe that there is another indicator of the scarcity of a resource relative to the demand for it that is considerably more reliable. This indicator is the price of the item in question. We can judge the abundance of a resource by the behavior of its price. So long as demand for the item is not shifting downward and market prices are not markedly distorted by interferences such as government intervention or international cartels, we expect that the real price of a resource will rise as its remaining quantity declines (in accord with Harold Hotelling's [1931] classic theorem). Certainly it is hard to believe that any resource whose price falls consistently and without regulatory interference is really growing scarce relative to prospective demand.

Statistical evidence on this issue was first assembled by Barnett and Morse [1963, part 3, chapters 8 and 9]. They found for a sample of 13 minerals that the real cost of extraction per unit had declined for all but 2 (lead and zinc) over the period 1870–1956. Using somewhat more recent data on *prices* of 15 minerals, Jack Frisch carried out for Baumol and Oates a parallel calculation for the period 1900–1975, using all minerals for which the required price series were readily available (see Baumol and Oates [1979, pp. 100–104, 108–110]). Frisch calculated the price of each resource measured in dollars of constant purchasing power. We have brought Frisch's figures up to date (using the producer price index to correct for the consequences of inflation). Representative results are depicted in figure 10.2 (for 3 fuels) and figure 10.3 (for 4 other minerals) for a period of more than eight decades. The fuel data show that until the energy crisis of the 1970s there was a negligible upward trend in the real (i.e., inflation-adjusted) prices of coal and natural gas, and virtually none in that of crude oil. These prices leaped upward under the pressures exerted by the Organization of Petroleum Exporting Countries (OPEC) in the 1970s, but they have since come back down a considerable part of the way toward their long-term level. While specialists seem to expect another rise some time in the 1990s, the longer-term prospects are rendered highly uncertain by the progress in new energy-producing techniques. An example is nuclear fusion, which, unlike the nuclear fission that is now in use, will, if it succeeds, have at its disposal virtually unlimited supplies of raw materials (sea water) and will apparently entail no serious waste disposal or other environmental problems. This, and other energy sources still in the process of exploration or development, may be able to bring energy prices back to their long-term real levels or even below them. The history of the prices of nonfuel minerals, as depicted in figure 10.3, is even more striking. Some, like iron ore, have manifested a slow long-period rise. Others, like lead, appear to have ex-

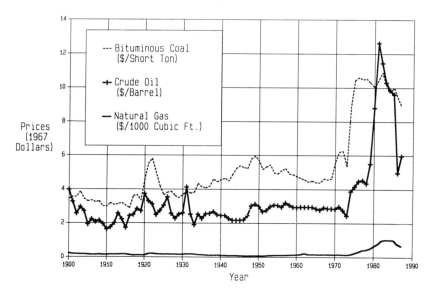

Figure 10.2

Fuel prices, 1900–1987. Sources: 1900–1955 data, Schurr and Netschert [1960, pp. 545–547]; 1956–1965 data, U.S. Bureau of Mines, *Minerals Yearbook* (various issues); 1966–1987 data, U.S. Department of Energy, *Annual Energy Review* [1987, tables 61, 72, and 81]; Producer Price Index, *Economic Report of the President* [1988].

hibited no long-term movement. But then, there are dramatic cases, like that of aluminum and magnesium, for which today's real prices are strikingly lower than they were 70 years ago.

The most noteworthy fact that emerges is that, over the long period considered, the prices of about half of the mineral resources investigated actually fell *after correction for changes in the value of the dollar*. None of the price rises, aside from those of fuels in the 1970s, can really be considered very substantial; in constant dollars most of them rose at a rate of less than 1% per year. We should note that the price decreases tend to be concentrated toward the beginning of the period, while increases begin to preponderate toward its end. This may suggest increasing scarcity in recent years (particularly since 1960), but is hardly evidence of imminent exhaustion. Very similar results were recently obtained from other calculations for seven minerals extending from 1900 to 1982, with three of the seven prices declining, and none of the others rising more than 0.7% per year on the average. This is surely below the real rate of interest during the period— the amount by which, the accepted theoretical analysis of the subject tells us, the price of a fixed depletable resource should be expected to rise each year in a competitive market.

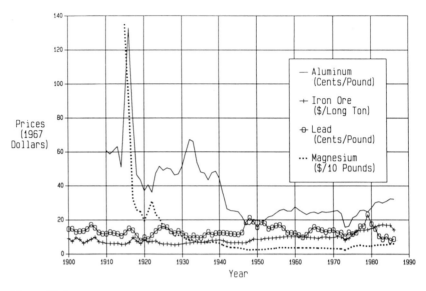

Figure 10.3

Mineral prices, 1900–1986. Sources: 1900–1955 data, Schurr and Netschert [1960, pp. 545–547]; 1956–1965 data, U.S. Bureau of Mines, *Minerals Yearbook* (various issues); 1966–1987 data, U.S. Department of Energy, *Annual Energy Review* [1987, tables 61, 72, and 81] and American Metal Market, *Metal Statistics* (various issues); Producer Price Index, *Economic Report of the President* [1988].

This is not the first time such a phenomenon has been observed. For example, "Between the later fifteenth and the mid-seventeenth century [when English timber supplies were reportedly being exhausted], while the prices of agricultural products in general [which then constituted the bulk of GNP] rose over six-fold, timber prices rose only just over five-fold" (Coleman [1975, p. 43]). In other words, the price of wood in terms of pounds of constant purchasing power probably fell (slightly) despite the depletion of the English forests. What is one to make of such price behavior? It is tempting to jump to the startling conclusion that in such cases the market is behaving as though the supplies of these resources—lumber, aluminum, copper, lead, mercury, magnesium, liquid natural gas, and natural gas—were actually increasing. As we shall see, there may in fact be some convoluted substance to this view; but there is more to the story. There is some evidence suggesting that whatever may have happened to inventories, a significant portion of the fall in the prices of the minerals in question is attributable to technical improvements in the extraction process.[2] We have no intentions of casting doubt on this conclusion, but for the purposes of the analysis here some interpretive discussion is essential.

10.3   Increasing the Effective Stocks of a Natural Resource: Reduced Extraction Costs

For our purposes it is useful to divide the savings resulting from an improved extraction process into two types: reduced use of labor, fuel, capital, etc., per unit of the resource extracted, and decreased "waste" of the resource in the extraction process. Examples of the latter are easy to find. Normally, when an oil well is abandoned a considerable quantity of oil will remain unextracted because it does not flow out unaided, and artificial means to force the petroleum to the surface grow increasingly expensive as 100% recovery is approached. The same is true of the separation of various solid minerals from the rock formations in which they are found. But, if the price of a resource rises enough, technological progress can make it feasible both absolutely and in economic terms to obtain an ever-increasing total amount of usable resource from a given site (such as an oil well).

In this sense, it is clear that a reduction in the cost of extraction of the second type (a decrease in waste) is tantamount to a rise in what we may call the *effective supply* of a resource. Thus, suppose that in 1960, with known extraction techniques, no more than 40% of the oil in a well could conceivably have been extracted at a cost ever likely to be acceptable, while by 1980 this figure has risen to 80%. Suppose in the meantime, say 5% of the initially available petroleum, X billion barrels, had been used up. Then the effective supply would have risen from its initial level, 40% of X billion barrels, to 80% of X (X having been reduced by 5%), yielding a net rise of effective supply equal to $0.8X \cdot (1 - .05) - 0.4X$ which constitutes a rise of 90%! That is, despite the 5% decline in the physical quantity of the resource remaining on our planet, its availability to consumers in the current and all future generations together will almost have doubled. A price fall in these circumstances is surely not difficult to explain. What has happened here is, in essence, not a rise in the quantity of oil, but an increase in the *productivity of the remaining supply*. This, incidentally, is what may underlie the reported fall in the price of timber between the fifteenth and seventeenth centuries when, according to recent research, "... in the whole process of smelting and conversion of pig into bar-iron there was approximately a threefold improvement in the amount of iron produced with a given amount of charcoal" (Coleman [1975, p. 42]). Since the depletion of the forests was, allegedly, "... largely, if not wholly, consequent upon the gobbling up of woodlands by the demands of the blast-furnaces and similar wood eaters ..." (Coleman [1975, p. 41] in a skeptical passage), this story may well be consistent with ours.

10.4 Increasing the Effective Stocks of a Natural Resource: The Opportunity (Substitution) Costs of Other Inputs

It should now be obvious how the effective supply of a depletable resource can be expanded by a decrease in wastefulness of the extraction process (or, for that matter, by a decrease in the wastefulness of any part of the process through which the resource is brought to the ultimate consumer) or by some other direct rise in its productivity. But we want to show now that even a decrease in extraction cost of the first type—a decline in the quantities of labor, capital, and other inputs used up in bringing the resource forth—may also add to the effective inventory of the resource, albeit indirectly. The point here is rather more subtle than that in the preceding section. It involves the (partial) substitutability of virtually all resources for one another. This means that a saving of labor, copper, or any other input is at the same time tantamount to a saving of (say) petroleum.

During the "energy crisis" of the 1970s this was illustrated dramatically in a number of ways. For example, the increased expenditure on home insulation to save on heating fuel represented the substitution of insulating materials (and the labor devoted to their installation) for petroleum and other sources of energy. A more romantic illustration was provided by newspaper reports that there was a partial revival of the cattle drive, with cattle more frequently being brought to market on the hoof rather than by truck, thus substituting cowboy labor for gasoline. Jacob Viner used to point out that there was, both in theory and in practice, very real substitutability between labor and the quantity of gold used in producing, say, a square yard of gold leaf of given thickness and refinement (i.e., number of carats). For when the price of gold increases, more labor is devoted to the recovery of scraps and gold dust from mineworkers' clothing. Thus, substitutability of inputs, rather than constituting an exceptional case, must be judged, at least in the long run, to represent the normal state of affairs.

To see the relevance of this observation to the basic issue with which we are concerned here, we need only note that if there is an increase in the efficiency of the extraction process of a resource such as oil that reduces the amount of labor or electricity used up in the activity, the labor and electricity inputs saved in this way can, *and to some extent will*, be substituted for oil elsewhere in the economy. The end result is, in substance, no different qualitatively from an outright decrease in waste of oil during extraction. As electricity that would formerly have been used up in drilling or mining is released from this use, either other forms of employment will be found for it and some of those uses will entail its substitution for petroleum or, instead, there will be a corresponding net reduction in electricity output, which also entails a saving of oil via reduced use of petroleum to generate electricity.

We conclude, then, that the use of *any* input in the extraction of a resource involves an *opportunity cost* in terms of the extracted resource. The labor used in bringing oil to the surface could, instead, have served as a substitute for oil in other uses. As a result, any decrease in the use of labor per unit of oil brought out of the ground to some degree constitutes an indirect addition to the economy's effective oil reserves. For, to the extent that the labor released serves to replace oil in the production of final outputs, the amount of output supportable by a given quantity of oil in the ground is enhanced correspondingly.

10.5 Increasing the Effective Stocks of a Natural Resource: Recycling

Finally, the effective reserves of a natural resource can be extended by technological changes that facilitate recycling. If, for example, an innovative recycling technique increases the number of times it pays to reuse copper from, say, two to three before it is finally abandoned, then the effective reserves of copper will clearly also have been raised by 50%, aside from any resources used up in the recycling process. Here it is important to stress the role of technical change or other forms of innovation as the source of expanded recycling in the economy. Recycling adopted without regard for its economics can actually waste resources rather than save them, and even result in a *negative* net energy flow. For example, some observers worry that the burning of municipal solid wastes to produce electricity will use up more energy than it creates, just as some solar energy techniques apparently can use up far more energy in the manufacture of the required equipment than they will produce during their expected life[3]. Thus, our discussion focuses once again on innovation and technical change as the source of increased productivity of natural resources, or reduced extraction costs, all of which help to increase the effective reserves of unreproducible resources and push in the direction of secular reductions in the real prices of those resources.

10.6 Price Trends, Extraction Costs, and Effective Reserves

This is an appropriate point to generalize the preceding discussion. What we have emphasized is the possibility that the effective supply, i.e., the effective performance capacity of an exhaustible resource, can be increased by technological innovation that reduces the waste (inefficiencies) that occur in the process of extraction of a resource, in its processing toward a final product and perhaps above all in its consumption (either directly, as in increased fuel efficiency of automobiles or increased productivity in its industrial uses, or as affected by the opportunities for financially viable recycling). All this is reflected in the trend in the price of such a resource, which is influenced both by the costs of extraction and the effective inventory of the item.

That is straightforward enough. Indeed, so far, only two observations have emerged that go beyond the obvious: First, there is little substantive distinction between decreased extraction cost and enhancement of the effective inventory of a resource, or, rather, the former turns out to be one of the avenues through which the latter occurs; and second, we have shown by example that inefficiency-reducing innovations not only help to offset the decrease in the physical stock of a resource that results from its consumption, but may actually lead to a net increase in its effective inventory —that is, during a given time period such changes can enhance the prospective economic contribution of the current inventory by an amount more than sufficient to offset the consumption of the resource that occurs during this period. Two questions arise naturally: whether the rate of technical change required to achieve this second result is so large as to remove it from the realm of plausibility and, even if it is plausible for a while, whether such developments can conceivably continue for a substantial time period, or even for the indefinite future. These are the issues to which we turn next. For their resolution it is necessary to construct a (very rudimentary) model, described in the appendix to this chapter. Here we shall briefly summarize its main results:

i. Given the initial quantity of a depletable and nonrenewable resource, there exists an infinity of time-sequence scenarios involving continuous and uninterrupted consumption (depletion) of the resource but also constant increases in its productivity that lead to perpetual increases of the *effective* inventory (supply) of that resource.

ii. In any of the scenarios just described, if productivity cannot increase beyond limit, then the effective inventory of the resource must also be bounded, and the rate of consumption (depletion) per year must ultimately grow smaller and smaller, finally approaching zero.

In commonsense terms, these propositions assert that, in a future in which the productivity of finite resources rises with sufficient persistence and rapidity, the effective quantity of the resource can continue to rise forever, despite uninterrupted consumption of the resource. However, in this process, if there is any ceiling on the possible level of productivity of the resource in question—if, say, the laws of physics make it impossible to transport someone from New York to San Francisco on less than one drop of gasoline—then even the *effective* stock of the resource can not be increased beyond some fixed and finite amount, and for the effective stock of the resource to remain on a permanent growth path, its consumption per annum must, ultimately, tail off toward zero.

10.7 Conclusions

It has been suggested that part of what has permitted the burst of productivity and living standards of the past 150 years in the industrialized countries of the world is the willingness of mankind to deplete its natural heritage, obtaining its current prosperity at the expense of future generations. In this chapter we have shown that such a conclusion is far from self-evident. Rising productivity, rather than drawing down humanity's stock of natural resource capital, may, in an effective sense, actually augment it, and may be able to continue to do so for the indefinite future. Resources that are not reproducible and whose quantities are finite may nevertheless be increased by technological advance in terms of their prospective economic contribution, and may do so, for all practical purposes, "forever." What we have shown is that in an economy characterized by pervasively rising productivity, the productivity of its finite resources is also likely to grow, and that their productivity may actually grow to a degree more than sufficient to offset the continuing decline in their remaining physical quantities.

This is not only possible in theory. The evidence of trends in resource prices suggests that something of the sort is in fact going on. Indeed, it would seem that the real unresolved issue is the magnitude of the phenomenon and whether it is sufficient to result, on balance, in an actual expansion of the effective inventories of a substantial proportion of the world's resources.

Notes

1. For an excellent earlier statement of much of this proposition, see Brems [1980]. A very similar position based on historical evidence can be found in Rosenberg [1976, papers 13 and 14].

2. See, for example, Barnett and Morse [1963]. Their conclusions are supported by the results of recent interviews of our associates with minerals specialists at the U.S. Bureau of Mines.

3. Another possible example of more energy being used up than produced in a purportedly energy-saving project is the construction of municipal subway systems; a number of researchers have concluded that the high energy cost of building these systems can far surpass any energy saving from reduced private automobile use (for more on these issues, see Baumol and Blackman [1980]).

11

Productivity Yardsticks:
Alternative Measures and
Their Appropriate Uses

"The question is," said Alice, "whether you can make words mean so many different things."
"The question is," said Humpty Dumpty, "which is to be master—that's all."
Lewis Carroll, *Through the Looking Glass*

Having now employed the concept of "productivity" rather loosely over the course of 10 chapters, for the interested reader we now pause, before our concluding chapter, to examine more carefully the various connotations that have been assigned to the term, and to glance at some of the associated measurement issues. The discussion will be fairly abstract and many readers will prefer to skip it and go directly to chapter 12. As is true of every inherently aggregative measure, we shall find that there exists no one unambiguously acceptable productivity concept. Rather, every available working definition unavoidably entails some degree of compromise. But the fairly eclectic position that we shall take here goes beyond mere recognition of the imperfection inherent in the use of the concept. Conventional wisdom in the field of productivity growth seems to accept a standard hierarchy, taking one type of productivity measure to be inherently superior to another. For example, it seems widely held that total factor productivity, since it seeks to take account of improvements in the performance of every type of productive input, and not just that of labor alone, is a concept inherently superior to the labor productivity measure. Similarly, it seems to be accepted that a productivity measure that includes explicit adjustments for improvements in the *quality* of the final product is necessarily more desirable than one that makes no such adjustment (here we shall refer to a measure that makes no quality adjustment as an index of "gross productivity"). Those who take such positions seem to imply that one only deals with statistics on labor productivity or gross productivity *faut de mieux*, that is, only because of an unfortunate paucity of information that precludes the use of something better. We, on the contrary, hold the view that such a ranking in terms of the comparative virtues of the different productivity concepts is quite unjustified. Rather, we shall undertake to show that even the supposedly "inferior" measures have their legitimate uses, for which the "superior" concepts constitute no acceptable substitutes. Thus, we shall argue in this chapter that labor productivity, and even gross productivity, each offers us vital information that would be lost without it.

11.1 Productivity Measurement: Labor Productivity versus Total Factor Productivity

Labor productivity is, of course, defined as output per unit of labor input, but even this simple concept introduces some ambiguities because neither the proper measure of output nor even the appropriate measure of labor input is uniquely preordained. The fact that every business firm and every industry, as well as the economy as a whole, produces a multiplicity of goods and services whose outputs generally increase at different rates usually makes it impossible to say categorically that "output is rising at an annual rate of x percent." For the economy as a whole one must choose among gross national product, gross domestic product, net national income, and the other standard macroeconomic concepts as the output measure to be used in a productivity calculation, and for a business firm or an industry a similar choice must be made. As the labor input quantity one can select number of workers, number of work-years, and number of work-hours, among others. These can all yield rather different results. For example, in an economy in which the number of hours worked per year by a typical person is declining rapidly, constancy of output per labor hour will mean that output per worker-year must be falling sharply. In addition, some way must be found to aggregate different worker skills and different levels of training. Still, the measurement of labor productivity generally entails relatively few intractable conceptual problems, and whatever the choices that are made among the options in the preceding list, one generally understands the implications and the proper interpretation of the resulting figures.

  The qualms expressed about the use of labor productivity, then, do not stem from the workability of the measure, but arise rather from what, for some purposes, constitutes an analytical inadequacy. It seems clear that in an economy whose labor force in some sense maintains constancy of skills and standards of performance, labor productivity can nevertheless increase because of technological changes that improve the quality of the capital stock, or simply as a result of increases in the amounts of equipment per worker. Where this occurs, standard measures of labor productivity can be expected to increase, even though in these circumstances it is plainly improper to interpret this change as a measure of *labor's* contribution to output expansion. One can persuasively maintain that what is being measured here is not the change in productive capacity or contribution of labor, which is zero in this hypothetical scenario, but rather that the contribution of capital is being implicitly misattributed to labor. The point is quite valid, and it is the main reason that the additional effort required to arrive at an evaluation of total factor productivity (TFP) is justified. But this is merely a legitimate criticism of an improper interpretation of labor productivity; it does not deprive the concept of other more proper interpretations.

Labor productivity is, instead, more usefully taken as an indicator of the *prospective consumption* that can be promised as the reward for an hour of labor. As was just recognized, it is not an indicator of the source of that potential output reward. However, as Karl Marx emphasized, labor, interpreted in the broadest sense, is the one human input in the productive process. Inanimate inputs undoubtedly also contribute, but the success of the productive process presumably is to be judged in terms of what it accomplishes for its human participants. Thus, while total factor productivity is undoubtedly the better index of *efficiency* of input use, it would appear that labor productivity is the more illuminating measure of the *result* of the process for its human participants. An easy way to see this is to consider the special case in which there is no change in the ratio of the size of the population and the size of the labor force (or, perhaps better, the number of labor-hours expended). In that case it is clear that the rate of growth of labor productivity must be identical with the rate of growth of per capita output. Since per-capita output has an obvious claim as a legitimate indicator of current standard of living (i.e., of overall economic welfare), the relation of labor productivity to economic welfare readily suggests itself. It was, presumably something of this sort that the consummate entrepreneur, Robert Fulton [1796], had in mind when he wrote, "The produce of labour is the real wealth of a country, the more the labourer will produce so much more the nation improves" (Philip [1985, p. 49]).

But labor productivity and per-capita output obviously do not, in general, tell us the same thing. What is special about the labor productivity concept is that it indicates how hard humanity must work to achieve the current economic yield. It tells us neither the reasons for the current state of affairs in this regard nor anything about the equity of the associated distribution. A nation may attain a high level of labor productivity either because its labor force is highly skilled or because its machines are ingenious, but in either case the result is the same—there is a high *potential* reward to an hour of labor. That reward may in fact go preponderantly to others, but unless labor productivity is high, a substantial reward for the outlay of labor is not even a possibility. High labor productivity, then, is the key *necessary* condition for general prosperity of the populance. We conclude that labor productivity is the proper measure of the *capacity* of a productive unit (a firm, an industry, or an entire economy) to reward its labor force, and that total factor productivity, or some other measure, cannot serve that purpose as well, being designed for another role.[1]

11.2   Total Factor Productivity (TFP): Its Purpose and Measurement

Total factor productivity (sometimes referred to more conservatively as "multifactor productivity" when only some limited subset of the economy's inputs is taken into account) is intended as a measure of the efficiency of an economy's productive mechanism. It is meant to provide an index of the rate of expansion of an economy's (or some productive unit's) capacity to produce, over and above the portion attributable just to expansion in its input quantities. That is, if a doubling of the quantity of labor, capital, and natural resources used up by an economy were to be associated with precise doubling of each of its product quantities, then one would be inclined to say that while output had risen, TFP had not increased at all. Only any excess in output growth over and above mere doubling would, in this case, be taken to constitute an expansion in TFP, on the implicit assumption that the relationship is not complicated by the presence of either economies or diseconomies of scale.

This immediately suggests one way in which one may wish to go about the measurement of TFP, a method that is in fact utilized in practice. This procedure, referred to as the method of *the residual*, simply starts off from some measure of expansion in aggregate output (for example, the rise in GNP during some time period) and then deducts from that figure the part of the increase that can be attributed by standard statistical analysis to the sheer expansion in input usage. The residual is then used as the basis for the TFP calculation. Thus, to continue with our previous example, if the doubling of each and every input quantity had multiplied all outputs by a factor of 2.3, one would normally attribute the doubling portion of the expansion to the increased input usage, while the residual, the 0.3, would be taken to constitute growth in TFP. To calculate the growth rate of TFP only one more step is required. This 0.3 residual must be divided by the growth in the inputs (relative to the initial input quantities) to determine how much the productive capacity of the original input quantities had expanded, and this gives us 0.3/2 = 0.15, i.e., a 15% growth figure for TFP.

The calculation might be a simple affair if it were not for the fact that input quantities virtually never increase in the same proportions, and the same is obviously true of output quantities. If the quantity of capital used in a production process goes up 23%, raw material usage rises 6%, and the quantity of labor used actually falls 2%, what are we to conclude about the quantity by which aggregate input use has changed? This, of course, is the standard problem besetting the construction of any economic index, that is, the selection of a single number to represent a multiplicity of disparate quantitative developments. And, as is now generally recognized, there can be no single formula that serves the purpose best in all circumstances—that is, there can be no "ideal index number." Only in particular circumstances, that is, under special assumptions, can one deduce that one such formula unambiguously serves the purpose at hand better than others. Let us, then, examine in a bit more detail some of these methodological issues entailed in the calculation of TFP, and some of the means that are commonly used to deal with them.

11.3   General Methodological Issues in the Measurement of Total Factor Productivity

Total factor productivity growth is intended to measure the increase of outputs that can be produced with various *combinations* of inputs. If an industry were to produce only one output and continued to use exactly the same amount of each input over time, there would be no problem in measuring the growth in TFP. One could simply divide the new output level by the previous output level.

There are two other special cases that present no problem in measuring productivity growth. In the first case, there is only one input, say, labor. Then productivity is defined as the quantity of output produced per unit of labor. Here, productivity growth is measured, simply, by the change in output divided by the change of labor usage. The other special case, as we have seen, occurs when there is more than one input but all inputs grow in the same proportion. In this case, productivity growth can be defined as the

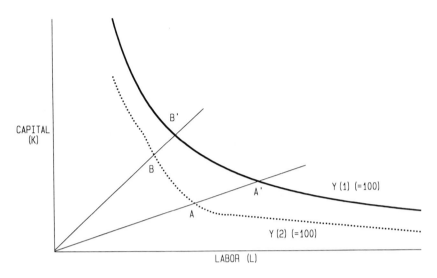

Figure 11.1
Input combinations yielding 100 output units, time periods 1 and 2.

change in output divided by the change in input usage. But even the calculations in these last two cases perform ideally only on the special assumption of constant returns to scale, which means that in the absence of technological change a doubling of input quantities is capable of yielding a precise doubling of all output quantities. (In our earlier numerical example, where output was assumed to have risen by a factor of 2.3, it was this premise that permitted us to attribute 0.3 of that amount to technological change because the 2.0 increase in output was ascribed to the doubled input quantities.) In contrast, for example, the presence of scale economies would have required a larger share of the output growth to be attributed to this influence, and, hence, less of it to technical change.

Except for these special cases, the measurement of total factor productivity growth is not so straightforward because, generally, more than one input is used and inputs do not all grow in the same proportion over time. Moreover, most industries produce more than one output. As a result, in seeking to measure TFP growth we want to know at what rate the amounts of output that can be produced with *each* pertinent combination of inputs increase over time. The immediate problem that now arises is that, in general, this will be *different* for different combinations of inputs. A simple diagram can be used to illustrate this problem. We assume that there are two inputs, labor L and capital K. The curve labeled $Y(1)$ in figure 11.1 shows various combinations of labor and capital, each combination being capable of producing 100 units of output in the first time period, 1. This curve can be used to evaluate productivity growth when it is compared with the next period's curve, $Y(2)$, showing all combinations of capital and labor capable of producing 100 units of input in the second time period. If there has been some technological progress, $Y(2)$ will generally lie below $Y(1)$, because the resulting rise in productivity means that less labor and less capital are required to produce 100 units of output in the second year than in the first year. However, the saving in labor and capital with one combination of inputs will usually be different from that achievable with another combination of inputs. That is why curve $Y(2)$ is shaped so differently from curve $Y(1)$. We see, for example, that with the labor-capital ratio corresponding to point A, productivity grows substantially [point A on $Y(2)$ is well below point A' on $Y(1)$], while the productivity growth at labor-capital combination B is far more modest.

As a result of such complications, no single number, such as a calculation of the increase in TFP, will be able to describe the full range of expanded production possibilities offered, say, by technical progress. Productivity growth can be measured in such a way only if some special assumptions about the nature of the pertinent technology and the way it changes over time are satisfied. In particular, it is helpful if neither economies nor diseconomies of scale are present, and, in order for the same productivity number to represent productivity growth accurately—whatever the pertinent input combination—it is clearly necessary for it to be true that (i.e., it must be assumed that) productivity grows at the same rate for each combination of inputs. Though this is not always recognized, these assumptions, while obviously not always realistic, are in fact implicitly adopted in most of the models that form the basis of statistical studies of total factor productivity.

11.4   Some Commonly Used Formulas for Total Factor Productivity Growth

The remainder of the chapter is addressed primarily to economists, and the general reader may well wish to proceed directly to chapter 12. In this section and the appendix to this chapter we describe several commonly used measures of TFP and discuss, in each case, the underlying corresponding restrictions on the production structure of an industry. We also comment on the methodological problems entailed in their use, and their relative advantages and disadvantages.

A. *Crude TFP Growth*. We begin with what would seem to be the productivity concept whose measurement is most straightforward, which we refer to as "crude productivity." Crude productivity growth measures the increase of output that can be produced with various combinations of inputs, making no attempt to separate out or adjust for the different sources of such growth. Because almost all industries produce many outputs and use many inputs whose quantities expand in different proportions, to measure crude productivity growth it is necessary to define it as the difference in the rate of growth of an output *index* and a rate of growth of an input *index*. We can define an output index $Y(t)$ and an input index $X(t)$ at time t as, respectively, weighted averages of the respective output quantities $y_i(t)$ and input quantities $x_j(t)$, so that

$$Y(t) = v_1 y_1(t) + v_2 y_2(t) + \cdots + v_m y_m(t), \qquad \text{all } v_i \geq 0, \quad \sum v_i = 1,$$

and

$$X(t) = w_1 x_1(t) + w_2 x_2(t) + \cdots + w_n x_n(t), \qquad \text{all } w_j \geq 0, \quad \sum w_j = 1.$$

Crude TFP at time t is, then, given by

$$CTFP(t) = Y(t)/X(t)$$

and crude productivity growth by

$$CTFP(t)/CTFP(t-1) = \{Y(t)/Y(t-1)\}/\{X(t)/X(t-1)\}.$$

There is, unfortunately, no uniquely preferable set of weights either for the input index or the output index. Four sets of weights in common use for the input index are (i) first-period cost share weights, (ii) last-period cost share weights, (iii) an average of first-period and last-period cost shares, and (iv) a "chain index," in which average period weights are updated for successive periods. On the output side, revenue shares are used as weights. As with input weights, one can use various periods to calculate the appropriate shares.

The advantage of the crude TFP index is that its magnitude can be calculated directly from the data usually on hand. In particular, with appropriate statistics on input quantities, input prices, output quantities, and output prices, one can construct this index directly. Moreover, unlike some other indices to be discussed in the appendix to this chapter, no econometric estimation procedure is required as part of the calculation process. Furthermore, experiments based on appropriate data for the railroad industry for the 1951–1974 period indicate that estimates of both annual and annual average crude productivity growth are relatively insensitive to the choice of weights (see section 11.10).

A central weakness of this measure is that its estimate of productivity growth depends on the quantities of the different inputs actually used in the various periods. If, in fact, technological change is uneven and the production curve moves inward at different rates for different input combinations over time (as illustrated in figure 11.1), then the value of the crude TFP index will vary, depending on the actual input combinations used in the periods (for example, whether they are represented by point A' or B' in period 1 and A or B, respectively, in period 2). As a result, there can, in general, be no unique measure of crude productivity growth for the industry, irrespective of the input quantities that happen to have been used. In principle, it may then be more desirable to construct a measure that somehow averages the productivity growth figures corresponding to different pertinent input combinations than to base the measure on the input levels actually employed. However, in practice, it is not usually possible to obtain data on the output realizable from input combinations other than those that were in fact used.

B. *The Divisia Index.* An alternative approach widely favored by those who start their work from a theoretical basis seeks to measure what we shall call growth in "productive capacity," a general concept to which we shall return presently. The Divisia index variant of this approach to measurement of TFP growth (named after the inventor of the indices utilized) differs from that of crude productivity in that it takes into account the rates of expansion of the amount of output that can be produced with *each* possible combination of inputs. Since, in general, these will be *different* with different combinations of inputs, the Divisia approach is fully workable and satisfactory in its results only under fairly restrictive assumptions about the nature of the productive techniques available to an industry and the way they change over time. In particular, it is helpful to assume that productivity grows at the same rate for each combination of inputs. But even this assumption does not yield a unique productivity growth figure, unless at the very least (for reasons we have seen) an assumption of constant returns to scale (or some substitute for it) is also adopted.

The standard Divisia TFP index can be shown to be a precise and defensible measure of TFP growth for all input and output combinations when the pertinent facts satisfy a fairly restrictive set of assumptions (for a derivation, see Hulten [1978]). These premises include

1. constant returns to scale,

2. technical progress proceeds continuously with the passage of time (no abrupt changes in technology),

3. technical progress does not require expansion in input quantities and, in particular, does not necessitate any increases in capital stock,

4. all input prices are determined in accord with the rules of behavior of perfectly competitive markets, and

5. all firms are perfectly efficient, minimizing the cost of whatever inputs they produce.

Given these premises and, in addition, premises that are consistent with the standard procedures for maximization of output,[2] it can be shown that productivity growth is measured correctly for each and every input combination by the Divisia formula for TFP growth

$$\text{DTFP} = \partial(\textstyle\sum v_i \ln y_i / \sum w_i \ln x_i)/\partial t,$$

where, for example, $d(\ln y_i)/dt \equiv (dy_i/dt)/y_i$ is the percentage rate of growth of input i, and $\sum v_i d(\ln y_i)/dt$ is a weighted average of the percentage growth rates of the various outputs, where q_i is the price of output i, the weight v_i that is assigned to output i is the ratio of $q_i y_i$, the market value of output y_i, to $\sum q_k y_k$, the total market value of all outputs, i.e., $v_i = q_i y_i / \sum q_k y_k$. The Divisia input growth index, $\sum w_j d(\ln x_j)/dt$, is, of course, to be interpreted similarly.

The Divisia index, like the crude productivity measure, has the advantage that it can be evaluated directly from the pertinent data, without any intermediate steps of econometric estimation. Input quantities and prices and output quantities and prices are all that is required. The major shortcoming of the Divisia index is the set of strong assumptions required for its validity. The appendix to this chapter describes some alternative TFP indices that have been constructed to avoid some of those premises, notably the assumption that rules out economies of scale, the premise of perfect efficiency, and the assumption that the input and output prices are those that would emerge under perfect competition.

11.5 Additional Conceptual Issues in Measuring Productivity

The literature on productivity devotes considerable and deserved attention to a variety of measurement problems and to distinctions such as that between labor productivity and total factor productivity. Some of this material has just been reviewed. However, there are some additional and rather basic definitional issues that arise implicitly in many of the discussions and that do not seem to have been examined to the degree they merit. To bring out the issues, the remainder of this chapter will contrast several basic interpretations of the productivity concept, discuss the differences in their uses and significance, and then demonstrate empirically that these various notions of productivity can yield very different measurements of productivity growth.

In writings on productivity growth at least three different connotations are implicitly assigned to the term. Most often, it is interpreted as a measure of the increase in productive "capacity" *attributable to technical change*—the shift in the production frontier. Sometimes it seems to be interpreted implicitly as a measure of the increase in consumer and producer welfare produced per unit of input, regardless of the source of the improvement (whether technical change, improved allocation of resources given the state of technology, or some other influence). Finally, usually with some embarrassment, statistical studies sometimes deal with changes in what we shall call "gross productivity"—the number of units of output produced per unit of input, *with no attempt to adjust for any accompanying changes in product quality*. We shall refer to these, respectively, as growth in productive capacity, welfare productivity, and gross productivity. We shall show in the next few sections that the (monotonically descending) pecking order that seems, at least implicitly, to be assigned to these three concepts in the literature is misleading. For, as will be demonstrated, each of them has its legitimate and significant use both in analysis and in application. Even the gross productivity measure, the least reputable of the concepts, will be shown to be extremely important in explaining the behavior over time of the relative prices of different goods and services, in budgetary planning for various public sector activities, and in planning to meet future manpower requirements. It will also be seen that, in some cases, the productive capacity measure may deviate systematically from the welfare productivity measure, and in those circumstances it will be argued that the former will be inappropriate for an analysis of standard of living.

Perhaps surprisingly, it will transpire that a welfare productivity figure, at least in principle, may prove to be easier to evaluate approximately than a change in productive capacity, despite the important role in welfare productivity of changes in the quality of the products in question—changes that are, of course, difficult to identify and describe, and sometimes all but impossible to quantify.

11.6 Productivity Growth as Measured by Productive Capacity

One frequently encounters the view that a pure measure of productivity growth should confine itself to the consequences of technical change and changes in the quality of the available inputs, for example, in the skills of

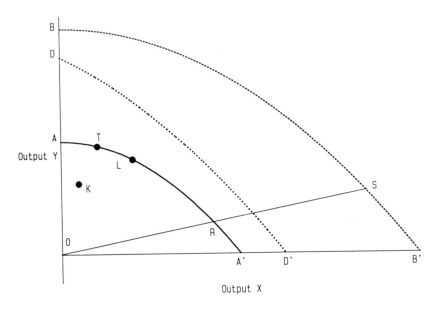

Figure 11.2
Three production frontiers.

the labor force, and that such a measure should leave out of consideration changes in output per unit of input that result, for example, from elimination of (mere) inefficiencies.[3] On this view, then, productivity growth occurs when there is an outward shift in the production frontier like that when AA′ is replaced by BB′ as a result of technical change (figure 11.2). But productivity does not increase, in terms of this concept, when the economy moves from an inefficient point like K, inside frontier AA′, to an efficient point, such as T, on that frontier.

For reasons that have already been discussed, matters are not so straightforward when the outward shift is uneven, as is that from AA′ to DD′ in figure 11.2. Then there simply exists no one number that can adequately measure the enhanced productive capacity. The problem is exacerbated when a new production technique expands the ability to produce one good at the expense of another, so that what may be described (somewhat barbarically) as the new technique-specific frontier (EE′ in figure 11.3) crosses the old frontier, AA′. One may then, perhaps, assume that the new production frontier for the economy will be the envelope, EHA′, of EE′ and AA′, and in these circumstances, while no part of the economy's frontier will have shifted inward, only some portion of it will have shifted outward.[4]

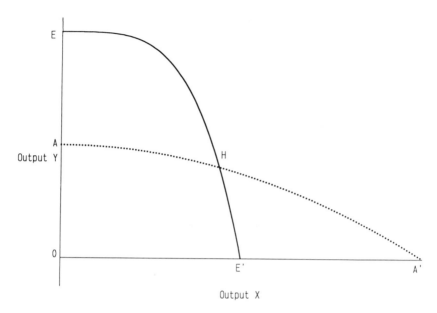

Figure 11.3
Intersecting production frontiers.

This indicates, once again, why those who seek to estimate some measure of growth of productive capacity usually adopt assumptions of some degree of severity about the nature of the production set and the character of technical change. Their premises are designed to offer them an expansion path for the production frontier that can be described uniquely by a scalar measure (i.e., a single number), as in the shift from AA' to BB' in figure 11.2. Unfortunately, reality need not follow follow such a simple course, and then *any* scalar measure of productivity growth as an index of expansion of productive capacity per unit of input becomes at best a rough indicator of a development that can only be described fully by a multiplicity of numbers or by a functional relationship.

11.7 The Imperfect Association of Productive Capacity and the Standard of Living (Welfare)

However one may choose to define the standard of living or the level of welfare (more will be said about that presently), it is clear that there are ways other than an increase in productive capacity to enhance them. For one thing, allocative or X-inefficiency may be reduced without any technological change. This moves the economy from a point inside the produc-

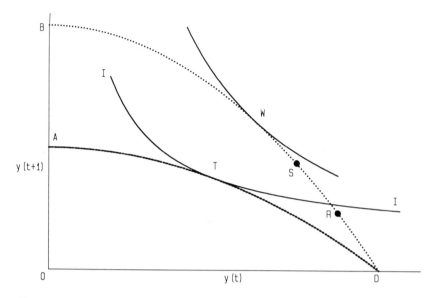

Figure 11.4
Welfare productivity versus productivity capacity.

tion frontier to another point closer to the frontier, but involves no shift in the frontier itself. In addition, a change in output proportions can constitute an improvement in terms of consumer preferences among products, thereby clearly contributing to consumer welfare, even if it is not accompanied by any new technology. Consequently, it should not be surprising that the association between growth of productive capacity and growth in welfare productivity is imperfect.

Disparities between the measures need not occur only haphazardly. An illustration will show how systematic differences between the two can arise. Consider the use of a patent system to stimulate economic growth. To permit the use of a two-dimensional diagram, we employ a model with a single commodity and a two-period horizon, though our conclusions will be perfectly general. In time period 1 the community has a choice between adoption or rejection of a patent law. The patent system will yield innovations that enhance productive capacity, but it will employ as its incentive a temporary grant of monopoly power to the innovator. The innovator will use that power to influence prices, thereby distorting the allocation of resources. Let us also assume that without patents the economy will be perfectly competitive. Figure 11.4 describes the consequences of society's choice between adoption and rejection of the patent policy. The axes represent $y(t)$ and $y(t + 1)$, outputs in the initial and the subsequent periods. In the absence of the patent arrangement, the production frontier is AD. With a patent system, the frontier shifts outward to BD. Clearly, with the economy's resources given, patents increase productive capacity.

Welfare productivity, however, is another matter. Without patents, the economy's (competitive) equilibrium point is T, the point of tangency between production frontier, AD, and an indifference curve, II, of the social welfare function. But under a second-period monopoly instituted via the patent system, output is distorted. Second-period output, $y(t + 1)$ is restricted below its optimal level so that instead of the optimal point, W, the equilibrium lies to its right at a point such as R or S. If it happens to fall at R, which lies below II, the indifference curve through the patentless equilibrium, welfare productivity will clearly have fallen, even though productive capacity has grown. Thus, patents can force a trade-off between growth in productive capacity and growth in welfare productivity.

11.8   On Welfare Productivity and Its Measurement

The preceding discussion may suggest, with good reason, that welfare productivity, however it may be defined, is the appropriate measure of the effectiveness with which the economy is pursuing the goals of the people who compose it. After all, we are not concerned, ultimately, with the mere size of the collection of physical objects (and services) the economy turns out, but with the standard of living they yield. Growth in welfare productivity is in some ways a more amorphous concept than growth in productive capacity. Yet in one important sense we shall see that it is more easily observable and measurable. It is more difficult to get at because welfare productivity can be increased in so many ways—via a change in output composition or a change in product quality as well as by elimination of inefficiencies. However, it is a simpler concept because, unlike productive capacity growth, it undertakes to find a number that measures the size of a move from one given point to another point in output space, not of the shift of an entire frontier. We ask by how much the move from point K to point L in figure 11.2 has increased welfare, not by how much an entire production frontier has shifted when it moves from AA' to DD'. Thus, a single number may be able more adequately to represent a change in welfare productivity than it can a shift in productive capacity. Still, since welfare productivity depends on product quality, this feature alone would appear to be a source of intractable difficulties. After all, it is a formidable task just to enumerate the quality changes that must be taken into account in determining what has happened, say, to the productivity of the phonograph industry or the medical profession since 1930, and all but impossible to quantify and aggregate the changes in quality of their products. This has been the bane of economists engaged in measurement of productivity in practice.

Curiously, however, an attempt to evaluate welfare productivity need not enmesh us deeply in the intractable complexities of measurement of quality changes. On the contrary, the welfare productivity approach, at least in principle, automatically solves those problems in a single stroke. Here, as in so many other areas, the price mechanism again displays its amazing efficacy as a conveyor of information. In an economic sense, an improvement in product quality, after all, is not a mere concatenation of modified technological specifications—higher-quality transistors, reduced lubrication requirements, and the like. Rather, the improvement is constituted by the utility that these changes offer consumers. And on our usual premises, that contribution to utility is unambiguously measured by the behavior of a product's relative price. If a product has become better, consumers will be willing to pay more *for a given quantity* of the item. There is no need to go behind the change in this component to seek to determine what part of it is attributable to which element in the complex set of quality changes that the product may have undergone. One may even suspect that further inquiry into quality measurement can prove misleading.

Thus, price analysis can well be considered *the* proper way of dealing with the measurement of changes in product quality. Yet, there is a complication. It is not legitimate simply to use the magnitudes of actual market prices as direct indicators of product quality. True, market prices do tell us what happens to the relative *marginal* utilities of various items as a result of improvements in their quality. But marginal utility is not the pertinent criterion. It can even be totally misleading if not interpreted with care. For example, suppose an improvement in the quality of some product increases the quantity that is sold, which, in turn, elicits scale economies and consequently, in the long run, leads to a reduction in price. Are we to conclude, because the product's relative price and marginal utility have fallen, that its quality, and hence its welfare contribution, has deteriorated? The answer, of course, is that the fall in price has added to (and certainly not reduced) the consumers' surplus contribution of the change in product quality, which is, ultimately (together with its producers' surplus effect), the most reasonable measure of the change. That is, for a particular industry, it would appear that the proper measure of developments in its welfare productivity is the behavior of the sum of producers' and consumers' surplus per unit of input.

The need to measure changes in consumers' and producers' surpluses complicates empirical evaluation of quality changes considerably, but it certainly does not amount to total retreat to the impossible task of identification and evaluation of all of the changes in the attributes of a product that occur with the passage of time. Measurement of changes in these surpluses is a far more manageable task than that. This is definitely true in principle, and to a considerable degree it is so in practice. To calculate welfare productivity growth in automobile production, for example, one need not undertake the (perhaps even undefinable) task of evaluating the degree of improvement in quality of a 1989 model over, say, its 1959 counterpart, including the modifications in comfort, safety, reliability, appearance, etc. In theory, for the purpose one need only estimate the relevant demand and cost relationships and use them to calculate the change in consumers' and producers' surpluses, armed with Robert D. Willig's [1976] assurance that the procedure is (almost perfectly) legitimate. That is, one can use the definable and conceptually observable cost and demand functions to evaluate the indefinable and unmeasurable quality changes. Moreover, in practice, as a good deal of work on hedonic indices has shown, it is actually possible to obtain reasonable econometric estimates of the required magnitudes. Thus, the procedures just described transform measurement of quality changes from a mysterious and ill-defined exercise into one whose outlines, at least, are clear.

11.9   Gross Productivity and the Service Sector of the Economy

Anyone who has thought about the subject is apt to be uncomfortable about discussions of productivity in the services because the very concept is so elusive. Just what is the "product" of education or medical care, and how does one measure it? Is one really forced, as is often done in the services, to measure output quantities via the quantity of input used in their production so that *calculated* productivity remains stagnant, just because of the way it is measured? Fortunately, for many purposes we do not have to face up to these difficulties. To explain why, we must turn to the concept of gross productivity. Gross productivity, in whose calculation absolutely no effort is made to adjust for quality changes, is often easy to measure; but it is, fortunately, also the correct information required for *some* significant types of analysis.

Gross productivity is simply a measure of the number of units of observable "output" per unit of input. For example, in musical performance we can define gross productivity of labor as the number of audience members (or the number of concert performances) per musician labor-hour. Similarly, in the case of higher education, the gross measure of labor productivity can be taken simply as the number of students attending colleges and universities divided by the number of faculty hours devoted to teaching, that is, the student/teacher-time ratio. These are obviously easy to measure and the figures readily available. Analogous measures of gross multifactor productivity in musical performance and education, taking into account other inputs besides musician or teacher time, are also easily constructed.

Why should we ever be interested in gross productivity rather than in a measure that is adjusted for quality changes? The answer is that gross productivity is the primary determinant of the budgets, costs, and prices of the products in question. For example, ignoring other inputs, the cost of education per student is simply the wage per faculty-hour multiplied by the number of faculty hours used, all divided by the number of students. But most of this information is given by gross productivity, which, here, equals the number of students divided by the number of faculty-hours. Therefore, the cost per student is simply the reciprocal of the index of gross productivity multiplied by the average hourly faculty salary. Moreover, this salary figure, unlike the gross productivity component, is determined largely outside the field of endeavor under consideration. Immobility of labor often permits faculty salaries to lag behind other wages and salaries in the economy. But, in the long run, trends in faculty salaries seem to be determined preponderantly outside the university, because of the long-run mobility of labor; and so salary trends tend, over long periods, to be similar everywhere. This means that, in the long run, the only way that university administrations can substantially affect the ratio between education cost per student and cost per unit of output in the remainder of the economy is by changing the rate of growth of gross productivity in colleges and universities. If gross productivity in education lags behind that in the rest of the economy, the cost per student *must* rise faster than cost per unit of output elsewhere, and university fees and total budgets must follow along commensurately.

An oversimplified example will explain most clearly the implications of the preceding observations, suggesting some applications of productivity measurement for which it is simply wrong to take quality changes into account. In particular, we shall see why this is true of certain types of budgeting decisions affected by differentials in productivity growth and for associated resource allocation decisions. Consider an economy that produces only two outputs—call them performance of string quartets and electronic (video) game machines. Suppose the quartets are all written for a

half-hour performance, so that they always require just four musical instruments and two person-hours of labor input per performance. Consequently,
whatever the changes in quality of the product, gross labor productivity
and total factor productivity must both remain absolutely fixed and immutable. Suppose also that electronic games improve in quality, in some
sense, with the passage of time, and that, in addition, gross total factor
productivity in their manufacture grows at a rate of 7% per year (hence
doubling every decade). Let this economy be perfectly competitive and its
overall price level, P_t, stationary so that

$$P_t = P(P_{ct}, c_t, P_{gt}, g_t) = k \tag{1}$$

(where P_{ct} is the price of admission to a concert, c_t is the number of concerts
performed, etc.). Suppose, finally, that both industries use similar inputs
with identical input prices and that income and price elasticities of demand
are such that the output proportion (i.e., the machine-concert ratio) remains
absolutely constant.

Several conclusions follow. First, the price of electronic games, P_g, must
fall and the price of concerts, P_c, must rise at constant percentage rates
satisfying (1) and

$$\left(\frac{\dot{P}_c}{P_c}\right) \bigg/ \left(\frac{\dot{P}_g}{P_g}\right) = 1.07. \tag{2}$$

That is, the price of concerts must rise at an annual rate of 7% relative to
the price of the games. Second, with output proportions constant, the share
of the economy's *inputs* devoted to concerts must increase steadily, at a
rate given by the difference in gross productivity growth of the two
outputs. It should be obvious that to calculate this change in allocation of
inputs there is no need to measure the change in quality of either concert
performance or electronic games.

Next, let us consider the following two applications based on the preceding example:

i. Schools in our imaginary economy need to plan how many classrooms
to build for the training of musicians vis-à-vis the number they need for the
training of electronic game assemblers. A moment's consideration confirms
that *gross* productivity growth is the only required productivity datum. For
example, if labor were the only input, and *in 1980 the labor force had been
divided equally between the two outputs,* by 1990, since gross productivity in
games doubles each decade while gross productivity in music remains
constant, the fixity of output proportions requires that

$$\frac{L_{c90}}{2L_{g90}} = \frac{L_{c80}}{L_{g80}} = 1, \tag{3}$$

where L_{g80} is the size of the 1980 labor force in game production, etc. Hence, we know from our calculation of gross productivity growth alone that two-thirds of the economy's 1990 labor force must be trained as musicians *regardless of developments in quality*. The arithmetic of gross productivity growth dictates beyond dispute the input requirements of each product, given the demand for that item.

ii. As a second application, suppose that half the cost of each concert is paid for by government subsidy. Then budget planning by, say, the National Endowment for the Arts, can be carried out completely with the aid of (1), (2), and (3), which determine *exactly* the growth in real cost of each concert and the number of concerts on the basis of gross productivity growth data alone. In commonsense terms, since gross productivity dictates the input requirements of each output, it also determines that item's budget requirement.

It is true, of course, that developments in quality enter the matter implicitly by determining the course of the relative demands for the two products, which were here subsumed in the premise that output proportions remain fixed. However, the point is that nowhere do we have to *measure* or even define or describe quality change (something we do not even know how to do for the past, much less for the future) in order to calculate the required input-training proportions or the arts subvention budget. For this we need only know *gross* productivity growth and changes in output proportions—both directly observable magnitudes.

11.10   The Choice of Productivity Measure: Some Empirical Comparisons

We shall show now, using actual statistical data, that the concepts discussed in this chapter can yield very different measurements of both annual and average annual productivity growth. More than that: We shall show that because of ambiguities in the notion of growth in productive capacity, different but legitimate measures of this one concept can yield values that vary widely. We use data for the railroad industry, which have been compiled with care by Caves, Christensen, and Swanson [1980] and have already been employed extensively by them and others. We shall only offer estimates of growth in gross productivity and in productive capacity, since welfare productivity is more difficult to measure.[5] We shall show, in particular, that the estimated value of growth in productive capacity is quite sensitive to the procedures used to impose equiproportionate movements upon the production frontier over time. It should be noted that although the analysis is carried out for just a single industry, the conclusions apply with equal (if not greater) force to an aggregate production function; that is, the measurement of productivity growth for an entire economy must also be very sensitive to the procedures used to impose equiproportionate growth.

We begin with what would seem to be the total factor productivity concept whose measurement is most straightforward—crude total factor productivity—a concept that has already been defined here. We have used three sets of input weights in measuring crude TFP growth in the railroad industry: (i) first-period cost share weights, (ii) last-period cost share weights, and (iii) an average of first-period and last-period cost shares. Five inputs are included in the input index: (i) labor, (ii) way and structure, (iii) equipment, (iv) fuel, and (v) materials. Two outputs enter the output index: (i) freight ton-miles and (ii) passenger miles; revenue shares are used as weights. Estimates of annual crude TFP growth rates as well as the average figure for the entire period, 1951–1974, are shown in table 11.1 for each of the three indices. Estimates of annual rates of crude TFP growth turn out to be relatively insensitive to the choice of weights. The maximum difference for any single year in the estimates resulting from the substitution of first-year for last-year weights is 0.53 percentage points (1957–1958) and in only one other case (1951–1952) does the difference exceed 0.3 percentage points. There is only one case in which the sign is different (1956–1957). Except for 1956–1957, where the signs differ, there are only two cases where the percentage difference between estimates of crude TFP growth yielded by the use of the two sets of weights differs by more than 10%: 1951–1952 and 1957–1958. The two estimates of average annual crude TFP growth over the entire period 1951–1974 differ by only 0.09 percentage points, or 3%. It is to be noted that in none of the preceding calculations is there any attempt to make any adjustment for changes in product quality. Consequently, all of the figures derived from those calculations can be described as estimates of what we have called "gross productivity" growth.

Next, we compare three measurements of growth in productive capacity. The first uses a standard Divisia index. The other two are measures described in the appendix to this chapter that were constructed by Caves, Christensen, and Swanson [1980] explicitly for use in the railroad industry. They are designed to avoid some of the more restrictive assumptions that underly the validity of the Divisia index.

Table 11.1
Estimates of annual rates of crude productivity growth in the railroad industry,
1951–1974

Year	First-year weight (%)	Last-year weight (%)	Average weight (%)
1951–1952	2.405	2.021	2.214
1952–1953	1.079	0.995	1.038
1953–1954	2.000	1.762	1.882
1954–1955	7.813	8.080	7.946
1955–1956	3.844	3.830	3.837
1956–1957	0.026	−0.153	−0.063
1957–1958	−0.653	−1.177	−0.914
1958–1959	3.884	3.929	3.907
1959–1960	1.932	1.840	1.886
1960–1961	3.187	2.911	3.050
1961–1962	5.435	5.466	5.451
1962–1963	4.361	4.403	4.382
1963–1964	4.481	4.433	4.457
1964–1965	6.544	6.576	6.560
1965–1966	4.734	4.685	4.709
1966–1967	−1.325	−1.449	−1.387
1967–1968	2.462	2.502	2.482
1968–1969	2.352	2.315	2.334
1969–1970	−2.055	−2.012	−2.034
1970–1971	−2.014	−1.917	−1.966
1971–1972	7.608	7.906	7.756
1973–1974	5.045	4.999	5.022

Average annual productivity growth, 1951–1974 (%)		
2.927	3.014	2.940

Source: Authors' own computations based on Caves, Christensen, and Swanson [1980].

The reader may be surprised at how different the estimates are from each other and from the crude productivity measurements. To show this, we use the data provided in Caves, Christensen, and Swanson [1980, pp. 171, 172, 175]. Three measures will be employed as estimates of annual productivity growth. The first, which we have called the "full Divisia index," measures productivity growth as the difference between a Divisia index of output and a Divisia index based the on five inputs already listed. Our second measure is also a Divisia index. It differs from the first in that only two inputs, labor and capital, are used in the index and the inputs are weighted by the share of labor and capital in the national income generated in the railroad industry. The third measure is the Caves-Christensen-Swanson index ETFP, based on five inputs and two outputs [see appendix, equation (3)]. Finally, for a more limited period, we shall provide estimates of two other Caves-Christensen-Swanson measures. The first of these is π_y^*, which is defined as the maximum rate at which outputs can grow when all input quantities are held constant [see appendix, equation (4).] Similarly, the second measure, π_x^*, indicates the rate at which input quantities can all be decreased proportionately, with the passage of time, when all output quantities are held constant [see appendix, equation (5).]

The estimates are shown in table 11.2. First, it is instructive to look at the estimates of annual average productivity growth over the period 1951–1974. These estimates range from the 1.5% value of ETFP to the 3.6% value of the two-input Divisia index, a 240% difference. Moreover, the two Divisia indices differ by 0.9 percentage points, or by 40%. The estimate of crude productivity growth over this period is about 3% per year, which also differs significantly from each of the three productive capacity growth measures.

Estimates of annual productivity growth are even more sensitive to the choice of measure. For 1952–1953, estimates vary from *negative* 0.6% per year to positive 0.7%. In 1953–1954, they range from −0.2% to 2.3%. In 1956–1957, they range from −1.0% to 0.6%; in 1957–1958, from −2.6% to 1.4%; in 1958–1959, from 2.6% to 4.6%; in 1959–1960, from 1.3% to 2.7%; in 1964–1965, from 4.4% to 8.5%; in 1966–1967, from −2.3% to 1.2%; in 1967–1968, from 0.1% to 3.6%; in 1968–1969, from 0.9% to 2.9%; in 1970–1971, from −4.4% to 1.0%; and in 1973–1974, from −0.6% to 1.3%. There is almost no consistency between any two of these measures.

Estimates of π_y^* and π_x^* are available only for average annual productivity growth for the period from 1955 to 1974. Comparisons of these with the three measures in table 11.2 are provided in table 11.3. The estimates of π_y^* and π_x^* based on the total cost function [equations (4) and (5) in the

Table 11.2
Estimates of annual rates of productivity growth in the railroad industry, 1951–1974, using three different capacity productivity indices

Year	Full Divisia index (DP*) (%)	Divisia index using national income weights (DP*) (%)	Caves-Christensen-Swanson [1980] measure (%)
1951–1952	−0.3	0.5	0.1
1952–1953	0.0	0.7	−0.6
1953–1954	−0.2	2.3	0.1
1954–1955	9.1	9.0	6.7
1955–1956	3.8	4.3	3.1
1956–1957	−0.5	0.6	−1.0
1957–1958	−2.2	1.4	−2.0
1958–1959	4.2	4.6	2.6
1959–1960	1.7	2.7	1.3
1960–1961	2.8	4.1	2.3
1961–1962	5.7	5.9	4.6
1962–1963	4.6	5.0	2.9
1963–1964	4.4	4.3	3.4
1964–1965	6.4	8.5	4.4
1965–1966	4.6	5.5	3.4
1966–1967	−1.5	1.2	−2.3
1967–1968	2.5	3.6	0.1
1968–1969	2.3	2.9	0.9
1969–1970	−2.0	−1.4	−3.5
1970–1971	−1.9	1.0	−4.4
1971–1972	7.9	10.9	7.0
1972–1973	5.5	5.2	4.6
1973–1974	−0.2	−0.6	1.3
Average annual productivity growth rate, 1951–1974 (%)			
	2.5	3.6	1.5

Source: Authors' own computations based on Caves, Christensen, and Swanson [1980].

Table 11.3
Estimates of annual average productivity growth in the railroad industry, 1955–1974, using different capacity productivity indices

Measure	Productivity growth (%)
1. Full Divisia index (DTFP)	2.5
2. Divisia index using national income weights (DTFP)	3.7
3. Caves-Christensen-Swanson [1980] measure ETFP	1.5
4. Caves-Christensen-Swanson [1981] measure π^*	
a. π_y^* (equation (4): total cost function)	0.9–1.0
b. π_x^* (equation (5): total cost function)	0.8
c. π_y^* (equation (4'): variable cost function)	1.8–2.0
d. π_x^* (equation (5'): variable cost function)	1.8

appendix] range from 0.8% to 1.0% per year,[6] which are considerably lower than the Divisia estimates and lower than the ETFP index. The estimates of π_y^* and π_x^* based on the variable cost function [equations (4') and (5')] fall in the range 1.8–2.0% per year, about twice the total cost function figures but still lower than the Divisia-based estimates of productive capacity growth.

11.11   Conclusions

We have shown that various basic concepts of productivity growth— labor productivity, total factor productivity, welfare productivity, productive capacity and gross productivity—have very different meanings and uses and can behave very differently. All of them have been shown to be significant—even the gross productivity growth measure, which makes no adjustments for quality changes and which may seem basically indefensible on first consideration. We have seen also why it may be impossible to devise any robust single-number representation of growth in productive capacity. We saw why explicit adjustments for changes in product quality may be unnecessary. That is, at least in principle, one can hope to deal with the quality change problem through reasonably accurate measurement of growth in welfare productivity. This, moreover, may in some ultimate sense have the best claim as the true measure of productivity growth for purposes of economic analysis.

The empirical results demonstrate that estimates of both annual and annual average productivity growth over fairly long periods are highly sensitive to the choice of productivity concept. Measures of gross productivity differ greatly from those of productive capacity. Moreover, estimates of productive capacity growth are very sensitive to the assumptions used to impose equiproportionate shifts on the production frontier over time. In the empirical literature of productivity growth, no one measure can be employed with confidence as a substitute for or even as an approximation to another. The concept selected should obviously be chosen with care in light of the use that is to be made of it.

Notes

1. The next two sections are intended as expository discussions of TFP, and so they may have little interest for economists, particularly those specializing in productivity analysis. They may, therefore, want to skip directly to section 11.4.

2. That is, maximization of the output of some one good, y_1, given all the other output and input quantities. Specifically, the pertinent premise is that the production relationship is strictly quasi-concave and continuously differentiable.

3. Where we deal with multifactor productivity the concept of a unit of input clearly involves serious aggregation problems. For the discussion here, however, that is an irrelevant complication and it will therefore be ignored. We shall, in effect, proceed on the assumption that all input is homogeneous or that we are concerned with labor productivity. We shall however, return to the aggregation issues later.

4. It is even arguable that a new technique sometimes literally reduces the economy's ability to produce some outputs. For example, the use of concrete in the construction of buildings has probably reduced the opportunities for on-the-job training of stonemasons, whose quality of work on churches and Gothic college buildings may thereby have been impeded.

5. The calculation of the consumers' surplus clearly requires estimates of the demand schedules for railroad output. We will also make no attempt to measure levels of or change in X-inefficiency over time.

6. Two measures of π_y^* were provided, based on alternative methods of estimation of the returns to scale (RTS).

12

Toward Policy for the Longer Term

The future is like everything else; it isn't what it used to be.
(Attributed to Simone de Beauvoir)

A characterizing feature of our work is its preoccupation with the long run. Like many writings on productivity, this book will end with a discussion of policy, but with one (predictable) difference—here there will be little emphasis upon the immediate future. Rather, the discussion will focus upon a rather longer period, which, for the sake of concreteness, we shall arbitrarily take to terminate 30 years hence. The selection of a 30-year interval can be justified only in broad impressionistic terms. On the one side, it clearly exceeds the length of time ordinarily considered in the standard macroeconomic literature, and from that point of view certainly extends beyond what, in a nontechnical sense, is considered to be the short run. Still, it is not so far in the future as to condemn anything written about it as pure science fiction. Indeed, many of the readers of this book may well consider an equal 30-year period in the past—about 1960, when John F. Kennedy was elected president—to lie well within the current era.

We shall begin the chapter by formulating what can, perhaps, be considered to constitute a set of ambitious but not unattainable goals for the American economy in the year 2020. In conformity with the book's orientation, these will relate primarily to productivity and output per capita. We shall then seek to provide a policy program that there is some reason to hope will prove *sufficient* to permit attainment of these goals. That is, our objective will be, not merely to offer a set of policy measures that will work in the right direction, but to formulate a program sufficiently powerful that, if carried out fully, can offer hope that the economy will actually attain the proposed goals.[1]

We shall also take note of empirical evidence, where such evidence is available, that indicates whether the proposed policy measures are likely to move the economy in the desired direction. In addition, where possible, we shall indicate what the available evidence suggests about the (quantitative) effectiveness of the proposed measures, and we shall try to deduce from that how strong a dosage of the proposed medication (that is, what values of the parameters in the proposed policies) is apt to prove sufficient for achievement of the desired goals. Unfortunately, we shall not be able to proceed as far in this direction as we would have liked, because it transpires that much of the requisite empirical evidence is either unavailable or has led to analyses whose results are all too often either ambiguous or mutually contradictory. Still, by proceeding this way we shall go somewhat beyond what is often done in writings on economic policy, where one is frequently left to rely on the author's experience, judgment, or even pure hunches as the basis for the proposals offered. Not that we shall altogether avoid policy proposals supported by little more than our own intuition; but where this occurs we undertake to label the suggestion clearly, indicating explicitly the absence of objective evidence for the policy proposal in question.

12.1 Candidate Goals for Productivity and Per-Capita Output

Obviously, there can be no such thing as the "right" goals for productivity and per-capita output. The notion of an optimal goal is either circular (by what criterion does one judge one target to be superior to another?) or must be taken to imply the existence of some set of "metagoals" (whose choice itself must ultimately be arbitrary) that can be used to evaluate the proximate targets under consideration. All this is to say either that the reasons underlying the choice of objectives about to be proposed must be taken to be self-evident or that those goals themselves must necessarily be treated as arbitrary and without any special standing. Having said this, we venture without further qualifications to suggest a set of targets that at least have the virtue of historical underpinnings.

First, we propose as minimum overall goals the levels of our two key variables that would have obtained if the long-term historical growth rate of the United States would have persisted, without interruption, since 1870, when most of our calculations begin. As a complementary minimum set of goals we propose the levels of productivity and per-capita outputs that one can forecast for the leading industrialized economies—our main economic competitors. Thus, we propose in this chapter to inquire into

Table 12.1
Historically based goals for the United States in the year 2020[a]

	1870 ($)	1979 ($)	Growth rate (%)	2020 projection ($)
GDP/work-hour	0.70	8.28	2.27	21.00
GDP/capita	764	6,055	1.90	13,200

Source: Maddison [1982, pp. 8, 212.]
a. All figures are in 1970 U.S. dollars.

what will be necessary in order to achieve whichever of these two targets turns out to be the more demanding for the year 2020. This compound standard of achievement will have to be satisfied if the United States is to remain among the world's economic leaders and is, at the same time, to experience no long-term slowdown below its own historical performance.

Before turning to details, one more preliminary point must be made. With countries such as Japan and West Germany having recently grown so much faster than we, it follows that straightforward extrapolation of their postwar growth rates must inevitably make their performance, if predicted mechanically in that way, the more difficult of our two subtargets to meet; indeed, it can constitute a target that may prove altogether unrealistic and perhaps even unattainable. But if there is any valid ground (as discussed in chapter 5) for the convergence hypothesis (which holds that many leading industrial economies can be expected to approach similarity in growth rates because the previous laggards will largely have run out of technological practices to learn from the industrial leaders), then this must be taken into account in making our forecasts for the Japans and the West Germanys of the future. Specifically, it means that while our forecasts must take into account the relatively rapid growth rates those countries have already achieved, they must also incorporate any tendency toward deceleration exhibited by those growth rates.

Let us turn, then, to our goals for American productivity and per-capita output, and to the calculations that underlie them. First, let us consider what follows from the historical growth record. Using Maddison's [1982] figures once again (table 12.1), we find that between 1870 and 1979 U.S. gross domestic product per work-hour (labor productivity) grew at an average annual rate of 2.27% (continuously compounded). The corresponding figure for gross domestic product per capita is 1.9%. In 1970 dollars, GDP per work-hour in 1979 is reported to have been a bit more than $8.25, which, when projected forward at the historical annual growth rate, means that in the year 2020 the American economy should be turning out approximately $21 in GDP per work-hour if there is to have been no long-term slowdown. This calls for an increase of some 150% in 41 years, which will be remarkable if achieved, but it follows from the historical basis of this growth-rate goal that it is by no means unprecedented. Similarly, the target for American GDP per capita, dictated by its historical growth rate, is a bit more than $13,000 1970 dollars, approximately a 120% rise from its $6,000 level in 1979.[2]

So much for the performance requirements that follow from the goal that the economy not fall behind its historical growth in labor productivity and per-capita output. The second part of our goal, continued international economic leadership, as one may suspect, is perhaps even more demanding. The word "perhaps" is used here because this time our target must unavoidably be still more elusive and conjectural. This has to be so because in order to estimate what performance is entailed in keeping up with other countries it is necessary, somehow, to predict (or assume) what those other countries will turn out to have achieved by the year 2020. Since no one is really in any position to make such a forecast (even if it is hedged by a plenitude of *caveats*), we have chosen to employ a strictly mechanistic projection procedure, whose shortcomings are obvious, but whose virtue lies in its relative neutrality. All the numbers reported will be rounded severely, with a plus or a minus used to indicate whether the number actually calculated is slightly higher or slightly lower than the number shown.

We experimented with different projection methods, ranging from an assumption that each country's labor productivity and GDP per capita would continue to grow at its average 1950–1979 rates, to the opposite extreme, taking each country to slow down to the long-term U.S. rate of growth. A moderately attractive compromise seemed to be the following: Since nearly 40 of the 70 years between 1950 and 2020 have already elapsed, one can take 4/7ths of each country's growth rate to be equal to that experienced between 1950 and 1979 (or 1980—depending on the data source, as will be seen presently). The remaining 3/7ths—that is, a particular country's growth rate for the 30 years between 1990 and 2020 —is then taken to be the average of its own growth rate for the period 1950–1979(80) and the historical growth rate figure for the United States that is given in table 12.1. In other words, this compromise calculation assumes that during the next 30 years each other country in the comparison group will have caught up sufficiently to cut its advantage of backwardness relative to the United States to the point where its growth rate will have fallen to the midpoint between that of the United States and the rate it itself had previously experienced. Later, we shall provide some (casual) empirical observations that will help us slightly in evaluating this premise.

Table 12.2 and figure 12.1 sum up the results of these calculations for GDP per work-hour. The table repeats the U.S. figures based on the historical extrapolations in table 12.1 and, in addition, provides the estimates just described for the 15 other industrialized countries included in the basic Maddison tables. The countries other than the United States are listed in descending order of extrapolated level of GDP per work-hour for the year 2020. The extrapolated figures are shown in the fourth column of the table; for example, projected German GDP per work-hour in 2020 is equal to nearly 35 1970 dollars. The fifth column of the table shows for each country the average annual growth rate for the period 1979–2020 necessary for it to achieve the projected productivity level. Thus, Germany is taken to achieve an annual growth rate of more than 3.9%. Finally, the last column shows what rate of productivity growth the United States will have to maintain on the average over the next 30 years in order not to fall behind each country's projected productivity level in 2020. Thus, this last column indicates that to stay abreast of Germany, American labor productivity will have to grow at an annual rate of 3.5%. Because of its head start in 1979, this figure is not as high as the 3.9% figure forecast for Germany itself, but it is considerably larger than the 2.27% historic American growth rate.

This immediately suggests the basic moral of table 12.2 and its companion figure 12.1. Both indicate that the historic U.S. growth rate is apt to prove insufficient to maintain America's productivity leadership. With that growth rate, 9 of the 15 other countries in the table are projected to surpass the American economy in labor productivity level by 2020. One may well wish to reject the German projection, which is quite out of line with the others, as an artificial result of the low economic position of that country right after World War II. This permitted it an extraordinary growth rate during its recovery period, one that it could not hope to sustain thereafter. Recent data do, indeed, suggest that Germany's long-run productivity growth rate may be overestimated by the calculation here. However, the table indicates that there are 4 other countries whose projected productivity levels will require the United States to achieve a productivity growth rate of 3–3.1% per year if it is not to fall behind. This is by no means an easy target. It calls for U.S. productivity growth about 0.8 percentage points higher (about 35% higher) than what it was able to achieve on the average over the period 1950–1979. This, then, is the productivity growth

Table 12.2
GDP per work-hour, projections for the year 2020 (in 1970 U.S. relative prices)

	1950 ($) (1)	1979 ($) (2)	Growth rate 1950–1979 (%) (3)	2020 projection ($) (4)	Growth rate 1979–2020 (%) (5)	Rate for U.S. parity (%)[a] (6)
U.S.	4.25	8.28	2.30	21 −	2.27	2.27
Germany	1.40	6.93	5.52	35 −	3.93	3.50
France	1.85	7.11	4.64	30 −	3.49	3.11
Japan	0.59	4.39	6.92	30 −	4.65	3.10
Austria	1.25	5.89	5.35	29 −	3.85	3.01
Belgium	2.11	7.31	4.28	28 +	3.30	3.00
Holland	2.27	7.48	4.11	28 −	3.21	2.97
Italy	1.37	5.83	4.99	26 +	3.67	2.81
Norway	2.03	6.65	4.09	25 −	3.20	2.67
Sweden	2.34	6.71	3.63	23 −	2.97	2.46
Finland	1.48	5.26	4.37	21 −	3.35	2.24
Canada	3.33	7.03	2.58	19 +	2.43	2.03
Denmark	1.82	5.27	3.67	18 −	2.99	1.88
Australia	3.05	6.48	2.60	18 −	2.44	1.84
U.K.	2.40	5.48	2.85	16 −	2.57	1.56
Switzerland	2.21	5.12	2.90	15 −	2.59	1.42

Source: Maddison [1982, pp. 8, 212] and our own calculations.
a. Rate of productivity growth that the United States will have to maintain on the average over the next 30 years in order not to fall behind each country's projected productivity level in 2020.

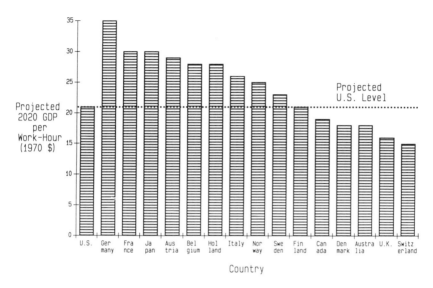

Figure 12.1
GDP per work-hour, 2020 projections, 1970 dollars.

goal for the United States to which the remainder of the chapter will address itself.

A word should be said here about the plausibility of the projections on which the preceding calculation is based. Viewed in one way, the extrapolations for the countries other than the United States can be considered very conservative, because the underlying calculation assumes those economies to be converging with some rapidity toward the historic U.S. growth rate. Moreover, a comparison of column 5 with column 3 of table 12.2 indicates that the projected growth rates are in every case well below the same country's actual growth rate during 1950–1979. On the other hand, the projected growth rates are not so low as to rule them out of the question on grounds of excessive conservatism. Recently, Maddison [1987] published a set of more up-to-date estimates of productivity growth rates for 6 of the countries in the table. These estimates indicate that for France, Germany, Japan, Holland, the United Kingdom and the United States actual productivity growth in the period 1973–1984 was below, and sometimes well below, the projected growth rates in column five of table 12.2.[3] Here it is also suggestive, though dangerous if taken as an indicator of a long-run metamorphosis, to note that according to recent estimates of the U.S. Bureau of Labor Statistics, the growth of labor productivity in U.S. manufacturing exceeded that of both France and West Germany, though it remained somewhat behind that of Japan as well as those of Italy and the United Kingdom.[4]

Table 12.3 and figure 12.2 show the corresponding projections for real GDP per capita, this time using data provided by Summers and Heston [1984] for 1950 and 1980, calculated in what they describe as "1975 international dollars." We follow their terminology in referring to their statistics for real GDP per capita as *RGDP*. The U.S. figures in table 12.3 are based on those in table 12.1, but after some slight readjustment, since table 12.1 is calculated in 1970 dollars while table 12.3 is in 1975 dollars, so that the numbers required modification for the inflation that had taken place in the interim. The RGDP calculations also suggest that the historic U.S. growth rate is apt to prove insufficient to retain U.S. leadership in 2020. This time only 5 of the 15 other countries are projected to run ahead of the United States by 2020 if the United States does not exceed its historic growth rate. Here, the challenge is perhaps not as great as that in labor productivity, except for Japan. We may wish to reject the Japanese projection, which is a result of its low output level right after World War II. As a result, we obtain a target RGDP growth rate for the United States of perhaps 3.1% per year, compared with its 1950–1980 average of nearly 2.3%.

Still, one must be under no illusion that achievement of such a target will be easy. The 1950–1980 period includes what Maddison has referred to as "the postwar golden age" because of its extraordinary growth performance. The targets now under discussion are even higher than the growth rates achieved during that period. Even the recent period of recovery in productivity growth has so far not brought us near that target, and the most recent data available suggest leveling off, rather than continuation of the upward movement. All this indicates that strong policy measures, representing considerable departures from business as usual, will be required to attain these goals.

12.2   Toward Policy Measures Sufficient to Attain Our Productivity Goals

Before turning to the details of the program that will be examined here, it may be useful to offer an outline of its contents. Conventional discussion of productivity growth usually emphasizes three prime determinants of an economy's productivity performance: the investment rate, the magnitude

Table 12.3
GDP per capita (RGDP), projections for the year 2020 (in 1975 "international dollars")

	1950 ($) (1)	1980 ($) (2)	Growth rate 1950–1980 (%) (3)	2020 projection ($) (4)	Growth rate 1980–2020 (%) (5)	Rate for U.S. parity (%)[a] (6)
U.S.	4,550	9,089	2.29	19,000 –	1.90	1.90
Japan	910	5,996	6.28	31,000 –	4.09	3.05
Germany	1,888	6,967	4.35	24,000 +	3.13	2.46
Austria	1,693	6,052	4.25	21,000 –	3.07	2.06
France	2,221	6,678	3.67	20,000 +	2.78	2.01
Norway	2,403	6,825	3.48	20,000 +	2.69	1.97
Finland	1,970	5,939	3.68	18,000 +	2.79	1.73
Canada	3,596	7,521	2.46	18,000 –	2.18	1.71
Sweden	3,184	7,142	2.69	18,000 –	2.30	1.69
Denmark	2,876	6,748	2.84	17,000 +	2.37	1.63
Belgium	2,454	6,293	3.14	17,000 +	2.52	1.60
Switzerland	3,116	6,610	2.51	16,000 –	2.20	1.41
Holland	2,332	5,856	3.07	16,000 –	2.48	1.39
Italy	1,379	4,661	4.06	15,000 +	2.98	1.31
Australia	3,324	6,308	2.14	14,000 +	2.02	1.10
U.K.	2,700	4,990	2.05	11,000 –	1.97	0.47

Source: Summers and Heston [1984] and our own calculations.
a. Rate of growth that the United States will have to maintain on the average over the next 30 years in order not to fall behind each country's projected RGDP level in 2020.

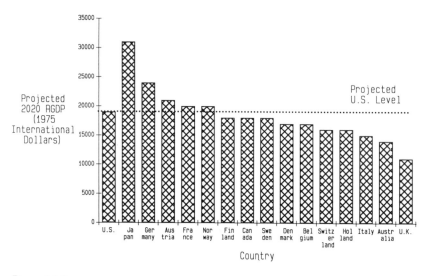

Figure 12.2
Real GDP per capita, 2020 projections, 1975 "international dollars."

of the effort devoted to basic and applied research, and the education of the labor force and managerial personnel. We do not differ from this judgment, and shall propose some policy programs, most of them rather conventional, to deal with each of these.[5]

In addition to these three determinants, the role of *entrepreneurship* also usually figures in discussions of the forces that drive productivity growth. While the subject of entrepreneurship is broached repeatedly, its discussion is generally short because, for very good reasons, it is difficult to say much about it. As in Mark Twain's remark about the weather, everyone is concerned about entrepreneurial performance but no one seems to know what to do about it. It seems to be widely held that the number, capability, and performance of a country's entrepreneurs depend on its cultural traditions, current social climate, prevailing psychological propensities, and other such influences about which we know little by way of effective measures for their modification. While we accept the view that these influences are important, we do not believe that they are the only significant determinants of the availability and performance of entrepreneurship. Though the details will be left for a companion volume devoted exclusively to the entrepreneur (Baumol [forthcoming]), our revised view of the subject will permit us to offer some policy proposals for this arena, proposals that, while not at odds with what has already been said elsewhere about productivity policy, appear to go somewhat beyond the bounds that have so far circumscribed the discussion. We shall refer to these as our more unconventional policy proposals. We believe that it will be possible to make a good case for the policy measures that will be suggested here, but, unfortunately, quantification in this area will elude us, in part because of the nature of this portion of the proposed program and perhaps partly because its comparative novelty has so far precluded systematic exploration by others.

In addition to our more unconventional proposals relating to entrepreneurship, we shall end by describing a policy measure that can well be considered to be quite heterodox. While not advocating its adoption, certainly not without further evidence indicating that it really is needed and without further study of its probable consequences, we shall offer it as a standby proposal, as a program to which one can turn if steps that are less radical turn out to bring us short of achievement of suitable objectives. This program, like one of those that will be proposed in the set relating to entrepreneurial performance, entails changes in the structure of the rewards offered for different sorts of entrepreneurial activity, so as to provide incentives for the reallocation of entrepreneurial effort in the direction of enhanced productivity growth. Our heterodox proposal calls for restructuring of the tax system to minimize all disincentives for any activity directed toward that goal, and to offer incentives for a shift in that direction. All of this will be explored in some detail in the remainder of the chapter.

12.3   A Program for Investment in Productive Capacity

As has been noted (see, for example, Solow [1988]), while investment is not the only means to enhance the growth of output, it is clearly one of the most direct measures available to increase the productivity of labor. Offering the work force more, better, and more up-to-date plant and equipment enables each hour of labor to turn out more of what it could previously produce.

Even a preliminary glance at the relevant statistical data suggests that there must be a strong relationship between the two. Table 12.4 indicates for seven countries the average growth rates over the postwar period of the nonresidential capital stock of each country, of its capital-labor ratio, and of its GDP per work-hour. The first thing to be noted from this table is the remarkably close correlation between its first and last columns, that is,

Table 12.4
Annual growth rates: capital-labor ratio, capital stock, and GDP per work-hour,
7 countries, 1950–1979

Country	Growth in capital-labor ratio (%)	Growth in nonresidential capital stock (%)	Growth in GDP per work-hour (%)
U.S.	2.44	3.61	2.30
Canada	2.95	5.03	2.58
U.K.	3.55	3.29	2.85
France	4.18	4.11	4.64
Italy	5.10	4.82	4.99
Germany	5.66	5.28	5.52
Japan	7.11	8.36	6.92

Source: Maddison [1982].

between the rates of labor productivity growth and the growth of the capital-labor ratio. Not only is it invariably true that the higher the one of these figures is, the higher the other is also, but, in addition, with the exception of France, that the ratio of the two figures hardly varies from country to country.[6] Now, we are well aware that correlation does not imply causation, and in chapter 8 considerable discussion has already been devoted to the highly plausible hypothesis that rapid productivity growth stimulates growth of a nation's capital stock, as well as the other way around. Nevertheless, it seems farfetched to discount altogether an association as tight as that exhibited in table 12.4 as some indication of the power of capital accumulation to enhance the growth of labor productivity.

It is, perhaps, useful at this point to perform a standard statistical analysis to estimate the relation between labor productivity growth and the growth in the capital-labor ratio.[7] This calculation (described in note 7) led to the conclusion that a 1-percentage-point increase in the growth rate of labor productivity is associated with a 3-percentage-point increase in the growth rate of the capital-labor ratio. That is, if one believes that the former is caused by the latter, it follows that one must raise the amount of capital per worker by 3 percentage points in order to achieve a rise in labor productivity growth of 1 percentage point. However, this is, perhaps, a very conservative estimate, since the statistical procedure that we utilized assumes implicitly that no technological changes were automatically introduced in the process of acquisition of new capital equipment. But that is surely implausible, since new plant and equipment usually embodies the latest (more productive) technology. In particular, if one country borrows

technology from another during the catching-up process, then technological change is normally heavily dependent on the purchase of the new
capital that is adapted to the transferred techniques. Indeed, the conservatism of the preceding estimate is also suggested by the regression results
shown in note 6, which suggest that a 1-percentage-point increase in the
capital-labor ratio is associated with a 1-percentage-point increase in labor
productivity growth—an estimated effect three times as great as the one
that was reported here. It is not implausible that the actual rise in labor
productivity attributable to a percentage point increase in capital per worker
probably lies in between these two figures (0.33 and 1.0), and we shall
conservatively assume the correct approximation of the effect to be 0.5,
meaning that a 1-percentage-point rise in the capital-labor ratio is required
to achieve a half-percentage-point rise in the growth of labor productivity.

We can use the preceding figures to arrive at an exceedingly crude
estimate of the rise in investment or savings performance that will be
required to enable the United States to achieve the increase in productivity
growth suggested as a reasonable target earlier in this chapter. Roughly
speaking, this calls for a rise of nearly 1 percentage point, that is, almost a
50% rise in the 1950–1979 growth rate of labor productivity, which was
2.3%. The preceding paragraph suggests (if we assume it to constitute an
approximation to a causal relationship) that this can be achieved via a 2-
percentage-point (1/0.5) increase in the growth rate of the U.S. capital-
labor ratio. Since employment has grown at 1.5% per year since the beginning of this century, this would entail a 3.5-percentage-point growth rate in
the capital stock if employment continues to grow at this historical rate.
The reason for the larger size of the growth rate of capital stock is, of course,
the increase in employment, which must be *surpassed* by the capital stock if
there is to be any increase in the growth of the capital-labor ratio. Since the
nonresidential capital stock of the United States has been growing over the
postwar period at an annual rate of about 3.6% per year, this means that if
the proposed productivity target is to be achieved *exclusively* through a rise
in domestic investment (saving), the growth rate of these must expand by
almost 100% (3.5/3.6). While the preceding discussion cannot seriously be
proposed as a piece of watertight analysis, it *is* intended to suggest the
order of magnitude of the effort that will be required.[8] Yet we must warn
the reader that even so modest an interpretation of our estimated figures is
exceedingly perilous. One of the main reasons is a fact we have repeatedly
emphasized: there is a two-way relationship between capital formation and
productivity growth—the latter undoubtedly stimulates the former, as
well as the other way around. Consequently, statistics showing that the

one figure rises whenever the other does give us no indication of how much productivity growth has really been contributed by investment. After all, it is conceivable that the bulk of the association we observe may arise from the investment stimulated by productivity growth and that it, therefore, tells us little of the (reverse) effect of investment on productivity growth, which may possibly even be negligible. Unfortunately, while a number of statistical studies have attempted to disentangle the two components of the two-way relationship, their results have been inconclusive, and the conclusions of some of these have literally contradicted those of some others.[9]

What instruments do policymakers have at their disposal to work toward an increase in investment such as we have suggested may be appropriate? Unfortunately, the determinants of the investment and savings rates seem to have been studied only sporadically. Moreover, several authoritative surveys of the literature concur in the conclusion that the statistical studies have yielded results that contradict one another and that are certainly not conclusive (see Aaron [1982, esp. pp. 40ff], Sturm [1983, pp. 175–178], Lindsey [1987, pp. 9–19], and Lipsey and Kravis [1987b, pp. 47–55]). Investigators have examined the effects on savings rates of taxation in general, of capital gains taxes in particular, of government rules requiring people to save via a social security system, and of the competition for investment resources between government and private saving. In almost every one of these areas the results have been, in Aaron's [1982] words, "statistical cacophony." Lipsey and Kravis [1987b, p. 55] provide a useful summary of the few conclusions that do emerge:

... these analyses point to [intercountry] differences in growth rates as the main source of differences in savings rates, with faster growth associated with higher ratios. There is some much less conclusive evidence that high levels of social security or other pension payments are associated with lower household savings rates.

The level of capital taxation [is] often thought of as a suitable policy variable for influencing saving rates.... But the relation to investment rates remains obscure.... There does seem to be a preponderance of evidence that the level of government saving or dissaving does affect the level of national saving.... Large deficits, because they are not offset or not fully offset by private saving, do reduce the national saving rate.

These are weak conclusions, and certainly offer us little quantitative basis on which to arrive at firm estimates of magnitudes such as appropriate changes in tax rates. We seem, after all, to be left largely with intuition and conclusions stemming from common wisdom for the details of our policy recommendations. As Aaron [1982] sums up the strength of the empirical evidence and its usefulness as a basis for the design of policy, "Using the best that economic theory and statistical techniques have to offer, [economists] have produced a series of studies that can be selectively cited by the true believers of conflicting hunches or by people with political agendas that they seek to advance" (p. 51). We seem obviously to have been left to our own devices in the formulation of the details of a program for the stimulation of savings and investment.

Four policy measures that have been considered as means for the public sector to stimulate the growth of investment and savings include the adoption of a real (inflation-adjusted) rather than a nominal rate of return as the basis for the calculation of the capital gains tax, a sharp reduction (over the long run) of nonproductive government investments such as military outlays, in order to reduce the magnitude of the "crowding out" effect upon productive investment, a reduction in the considerable tax incentives for investment in private housing, and further moves modifying the system of personal taxation in the direction of an expenditure rather than an income tax.

1. *Real Capital Gains Taxation.*[10] The entire American tax system, like those of most other countries, has been based on nominal values, using actual dollar figures from different years as though inflation had caused no changes in their purchasing power; and in an inflationary period, this has automatically introduced a variety of distortions and disincentives. Yet, there are good reasons for *particular* concern over the effects of failure to index tax rates in the case of capital gains. It is clear that capital gains are a major component of the return on investment. Therefore, it is certainly plausible that excessive taxation on this type of earning will be a substantial disincentive to capital formation. Most important, because a capital gains tax is a tax on a *differential* in value (the value of the asset when it is sold minus its value when acquired), whereas most taxes (e.g., sales and income taxes) are based on an absolute economic magnitude (the price of the taxed item or the taxpayer's income), the capital gains tax is particularly vulnerable to severe distortion by inflation. An individual whose real income has fallen because of inflation will nevertheless be subject to income taxation only if the real income is positive, *but the sale of a capital asset is subject to taxation on the nominal capital gain even when there is a real capital loss.* An example should help to make the point clear. If, over the course of two decades when the general price level has risen 150%, an asset's price has risen only 100%, the holder of that asset will have suffered a purchasing power loss of one-third of the funds invested. Yet the holder will be taxed

as if the asset's value had actually *risen* 100%. It is difficult to doubt that this significantly discourages investment, so that a shift toward the use of real (inflation-adjusted) figures as the basis for *capital* gains taxation will substantially enhance investment. Here, it should, of course, be stressed that equity considerations may call for a move in the opposite direction. Yet it is surely possible to avoid any shift in the tax burden from the rich to the middle class and the poor while reducing the (marginal) disincentive effects of taxation on savings, that is, by cutting the tax rate on any *additions* to an individual's income that are attributable to a rise in savings.

While this proposal has been advocated widely, several reservations must be noted. First, as was observed earlier, there seems to be no compelling empirical evidence showing that reductions in taxes on capital gains or any other tax rates exert a substantial stimulative effect on total saving. Second, since the rate of taxation of personal income in the United States is, in fact, *below* that in most industrial free-market economies, it seems difficult to attribute American's apparently low savings rate to this influence. The same arguments suggest caution in evaluation of the frequently proposed move toward taxation of actual consumer expenditures, rather than total income, as a means to decrease the burden of taxation on savings.

Finally, some care must be exercised, on somewhat analogous grounds, in dealing with the suggestion that an appropriate measure to stimulate productive investment in the United States is to reduce tax incentives for investment in private housing. As was indicated in chapter 8, Americans do not devote a higher percentage of their incomes to private housing than the residents of other high-income countries do. If anything, the United States is relatively low on that score. Thus, private housing does not seem to be a specially serious source of "crowding out"—that is, of competition for funds that might otherwise go into private investment in that country. This is in marked contrast to the arena of military expenditure to which we turn next.

2. *"Crowding Out" and Nonproductive Government Investment.* Many economists believe that, except in periods of recession, a large government deficit and the borrowing it necessarily entails can be a substantial impediment to private investment in plant and equipment. The process entails competition between the public and private sectors for real resources—the labor, raw materials, and other inputs needed by private enterprise if it is to produce new plant and equipment. Government borrowing is then said to "crowd out" private investment from the markets for such resources. This

Table 12.5
Defense expenditure as percentage of GNP for 1983, 13 industrialized countries

Country	Defense as % of total expenditure	Total expenditure as % of GNP	Defense as % of GNP
U.S.	23.7	25.3	6.00
Norway	8.6	39.7	3.41
France	7.3	44.8	3.27
Sweden	6.9	46.9	3.24
Netherlands	5.3	59.4	3.15
Belgium	5.2	56.7	2.95
Germany	9.3	31.1	2.89
Australia	9.7	26.7	2.59
Canada	8.0	25.6	2.05
Switzerland	10.4	19.4	2.02
Italy	3.5	52.8	1.85
Finland	5.5	31.6	1.74
Austria	3.2	39.9	1.28

Source: *World Bank* [1987, p. 223].

rivalry between government and business manifests itself most obviously in the form of high interest rates, as government borrowing drives up the cost of funds, making business investment more costly and less profitable than it would have been otherwise. Restraining public expenditure, then, can make private investment easier and more rewarding financially.

The United States is not alone in experiencing expansion of the share of public sector outlays as a proportion of its gross national product. The spread of the welfare state and the rising cost of many public services (as a consequence of the cost disease) are among the influences to which this trend can be attributed. Only in terms of one major expenditure is the experience of the U.S. public sector since World War II unique—in its military outlays. Among the free-enterprise, industrialized economies none has approached the United States in terms of proportion of GNP devoted to the defense establishment in the postwar era. Thus, table 12.5 and figure 12.3 show that in 1983 the American share of GNP devoted to military purposes was more than 1.75 times as high as the closest runner up among 13 free-market, industrial countries, and nearly 2.5 times as high as the average for the remaining 12.

We obviously can claim no expertise on military matters and can therefore only go so far as suggesting that productive investment in the United

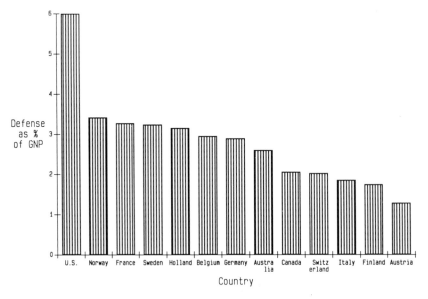

Figure 12.3
Defense expenditure as percentage of GNP, 1983. Source: *World Bank* [1987, p. 223].

States (as well as that in the Soviet Union) can benefit substantially from further progress on mutual disarmament. Given the spread of prosperity among the industrial nonsoviet economies, the United States may also be able to reduce its contribution to the cost of military preparation within the North Atlantic Treaty Organization (NATO). Either of these developments might contribute materially toward attainment of the long-term American productivity-growth goals proposed here.

12.4   Strengthening Research and Development

Because innovation is a key element in the stimulation of productivity, an obvious step toward enhancement of productivity growth is facilitation of the research that makes innovation possible. There is an extensive literature that attempts to estimate the "return" to R&D. The basic technique is the use of a statistical regression analysis in which the rate of productivity growth is assumed to depend on the ratio of national R&D expenditures to national output. Estimated (direct) returns generally fall in the range from 20%–30% (see National Science Foundation [1977], Nadiri [1980], Griliches [1979, 1980a,b], Mansfield [1980], Griliches and Lichtenberg [1981], and Wolff and Nadiri [1987]) and, more recently, on the order of 40–50% (see

Griliches [1986]). If we use a 25% rate of return as a compromise, then it follows that a 4-percentage-point increase in R&D expenditures as a proportion of GNP would be required to raise productivity growth by 1 percentage point. However, estimates of the so-called "social rate of return" to research and development (in which the effect of R&D on both the productivity of the firm engaging in R&D and that of other firms in the industry and associated industries are included—the so-called "spillover" effect), are typically much higher and range from about 40% to 75% (see Terleckyj [1974, 1980], Scherer [1982], or Wolff and Nadiri [1987], for example). If we take a 50% figure as a plausible guess, it follows that research and development expenditures would have to increase by 2 percentage points in relation to output in order to raise productivity growth by 1 percentage point.

The United States spends a slightly higher proportion of its output on research and development than other industrial countries do. Since the mid-1960s, however, several other countries, notably West Germany and Japan, have devoted an increasing share of their output to R&D, and the proportion of their GNP spent on these activities is now only slightly smaller than that of the United States. In absolute expenditures, however, the United States still dominates the industrial world in volume of resources devoted to research and development.

In discussing R&D it is helpful to distinguish between basic and applied research:

1. *Support for Basic Research.* A hallmark of basic research is the unpredictability of the uses to which its results will be put and, consequently, of the identity of those who will benefit from it. This gives rise to a variety of issues. The first is the nature of the gains that basic research offers to the country that carries it out. It has been argued that basic research expenditures purchase little advantage in the productivity race because, usually, the research results soon become available to everyone and other economies may be able to appropriate the bulk of the benefits by concentrating their research resources on application and development.

It is suggestive that the United States appears to have been the world leader in basic research, according to indexes such as shares of gross national product devoted to this activity and share of Nobel prizes, throughout the period when the country's productivity growth fell behind that of its commercial rivals. There is something to the argument, although matters are not quite so simple as it suggests. For example, basic research activity contributes to the process of scientific and technical training and helps to provide the skilled labor force necessary for success in innovation. Familiarity with the details of current basic research may also suggest applications more quickly. Whatever the validity of these qualifications, however, they are not the main point. The primary productivity contribution of basic research is *not* the advantage it confers on one economy relative to others. We have emphasized earlier that the United States faces two rather different productivity issues: the slowdown in its own productivity growth and its lag behind other countries. While closer inspection has revealed both these problems to be less serious than is often supposed, they probably are not altogether absent, and their future threat can certainly not be ruled out. Now, while basic research outlays may or may not make a large difference in the degree to which the United States will succeed in its attempt to catch up with other economies, it is surely vital for a durable reversal of the fall in overall U.S. productivity growth.

The unpredictability of the beneficiaries of basic research has a second and more familiar implication: Private enterprise cannot be relied on to devote to this activity the quantity of resources called for by the public interest. Basic research is the illustration *par excellence* of the "free-rider" problem—that is, the opportunity it presents for beneficiaries to avoid payment of a suitable share of the costs. When it is difficult or impossible to collect payments from the users of a product, that product is obviously not one that will prove attractive to firms operated on the profit motive. This implies that if society is to have the basic research activity that its own interests call for, then the government will have to pay most of the bill. This has, of course, long been recognized.

In the United States, the bulk of basic research has been carried out at universities and research institutes, with funding provided by the public sector. There is little prospect that this arrangement will change and probably no reason that it should. The complementarity of the research and teaching activities and the availability of scientists and scholars of outstanding ability at universities may make it desirable that much of the nation's basic research continues to be carried out at those institutions. Given these conclusions, it has been recommended that the government undertake a commitment to a high level of funding of basic research, particularly that which is carried out in the nation's universities. Moreover, it has been urged that such funding achieve an increased degree of consistency and precommitment of support for substantial periods in order to facilitate long-term planning by researchers and to encourage projects that cannot be expected to yield rapid results.

2. *Applied Research.* Whereas basic research may contribute primarily to the nation's effort to grapple with the productivity slowdown rather than with its lag behind other countries, applied research and development almost undoubtedly serves both causes. Yet, despite its importance, this activity can, to a far greater degree, be left to the private sector to finance and carry out. Here, in general, there is little reason to question the efficacy of the profit motive as the requisite stimulus. Later, however, we shall suggest a substantial exception to this conclusion.

It is, of course, appropriate for government to carry out or finance research and development in defense, air traffic control, and other areas whose results are likely to have direct uses by the public sector and also to do so in such fields as health and environmental protection, which serve the public interest but are unattractive commercial propositions. But aside from these kinds of direct government participation, the public sector can, in general, probably encourage applied R&D activity most effectively by explicit removal or modification of policies (such as the threat of disapproval, on antitrust grounds, of joint ventures in research by several firms in an industry) that impede or discourage private efforts.

12.5   Entrepreneurship and Technology Transfer

Since Joseph Schumpeter's monumental contributions on the theory of entrepreneurship, economists have tended to identify the work of the entrepreneur with the completely novel innovation—with the putting into practice of some technique of production, marketing, or business administration that had never been employed before. But anyone studying the history of technological advance cannot fail to be impressed rather rapidly with the critical role of those enterprising individuals whose specialization is the introduction to new geographic locations of techniques that have been practiced elsewhere, sometimes for considerable periods. This activity, which is often referred to as "technology transfer" by the recipient economy, and as "imitation" or even as "stealing of ideas" by the country from which they are derived, has fueled productivity throughout the Western world long before the Japanese attained mastery of the approach. The sixteenth-century Dutch, on the verge of becoming economic leaders of the world, borrowed heavily from the techniques of the Italians, the outgoing leaders. By then, the English were already learning not only from the Low Countries but also from other parts of the continent. The Americans borrowed heavily from the English and from other European sources, particularly from the time they achieved independence up until the middle of the nineteenth century. And even as the United States was learning from Britain, the favor was being reciprocated: America, for example, learning about canal building, the steam engine, and the railroad locomotive from Great Britain, but the steamboat and the critical notion of uniform inter-changeable components for guns, clocks, and other machines having mi-grated in the other direction. (For references on these matters see, e.g., North and Thomas [1973, p. 153], Hobsbawm [1969, p. 137], and Stapleton [1987].)

The essential fact, then, is that no industrialized nation has failed to benefit from the transfer of technology from elsewhere. Moreover, there is reason to believe that the search and seizure of opportunities for such transfer is among the most valuable contributions of the entrepreneur to the productivity of an economy. The entire world benefits from the activ-ity. Indeed, it is arguable that the bulk of the improvement in the standard of living in each and every one of the industrialized economies that has occurred since the Industrial Revolution is attributable to innovations that derived from foreign rather than domestic sources. Certainly, among the dozen or so countries that are in the world's economic vanguard, each constantly is in the process of modifying and improving its economic practices, that is, in generating new techniques and procedures. Each can then benefit from the new ideas that it itself is generating; but on the average it can clearly benefit even more by rapid absorption and adoption of the new ideas that the 11 or so other leader countries are simultaneously generating. Obviously, there is more to be learned from 12 countries than from just 1.[11]

There is reason to suspect that the United States has been relatively remiss, in the postwar period, in taking advantage of opportunities for the absorption of foreign innovations. One has the impression that in the past few years this has begun to change, with American firms or industry organizations appearing to send an uninterrupted flow of visiting groups to study the equipment and the management practices of the Japanese, a process the Japanese have not failed to reciprocate. But the U.S. govern-ment seems to have been reticent to enter this arena. While Japan has an active and hard working government office devoted to technology trans-fer, the U.S. government offers little that can be taken as a counterpart.

The moral that follows from the preceding discussion is that the United States may be able to contribute substantially to the rate of improvement of its technology and to the effectiveness of the work of its entrepreneurs by the establishment of an agency that works systematically to encourage the transfer of foreign technological developments to the American economy. This can entail an enormous task of gathering and dissemination of information. In addition, it may entail the provision of technical assistance in the adaptation and absorption of foreign innovations, legal assistance in securing rights to use them with minimal cost and delay, and perhaps even the occasional provision of incentives for their adoption by American firms, where special circumstances call for such incentive measures. History and the experience of other industrialized economies suggest strongly that there is much to be gained from such a measure, and while it is probably impossible to estimate its contribution quantitatively, it is difficult to believe that it would not serve to enhance noticeably the rates of growth of productivity and of output per capita in the United States.

12.6 "Rent-Seeking" Opportunities and the Misdirection of Entrepreneurship

A second rather misleading association with the concept of entrepreneurship is the impression that the entrepreneur's activities, whatever their character happens to be in any particular case, will almost always contribute to the productivity of the economy. Even Adam Smith's invisible hand doctrine makes a claim that is far weaker than this, asserting only that self-interest leads the business person to contribute to economic welfare, *provided that there is no impediment to the competitive process and no opportunity to interfere with its workings.* A moment's consideration suggests that an even broader caveat applies to the activities of the entrepreneur. If we follow general usage to define the entrepreneur as a person who displays extraordinary initiative and imagination in economic activity, doing so in pursuit of profit, power, and position, it becomes clear that successful productive innovation is very much an entrepreneurial act, but it is by no means the only option open for pursuit of the entrepreneur's purposes. For one thing, a successful and innovative act of monopolization is surely enterprising and profitable, but it is hardly productive. There can be little doubt that no negligible portion of the great American fortunes is attributable to entrepreneurial acts of this variety. The colorful label "the robber barons" that critics have assigned to them is meant to draw attention to that side of their activities, whether or not it is fully justified.

The central point is that for many entrepreneurs, the productive contribution of their activities, if any, is only an incidental by-product of pursuit of their ultimate profit objective. If that objective is most effectively pursued by means that add to productivity and output, all is well and good. But if other avenues that are less beneficial to the economy bring the entrepreneur more quickly toward the profit goal, then the entrepreneur may have no qualms about pursuing those avenues too. We are not suggesting that entrepreneurs are a particularly amoral or even immoral lot. The capacity of humans to convince themselves that whatever serves their own purposes also contributes to virtue seems unlimited, and in this the entrepreneur is no different from the professor, the lawyer, or the doctor. Adam Smith, then a retired professor, once suggested that a university faculty left completely to govern itself, if given no special incentive to prevent it from happening, might give up "... altogether even the pretense of teaching" [1776/1925, p. 251] (indeed, he claimed that this had already occurred at Oxford). Surely, there is no less reason to rule out an analogous possibility in the case of the entrepreneur.

History, once again, offers support for this observation. For example, the most successful and enterprising individuals in England in the seventeenth century and in France in the eighteenth were those who engaged in activities such as pursuit of a grant of a monopoly by the monarch over some line of business enterprise or the acquisition of the position of "tax farmer" (collector of taxes)—with a considerable proportion of the taxes paid expected to remain in the hands of the farmer. The fortunes accumulated by such means are reported by historians to have been a considerable multiple of those accumulated by the wealthiest merchants, which, in turn, were far higher than those acquired in industrial activity (see, e.g., Hobsbawm [1969, pp. 30–32] and Stone [1985, p. 85]). This may help to some degree to explain why the Industrial Revolution did not break out in earnest in England until the end of the eighteenth century, and in France until well into the nineteenth.

Economists refer to the pursuit of financial gain by such nonproductive means as "rent seeking," where "rent" in economic jargon refers to a payment that is not needed to elicit productive labor or the productive services of some other input. The issue is relevant for us because the United States in recent decades seems to have presented the business community with expanded opportunities for a variety of rent-seeking activity that was, apparently, far less common earlier. Lawsuits and other related actions have become a means frequently resorted to by business firms to protect themselves from the pressures of competition, to wring concessions from rivals and from other firms, and even to extract sizable payments from them. In an era when firms not infrequently sue one another for billions of dollars, it is clear that this activity can be more promising to the plaintiff and can threaten more financial damage to the defendant than is entailed in a considerable period of normal productive activity. When involved in such an undertaking it is naturally to be expected that top management will devote more attention to its lawyers and its "expert witnesses" than to its engineers. And, predictably, it is the productive activity of the firms involved that will lose out in the process. A recent study of one such case (the Texaco-Pennzoil lawsuit, with its $3 billion out-of-court settlement) indicates that the combined value of the stocks of the two corporations declined substantially throughout the period of the lawsuit and until the announcement of the settlement, losing over 20% of their total market value (see Summers and Cutler [1988]). This makes no allowance for the losses sustained by the bondholders, but it does suggest that there must have been a real economic loss of substantial proportions. If this had been an isolated affair it could have been regarded as a curiosum, but the fact that virtually every major firm in the economy seems now to be embroiled in lawsuits of greater or lesser magnitude puts a different complexion on the phenomenon.

The seriousness of its implications is perhaps suggested better in another arena—the work of government regulatory agencies in their oversight of the prices and investments of the firms under their supervision. Over most of the postwar period, and certainly before the onset of the moves toward deregulation toward the end of the 1970s, these agencies devoted much of their time and attention to cases stemming from complaints by competitors that the prices of the regulated firms were excessively low! Thus, one had the curious spectacle of a group of government agencies supervising pricing in rail transportation, passenger air transport, telecommunications, oil pipelines, and a variety of other fields, agencies part of whose *raison d'être* was presumably to protect the public from the market power the regulated firms were taken to possess, repeatedly forcing those firms to *raise* their prices against their will. Of course, the explanation is that competitors had found that complaints to the regulatory agency were a promising means to protect themselves from the threat of effective competition, and that an enormous outlay of resources for the purpose was justified by the promise of success in rent seeking by such means.

Rent-seeking activity also seems recently to have attained a new level of intensity in the financial markets. The imaginative devices concocted for the financial benefit of those immediately concerned in takeover activities has elicited a suitably colorful vocabulary. "Golden parachutes," "greenmail," and "poison pills" all suggest correctly that the activities involved hardly qualify as what the courts, in another context, have dubbed "honestly industrial." The outbreak of scandals connected with insider trading and the activity referred to as "risk arbitrage" has led to the downfall and even the imprisonment of some of the entrepreneurs who, until their undoing, were undoubtedly among the most successful in the nation, rewarded by great wealth and public honors. But for our purposes these scandals are pertinent because they bring out the fact that, while the activities involved were undoubtedly innovative, enterprising, and successful in pursuit of their goals, they were hardly such as to add much to the growth of productivity. In particular, by absorbing the time and talent of the clever and able individuals who undertook them, these activities served as a direct drain upon the stock of productive entrepreneurial talent available to the economy. Battalions of business persons, lawyers, and economists were diverted from productive contribution in pursuit of their share of the available pool of rent.[12]

Of course, the U.S. economy is not alone in manifesting the phenomenon of rent seeking through litigation and financial manipulation. Indeed, no free-market economy is completely immune from it. But it seems to be widely agreed that it takes its most extreme form in the United States, with Europeans reportedly (and regrettably) bringing up the van, gradually absorbing these latest techniques of rent-seeking entrepreneurship. One explanation proposed is that the United States through its cultural antecedents, is a particularly litigious society, and that such activities are rare in Japan for reasons equally rooted in that society's culture. There may be much truth in this judgment, but fortunately there is more to the story. For, while no one knows much about what can be done to modify a cultural tradition, we do know of policy measures that promise to be able to modify its consequences. Here the Japanese case is instructive, once again. It is true that cases in which Japanese firms sue one another on antitrust grounds are exceedingly rare. And while a tradition of aversion toward litigation may have much to do with it, the pertinent provisions of Japanese law are surely not irrelevant. For a Japanese firm to sue another on antitrust grounds, it must first be granted permission by the Japanese Fair Trade Commission, and such permission is hardly ever granted. Moreover, once denied, the plaintiff firm has no legal ground for appeal.[13]

The conclusion from all this is that the United States may well not be suffering from a loss of entrepreneurial talent and initiative, as has sometimes been suggested. Rather, if there is a problem in this arena (a conjecture that is, in any event, very difficult to test), much of the difficulty may be a misdirection of entrepreneurial talent rather than its disappearance. Moreover, whether conditions on the entrepreneurial front have or have not deteriorated, surely an injection of productive entrepreneurship should contribute to productivity. And this can be achieved by closing off, to the extent that is practicable, the most attractive opportunities for rent seeking. The Japanese example shows how this can be done by suitable alterations in the economic "rules of the game." Even if we do not want to go as far as Japan has in discouraging private antitrust suits, for example, more moderate rules of a similar sort are easily formulated. And one can be quite sure that, once suitable measures have closed off or at least impeded access to the avenues for unproductive entrepreneurship, entrepreneurial energy and talent will automatically be redirected to the productive means that still remain open. Such measures can benefit other industrialized countries, and not just the United States. However, as we have seen, there is reason to suspect that in this area it is the United States that has the most to gain.

12.7 Improving the Education of Minorities

While it is not, strictly speaking, consistent with the lines of policy to which this chapter is devoted, it would be unfortunate if we were not to remind the reader of the threat to productivity growth that, according to the analysis of chapter 9, is constituted by the educational deprivation of American minority groups. We have seen that for the foreseeable future the majority of the additions to the U.S. labor force are likely to derive from the black, the Hispanic, and the native American sectors of America's population. Moreover, we have seen the evidence suggesting that education—particularly at the high school level and, presumably, with some technical or scientific orientation—can make a crucial difference for the economy's productivity performance. Finally, we have reviewed some of the evidence showing the dramatic inferiority of the education that American minority group members as a whole are currently receiving.

All of this adds up to a lurking threat to the future productivity achievement of the United States, and it surely calls urgently for preventative countermeasures. This is hardly the place, and we are hardly the qualified persons, for an extensive discussion of the appropriate educational steps. We are convinced, however, that it is time for an investigation into the design of a workable, replicable, and financially feasible educational program that is based solidly on evidence and controlled experimentation rather than (as often seems to be the case) unsupported intuition accompanied by ever more requests for larger school budgets, almost as an end in themselves. Undoubtedly, much more money *will* have to be spent for the purpose; but this should only be agreed to after one is clear about the uses to which it will be put, and after concrete evidence has been assembled showing that the things on which it is proposed to expend the funds offer demonstrable promise of achieving their purpose. To do less than this not only invites further disappointment. It also shortchanges the next generation of minorities as well as the economy as a whole.

12.8   A Failsafe (Reserve) Measure for Stimulating Productivity Growth

Beginning with our discussion of the role of investment stimulation in long-run productivity policy for the American economy, it seemed to become clear that while a substantial and determined effort will have to be committed for the purpose, no really radical measures departing even in spirit from anything that has been done in the United States before, will be required for the achievement of the illustrative goals that have been formulated to give concreteness to our discussion. Thus, it would appear that, as we had hoped, our productivity goals, while demanding enough, will require no radical upheaval for their attainment. We believe that a suitable combination of the measures that have already been described in this chapter will suffice for the purpose. Nevertheless, there is no way one can be certain that this will prove to be so. With so much at stake for the economic welfare of our society it is, therefore, appropriate to seek some supplementary mechanism to which one can turn should it transpire that the other, more conventional, policy measures are insufficient for the purpose. It is to such a failsafe mechanism to which we shall turn next. For many reasons, we hope that recourse to such a program will prove unnecessary. Yet we believe that it has two virtues that are desirable in such a standby mechanism. First, it does not threaten to cause any fundamental upheaval in any of our institutional arrangements or in the way the economy or the society operates. Second, it rests on parameters whose values can be selected by the designers of policy, and it seems clear that if sufficiently demanding values are chosen for those parameters, one can be reasonably confident that the desired consequences will be elicited. In simpler words, the policy is designed so as to be virtually guaranteed capable of achieving the proposed increases in rate of productivity growth, if only the program is set up to be sufficiently demanding and is carried out with sufficient determination.

Among the clear intermediate objectives of productivity policy one can, for obvious reasons, include enhancement of the flow of capital resources into areas of the economy where the prospects for productivity growth are greatest, and stimulation of more effective exercise of managerial and entrepreneurial abilities. The policy measures that will be discussed next promise to contribute to the achievement of both of these goals.

It may well seem that the forces of the free-market mechanism should be perfectly capable of directing capital flows precisely in the manner required by productivity policy. The threat of declining profits should deter investors from keeping their resources in enterprises in which prospects for increased productivity are poor, and it should attract those resources to lines of activity where the opportunities for productivity growth are brightest. In principle, the logic of this position is impeccable. Yet the experience of the Japanese and the French seems to indicate that productivity growth can be helped along, perhaps even significantly, by the employment of systematic stimuli designed to speed up the process. In both these countries government agencies have for years undertaken to determine which sectors of the economy offer the greatest promise for growth, and have sought to induce private investment to flow accordingly. Apparently, business communities have not found this form of intervention by government to be onerous, and it may well have contributed to the remarkable postwar growth records of the two countries.

There are several reasons why it may, in practice, be possible to improve on the performance of the market in terms of the allocation of capital resources. Various forms of government interference impede the flow of capital resources. For example, in industries subject to public utility regulation, firms have often been prevented by regulators from withdrawing their capital from unprofitable lines of activity. Managements themselves, understandably, are reluctant to leave familiar lines of activity in which they have been engaged profitably for long periods in the past, even when their future is now grim. Reluctance to enter unfamiliar territory and the eternal persistence of hope can delay the flow of resources in the directions that a dispassionate assessment of the portents would require. In many cases, rather than shift their investment to new and more promising areas of endeavor, firms in desperate straits prefer to seek protective measures from government or even outright financial assistance.

It is for reasons such as this that it may not be inappropriate to adopt some sort of program to stimulate the prompt flow of capital resources in the directions that enhance the economy's productivity. Nevertheless, given the nature of the U.S. economy and prevailing attitudes toward intervention by government in this country, one may well want to explore means to use the free market for this purpose as an alternative to intervention by the public sector, on the French or Japanese model. As we shall see now, it also may be quite unnecessary for the purpose to supersede the market mechanism in any way. On the contrary, one can make use of it to deal with the problem, merely by sharpening the incentives it offers to firms for assiduous pursuit of enhanced productivity.

There is an approach that seems well suited for that purpose. Economists and other observers have long questioned the desirability of taxes upon business activities and, in particular, the taxation of corporate profits. Such a tax is clearly a disincentive for investment by the general public, and effectively precludes the corporate sector, even when it is the most efficient enterprise to carry out the job, from a variety of lines of activity open to other forms of business firms, activities that are socially desirable and would be profitable in the absence of such a tax. All of this argues for further and perhaps very substantial reductions in corporate tax rates. However, instead of a simple across-the-board decrease in corporate taxes, it is possible to structure the decrease in a way that will simultaneously offer an incentive through the market for allocation of capital resources in accord with the requirements of productivity growth. This can be done by instituting *a fixed schedule of tax rebates that are based on the percentage rate of growth of productivity in the previous year.* If the marginal rebate rate is sufficiently generous, it can offer an enormous competitive edge to firms that are successful in increasing their productivity.

The approach may appear to drag the economy into a morass of complexities and disputes over the proper definition and method of measurement of productivity. However, that is not so. A simple and workable index of productivity that is usable for this purpose is the relationship between the value of the firm's outputs, i.e., of its sales, and the value of its inputs, both after correction for inflation. In other words, an attractive measure of total factor productivity for the purpose of administration of the proposed system of tax rebates is the firm's *real* rate of profit. Or rather, the appropriate measure of growth of productivity is the *rate of growth* in the firm's profits after correction for inflation. It should be noted that because it is carried out entirely in pecuniary terms, this method of calculation readily permits the firm to take credit for any productivity growth it achieves by transfer of resources from a line of activity in which growth is difficult or all but impossible to another in which growth is relatively accessible. Moreover, the procedure imposes no additional bookkeeping or other administrative requirements upon the firm. The profit calculations it already supplies to the tax authorities are all that is required for the purpose, and it remains only to select some appropriate measure of the rate of inflation, such as the GNP deflator or the producer's price index, with which to make the required adjustment for inflation in the calculated rate of growth of profits. The choice of price index is, of course, arbitrary, but not terribly significant since its effects can be adjusted for in the schedule of rebate rates that is adopted.

The relevant growth rates in profit should probably not be based on a comparison of the current profit rate with that of the preceding year. Rather, it seems preferable to use an average of the firm's growth rates for a number of years in the recent past—say, the preceding 5 years. That is, it should probably be based on a moving average in the growth rate of profits. Such a provision offers three advantages: It offers the enterprise some protection from the effects of unfortunate and transitory reverses in its profits, it makes it easier for the firm to undertake measures that will pay off handsomely later, but that require it to give up profits initially, and, finally, it provides a direct incentive for management to pay greater attention to the long-run welfare of the firm rather than to its very short-run prosperity. By basing the firm's tax bill on its performance, say, over a 5-year period, it makes it more difficult for management to disregard the consequences of its actions upon the future, because stockholders will find the longer run to be a matter of far greater concern.

It should be emphasized that, by constituting a system of tangible and certain rewards for success in achieving productivity growth, the proposed rebate arrangement will not only encourage the proper allocation of capital resources but provide a powerful inducement to management to give higher priority to productivity growth. As a system of payment by results it will constitute a set of strong incentives for the appropriate measures. It will provide an enhanced reward for the selection of management personnel with an ability to stimulate productivity through improved labor-management relationships, through the search for and adoption of the most promising innovations and through the discovery of the most fruitful opportunities for reinvestment of the firm's capital. Thus, the program also provides tangible rewards for an achieving management, and for the exercise of entrepreneurial initiative.

Two other features of the proposal should be noted. First, it does not necessarily require a net reduction in the taxes levied on the business sector. Should it be decided for political or other reasons that an attempt to cut the taxes collected from this sector is ill-advised, it is easy to modify the arrangement in a way that leaves industry's net tax payments unchanged. For that purpose one can balance off any tax rebates collected by industry under the growth incentive plan by a suitable upward readjustment in the conventional business tax rates. We are obviously not recommending such an adjustment (or arguing against it, for that matter). Our purpose in raising the issue is to emphasize that the proposal neither stands nor falls with a net reduction in total business tax payments. All that it requires is that the basis upon which an individual firm's tax payments are assessed provide a substantial relative reward for successful growth in productivity.

The second feature of the proposal that requires emphasis at this point is an attribute to which physical scientists refer as "tunability of its parameters." That is, the influence of this policy upon the economy's rate of productivity growth is not something that is, as it were, imposed upon it by some outside influences; rather, the magnitude of its influence can, at least within considerable limits, be selected by the policy designers through their choice of the magnitudes of the pertinent tax and rebate rates. By increasing the marginal rebate offered as a reward for a given percentage growth in productivity, the incentive for industry to devote additional effort for the purpose will obviously be enhanced. At least in theory, this incentive can be strengthened virtually indefinitely. For it is possible to raise both the normal business tax rates and the rebate rates so far that achievement of substantial productivity growth becomes a life and death matter for the firm. That is, these two rates can be set sufficiently high that it will be virtually impossible for a firm with a mediocre productivity record to emerge with positive after-tax profits. Once again, this possibility is not raised because it is necessarily to be desired. Rather, the point is to dramatize the flexibility of the proposal under discussion. It can give considerable control over its degree of effectiveness by the proper selection of the values of its parameters—the tax and rebate rates. It can be used to supplement the more conventional stimuli to productivity that have been discussed in the previous parts of the chapter, augmenting them to whatever degree turns out to be necessary to achieve the appropriate long-run productivity targets.

The conclusion of this chapter is that timid policy *can* prevent the attainment of the productivity goals that are required to preserve the international economic leadership of the United States—the goals that can keep it from becoming a comfortable, but distinctly second-rate, economic power. The message is that such decline is by no means manifest destiny. Rather, the long-term record, as this book has shown, offers much ground for optimism and indicates that a bright future remains within our grasp. It is for us to seize it.

Notes

1. The economist reader will recognize that by adopting this approach we shall have given up any attempt at optimization. Rather, we shall be following a "satisficing" approach (to use Herbert Simon's term for the procedure whose analysis he contributed). That is, we shall seek to find a course of action that there is reason to believe is capable of producing results "satisfactory" in terms of the goals that will be proposed. In macroeconomics it has often been found that an optimality approach is not easy to define, let alone to analyze formally. Thus, it is hard to imagine what might be considered to constitute an "optimal degree of unemployment," or an "optimal rate of productivity growth," and though models of optimal population have been formulated, we suspect that they raise more questions than they answer.

2. The difference between the rate of growth of GDP per worker and GDP per capita depends in large measure on the rate of population growth by age cohort and labor force participation rates by cohort. These two factors are both difficult to forecast. As a result, we shall use the historical difference between the rate of employment growth and that of population growth as the basis of our projection.

3. The figures are summed up in the following table:

	France	Germany	Japan	Holland	U.K.	U.S.
Maddison [1987] estimate: labor productivity growth rates for 1973−1984	3.4	3.0	3.2	1.9	2.4	1.0
Our table 12.2: projected growth rate for 1979−2020	3.49	3.93	4.65	3.21	2.57	2.27

4. Interpretation of such short-period developments is, as always, complicated by a variety of special attendant circumstances. For example, Assar Lindbeck, in an oral presentation to New York University's C. V. Starr Center for Applied Economics, emphasized the differences between recent events in the labor markets of the United States and Europe that led to relative constancy of real wages in the former while they continued to rise in the latter. That, in turn, served as an added incentive for European firms to reduce their use of labor relative to output, thereby making for a relative rise in labor productivity in Europe. If in the face of this powerful influence the United States was nevertheless able to narrow the manufacturing productivity growth gap between itself and Europe during the 1980s, it suggests even more strongly that retention of its leadership position in the long run is hardly an unattainable goal.

5. Much of what will be said in this portion of the discussion follows what has already appeared in a statement issued by the Trustees of the Committee For Economic Development [1983], an organization largely composed of business leaders and economists concerned with public policy. All of the authors of the present volume participated in the preparation of that statement, and one of us

served as its director of research. The material is expanded further in Baumol and McLennan [1985, especially chapter 8].

6. It is not surprising that a simple regression between the two variables yields an R^2 equal to 0.96. The regression equation is

growth rate: GDP/work-hour $= -0.33 + 1.035$ (growth rate: capital/labor),

and the standard error of the coefficient of the independent variable is 0.093. With only seven observations and so simple a relationship, obviously, no great weight can be given to this result.

7. For this purpose, we used as the estimating equation the Cobb-Douglas production function, whose basic formula is

$$Y_t = Ce^{rt}L_t^{\alpha}K_t^{(1-\alpha)},$$

where Y_t is output at time t, C is a constant, r is the rate of (disembodied) technological change, L_t is the labor input at time t, K_t is the capital input at time t, and α is a technological parameter. There are several implicit assumptions in this formulation, among them that there are constant returns to scale and that technological change is not embodied in either the labor input or the capital input. Moreover, under the assumption of perfectly competitive markets and profit maximization on the part of the producers, it can be shown that the parameter α will equal the share of labor in GDP. With some algebraic manipulation, we obtain:

LPGRTH $= r + (1 - \alpha) \cdot$ KLGRTH,

where LPGRTH is the rate of labor productivity growth and KLGRTH is the rate of growth in the capital-labor ratio. During the postwar period, the share of labor in output of the United States has been on the order of two-thirds and the share of capital, $(1 - \alpha)$, one-third. This yields the estimate reported in the next sentence of the text.

8. Actually, employment grew a little faster in the postwar period, at 1.7% per annum, which would entail an even higher growth rate in the capital stock. On the other hand, total hours worked grew more slowly (0.8% over the 1900–1979 period and 1.2% over the 1950–1979 period), as did population (1.3% since 1900 and also since 1950). If we base the capital stock projection on these figures, the estimate of the required rate of growth in the capital stock is correspondingly lower.

9. For a very recent discussion and a brief review of the literature, see Lipsey and Kravis [1987b, pp. 60–64].

10. Some of the following material is based directly on Baumol and McLennan [1985, pp. 208ff].

11. As we noted in chapter 5, this learning process has become an exceedingly rapid affair. For example, one study of the major developments in semiconductor technology that have occurred since the introduction of the device concluded that

in no case did the process of international dissemination require more than 4 years and that the average transfer period was 2.5 years (Tilton [1971]). In another study of 10 industries, the median rate of diffusion was found to be 6–18 months (Mansfield [1985, p. 221]).

12. In a recent book by one of us, such legal, financial, and other business services were, in fact, labeled "unproductive activities." See Wolff [1987a] for a related discussion of several of these issues, as well as a detailed analysis of the economic impact of such unproductive activity on productivity growth in the United States.

13. As noted in Wolff [1987a, p. 25], in 1983 the United States had about 3 times the number of lawyers per capita as West Germany, 10 times that of Sweden, and 20 times that of Japan.

Appendix to Chapter 4:
Time Series Regressions
for Productivity Growth,
1947–1976

A. Regressions for the 11 Major Sectors

For the economy as a whole and for 11 sectors, linear, quadratic, and three types of cubic regressions were run using two different productivity growth series for the period 1947–1986 (gross national product per full-time equivalent employee and gross national product per person engaged in production). There are three reasons for use of the cubic form. First, it is needed to test the hypothesis on the time path described in section 4.6. Second, for some sectors productivity growth over the 1947–1986 period seems to have had two turning points. Third, for most of the other sectors, productivity growth has first fallen and then risen during the period 1947– 1986, but by no means symmetrically. The cubic form allows this U-shaped pattern to take an asymmetrical shape, whereas the quadratic form imposes a symmetric shape.

The first cubic form used by us is the most general and is particularly apt to be appropriate for the sectors with two turning points in their productivity growth series:

$$PRODGRTH_t = b_0 + b_1 \, TIME + b_2 \, TIME^2 + b_3 \, TIME^3 + \varepsilon_t. \qquad (1a)$$

The other two forms permit asymmetry in the U-shaped pattern of productivity growth:

$$PRODGRTH_t = b_0 + b_1 \, TIME + b_2 \, TIME^3 + \varepsilon_t, \qquad (1b)$$

$$PRODGRTH_t = b_0 + b_1 \, TIME^2 + b_2 \, TIME^3 + \varepsilon_t. \qquad (1c)$$

We chose the form with the best fit (as measured by the adjusted R-squared statistic) for GNP per full-time-equivalent employee. The results for the major sectors are shown in table A4.1.[1] They can be characterized as follows:

Table A4.1
Best fit regression results: productivity vs. time—linear, quadratic, and cubic forms, 1947–1986, by major sector for GNP per full-time-equivalent employee[a]

Sector	Constant	Time (×100)	Time² (×1,000)	Time³ (×10,000)	R^2	Adjusted R^2	Standard error of regression	Turning point Trough	Turning point Peak
Total (GNP)	0.026 [6.17]		−0.065 [2.32]	0.014 [1.89]	0.24	0.20	0.013	1978	
Domestic economy (GDP)	0.026 [6.11]		−0.070 [2.48]	0.016 [2.10]	0.23	0.19	0.013	1977	
Private economy	0.031 [6.82]		−0.088 [2.90]	0.020 [2.44]	0.30	0.26	0.014	1977	
Agriculture	0.036 [1.67]		−0.167 [1.15]	0.049 [1.25]	0.05	−0.01	0.065	1971	
Mining	−0.002 [0.05]	2.158 [3.12]	−1.669 [4.08]	0.303 [4.39]	0.51	0.46	0.044	1976	1956
Construction	0.042 [4.09]		−0.274 [3.96]	0.064 [3.45]	0.40	0.37	0.031	1976	
Durable manufactures	0.034 [2.69]		−0.135 [1.60]	0.042 [1.83]	0.12	0.07	0.038	1969	
Nondurable manufactures	0.040 [4.66]	−0.049 [1.30]			0.04	0.02	0.026		
Transportation and public utilities	0.011 [0.71]	0.919 [2.74]	−0.463 [2.33]	0.063 [1.87]	0.29	0.23	0.021	1984	1962
Wholesale trade	0.005 [0.23]	0.757 [1.55]	−0.529 [1.82]	0.094 [1.91]	0.12	0.04	0.031	1976	1958

Retail trade	0.022 [2.63]		−0.091 [1.63]	0.022 [1.44]	0.09	0.04	0.025	1976
Finance, insurance, and real estate	0.010 [1.37]	0.297 [1.83]	−0.221 [2.30]	0.035 [2.18]	0.52	0.48	0.010	1981 1956
Services	0.004 [0.50]	0.248 [1.51]	−0.172 [1.76]	0.028 [1.69]	0.26	0.19	0.010	1980 1957
Government and government enterprises	−0.001 [0.34]	0.009 [1.20]			0.04	0.01	0.005	

a. The best fit regression form is chosen on the basis of the highest adjusted R^2. t-ratios are shown in brackets beneath the respective coefficients. The sources of the data are Bureau of Economic Analysis, *National Income and Product Accounts* (various issues): (i) table 6.2, GNP by industry in constant dollars; (ii) tables 6.7A and 6.7B, full-time-equivalent employees by industry.

1. *The Aggregate.* For the economy as a whole, the regression results are generally insignificant for forms (1a) and (1b), but significant for form (1c). For GNP/FTE, the coefficient of TIME^2 is significant at the 5% level (2-tail test), while the coefficient of TIME^3 is significant at the 10% level (2-tail test). For GNP/PEIP, both coefficients are significant at the 5% level. Moreover, in both cases, the coefficient of TIME^2 in negative and that of TIME^3 is positive, indicating that the time path of productivity growth was roughly U-shaped over the period. The minimum occurs in 1978 for GNP/FTE and in 1979 for GNP/PEIP. This result contrasts strongly with the quadratic form, for which the TIME coefficients are insignificant. Moreover, the adjusted-R^2 statistics are slightly higher than those for the straight linear form, indicating that the cubic form fits the data better than the linear time trend regression.

2. *Agriculture.* For the agriculture sector, none of the cubic forms have significant time coefficients. Since this also holds for the linear and quadratic forms, we can conclude that this sector has no noticeable time trend over the 1947–1986 period.

3. *Mining.* For the mining sector, the most significant of the cubic forms is the general cubic form (1a). All three time coefficients are significant at the 1% level (2-tail test) for the two productivity measures. The results show productivity growth rising from 1947 and peaking in 1956, then falling until 1976, thereafter rising between 1976 and 1986. This general cubic form provides the best fit of all the time trend forms, with an adjusted R^2 of 0.46 (for both productivity variables).

4. *Construction.* For the construction sector, the general cubic form (1a) is not significant, but the other two cubic forms are. Of the two, the best fit is provided by (1c). Both time variables are significant at the 1% level (2-tail test). This is also the best fit of any of the time trend forms, with an adjusted R^2 of 0.37 for GNP/FTE and 0.55 for GNP/PEIP. The results show productivity growth falling after 1947, reaching a minimum in 1976 and then rising thereafter.

5. *Durable Manufactures.* For durables, the best cubic fit and the best fit among all the forms is form (1c). The two time coefficients are significant at the 10% level (2-tail test). The results show productivity growth falling from 1947, reaching a minimum in 1969, and then rising thereafter. However, the adjusted R^2 is only 0.07 for GNP/FTE and GNP/PEIP (these are slightly better than for the quadratic form), so that the U-shaped pattern is not very strong.

6. *Nondurable Manufactures.* For the manufacture of nondurables, on the other hand, none of the cubic, linear, or quadratic results is significant. Thus, for nondurables, there is no significant time pattern over the 1947–1986 period.

7. *Transportation and Public Utilities.* For this sector, the general cubic form (1a) provides the best results of any of the time regressions. The TIME and TIME^2 variables have coefficients significant at the 5% level (2-tail test) and the TIME^3 variable has a coefficient significant at the 10% level (2-tail test). The adjusted R^2 is the highest of all the forms—0.23 for GNP/FTE and for GNP/PEIP. The results show productivity growth rising after 1947, peaking in 1962, falling after 1962, reaching bottom in 1983 (1982 for GNP/PEIP), and then rising thereafter. In the quadratic form, the fitted results show productivity growth rising between 1947 and 1966 and then falling thereafter.

8. *Wholesale Trade.* For wholesale trade, the best fit of all the forms is the general cubic form (1a). However, only two of the three time coefficients are significant at the 10% level (2-tail test), and the adjusted R^2 is only 0.04. The results show productivity growth rising between 1947 and 1958, reaching a peak in 1958, declining until 1976 (1977 for GNP/PEIP), and then rising again.

9. *Retail Trade.* For retail trade, the best cubic form is form (1b), but the best overall fit is the quadratic form, with an adjusted R^2 of 0.04 for GNP/FTE and 0.05 for GNP/PEIP. In this fit, productivity growth falls between 1947 and 1976 for GNP/FTE (1977 for GNP/PEIP), and then rises thereafter.

10. *Finance, Insurance and Real Estate.* For this service subsector, none of the cubic forms has significant coefficients for any of the TIME variables in their equations. The best overall fit is the linear form, with an adjusted R^2 of 0.48 for GNP/FTE and 0.47 for GNP/PEIP. The results show a significant downward trend in productivity growth over the entire period 1947–1986.

11. *Other Services.* For these services, the best fit among the cubic forms and, in fact, among all the forms is the general cubic form (1a). However, only two of the three coefficients of the TIME variables are significant at the 10% level (2-tail test) and the adjusted R^2 is 0.19. The fit is appreciably better for GNP/PEIP, with all three time coefficients significant at the 5% level and an adjusted R^2 of 0.26. Productivity growth rises after 1947, peaks in 1957 (1958 for GNP/PEIP), falls until 1980, and then rises again.

12. *Government.* Finally, for the government sector, none of the cubic forms yields significant coefficients for the TIME variables. Though the highest adjusted R^2 among all the forms is the general cubic form (1a), probably the best fit is achieved by the linear form, which shows a slight though statistically insignificant upward trend in productivity growth over the entire period.

We may note from all this that the only sector for which the best regression fit shows a significant downward trend in productivity growth over the entire period 1947–1986 is finance, insurance, and real estate.

B.   Regressions for the 75 Sectors and Subsectors

Similar regressions were also run with a finer breakdown of sectors. We again used data from the national income accounts tables of the U.S. Bureau of Economic Analysis. The series span 38 years, not 39 years as for the major sectors, since subsector data for 1947 do not conform with those for later years. Thus, the first point in the series represents productivity growth between 1948 and 1949. The number of subsectors varies from one sector to another—thus: agriculture, forestry and fisheries (2 subsectors); mining (4 subsectors); construction (no subsectors); manufacturing (21 subsectors); transportation, public utilities, and communications (10 subsectors); wholesale trade (no subsectors); retail trade (no subsectors); finance, insurance, and real estate (7 subsectors); services (13 subsectors); government and government enterprises (4 subsectors). As before, two different productivity series were calculated for each subsector, one for the change in gross national product per full-time equivalent employee (GNP/FTE) and the other for change in gross national product per person engaged in production (GNP/PEIP). Straight time trend, quadratic trend, and cubic trend regressions were run for all sectors for both employment series. Since the results for the two are, again, quite similar, we shall, generally, report only the former.

First, it is instructive to note that of the 75 sectors and subsectors for which the time trend regressions were run, only 19 have significant time coefficients for GNP/FTE. Of these 19, 17 are negative (out of 49 sectors with a negative time coefficient), while 2 are positive (out of 26). While the subsectors with a negative, significant time coefficient are dispersed throughout the major sectors of the economy—with the exception of agriculture, durable goods, wholesale trade, and retail trade—there is a relatively large concentration in transportation and public utilities and in other services. The sector with the highest adjusted R^2 is real estate, with a value of 0.60. The 2 sectors with a positive, significant time coefficient are machinery, except electrical, and the federal government sector. For the quadratic form, the coefficients of the TIME and TIME^2 variables are both significant in only 8 regressions. Of these, 2 are for major sectors, construction and transportation and public utilities. The remaining 6 are subsectors of agriculture, durables, services, and government. Of the 75 quadratic regressions run for this employment series, 45 yielded extrema that are minima.

The subsector regression results with the best fit, as measured by the adjusted R^2 statistic, are shown in table A4.2. In cases where alternative forms yielded adjusted R^2 values close to one another, we chose the form with the highest t-values for the trend variables. First, let us consider the number of cases with significant downward trends in productivity growth throughout the period 1948–1986 in the equation of best fit. Of the 75 (sub)sectors, there are only 6 that meet this criterion—printing and publishing; air transportation; pipelines (except natural gas); electrical, gas, and sanitary services; personal services; and auto repair services, and garages. Of the 6, only 1 is part of manufacturing, 3 are components of transportation and public utilities, and 2 are services.

Turning to individual subsectors, we see that for the farm sector there was no significant time trend. But for the agricultural services, forestry, and fisheries industry, the quadratic form is significant, indicating that productivity growth fell after 1947, reached bottom in 1969, and rose thereafter. Of the mining subsectors, 3 out of 4 displayed a cubic pattern, with productivity growth rising after 1947, peaking in the mid-1950s, falling until the mid-1970s, and rising thereafter. The exception is nonmetallic mineral mining, which shows no significant time trend of any form. Of the 21 manufacturing subsectors, 17 show no significant time pattern of any form. The 4 exceptions are nonelectrical machinery, which generally has a cubic fit, with productivity growth increasing until 1955, falling until 1970, and then rising thereafter; apparel and other textile products, which show the opposite pattern, with productivity growth falling between 1948 and 1959, rising until 1976, and then falling after that; petroleum and coal products, with a pattern similar to that of nonelectrical machinery, with productivity growth rising until 1957, falling until 1977, and then increasing again; and printing and publishing, which shows a significant downward trend.

Within transportation, there is considerable variation in pattern. Railroad transportation shows a cyclical time pattern, with productivity growth rising after 1947, peaking in 1960, falling until 1977, and then increasing.

Table A4.2
Best fit regression results: productivity vs. time—linear, quadratic, and cubic forms, 1947–1986, by subsector, for GNP per full-time-equivalent employee[a]

Sector	Constant	Time (× 100)	Time² (× 1,000)	Time³ (× 10,000)	R²	Adjusted R²	Standard error of regression	Turning point Trough	Peak
1. Agriculture									
Farms	0.040 [1.49]		−0.187 [1.03]	0.062 [1.26]	0.08	0.03	0.081	1968	1957
Agricultural services, forestry, fisheries	0.027 [1.99]	−0.55 [3.39]	0.130 [3.19]		0.25	0.21	0.027	1969	
2. Mining									
Metal mining	−0.044 [0.80]	2.550 [2.11]	−1.852 [2.59]	0.348 [2.89]	0.25	0.18	0.077	1974	1957
Coal mining	−0.032 [0.63]	2.964 [2.64]	−2.127 [3.20]	0.386 [3.44]	0.29	0.23	0.071	1975	1957
Oil and gas extraction	−0.083 [1.98]	3.375 [3.70]	−2.277 [4.22]	0.392 [4.31]	0.40	0.35	0.058	1977	1958
Nonmetal minerals	0.035 [2.27]	−0.040 [0.58]			0.01	−0.02	0.047		
4. Durable manufacturing									
Lumber and wood products	−0.035 [0.78]	1.638 [1.68]	−0.883 [1.53]	0.131 [1.34]	0.09	0.01	0.062	1980	1961
Furniture	0.023 [1.46]	−0.023 [0.34]			0.00	−0.02	0.047		

Stone, clay, and glass products	0.040 [2.07]	−0.159 [0.99]		0.009 [0.86]	0.03	−0.03	0.043	1972 1924
Primary metal products	0.029 [1.26]		−0.163 [1.04]	0.046 [1.08]	0.03	−0.02	0.070	1972
Fabricated metal products	0.023 [2.02]	−0.009 [0.18]			0.00	−0.03	0.034	
Machinery, excluding electrical	0.004 [0.11]	0.854 [1.16]	−0.809 [1.85]	0.189 [2.56]	0.52	0.48	0.047	1970 1955
Electrical equipment	0.038 [2.51]	0.033 [0.49]			0.01	−0.02	0.046	
Motor vehicles	0.069 [1.68]	−0.159 [0.86]			0.02	−0.01	0.125	
Other transportation equipment	0.040 [2.01]		−0.169 [1.25]	0.046 [1.24]	0.04	−0.01	0.061	1973
Instruments	0.043 [2.93]		−0.108 [1.11]	0.032 [1.20]	0.04	−0.01	0.044	1971
Miscellaneous manufactures	0.021 [0.72]	0.065 [0.49]			0.01	−0.02	0.090	
5. Nondurable manufacturing								
Food and kindred products	0.034 [2.77]	−0.020 [0.37]			0.00	−0.02	0.037	
Tobacco products	0.020 [0.81]	0.213 [1.04]		−0.03 [1.83]	0.15	0.10	0.054	1931
Textile mill products	0.047 [2.20]	0.007 [0.08]			0.00	−0.03	0.065	1965

Table A4.2 (continued)

Sector	Constant	Time (× 100)	Time² (× 1,000)	Time³ (× 10,000)	R²	Adjusted R²	Standard error of regression	Turning point Trough	Turning point Peak
Apparel and other textiles	0.056 [2.67]	−0.854 [1.84]	0.531 [1.94]	−0.09 [1.94]	0.10	0.02	0.029	1959	1976
Paper and allied products	0.032 [1.41]	−0.007 [0.07]			0.00	−0.03	0.068		
Printing and publishing	0.031 [3.20]	−0.097 [2.24]			0.12	0.10	0.029		
Chemical and allied products	0.052 [2.46]	−0.054 [0.57]			0.01	−0.02	0.064		
Petroleum and coal products	0.002 [0.06]	1.618 [1.85]	−1.146 [2.22]	0.202 [2.31]	0.18	0.11	0.055	1977	1957
Rubber and plastics	0.027 [1.48]	−0.007 [0.08]			0.00	−0.03	0.056		
Leather products	−0.020 [0.60]	0.465 [1.19]	−0.108 [1.11]		0.04	−0.02	0.064		1970
6. Transportation and public utilities									
Railroad transportation	−0.048 [1.25]	2.244 [2.69]	−1.360 [2.75]	0.224 [2.69]	0.18	0.11	0.053	1977	1960
Local passenger transit	−0.064 [2.97]	0.418 [1.63]	−0.088 [1.38]		0.09	0.03	0.042		1972
Trucking and warehousing	0.031 [2.37]		0.032 [0.37]	−0.0 [0.76]	0.14	0.10	0.039		1960

			1970	1980	1961	1976	1957
Water transportation	0.018 [0.67]	0.026 [0.22]			0.00	−0.03	0.080
Air transportation	0.099 [4.97]	−0.318 [3.58]			0.26	0.24	0.060
Pipelines excluding natural gas	0.116 [5.19]	−0.283 [2.84]			0.18	0.16	0.067
Transportation services	−0.020 [1.38]	0.061 [0.95]			0.02	−0.00	0.043
Telephone and telegraph	0.061 [5.95]	−0.026 [0.57]			0.01	−0.02	0.031
Radio and TV broadcasting	0.071 [2.28]	−0.645 [1.75]	0.144 [1.56]		0.09	0.03	0.061
Electrical, gas, and sanitary services	0.088 [8.78]	−0.238 [5.29]			0.44	0.42	0.030
9. Finance, insurance, and real estate							
Banking	−0.000 [0.28]	0.002 [0.52]			0.01	−0.02	0.002
Credit agencies	−0.010 [1.53]	0.032 [1.13]			0.03	0.01	0.019
Security brokers	0.012 [1.07]	−0.355 [1.45]	0.195 [1.34]	−0.03 [1.18]	0.08	−0.00	0.016
Insurance carriers	0.004 [0.40]	0.047 [1.15]			0.04	0.01	0.028
Insurance agents	−0.027 [1.10]	0.833 [1.55]	−0.600 [1.88]	0.108 [2.00]	0.13	0.06	0.034

Table A4.2 (continued)

Sector	Constant	Time (× 100)	Time² (× 1,000)	Time³ (× 10,000)	R²	Adjusted R²	Standard error of regression	Turning point Trough	Turning point Peak
Real estate	0.066 [8.84]		−0.226 [4.53]	0.047 [3.47]	0.62	0.60	0.022	1980	1957
Holding and investment companies	−0.005 [0.53]	0.016 [0.43]			0.01	−0.02	0.026		
10. Services									
Hotels and lodgings	0.007 [0.48]	0.123 [0.72]	−0.066 [1.56]		0.27	0.23	0.028		
Personal services	0.037 [4.01]	−0.130 [3.15]			0.22	0.19	0.028		
Business services	−0.011 [2.08]	0.024 [1.03]			0.03	0.00	0.016		
Auto repairs, garages	0.055 [5.35]	−0.195 [4.26]			0.33	0.32	0.031		
Miscellaneous repair services	−0.003 [0.24]	−0.008 [0.14]			0.00	−0.03	0.037		
Motion pictures	−0.005 [0.22]	0.078 [0.76]			0.02	−0.01	0.069		
Amusements	0.029 [2.77]		−0.209 [3.02]	0.056 [2.97]	0.21	0.16	0.031	1973	
Health services	−0.024 [1.57]	0.827 [2.44]	−0.563 [2.81]	0.099 [2.94]	0.22	0.15	0.021	1976	1958
Legal services	−0.057 [1.94]	1.524 [2.38]	−1.011 [2.67]	0.169 [2.65]	0.25	0.19	0.041	1978	1958

Educational services	0.002 [0.87]	−0.020 [1.57]			0.06	0.04	0.009		1968
Social services	0.002 [0.87]	0.004 [0.38]			0.00	−0.02	0.007		
Miscellaneous professional services	−0.011 [0.62]	0.119 [0.79]	−0.01 [1.01]		0.03	−0.02	0.040		1968
Private households	0.011 [1.85]		−0.075 [1.91]	0.024 [2.27]	0.21	0.16	0.018	1969	
11. Government and government enterprises									
Federal government	−0.005 [1.39]	0.054 [1.96]		−0.00 [1.21]	0.15	0.10	0.007		1976
Federal government enterprises	0.027 [1.98]	−0.181 [1.10]	0.045 [1.10]		0.03	−0.02	0.027	1968	
State and local government	−0.002 [0.79]	0.163 [2.53]	−0.100 [2.61]	0.016 [2.44]	0.25	0.19	0.004	1979	1959
S&L government enterprises	−0.123 [6.07]	1.625 [3.66]	−0.700 [2.67]	0.097 [2.18]	0.53	0.49	0.028	1977	1967

a. See notes to table 4.1.

Local and interurban passenger transit, trucking and warehousing, water transportation, and transportation services show no time trend of any form. Air transportation and pipelines (except natural gas), as noted above, show significant downward trends. On the other hand, no significant time trend is observable in either of the 2 communication subsectors. For utilities (electrical, gas, and sanitary services), there is a very significant downward trend in productivity growth over the 1947–1986 period. Of the subsectors of finance, insurance, and real estate, 5 of 7 show no significant time trend. The insurance agents, brokers, and service industry does show a pattern very similar to that of the sector as a whole, while the results for the real estate sector display a cyclical pattern, with productivity growth falling between 1947 and 1957, rising until 1976, and then falling thereafter.

Among the 13 service subsectors, there are only 2, health services and legal services, that have time patterns similar to that of the service sector as a whole, for which the best fit is the general cubic form (1a), which shows productivity growth first rising between 1948 and 1957, falling until 1980, and then increasing again. The results for the amusement and recreation service industry show a convex pattern, with productivity growth falling after 1948, bottoming in 1973, and then rising thereafter. The pattern for the private household sector (i.e., domestic servants) is similar, except that the minimum is reached in 1969. As was already noted, personal services and auto repair and services show significant downward trends in productivity growth over the full period 1948–1986. Seven service industries show no significant time patterns in productivity growth.

Finally, there is a significant upward trend in productivity growth in the federal government sector. However, this result must be interpreted cautiously, since "real" output of the federal government is measured as value added, which consists almost exclusively of wages and salaries, deflated by the GNP deflator. Thus, the measured increase in government productivity may simply be an artifact of the rise at an accelerating rate of government salaries relative to private wages and salaries over the period. In contrast, the federal government enterprise sector shows no trend in productivity growth. For the 2 subsectors of the state and local government sector, the best fit is the general cubic form (1a). In both cases, productivity growth first increases, then declines, and increases thereafter.

Note

1. Results for the series on GNP per person engaged in production are not shown in table A4.1 or table A4.2 because they are very similar to the series on GNP per full-time-equivalent employee.

Appendix to Chapter 5: Five Statistical Tests of Convergence Using the Summers-Heston Data

To avoid overstating our case, we tested the convergence hypothesis using the Summers and Heston [1984] data in literally every way we could devise. In this appendix we describe the five statistical tests that we employed for this purpose.

First Test: A Moving Average Approach

Figure A5.1 uses data points related to those of figure 5.5 to evaluate for what range of RGDP (if any) a negatively sloping (convergence) pattern holds and for what ranges the pattern is upward sloping (divergent). Because the data points in figure 5.5 are rather scattered, to obtain a coherent pattern, moving averages grouping countries into sets of 10 at a time were calculated. That is, the first set was made up of the 10 countries ranked lowest in terms of 1950 GDP per capita, the second set added the 11th lowest and removed the lowest, and so on. For each such group we graphed its average 1950 RGDP on the horizontal axis and the growth rate of RGDP between 1950 and 1980 on the vertical axis. The resulting graph constitutes an automatic *ex ante* stratification, since poorer countries at that date clearly must lie to the left of the graph, while initially wealthier countries lie to its right. Our hypothesis, consequently, entailed the conjecture that the moving average graph would be roughly positively sloping toward the left, and distinctly negatively sloping toward the right, meaning that per-capita incomes among less developed countries, selected *ex ante*, had diverged, while the opposite had been true among initially "industrialized" countries.

This is, indeed, something like what figure A5.1 shows. For nations with initial per-capita real GDPs below about $700, the curve's slope is highly erratic, and can, perhaps, be interpreted to be positive in slope overall. Beginning possibly with a $700 annual figure, and certainly above $1,300,

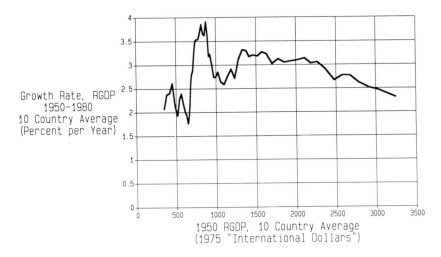

Growth Rate, RGDP
1950-1980
10 Country Average
(Percent per Year)

1950 RGDP, 10 Country Average
(1975 "International Dollars")

Figure A5.1
Growth rate, RGDP (1950–1980) vs. 1950 RGDP, 10-country moving average, 72 countries ranked by 1950 RGDP. Source: Summers and Heston [1984].

the slope is clearly negative. Correspondingly, of the 72 countries in the sample, something between 29 and 52 fall in this group represented in the downward sloping portion of the curve, while between 20 and 43 fall in the more or less positively sloping segment.

What all of this suggests is that somewhere near the median in our sample of countries the advantages of backwardness do indeed begin to overbalance the counteracting forces, sociological, educational, and other.

Second Test: Nonlinear and Piecewise Linear Regressions

To supplement the impressionistic procedure just described, a somewhat more formal regression analysis was undertaken. Both a nonlinear relationship and a piecewise linear relation composed of two line segments were fitted to the raw data of figure 5.5 Predictably, the closeness of the statistial fit fell far below that obtained in our *ex post* classificatory calculation.

The quadratic regression yielded the equation[1]

$$\ln \text{RATIO} = 0.586 + 0.00038 \text{ RGDP50} - (9.9/10^7) \text{ RGDP50}^2,$$
$$\qquad\quad [4.2] \qquad [2.1] \qquad\qquad\qquad [2.2]$$

$$R^2 = 0.07, \qquad N = 72,$$

where RATIO = 1980 RGDP divided by 1950 RGDP and RGDP50 =

per-capita 1950 GDP. The maximum of the equation occurs at a 1950 RGDP value of $1,900, approximately. Both variables are significant at the 5% level, with the predicted signs. The results indicate divergence among the lower income countries in 1950 and convergence among the higher income ones.

The piecewise linear regression was designed to attain its maximum near that of the nonlinear one, putting 17 countries into the *ex ante* upper income category and 55 countries into the other.

The resulting regression equation is

$$\ln \text{RATIO} = 0.658 + 0.00019 \text{ RGDP50} - 0.00044 \text{ D1900},$$
$$\qquad\qquad [5.8] \qquad [1.9] \qquad\qquad\qquad [2.2]$$

$$R^2 = 0.07, \qquad N = 72,$$

where $\text{D1900} = \text{RGDP50}$ if $\text{RGDP50} \geq \$1,900$ and 0 if $\text{RGDP50} < \$1,900$. The first variable is significant at the 10% level and the second at the 5% level, and both have the predicted signs, thus confirming the results of the quadratic equation. Finally, two separate regressions were run, one for the upper income sample and the other for the lower income group.

For the upper income group

$$\text{RATIO} = 3.3 - 0.00038 \text{ RGDP50}, \qquad R^2 = 0.30, \qquad N = 17$$
$$\qquad\quad [7.7] \qquad [12.5]$$

and for the lower income group

$$\text{RATIO} = 2.1 + 0.0005 \text{ RGDP50}, \qquad R^2 = 0.03, \qquad N = 55.$$
$$\qquad\quad [5.5] \qquad [2.3]$$

The results provide strong support for convergence among the countries in the upper income group but weaker support for divergence among the lower income group.

Third Test: Ratios of Coefficients of Variation for Country Samples of Different Sizes

Another way of testing the sensitivity of calculations on the convergence hypothesis to the choice of country sample is to rank the countries *ex ante* and then determine what happened to the coefficient of variation between 1950 and 1980 for each and every pertinent sample of countries. Accordingly, the Summers-Heston countries were ranked in terms of 1950 RGDP, and for various samples, which are about to be described, we calculated the

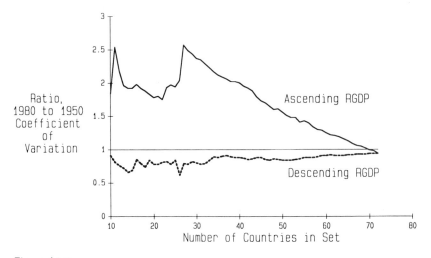

Figure A5.2
Convergence ratio, 1980 vs. 1950, sample of 10–72 countries, ranked by ascending and descending 1950 RGDP. Source: Summers and Heston [1984].

ratio of the 1980 coefficient of variation to its 1950 counterpart. Clearly, if the ratio turned out to have a value less than unity, one could judge convergence to have occurred among the RGDPs of the countries in that particular sample.

We then constructed 124 country sets, 62 in descending order of RGDP and 62 in ascending order. In the first group we started with the 10 most affluent countries in 1950. The next set was composed of the top 11 countries. Then we expanded the set to 12 countries and so on, continuing in this way until all 72 Summers and Heston countries were included in the final largest set. The second 62 country sets were constructed by starting with the 10 poorest countries in 1950, and then expanding the sets, one country at a time in ascending order of RGDP. The results of the calculation of 1980 to 1950 ratios of coefficients of variations for all these sets are shown in figure A5.2. It shows on the horizontal axis the number of countries included in each set. That is, in the descending RGDP curve, as one moves from left to right one deals with larger and larger samples with constantly declining 1950 RGDP on the average, as the set size increases. The vertical axis shows for each sample size of countries the ratio of 1980 to 1950 coefficient of variation. We see that in the descending RGDP curve this ratio has a value less than unity for every sample size, even though that ratio generally increases somewhat as one moves rightward. This means that inclusion of the top 10 countries is enough to engender convergence for *every* size sample of countries(!). However, this result grows weaker as ever-poorer countries are included.

The ascending RGDP curve, which starts off with the 10 poorest countries and then includes ever-wealthier ones (as of 1950), constitutes a remarkable contrast with the other curve. Here the ratio displays an odd pattern toward the left as the sample expands from the 10 poorest countries to the 27 least affluent. Thereafter it begins to decline steadily, as we had expected. However, its value remains consistently above unity until the sample size reaches 70 countries. That is, inclusion of the 10 poorest countries is sufficient to guarantee *divergence* in *any* of the samples of countries until the two most affluent countries in 1950 are finally included.

Thus, the results of this test, while not inconsistent with our convergence hypothesis, may possibly raise questions of its own. This and the preceding tests also entail a problem, because of the heavy weight they assign to the 1950 figures, comparing only 1950 and 1980, with no attention to intermediate-year figures. It can be argued that 1950 was characterized by atypical diversity in RGDP as a result of the great differences in damage done to various economies by World War II, notably to those of Germany, France, the United Kingdom, and Japan. Recovery of the most heavily damaged countries would naturally contribute abnormal convergence and would thereby bias the results of our calculation in the direction of our hypothesis.

Fourth Test: Year-by-Year Coefficients of Variation

To avoid such problems, we turned finally to our most exacting tests, involving calculation for different *ex ante* country samples of the time path of the coefficient of variation and the Gini coefficient *for each year* in the period 1950–1981 (1981 Summers-Heston data became available as we were carrying out the study reported here). The Summers and Heston countries were again ranked on a 1950 basis (it was also done on a 1960 basis with no noteworthy changes in results, though not all of the tests were replicated for the 1960 base). The time series of coefficient of variation was calculated for the top 10 countries as well as the top 12, 14, 16, 18, 22, 24, 26, 28, 30, 35, 40, 45, 50, 55, and 60 countries. (Various other related calculations were also carried out.) There is a sharp break in pattern of behavior between the samples that include fewer than 16 countries and those that include 16 or more. In figure A5.3 the curve for the sample of the top 14 countries is typical for the smaller country sets, i.e., the sets containing the countries with the highest RGDP values in 1950. We see that

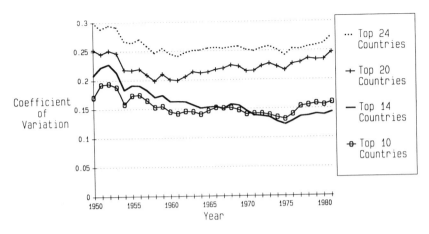

Figure A5.3
Coefficient of variation, RGDP, 1950–1981, for sets of countries by 1950 RGDP rank.
Source: Summers and Heston [1984].

the coefficient of variation falls quite steadily and sharply throughout the period, except at its very beginning and very end. Noteworthy is the fairly steady rise since 1975, a rise whose overall magnitude remains fairly modest—at least so far.

For larger samples of countries, divergence, as measured by the coefficient of variation, begins much earlier and continues far longer. In figure A5.3 the curve for the sample of the top 24 countries is not atypical (though for larger samples patterns become more erratic). In this curve we see a fairly steady rise in divergence ever since 1961. The coefficient of variation in 1981 was still about midway between its 1950 high and its 1961 low, but this means that about half of the initial increase in homogenization has been lost.[2] Before commenting on these results let us turn finally to our fifth test.

Fifth Test: Year-by-Year Gini Coefficients and Regressions

The calculations just described were repeated using Gini coefficients rather than coefficients of variation; only this time we used samples of 10, 15, 20, 30, 40, 50, 60 and all 72 Summers-Heston countries. Figure A5.4 illustrates the results for the first four of these cases. Essentially, and as is to be expected, it shows basically the same patterns as those that emerge via the coefficient of variation. For smaller sets of the top countries ranked by 1950 RGDP the graphs show an overall decline, albeit more modest than that

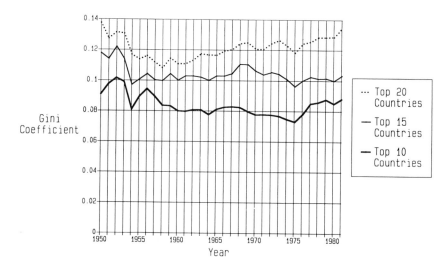

Figure A5.4
Gini coefficients, RGDP, 1950–1981, for sets of countries ranked by 1950 RGDP. Source:
Summers and Heston [1984].

yielded by the coefficient of variation. That decline is, however, replaced
by an ascent toward the end of the period. That is, for these top groups
there was clear convergence from 1950 until about 1970, when a period of
divergence set in, as, there is reason to suspect, also happened in earlier
economically troubled periods. When the sample is enlarged to include a
number of poorer countries, the pattern remains in most cases, but the
period of divergence sets in earlier, sometimes considerably so.

All of this was formalized and confirmed by a set of trend regressions
that were carried out for the time series of coefficients of variation and the
Gini coefficients over the period from 1950 to 1981. For each of the
samples two regressions were calculated, one linear and one quadratic
(involving the square of the independent variable, TIME). The linear regressions using the coefficient of variation as the dependent variable
yielded significant and negative coefficients for TIME for cases consisting
of the top 16 or fewer countries and those consisting of the top 24 or more
countries (see table A5.1 for selected results). The R^2 statistic ranged from
0.19 to 0.81. For the in-between cases, the coefficient of TIME was insignificant, and the R^2 very low. Linear regressions using the Gini coefficient
as the dependent variable yielded similar results, with significant and negative coefficients for TIME in cases involving the top 15 or fewer countries

Table A5.1
Time trend regression results

Dependent variable and sample	Constant	Independent variables[a] TIME	TIME^2	R^2	Adjusted R^2
		Linear regressions			
A. Coefficient of variation					
1. Top of 12 countries	0.192*** (44.6)	−0.00190*** (8.3)		0.70	0.69
2. Top 16 countries	0.208*** (48.8)	−0.00059** (2.6)		0.19	0.16
3. Top 20 countries	0.221*** (4.1)	0.00009 (0.4)		0.06	0.00
4. Top 24 countries	0.273*** (56.6)	−0.00077*** (3.0)		0.23	0.21
5. Top 30 countries	0.328*** (58.2)	−0.00117*** (3.9)		0.34	0.32
B. Gini coefficient					
1. Top 10 countries	0.091*** (41.2)	−0.00040*** (3.4)		0.28	0.26
2. Top 15 countries	0.109*** (56.5)	−0.00027** (2.7)		0.19	0.17
3. Top 20 countries	0.118*** (45.2)	0.00021 (1.6)		0.07	0.04
4. Top 25 countries	0.156*** (74.1)	−0.00004 (0.3)		0.04	0.00
5. Top 30 countries	0.181*** (65.5)	−0.00041*** (2.8)		0.20	0.18

Quadratic regressions

A. Coefficient of variation					
1. Top 12 countries	0.212*** (42.5)	−0.00534** (7.7)	0.000104*** (5.1)	0.84	0.83
2. Top 16 countries	0.224*** (40.8)	−0.00347*** (4.5)	0.000087*** (3.9)	0.46	0.43
3. Top 20 countries	0.249*** (48.7)	−0.00489*** (6.8)	0.000151*** (7.2)	0.64	0.62
4. Top 24 countries	0.299*** (68.4)	−0.00536*** (8.8)	0.000139*** (7.7)	0.75	0.73
5. Top 30 countries	0.361*** (90.2)	−0.00701*** (12.5)	0.000177*** (10.8)	0.87	0.86
B. Gini coefficient					
1. Top 10 countries	0.101*** (42.5)	−0.00227*** (6.8)	0.000056*** (5.8)	0.67	0.65
2. Top 15 countries	0.113*** (39.2)	−0.00102** (2.5)	0.000023* (1.9)	0.28	0.23
3. Top 20 countries	0.130*** (45.3)	−0.00196*** (4.9)	0.000066*** (5.6)	0.55	0.52
4. Top 25 countries	0.167*** (79.6)	−0.00186*** (6.4)	0.000058*** (6.7)	0.61	0.58
5. Top 30 countries	0.197*** (91.0)	−0.00319*** (10.6)	0.000084*** (9.5)	0.81	0.79

* Significant at the 10% level (two-tailed test).
** Significant at the 5% level (two-tailed test).
*** Significant at the 1% level (two-tailed test).

a. Estimated coefficients are shown, with t-ratios in parentheses. The sample size is 32 (years 1950 to 1981). The countries included in each sample are chosen on the basis of their 1950 RGDP ranking.

and those involving the top 30 or more nations. The in-between cases in terms of sample size failed to yield significant coefficients for TIME.

The quadratic regressions, which were able to take account of the recent period of divergence as well as the earlier period of convergence, produced much stronger results for all sample sizes. The coefficient of TIME was consistently negative and significant, the coefficient of $TIME^2$ was consistently positive and significant, and the adjusted R^2 values were uniformly greater than the corresponding linear regressions. For the quadratic form, the R^2 values ranged from 0.46 to 0.93 for the coefficient of variation regressions and from 0.28 to 0.81 for the Gini coefficient regressions.

The two sets of results suggest that the secular trend is toward long-term convergence in per-capita income levels for all samples of countries, except those involving the top 20 or so. This result holds up for both the coefficient of variation and the Gini coefficient measure of dispersion, even though the incremental change in the latter was much smaller in relative terms than the former. However, as we have seen, the secular movement toward convergence may reverse itself at least in the short or intermediate term. This seems to have been true in the mid- and late 1970s, perhaps because of the worldwide oil crisis and the accompanying recession.[3]

Notes

1. The t-ratios are shown in brackets under the respective coefficients.

2. Two variants were also tried. First, we used a slightly different concept of output per capita, which Summers and Heston call RGDP* and which incorporates a terms-of-trade adjustment. Second, we eliminated Japan and West Germany from the sample, since these countries had particularly low RGDP levels in the early 1950s because of the aftereffects of World War II. The resulting patterns were almost identical with those reported in the text.

3. In this appendix we have sought to emphasize (and try to deal with) every influence we could think of that would bias our calculations in the direction of (the appearance of) convergence. But Moses Abramovitz has called our attention to a bias in the other direction. The point is that, if we believe convergence is attributable to a considerable degree to the advantages of backwardness, which gives technological laggards the greater opportunity to learn, then to test convergence we should rank countries not by their initial levels of productivity but by their initial degree of technological sophistication. Unfortunately, we have no measure of the latter, and so we must use the former as a highly imperfect substitute. The result is that countries that are unusually productive because, say, they have large land endowments, may be technologically backward and nevertheless grow rapidly, thereby appearing to perform in a manner inconsistent with the basic hypothesis. Professor Abramovitz's discussion of the matter is, as always, illumi-

nating [personal correspondence dated August 18, 1987]:

It is unavoidable that, at this stage of the game, the empirical work should focus on levels, growth rates and variances of labor productivity or per capita output. In this treatment, however, there is a disjunction between the data we use and our underlying belief in the forces that lie behind the tendency to convergence. My belief—and I suppose yours—is that convergence arises from: (a) absorption of the technology of more (technologically) advanced countries; (b) opportunities for profitable capital accumulation, including human capital, that accompany such absorption; (c) the increase in product that occurs when redundant or underemployed workers are transferred from small-scale farming to urban industrial and commercial employment in the course of industrialization; (d) the enlargement of scale stemming from all the above. Given the necessary "social capability," we think the catch-up potential varies inversely with countries' existing levels of technology. We use levels of per capita product or labor productivity as proxies for "level of technology." That's the rub. Particularly in the early stages of countries' progress in modern economic growth or "industrialization," levels of labor productivity are heavily influenced by countries' endowments of cultivable land and other natural resources. That is because very large proportions of the countries' labor are still engaged in agriculture or other primary production. So labor productivity levels vary a great deal among countries for reasons that are independent of their degrees of technological backwardness. Levels of labor productivity are, therefore, erratic indicators of countries' catch-up potential. Therefore, in any sample of countries that includes large number of poor countries, the association between initial levels of per capita income or productivity and subsequent growth rates is likely to be weak. (Note that this is a consideration distinct from that of "error" in the labor productivity estimates of poor countries or early years. "Error" is a consideration that biases the correlation upwards.) You will remember that this point about the heavy dependence of labor productivity on natural resource endowment in early stages was one of the reasons I advanced in my paper to account for the relatively weak (not non-existent) evidence of convergence even among Maddison's 16 countries between 1870 and 1913.

Appendix to Chapter 6

A. Basic Theorems on Stagnant, Progressive, and Asymptotically Stagnant Outputs

We start with some results on stagnant and progressive activities, turning later to the case of asymptotic stagnancy. Our first proposition generalizes a result now well-known—that the unit cost of a product of a persistently more stagnant activity must rise without limit in comparison with that of a more progressive activity. This is, of course, the basic manifestation of what has been called the "cost disease" of the stagnant services. Now we show that, even if there is absolutely *no* shift in consumer tastes and demands toward the more stagnant sector, inputs and consumers expenditures will automatically move in that direction. The results will be shown to be consistent with the empirical evidence.

We use the following notation:

y_{it} = output of product i in period t,

x_{kit} = quantity of input k used in producing i in period t,

p_{it} = (real) price of i in period t,

w_{kt} = (real) price of k in period t,

$\pi_{fit} = y_{it}/\sum w_{kt}x_{kit}$ = total factor productivity in output i,

$\pi_{kit} = y_{it}/x_{kit}$ = the productivity of input k in production of output i, and

$^* $ = rate of growth, i.e., for any function $f(t)$, $f^* \equiv \dot{f}/f$.

Proposition 1 Let y_{1t} and y_{2t} be two outputs produced by single-product firms. Then, if $\pi^*_{f1t} \leq r_1 < r_2 \leq \pi^*_{f2t}$, so that output 1 is relatively stagnant (and output 2 is relatively progressive), the ratio of the average cost of output 1 to that of output 2, AC_{1t}/AC_{2t}, will rise without limit.

Proof By definition,

$AC_{1t}/AC_{2t} \equiv \pi_{f2t}/\pi_{f1t}$,

so that by the standard proposition on the growth rate of a fraction,

$(AC_{1t}/AC_{2t})^* = \pi_{f2t}^* - \pi_{f1t}^* \geq r_2 - r_1 > 0.$ QED

Proposition 2   Let the proportion between two outputs, 1 and 2, be constant so that $y_{2t} = v y_{1t}$. If, in addition, for any t,

$$\max_k \pi_{k1t}^* \leq r_1 < r_2 \leq \min_k \pi_{k2t}^*,$$

then product 1's share of any input k used in the production of both goods will approach the limit unity as $t \to \infty$. Moreover, for any value g however small, $0 < g < 1$, there will exist a T such that for any $t > T$ the input ratio satisfies $1 \geq x_{k1t}/(x_{k1t} + x_{k2t}) \geq 1 - g$.

Proof   Consider any input k. Then

$$(y_{1t}/x_{k1t})^* \leq \max_k \pi_{k1t}^* \leq r_1, \qquad (y_{2t}/x_{k2t})^* \geq \min_k \pi_{k2t}^* \geq r_2,$$

so that

$$y_{1t} \leq a_{1k} x_{k1t} e^{r_1 t}, \qquad y_{2t} \geq a_{2k} x_{k2t} e^{r_2 t}, \tag{1}$$

where

$a_{1k} = y_{10}/x_{k10}$, etc.

Then, writing $a = a_{1k}/a_{2k}$ and $x_{kt} = x_{k1t} + x_{k2t}$, we obtain dividing $y_{2t} = v y_{1t}$ by y_{1t} in (1),

$$av \geq e^{(r_2 - r_1)t}(x_{kt} - x_{k1t})/x_{k1t},$$

or

$$1 + e^{(r_1 - r_2)t} va \geq x_{kt}/x_{k1t} \geq 1.$$

That is, taking reciprocals,

$$1 \geq x_{k1t}/(x_{k1t} + x_{k2t}) \geq 1/[1 + e^{(r_1 - r_2)t}].$$

Since $r_1 < r_2$, the right-hand side will approach unity asymptotically, which yields our results.   QED

Proposition 3   Under the circumstances of proposition 2, competitive equilibrium requires the share of consumer expenditure on relatively stagnant product 1 to approach the limit unity as $t \to \infty$. Moreover, for any g however small, $o < g < 1$, there will exist a finite T such that for any $t > T$,

$$1 \geq p_{1t}y_{1t}/(p_{1t}y_{1t} + p_{2t}y_{2t}) \geq 1 - g.$$

Proof Let m be the value of k that minimizes $x_{k1t}/(x_{k1t} + x_{k2t})$ for the period t. In competitive equilibrium equality of total revenue and total cost require

$$1 \geq \frac{p_{1t}y_{1t}}{p_{1t}y_{1t} + p_{2t}y_{2t}} = \frac{\sum w_{kt}x_{k1t}}{\sum w_{kt}(x_{k1t} + x_{k2t})} \geq \frac{x_{m1t}\sum w_{kt}}{(x_{m1t} + x_{m2t})\sum w_{kt}}$$

$$= \frac{x_{m1t}}{x_{m1t} + x_{m2t}}.$$

The result now follows by proposition 2. QED

Intersectoral Shifts and the Economy's Productivity Growth

Proposition 2 tells us that there is a powerful force pushing toward absorption of increasing shares of an economy's inputs by its stagnant sectors. With fixed output proportions, this is an arithmetic tautology. Thus, imagine a two-sector economy that uses only one input, labor, where both sectors initially employ the same quantity of labor. If, in T years, sector A's hourly productivity doubles while B's is constant, fixed output proportions mean that at the end of the period stagnant sector B *must* employ twice as many worker-hours as A.

Next, we prove two results on overall productivity. First, where the productivity growth rates of the different sectors of the economy are unequal, *it is impossible for both input and output proportions to remain constant*. Second, even if productivity growth in each sector of the economy remains perfectly unchanged, and there is absolutely no change in the relative outputs, the resulting intersectoral input shifts must slow the economy's overall rate of productivity growth.

Proposition 4[1] In any economy in which the productivity growth rates of its different sectors are unequal, it is impossible for both output ratios and input ratios to remain constant.

Proof Proposition 4 follows immediately as a corollary to proposition 2. QED

For the remaining two propositions of this section we need additional notation, because they deal with productivity growth for the entire economy and, hence, require some aggregation of outputs and inputs with the aid of prices. First, we obtain some expressions for the overall productivity growth rates. Let

$y_t = \sum p_{i0} y_{it} = $ value of total output in period t using base period prices,

$x_t = \sum\sum w_{k0} x_{kit} = $ value of the inputs used by the economy in base period prices,

$r_{it} = \sum_k w_{k0} x_{kit} / x_t = i$'s share of the economy's total inputs, in base period prices,

$\pi_t = y_t / x_t = $ the economy's total factor productivity,

$\pi_{it} = p_{i0} y_{it} / \sum\sum w_{k0} x_{kit} = $ value productivity of inputs used to produce i,

$\phi_{it} = p_{i0} y_{it} / y_t = i$'s share of the value of total output in base period prices.

We value outputs in base period prices, because it follows wide usage and because it avoids the need to differentiate prices with respect to time. Before getting to the theorems on unbalanced growth and the productivity of the economy as a whole, we use the preceding expressions to provide a sharper variant of proposition 2, which we shall also need later:

Proposition 5   If its proportion of the economy's output is constant, activity i's share of the economy's inputs, r_{it}, will decline monotonically with π_{it}^*, the rate of growth of the activity's productivity. Its input share will be constant ($r_{it}^* = 0$) if and only if its productivity growth rate exactly equals that of the economy as a whole, π_t^*; i's input share will increase if and only if its productivity growth rate is below that of the economy, and decrease only in the opposite case.

Proof   By the definition we have immediately

$$r_{it} / \phi_{it} \equiv \pi_t / \pi_{it}. \tag{2}$$

Again, using the standard result for the percentage rate of growth of a fraction $[(A(t)/B(t)]^* = A(t)^* - B(t)^*$, we have from (2)

$$r_{it}^* - \phi_{it}^* = \pi_t^* - \pi_{it}^*. \tag{3}$$

But with output shares constant, $\phi_{it}^* = 0$. Thus,

$$r_{it}^* = \pi_t^* - \pi_{it}^*,\tag{4}$$

where $\pi_t^* - \pi_{it}^*$ is, obviously, the difference between the economy's productivity growth and that of activity i. QED

We obtain at once

Proposition 6   If output composition is fixed and the productivity growth rates of the various outputs are constant and unequal, the economy's rate of productivity growth must decline with the passage of time (because inputs will be shifted toward the more stagnant sectors).

Proof   Since output shares are constant, all $\phi_{it}^* = 0$ and (4) holds. Note also that since r_{it} is activity i's input *share*,

$$\sum_i r_{it} \equiv 1 \qquad \text{and} \qquad \sum \dot{r}_{it} = 0.\tag{5}$$

Multiplying (4) through by r_{it} and summing over i, we then have, by (5),

$$\sum \dot{r}_{it} = \pi_i^* \sum r_{it} - \sum r_{it}\pi_{it}^*, \qquad \text{or} \qquad \pi_i^* = \sum r_{it}\pi_{it}^*.$$

Differentiating with respect to time to see whether π_t^* is declining, we obtain

$$\dot{\pi}_t^* = \sum \dot{r}_{it}\pi_{it}^* + \sum r_{it}\dot{\pi}_{it}^* = \sum \dot{r}_{it}\pi_{it}^*,\tag{6}$$

because the sectoral productivity growth rates are constant ($\dot{\pi}_{it}^* = 0$).
   Since by (5), $\pi_t^* \sum \dot{r}_{it} = 0$, we have [subtracting this from (6)] by (4)

$$\dot{\pi}_t^* = \sum \dot{r}_{it}(\pi_{it}^* - \pi_t^*) = -\sum \dot{r}_{it}r_{it}^* = -\sum \dot{r}_{it}^2/r_{it} < 0. \quad \text{QED}\tag{7}$$

Corollary   Under the circumstances of proposition 6, except that the sectoral productivity growth rates are all the same, the economy's productivity growth rate will remain constant.

Proof   This follows by (7), since with uniform productivity growth we must have $\pi_{it}^* = \pi_t^*$ for all i. QED

We turn next to the asymptotically stagnant activities. Pure asymptotic stagnancy is the case of an activity whose inputs are used in fixed proportions, with one group of inputs produced by progressive activities while the others are produced by stagnant activities. Characteristically, these, like other asymptotically stagnant activities, are "high-tech" industries, at the frontier of technical progress.

Asymptotically stagnant activities have several noteworthy behavior patterns. In their early stages, when progressive inputs dominate their budgets, their costs and prices fall rapidly, like those of progressive activities. Later, their fixed input proportions and the rapid fall in the relative prices of their progressive inputs inevitably give the stagnant inputs an ever-rising share of the total budget of the asymptotically stagnant activity, as a simple matter of arithmetic. Third, as the stagnant component comes to dominate the budget, the price of the activity must approach that of its stagnant component, and therefore has to rise, so succumbing to the cost disease. Finally, the date when the activity sheds its progressive characteristics comes more quickly, the more rapid the decline in the price of its progressive component. That is, the more spectacularly successful is productivity enhancement in the production of the progressive inputs, the more rapidly they will extinguish themselves as significant components of the asymptotically stagnant activity's budget, and, consequently, the more rapidly the relative cost of this activity will begin to rise.

These results are encompassed in the following two propositions:

Proposition 7 Suppose an asymptotically stagnant activity, A, uses stagnant input x_1 and progressive input x_2 in fixed proportion v, so that $x_{2t} = v x_{1t}$. If w_{1t}, the unit price of x_{1t}, increases at a rate at least equal to r_1 and w_{2t} increases at a nonnegative rate no greater than r_2, where $r_2 < r_1$, then the share of total expenditure by A that is devoted to x_{1t} will approach the limit unity. Moreover, for any positive g, however small, $0 < g < 1$, there exists a T such that for all $t > T$,

$$1 \geq w_{1t}x_{1t}/(w_{1t}x_{1t} + w_{2t}x_{2t}) \geq 1 - g.$$

Proof We are given

$$w_{1t} \geq w_{10}e^{r_1 t}, \qquad w_{2t} \leq w_{20}e^{r_2 t}, \qquad x_{2t} = v x_{1t}.$$

Then, writing $k = w_{20}/w_{10}$,

$$1 \leq \frac{w_{1t}x_{1t} + w_{2t}x_{2t}}{w_{1t}x_{1t}} = 1 + \frac{v w_{2t}}{w_{1t}} \leq 1 + kve^{(r_2 - r_1)t}. \quad \text{QED}$$

Proposition 8 Let the asymptotically stagnant activity of proposition 7 be supplied under conditions of perfect competition, and let its outputs, y_t, satisfy $y_t = u x_{1t}$, $u = $ a constant, and let its price be p_t. Then p_t^* will approach w_{1t}^* asymptotically; i.e., the growth rate of p_t will approach that of the price of its stagnant input.

Proof $p_t = (w_{1t}x_{1t} + w_{2t}x_{2t})/y_t = (w_{1t} + vw_{2t})/u$. Then, writing $a = 1/u$, $b = v/u$, we have

$$p_t^* = \frac{\dot{p}_t}{p_t} = \frac{a\dot{w}_{1t} + b\dot{w}_{2t}}{\cdot aw_{1t} + bw_{2t}} = \frac{\dot{w}_{1t}}{w_{1t}} \frac{aw_{1t}}{aw_{1t} + bw_{2t}} + \frac{\dot{w}_{2t}}{w_{2t}} \frac{bw_{2t}}{aw_{1t} + bw_{2t}}.$$

But $aw_{1t}/(aw_{1t} + bw_{2t})$ approaches unity asymptotically by proposition 7, while $\dot{w}_{2t}/w_{2t} \leq r_2$ and $bw_{2t}/(aw_{1t} + bw_{2t})$ approaches zero asymptotically (since its reciprocal $= 1 + aw_{1t}/bw_{2t} \geq 1 + kae^{r_1 t}/be^{r_2 t}$). Consequently, from the preceding equation, p_t^* must approach $\dot{w}_{it}/w_{it} = w_{it}^*$ asymptotically. QED

Corollary The smaller the upper bound, r_2, on w_{2t}^*, i.e., the growth rate of the price of the progressive input of the asymptotically stagnant activity, the more rapidly the behavior of the latter's price will be forced to approximate that of its stagnant input.

B. Alternative Measures of Sectoral Output and Productivity Growth

Chapter 6 described the first two of the methods used to measure the outputs of the different sectors of the economy and to classify them as progressive or stagnant. This appendix describes the alternative methods used to test the robustness of the results.

U.S. input-output data for 1947 and 1976 were used to estimate the third set of growth rates[2] (column 3, table 6.2).[3] Since these are total factor productivity (TFP) growth rates, they are generally lower than the corresponding labor productivity measures because capital-labor ratios were increasing. The overall rate of TFP was 1.17% per year, about a point lower than that of labor productivity, and the sectoral rates behaved similarly. However, their relative magnitudes leave the classification of the sectors as progressive and stagnant unchanged from that of the preceding measure, with the exception of mining.[4] The rate of TFP growth in mining was nearly zero, and so by this measure the mining sector was stagnant.

So far, our productivity measures evaluate productivity improvements within any one sector; one can also examine the changes in total input usage, per unit of a sector's input suppliers per unit of (final) output.

Three such total factor requirement measures are reported in columns 4–6 of table 6.2. The measure λ shows the total (direct plus indirect) labor requirements per unit of final output:

$$\lambda = \ell(\mathbf{I} - \mathbf{a})^{-1}. \tag{10}$$

The measure λ_m in column 5 of table 6.2 differs from (4) only in λ_m's Marxian accounting framework. Capital, as produced means of production, is valued by its depreciation rate (see Wolff [1979]).

The measure in column 6 of tale 6.2, $\tilde{\rho}$, is the total factor requirement analog of ρ. Let

$$\gamma = k(I - a)^{-1} \tag{11}$$

be the total capital requirements per unit of final output. Then the rate of change of total factor requirements per unit of final output can be estimated from

$$\tilde{\rho}_j \equiv - (w\,d\lambda_j + r\,d\gamma_j)/p_j. \tag{12}$$

Productivity growth based on λ and λ_m is quite similar to that in column 2, table 6.2, since changes in total factor requirements are dominated by those in direct factor requirements.[5] The classification of sectors is therefore identical with that of column 2, except that the mining sector now falls into the stagnant category. Similarly, the classification of sectors on the basis of $\tilde{\rho}$ is identical with that based on ρ.

The last column in table 6.2 uses the change in the (real) relative price of a sector's output to measure its *relative* rate of productivity growth. (The variable p is based on the GNP deflator, whose rate of change over time is standardized to equal 0.0) For a decline in relative prices can be interpreted, in a competitive market, as a corresponding decline in the growth of total factor requirements.[6] Of course, in reality, other developments influence relative prices. Nevertheless, all sectors that were classified as progressive by the measure $\tilde{\rho}$ showed declines in relative prices (that is, positive values in column 7), and conversely, except for business services, where relative price increased. By this measure, all general services were classified as stagnant.

In table 6.3, an $\times$ indicates that a sector is classified as stagnant by the corresponding measure of relative productivity growth (panel A). The results in columns 3–7 are quite similar to those in the first two columns for the remaining panels. The average annual rate of productivity growth for the two aggregated sectors are shown in panel B. The rate of productivity growth of the stagnant sector is between 2 and $2\frac{1}{2}$ percentage points less than that of the progressive sector.[7] The percent of employed persons working in the stagnant sector (panel C) increased between 11% and 13% over the 1947–1976 period. The stagnant sector's real share of final output (panel D) and gross output (panel F) declined slightly, according to these measures, while its share in nominal terms (panel E and G) increased in the range from 6 to 12 percentage points.

C. The Postwar Evolution of Computer Prices

Between 1954 (when the first computer was delivered to a commercial customer) and 1984, computer prices fell at an average rate of 19% annually, according to a study by Robert Gordon [1987]. Moreover, the prices of personal computers (PCs) have declined even faster. Gordon estimates that PC prices fell 20–25% annually between 1982 and 1986, and prices of peripheral equipment fell even more during that period.

The first commercial computer had 20 kilobytes of memory, a machine cycle time of 2,400 microseconds, and cost $192,000. By contrast, a PC clone in 1986 had 640 kilobytes of memory, a machine cycle time of 0.2 microseconds, and cost less than $1,000.

In 1955, 150 computers were built; their total value was $62 million. By 1965, 5,350 computers worth $1.8 billion were produced. That represents an average annual growth rate in total sales of 44%.

Before 1965, virtually all computers were mainframes; since then, mini- and microcomputers have dramatically increased their share of the market for computers. In 1969, mainframes accounted for 97% of the total value of computer production of $4.3 billion. By 1984, mainframes were only 46% of the total value of computer production (not including PCs) of $2.3 billion.

Gordon notes that official government price indexes assume that computer prices were constant before 1969. Adjusting for the price declines that actually occurred before that year, and for other technical factors, he finds that government estimates of price increases for office, computing, and accounting machines overestimate the annual rate of price increase by 16.4% during 1957–1972, and by 4.4% during 1972–1984. Because spending on computers was a small percentage of total outlays before 1972, Gordon estimates that the government's treatment of computers causes the statistics to overestimate the true value of inflation for all producer durables by about three-fourths of a percentage point per year both before and after 1972. However, research by Gordon on a wide variety of other products suggests that there was a total overestimate of producers' durable equipment inflation of about 3 percentage points per year.

Notes

1. We are very grateful to David Dollar for this result.

2. Our third measure of productivity growth rates requires several new symbols to describe the input-output framework. Let

X = (column) vector of gross output by sector,

Y = (column) vector of final demand by sector,

a = matrix of interindustry technical coefficients,

ℓ = (row) vector of labor coefficients showing employment per unit of output,

k = (row) vector of capital stock coefficients showing the capital stock required per unit of output, and

p = (row) vector of prices showing the (current) price per unit of output of each industry.

In addition, we use the following scalars:

w = the annual wage rate, in current dollars,

r = the rate of profit on the capital stock,

$z = pY$ = gross national product at current prices,

$L = \ell X$ = total employment, and

$K = kX$ = total capital stock.

The aggregate rate of total factor productivity (TFP) growth is given by

$$\pi^* = (p\,dY - w\,dL - r\,dK)/z, \tag{8}$$

where d refers to the differential. The rate of TFP growth for sector j is given by

$$\rho_j \equiv -\left(\sum_i p_i\,da_{ij} + w\,dl_j + r\,dk_j\right)/p_j. \tag{9}$$

This is the continuous analog of Leontief's measure of sectoral technical changes [1953]. See Peterson [1979] and Wolff [1985] for more details. Because discrete time periods are employed, a Törnqvist-Divisia Index is used to estimate sectoral and the overall rate of TFP (see Gollop and Jorgensen [1980] or Wolff [1985]).

3. The 1947 input-output table is the standard 87-order Bureau of Economic Analysis version. (See, for example, U.S. Department of Commerce, Bureau of Economic Analysis [1974] for methods and a listing of sectors.) The 1976 table was estimated using the so-called R.A.S. (or biproportionality) method on the 1972 table, with the gross domestic output figures in U.S. Department of Commerce, Bureau of Labor Statistics [1979a]. Estimates of the total capital stock in each input-output sector appear in U.S. Department of Commerce, Bureau of Labor Statistics [1979b]. Full capital coefficient matrices for 1947 were obtained from the Brandeis Economic Research Center (BERC); sectoral 1947 depreciation rates from BERC and for 1976 by the Bureau of Economic Analysis. Additional details on data sources and methods are available from the authors.

The accounting framework was then modified in the following ways:

1. An "endogenous export column" was created to balance the noncompetitive import row (sector 80).

2. For the estimation of Marxian labor values, the depreciation row that is normally part of value-added was treated as an endogenous input row (sector 88), and an "endogeneous capital replacement" column was included to balance this row.

3. Five sectors—research and development (74), business travel (81), office supplies (82), scrap and used goods (83), and inventory valuation adjustment (87)—appeared in the 1947 table but not in the 1976 table. In order to assure consistency of the accounting framework, these sectors were eliminated from both gross and final outputs in 1947 by distributing their inputs to other sectors.

4. Indirect business taxes in value-added were eliminated in order to remove the biasing effect of indirect business taxes on relative prices.

5. The input-output matrices were finally converted to constant (1958) prices by multiplying each row of the matrix by the appropriate sectoral price deflator.

For details, see Wolff [1985].

4. This reflects a large postwar influx of capital equipment into mining and increases in intermediate inputs. The mining sector is rather different from a more standard stagnant sector, since it is a process industry whose output is not directly related to its labor (or capital) input. Its low rate of TFP growth is probably attributable primarily to the nature of extraction, in which more accessible ores and petroleum are mined first and less accessible deposits later. The increasing difficulty of mining would have yielded a negative growth rate in TFP if technology had remained constant. The fact that TFP growth was zero in this sector over the period 1947–1976 suggests that technical change (or the discovery of new accessible deposits) did occur.

5. It should be noted that the overall level of productivity growth corresponding to λ_m is the ratio of net national product to employment, since depreciation is treated as endogenous. The rate of growth is lower than that of GNP per worker.

6. In the Leontief framework, prices are the duals of the total factor requirements and are given by $v(I - a)^{-1}$, where v is the row vector of the value-added coefficient.

7. Both sector values of ρ are below the overall rate of TFP growth, π^*. This is correct, because as demonstrated in Peterson [1979] or Wolff [1985],

$$\pi^* = \sum \frac{p_i X_i}{z} \rho_i.$$

The ratio of total GDO to total final output (in current dollars) is about 2.0 in both years.

Appendix to Chapter 7:
Decomposition of
Employment Change

Let us begin by defining the following matrix and vector components:

$\mathbf{X}$ = column vector showing the total output (gross domestic output or GDO) by sector,

$\mathbf{Y}$ = column vector showing the final output by sector,

$\mathbf{M}$ = the employment matrix, where M_{ij} shows the total employment of occupation i in industry j,

$\mathbf{L}$ = a row vector showing total employment in industry j, where $L_j = \sum_i M_{ij}$, and

$\mathbf{B}$ = a column vector of total employment by occupation, where $B_i = \sum_j M_{ij}$.

Let us now define the following coefficients:

$\mathbf{a}$ = the square matrix of interindustry input-output coefficients, where a_{ij} indicates the amount of input i required per unit of output j,

$\mathbf{y}$ = a column vector showing the percentage distribution of total output (GDO) by sector, where $y_i = Y_i / \sum Y_i$,

$\mathbf{n}$ = an employment distribution matrix, showing the percentage distribution of employment by occupation within each sector, where $n_{ij} = M_{ij} / L_j$,

$\mathbf{m}$ = the employment coefficient matrix, showing employment by occupation per unit of output, where $m_{ij} = M_{ij} / X_j$,

$\mathbf{p}$ = a row vector showing the percentage distribution of employment by sector, where $p_j = L_j / \sum L_j$,

ℓ = a row vector of labor coefficients showing total employment per unit of output, where $\ell_j = L_j/X_j$, and

$\mathbf{b}$ = a column vector showing the percentage distribution of employment by occupation, where $b_i = B_i/\sum B_i$.

To derive our basic tautological relationship, we first express the matrix of occupational output-employment coefficients, $\mathbf{m}$, in terms of the vector of industry labor coefficients, ℓ, obtaining

$$\mathbf{m} = \mathbf{n}\hat{\ell}, \tag{1}$$

where a hat ($\hat{}$) connotes a diagonal matrix whose elements are those of the associated vector (ℓ). It follows from the basic Leontief identity $\mathbf{X} = (\mathbf{I} - \mathbf{a})^{-1}$ and (1) that

$$\mathbf{b^*} = \mathbf{m}(\mathbf{I} - \mathbf{a})^{-1}\mathbf{y}, \tag{2}$$

where $\mathbf{b^*}$ is the distribution of employment by occupation generated by the percentage output vector $\mathbf{y}$. Then by (1) and (2)

$$\mathbf{b^*} = \mathbf{n}\hat{\lambda}\mathbf{x},$$

where $\lambda = \ell(\mathbf{I} - \mathbf{a})^{-1}$ and λ_i shows the direct and indirect labor requirements per unit of output i. We have, directly,

$$\Delta\mathbf{b}(\mathbf{y}) = \Delta\mathbf{n}\,\hat{\lambda}\mathbf{y}/\sum\mathbf{b^*} + \mathbf{n}(\Delta\hat{\lambda})\mathbf{y}/\sum\mathbf{b^*} + \mathbf{n}\hat{\lambda}\,\Delta\mathbf{y}/\sum\mathbf{b^*}, \tag{3}$$

where $\mathbf{b}(\mathbf{y})$ is the percentage distribution of employment generated by the output vector $\mathbf{y}$. This equation, then, decomposes a change in occupational composition of employment $\Delta\mathbf{b}(\mathbf{y})$, into three parts:

i. $\Delta\mathbf{n}\,\hat{\lambda}\mathbf{y}/\sum\mathbf{b^*}$, which corresponds to the change in the n_{ij}, the shares of the different occupations, by industry. In other words, this term reflects, in part, the extent to which production processes within industries have changed their techniques so as to substitute information labor for labor of other types. However, as we saw earlier, this term also reflects in part any relative growth in productivity of noninformation labor that tends automatically to depress the relative demand for such labor—another variant of the productivity lag effect. We shall call this term in the equation the *input-substitution component*.

ii. The second term in (3) involves $\Delta\hat{\lambda}$, the change in the vector of quantities of direct plus indirect labor per unit of output, by industry, i.e., the change in the reciprocal of each industry's "total" labor productivity. We call this the *productivity-lag component*.[1]

iii. The final term involving the incremental change, Δy, in the shares of the total outputs of the different industries, we describe as the (final) *output-composition component*.

Thus, if the last term turns out to be significant and substantial in an empirical calculation, this will imply that the growth in information employment is indeed attributable to an information revolution. For a large third term indicates that buyers are typically turning increasingly to outputs whose production has a large information content. The same may also be true, in part, of a large first term, which may indicate that a typical production process has increased its reliance on information labor. However, if the second term turns out to be substantial and significant, it will suggest that a corresponding portion of the increase in share of information labor is attributable not to an upsurge in information use, but rather to unbalanced growth—the shift of labor out of activities whose productivity growth is atypically large.

Note

1. The second term can be further decomposed into two effects: one emanating from a change in the direct labor coefficients and the other from a change in the structure of the interindustry coefficients. The results indicated that the added effect from the change in the interindustry coefficient structure was not very important.

Appendix to Chapter 8

A. The Calculations of Total Factor Productivity and Investment[1]

We start with total factor productivity (TFP) and investment calculations based on data for the postwar period (actually, 1950–1979). There are two reasons: First, it is one of the longest stretches of time unbroken by a major war, major social changes, or economic depression, and thus provides a relatively long period for tests of such hypotheses as the convergence of productivity levels and that of the advantages of backwardness; second, it is also the period for which the available data are most abundant. This is true not only for capital stocks but also for the national accounting data necessary to estimate the wage and profit share required to calculate total factor productivity.

The analysis begins with the measurement of total factor productivity. Data limitations force us to use a measure that is really only a two-factor productivity index. We employed two basic measures:

$$\text{"crude" TFP} = Y/[\alpha L + (1-\alpha)K], \tag{1}$$

where Y is the total output of the country in question, L and K are the quantities of its labor and capital inputs, respectively, and α is the share of wages in national income. The time derivative of (1) was used as the measure of rate of growth of crude TFP. In addition, we calculated a growth rate of a Divisia measure of TFP given by

$$\rho = \dot{Y}/Y - [\alpha \dot{L}/L + (1-\alpha)\dot{K}/K], \tag{2}$$

where a superscript dot indicates a derivative with respect to time.

Table A8.1 shows various measures of (crude) TFP for the period 1950–1979 for Canada, France, Germany, Italy, Japan, the United Kingdom, and the United States. The ratio of employee compensation (EC) to GDP is employed to measure the share of wages, α, and the gross nonresidential

Table A8.1
Total factor productivity (TFP) levels and growth rates, 1950 and 1979

	TFP levels[a]		Crude TFP growth,[a] 1950–1979 (%)	Divisia TFP growth (ρ),[b] 1950–1979 (%)
	1950	1979		
Canada	0.87	1.18	1.02	1.15
France	0.59	1.22	2.53	2.45
Germany	0.47	1.04	2.78	2.68
Italy	0.51	1.16	2.88	2.37
Japan	0.27	1.00	4.56	2.97
U.K.	0.72	1.15	1.63	1.43
U.S.	1.00	1.37	1.09	1.30
Mean	0.63	1.16	2.35	2.05
Standard deviation	0.23	0.11		
Coefficient of variation	0.37	0.10		
Max/Min	3.75	1.37		
Correlation with				
TFP_{50}			−0.960	−0.939
$LPROD_{50}$			−0.918	−0.907
Correlation, excluding Japan, with				
TFP_{50}			−0.962	
$LPROD_{50}$			−0.937	
Adjusted correlation with natural logarithm of				
TFP_{50}			−0.961	

a. TFP levels are computed according to equation (1). The TFP measure has been standardized so that TFP in the United States in 1950 is equal to unity. Output is measured by GDP, the labor input by person-hours, capital by gross nonresidential fixed plant and equipment, and the wage share by the ratio of employee compensation (EC) to GDP. Average period wage weights are used in the calculation.
b. Divisia TFP growth is computed according to equation (2). Output is measured by GDP, the labor input by person-hours, capital by gross nonresidential fixed plant and equipment, and the wage share by the ratio of employee compensation (EC) to GDP. Average period wage weights are used in the calculation.

stock of fixed plant and equipment is used to measure K. Hours worked are used as the labor input. The TFP index has been scaled so that TFP in the United States in 1950 is set at unity.[2] We use the average wage share for the period in the calculation.[3] The results indicate that there was a dramatic convergence in TFP levels between 1950 and 1979. The standard deviation in TFP levels fell by half and the coefficient of variation by over two-thirds. Moreover, the ratio of maximum to minimum TFP level fell by about two-thirds over these years.

Table A8.1 also shows average annual rates of crude TFP growth [as defined by equation (1)] for the seven countries.[4] The bottom five rows show the correlation of TFP growth rates with country productivity levels in 1950, testing whether countries with initially low productivity levels tend to have relatively higher productivity growth rates, as is required for convergence. The first row shows the correlation with the 1950 crude TFP level (TFP). The correlation is very high (in absolute value), −0.96.

The second row shows the correlation of TFP growth rates with the country's labor productivity level in 1950. This was calculated for two reasons. First, the measurement of labor productivity does not involve the kinds of conceptual difficulties that the measurement of TFP growth entails. Second, part of the argument of this analysis is that countries that are technologically backward will also have low capital-labor ratios. Reciprocally, high rates of technological change are associated with high rates of capital formation. Therefore, a strong inverse relation between initial labor productivity level and TFP growth is to be expected. This is confirmed, though the correlation is −0.92, not quite as high as that between TFP growth and initial TFP level. The inverse correlation of TFP growth with the 1950 TFP level, which is higher than the inverse correlation of TFP growth with initial labor productivity, suggests that technological backwardness per se is a slightly stronger determinant of the borrowing of more advanced technology than is a low capital-labor ratio.

Since Japan is such a statistical outlier in many respects (for example, TFP growth, the rate of capital formation, and the investment rate), the same correlation was also calculated using data on all countries except Japan. The resulting six-country correlations are actually slightly higher in absolute value than the corresponding seven-country figures. This indicates that the test of the convergence hypothesis is not unduly influenced by the inclusion of Japan in the sample.[5]

Computations of TFP growth, based on the Divisia measure, are also shown in table A8.1. This measure, described by equation (2), has an illuminating interpretation under certain (restrictive) conditions. In particular, if all markets are competitive, all industries have smooth production functions with constant returns to scale, and producers minimize cost, then it can be shown that the aggregate production frontier will shift out at the same rate at each point. The Divisia index ρ will then measure this equiproportionate rate of technological advance (see chapter 11 for a more detailed discussion). Even if these conditions fail to hold, the Divisia index represents a reasonable way to measure aggregate TFP growth. Since wage shares typically change over a period, the Törnqvist-Divisia index, defined by setting α equal to the average wage share of the period, was employed. TFP growth rates calculated via this index are uniformly lower than those based on the crude TFP measure, though the difference is relatively small (about 0.2–0.3 percentage points). The correlation coefficients between TFP growth and 1950 productivity levels are slightly lower in absolute value using the Divisia measure than the corresponding crude TFP one.

In conclusion, the inverse correlation between TFP growth and initial productivity level remains very strong (correlations of at least −0.9) for the two measures used. Moreover, almost without exception, the inverse correlation between TFP growth and initial TFP level is stronger than that between TFP growth and initial labor productivity level.

B.   Total Factor Productivity Growth and the Growth in Capital Stock

The main results of the TFP study for the purposes of this chapter are those evaluating the relation between productivity and capital accumulation. Table A8.2 presents basic data on the growth in capital stock over the period 1950–1979. There clearly has been considerable variation in rates of growth of capital stock among the seven countries. They range from a low of 3.3% (United Kingdom) to a high of 8.4% (Japan). The arithmetic average is 4.9%, and the standard deviation 1.6%.

Growth rates are also shown for the capital-labor ratio. Growth rates for the ratio of gross capital to labor range from a low of 2.4% (United States) to a high of 7.1% (Japan). The rank order is very similar to that of gross capital stock growth. Investment rates are also shown in table 8.4. Gross investment rates range from 7.0% (United Kingdom) to 17.2% (Japan), with a mean of 11.6% and a standard deviation of 3.3%.

The main point for our discussion is that strong inverse correlations exist between the various growth rates of capital stock and the 1950 productivity levels (also see figure 8.3.). The correlation coefficient between gross capital stock growth and the 1950 TFP level is −0.73. There is an even stronger inverse correlation between initial TFP level and the rate of

Table A8.2
The average annual rate of growth of the capital stock, the capital/labor ratio, and the
average investment rate, 1950–1979[a]

	Annual growth rate of capital stock (%)	Annual growth rate of capital/labor ratio (%)	Average investment rate (%)
Canada	5.03	2.95	12.95
France	4.11	4.18	10.09
Germany	5.28	5.66	14.61
Italy	4.82	5.10	10.46
Japan	8.36	7.11	17.23
U.K.	3.29	3.55	6.96
U.S.	3.61	2.44	8.90
Mean	4.93	4.43	11.60
Standard deviation	1.56	1.52	3.27
A. Correlation with TFP_{50}			
	-0.734	-0.979	-0.640
B. Correlation with $\dot{TFP}/TFP$			
	0.816	0.971	0.676
C. Correlation with Divisia TFP growth (ρ)			
	0.663	0.927	0.628
D. Correlation with $LPROD_{50}$			
	-0.655	-0.942	-0.558

a. Capital is measured by gross nonresidential fixed plant and equipment. The wage
share is measured by the ratio of employee compensation (EC) to GDP, and the average
1950–1979 wage share for each country is used to compute the TFP level and TFP
growth.

change in the capital-labor ratios, of −0.98. This result is highly consistent with the hypothesis that low levels of TFP lead to high rates of capital formation. The correlation between the investment rate and the 1950 TFP level is −0.64, also negative, though lower in absolute value than the corresponding correlation with capital growth rates. Finally, the correlation coefficients between the 1950 labor productivity level and the various measures of capital stock growth and the investment rate are all strongly negative, though, as is to have been expected, slightly lower in absolute value than the corresponding correlations involving 1950 TFP levels.

Correspondingly, there is a high positive correlation between the rate of growth of TFP (both crude and Divisia) and the rate of growth of capital stock (also see figure 8.2).[6] The correlation coefficient for the crude TFP index is 0.82, and that for the Divisia index is 0.66. Even stronger are the correlations between TFP growth and the rate of change in the capital-labor ratio, with coefficients of −0.93 and −0.97. These results are consistent with the hypothesis that new technology must generally be embodied in new capital equipment and machinery. Finally, there are strong positive correlations between TFP growth and the gross investment rate, with coefficients of 0.63 and 0.68.

C. The Longer View

The postwar period from 1950 to 1979 is perhaps unique in recent history in its absence of major wars or depressions. This naturally raises the question whether the relations among initial productivity level, productivity growth, and capital formation that have just been described hold for longer periods of time that span major disruptions of normal economic growth. To answer this, these relations were investigated for the period from 1880 to 1979, one that includes two major depressions and two world wars. The surprising result is that, with relatively few exceptions, the same relations hold.

Because of data limitations, the cross-national average value of the ratio of employee compensation to national income was used as the measure of the labor share.[7] The calculations of TFP levels for selected years in the period from 1880 to 1979 are shown in table A8.3. It should be noted that because of unavailability of data the sample of countries diminishes the further back in time one proceeds. Both the ratio of maximum to minimum TFP levels and the coefficient of variation indicate that there was a relatively gradual convergence in TFP levels from 1880 to 1938. This was followed by a sharp increase in dispersion of TFP levels between 1938 and

Table A8.3
Total factor productivity (TFP) levels, 1880–1979[a]

	1880	1913	1929	1938	1950	1979
Canada	NA	NA	0.50	0.49	0.86	1.23
France	NA	NA	NA	NA	0.54	1.31
Germany	0.18	0.31	0.38	0.46	0.43	1.12
Italy	0.17	0.26	0.34	0.42	0.45	1.21
Japan	0.08	0.14	0.24	0.32	0.21	1.01
U.K.	0.32	0.44	0.53	0.57	0.72	1.15
U.S.	0.30	0.49	0.65	0.65	1.00	1.38
5-country statistics						
Mean	0.21	0.33	0.43	0.48	0.56	1.17
Standard deviation	0.09	0.13	0.15	0.12	0.27	0.12
Coefficient of variation	0.43	0.38	0.34	0.24	0.48	0.10
Max/Min	4.10	3.47	2.74	2.04	4.70	1.37
6-country statistics						
Mean	NA	NA	0.44	0.49	0.61	1.18
Standard deviation	NA	NA	0.14	0.11	0.27	0.11
Coefficient of variation	NA	NA	0.31	0.22	0.44	0.10
Max/Min	NA	NA	2.74	2.04	4.70	1.37
7-country statistics						
Mean	NA	NA	NA	NA	0.60	1.20
Standard deviation	NA	NA	NA	NA	0.25	0.11
Coefficient of variation	NA	NA	NA	NA	0.42	0.09
Max/Min	NA	NA	NA	NA	4.70	1.37

a. TFP levels are computed according to equation (1). The TFP measure has been standardized so that TFP in the United States in 1950 is equal to unity. Output is measured by GDP, the labor input by hours worked, and capital by gross nonresidential fixed plant and equipment (net for Germany). The wage share is the same for all years and is the average value of mean EC/NI in the United Kingdom and the United States over the 1880–1979 periods.

Table A8.4
Average annual rates of crude and Divisia TFP growth by country and subperiod, 1880–1979[a]

	1880–1979		1880–1929		1929–1979		1880–1950		1950–1979	
	Crude TFP (%)	Divisia TFP (%)	Crude TFP (%)	Divisia TFP (%)	Crude TFP (%)	Divisia TFP (%)	Crude TFP (%)	Divisia TFP (%)	Crude TFP (%)	Divisia TFP (%)
Canada	NA	NA	NA	NA	1.99	2.00	NA	NA	1.30	1.44
France	NA	NA	NA	NA	NA	NA	NA	NA	3.10	3.04
Germany	1.88	1.56	1.47	0.98	2.45	2.29	1.24	0.89	3.39	3.33
Italy	1.99	1.36	1.37	0.47	2.76	2.34	1.35	0.57	3.51	3.09
Japan	2.60	1.62	2.23	1.08	3.13	2.32	1.42	0.50	5.45	4.17
U.K.	1.30	1.09	0.99	0.72	1.72	1.56	1.14	0.91	1.68	1.48
U.S.	1.55	1.37	1.43	0.89	1.69	1.80	1.65	1.29	1.15	1.36
Mean	1.86	1.40	1.50	0.83	2.29	2.05	1.36	0.83	2.80	2.56
Correlation with										
TFP_0	−0.973	−0.832	−0.848	−0.325	−0.962	−0.813	−0.012	0.804	−0.965	−0.956
$LPROD_0$	−0.804	−0.531	−0.570	−0.054	−0.934	−0.769	0.409	0.961	−0.922	−0.912
$\ell n(TFP_0)$	−0.989	−0.803	−0.911	−0.412	−0.978	−0.798	−0.052	0.795	−0.991	−0.951
Adjusted correlation with										
$\ell n(TFP_0)$	−0.961		−0.697		−0.924		0.384		−0.969	

a. TFP levels are computed according to equation (1). The TFP measure has been standardized so that TFP in the United States in 1950 is unity. Output is measured by GDP, the labor input by hours worked, and capital by gross nonresidential plant and equipment (net for Germany for 1870–1950). The wage share differs by period and is set equal to the international average value of EC/NI of countries for which data are available over the whole period.

1950. This was primarily attributable to the effect of World War II on the German and Japanese economies, since, in both cases, absolute productivity actually declined in this period. Between 1950 and 1979, as documented in the previous section, there was very rapid convergence in average productivities. In sum, the dispersion of productivity levels, as measured by the coefficient of variation, fell by about half between 1880 and 1938, doubled between 1938 and 1950, and then fell by over three-quarters between 1950 and 1979. The 1979 dispersion stood at about one-fourth of its 1880 level.

Table A8.4 shows average growth rates of both crude and Divisia TFP growth for selected periods and their correlation with initial productivity levels (indicated by TFP_0 and $LPROD_0$) and the natural logarithm of initial TFP. The results support the convergence hypothesis for the full period 1880–1979 and for almost all subperiods. The correlation coefficients are stronger for crude TFP growth than for Divisia TFP growth, and for initial

Table A8.5
Average annual rate of growth of the capital-labor ratio by country and subperiod, 1880–1979[a]

	1880–1979 (%)	1880–1929 (%)	1929–1979 (%)	1880–1950 (%)	1950–1979 (%)
Canada	NA	NA	2.40	NA	2.95
France	NA	NA	NA	NA	4.18
Germany	2.80	1.71	3.87	1.38	5.66
Italy	3.16	2.38	3.93	2.36	5.10
Japan	3.76	2.68	4.81	2.37	7.11
U.K.	1.76	1.04	2.46	1.01	3.55
U.S.	2.27	2.45	2.09	2.19	2.44
Mean	2.75	2.05	3.26	1.86	4.43
Standard deviation	0.69	0.60	1.00	0.56	1.52
Correlation with					
TFP_0	−0.974	−0.585	−0.792	−0.528	−0.974
TḞP/TFP	0.983	0.752	0.976	0.751	0.973
ρ	0.831	0.188	0.844	−0.298	0.950
Adjusted correlation with					
ρ	0.890	0.490	0.894	0.196	0.963

a. Capital is measured by gross nonresidential plant and equipment (net for Germany for 1870–1950) and the labor input by hours worked. See the notes to table 8.6 for details on the measurement of TFP levels and growth rates.

TFP level than for initial labor productivity level. Using crude TFP growth and initial TFP level, the calculations show that convergence was particularly strong over the entire period 1880–1979 and the subperiods from 1929 to 1979 and 1950 to 1979. Correlation coefficients were somewhat lower in absolute value for the period 1880–1929, though still sufficiently high to support the convergence hypothesis. The only perverse case was the 1880–1950 period, for reasons already indicated.

Correlations between the growth in the capital-labor ratio and productivity are shown in table A8.5. With one exception, these strongly support the embodiment hypothesis. The correlation coefficients are all negative, as predicted. The correlations of productivity and the growth in the capital-labor ratio range from −0.53 to −0.97. Correspondingly, correlations between TFP growth and the growth in the capital-labor ratio are generally very strong and positive. Those between crude TFP growth and the growth in the capital-labor ratio range from 0.75 to 0.98. Correlations between the Divisia index of TFP growth and capital growth tend to be lower. However, there is a built-in positive bias in the correlation coefficient between the Divisia measure and the growth in the capital stock, since the Divisia index includes the growth in the capital stock as one of its terms [cf. equation (2)]. This bias can be corrected for, and the adjusted correlation coefficients, shown in the last row of table A8.5, indicate that the correlations are almost as strong as those using crude TFP growth (see Wolff [1987b] for details on the adjustment procedure). Moreover, all four sets of measures indicate that the relation between TFP and capital accumulation was considerably stronger in the period after 1950 than during the years from 1880 to 1938. This suggests that other factors peculiar to the postwar period have heightened the importance of the embodiment effect.

It should be emphasized again that the results of the calculations described in this appendix are based on a rather narrow and selective sample of countries, the "Big Seven." It is therefore not possible to say that the results hold universally or even generally. This will have to await the availability of additional data and additional analysis.

Notes

1. This section is adapted from Wolff [1987b]. See the paper for details. Data on output, gross capital stock, and hours worked are obtained from Maddison [1982]. Problems of comparability of measures among countries are discussed in Maddison. Since some of the data series are not complete for the full period 1870–1979, we have interpolated missing data points on the basis of average rates of growth for periods for which the data are available. Data on wage shares are computed from

the following sources: (i) Data for 1950–1979 are from the United Nations' *Yearbook of National Accounts Statistics*, selected years, except for the 1950–1960 period in Italy. (ii) Data for 1937–1950 and for 1950–1960 in Italy are from the International Labor Organization's *Yearbook of Labor Statistics*, various years. (iii) For Japan, data for 1920–1937 are from Ohkawa and Rosovsky [1973, pp. 316–317]. (iv) For the United Kingdom, data for 1870–1938 are from Dean and Cole [1964, p. 247]. (v) For the United States, data for 1870– 1938 are from Johnson [1954].

2. This was done by setting both U.S. labor productivity (Y/L) and capital productivity (K/L) in 1950 at unity. Since the choice of scale is arbitrary, we also tested the sensitivity of the results to the choice of base year and base country. The results show that relative total factor productivity levels are quite insensitive to the choice of base.

3. We also used first period, last period, and cross-national wage shares for the calculation. The results were very robust under variation in choice of wage shares. See Wolff [1987b] for details.

4. Computations were also made on the basis of the ratio of EC to GNP and EC to national income (NI). The results are almost identical to those based on the ratio EC/GDP.

5. Tests of the correlation between initial productivity level and the rate of productivity growth are, unfortunately, biased, because the same term is included in the two variables. For some of our calculations it was possible to adjust for the bias (see Wolff [1987b] for details). The adjusted correlation coefficient also indicates that there was a very strong inverse relation between initial total factor productivity level and the total factor productivity growth rate, and, indeed, it is almost of the same magnitude as the correlation coefficient between the 1950 TFP level and the TFP growth rate. There does not appear to be a straightforward way to adjust most of the correlation coefficients calculated, since the TFP growth rate is not linearly related to initial TFP or labor productivity levels. On the other hand, the bias in the correlation coefficients is probably less severe for this reason.

6. There is also a statistical bias problem in the correlation of Divisia TFP growth with the growth in the capital stock and the capital-labor ratio. See Wolff [1987b] for adjusted results.

7. For the years 1938 to 1979, this average is based on data for five countries: Canada, France, Japan, the United Kingdom, and the United States. For other periods, the average is based on data for the United Kingdom and the United States only. It should be noted that the wage share is recomputed for each period analyzed.

Appendix to Chapter 9: Convergence and Education—a Statistical Analysis

Our statistical study, as explained in the text of this chapter, undertook to extend our convergence analysis of chapter 5 via a set of regression calculations that related the rate of growth of a nation's real GDP per capita (the dependent variable) to the initial level of real GDP per capita and a measure of the level of education in that nation (the two independent variables). In this study, five different productivity series are used. The first is derived from the World Bank's World Development Report of 1986 and the remaining four from the Summers and Heston [1984] data. Each productivity series encompasses a different sample of countries. We used data only from countries for which figures giving beginning-of-period and end-of-period productivity levels are available. There were a few missing values for education levels, and these were imputed by using the mean value of the variable for the World Bank country group of which the specific country is a member.[1] Population growth estimates are available for all countries.

The first productivity series, from the World Development Report, is real gross national product (in 1984 U.S. dollars) per capita (which we call RGNP) and runs from 1965 to 1984 (see table A9.1 for a description of the variables). The series encompasses 105 countries (see table A9.2 for details on the samples). The second series, from the Summers and Heston data, is real gross domestic product (in 1975 international prices) per capita (which they label RGDP) for the 1950–1981 period. The sample covers 66 countries. The third is RGDP for the 1960–1981 period and includes 112 countries. The fourth, from the Summers and Heston data, is real per-capita gross domestic product (in 1975 international prices), with a terms of trade adjustment, for the 1950–1981 period (which they label RGDP*). The sample includes 57 countries. The last is RGDP* for the 1960–1981 period, which includes 103 countries.

Unfortunately, there is no information available on the educational attainment levels of the labor force or of the adult population (or even of the

Table A9.1
Statistical analysis of convergence and education: definitions and source of variables

Variable	Definition	Source
$RGNP_t$	Real gross national product (GNP) in 1984 dollars per capita, year t	World Development Report 1986, table 1
$RGDP_t$	Summers and Heston real gross domestic product (GDP) per capita, year t, in 1975 international prices	Summers and Heston data [1984]
$RGDP_t^*$	Summers and Heston real gross domestic product (GDP) per capita, year t, with terms of trade adjustment, in 1975 international prices	Summers and Heston data [1984]
R84/65	$\ln(RGNP_{1984}/RGNP_{1965})$	
R81/50	$\ln(RGDP_{1981}/RGDP_{1950})$	
R81/60	$\ln(RGDP_{1981}/RGDP_{1960})$	
R*81/50	$\ln(RGDP^*_{1981}/RGDP^*_{1950})$	
R*81/60	$\ln(RGDP^*_{1981}/RGDP^*_{1960})$	
POPGRT	Average annual rate of population growth, 1965–1983	World Development Report 1986, table 25
$PRIMARY_t$	Proportion of age group enrolled in primary school in year t[a]	World Development Report 1986, table 29
$SECONDARY_t$	Proportion of age group enrolled in secondary school in year t[a]	World Development Report 1986, table 29
$HIGHERED_t$	Proportion of age group enrolled in higher education in year t[a]	World Development Report 1986, table 29

a. For countries for which education data were missing, means for World Bank country groups were imputed.

population as a whole). As a result, we use data on the percentage of the student-age population currently enrolled in school as a proxy for the educational attainment of the labor force. There are three different variables provided in the World Bank data. The first is the percentage of children of primary school age enrolled in primary school (PRIMARY). The second is the percentage of children of secondary school age enrolled in secondary school (SECONDARY). The third is the percentage of college-age individuals enrolled in higher education (HIGHERED). Data on each of the three are available both for 1965 and 1983. Data on the earlier of the two years is a better indicator of the educational level of the labor force than that for the later year.

The last variable of interest in our analysis is population growth (POPGRT). This variable is included in order to control for any country whose population growth is so rapid as to swamp any gains from the advantages

Table A9.2
Statistical analysis of convergence and education: country samples for the five productivity series

		World Bank	Summers and Heston data			
		RGNP 1965–1984	RGDP 1950–1981	RGDP 1960–1981	RGDP* 1950–1981	RGDP* 1960–1981
Sample size		105	66	112	57	103
Country						
1	Afghanistan	× ×	× ×		× ×	
2	Algeria		× ×		× ×	
3	Angola	× ×	× ×		× ×	
4	Argentina					
5	Australia					
6	Austria					
7	Bangladesh		× ×		× ×	
8	Barbados	× ×	× ×	× ×	× ×	× ×
9	Belgium					
10	Benin		× ×		× ×	
11	Bolivia					
12	Botswana		× ×		× ×	
13	Brazil					
14	Bulgaria	× ×			× ×	× ×
15	Burkina Faso		× ×		× ×	
16	Burma					
17	Burundi		× ×		× ×	
18	Cameroon		× ×		× ×	
19	Canada					
20	Central African Republic		× ×		× ×	
21	Chad	× ×	× ×		× ×	
22	Chile					
23	China				× ×	× ×
24	Colombia					
25	Congo People's Republic		× ×		× ×	
26	Costa Rica					
27	Cyprus	× ×	× ×	× ×	× ×	× ×
28	Czechoslovakia	× ×			× ×	× ×
29	Denmark					
30	Dominican Republic					
31	Ecuador					

Table A9.2 (continued)

		World Bank	Summers and Heston data			
		RGNP 1965–1984	RGDP 1950–1981	RGDP 1960–1981	RGDP* 1950–1981	RGDP* 1960–1981
32	Egypt (United Arab Republic)					
33	El Salvador					
34	Ethiopia					
35	Fiji	× ×	× ×	× ×	× ×	× ×
36	Finland					
37	France					
38	Gabon	× ×	× ×	× ×	× ×	× ×
39	Gambia	× ×	× ×	× ×	× ×	× ×
40	Germany, Federal Republic of					
41	German Democratic Republic	× ×			× ×	× ×
42	Ghana		× ×		× ×	
43	Greece					
44	Guatemala					
45	Guinea		× ×		× ×	
46	Guyana	× ×	× ×	× ×	× ×	× ×
47	Haiti		× ×		× ×	
48	Honduras					
49	Hong Kong		× ×		× ×	
50	Hungary				× ×	× ×
51	Iceland	× ×	× ×	× ×	× ×	× ×
52	India					
53	Indonesia		×		× ×	
54	Iran	× ×	× ×		× ×	
55	Iraq	× ×	× ×		× ×	
56	Ireland					
57	Israel					
58	Italy					
59	Ivory Coast		× ×		× ×	
60	Jamaica		× ×		× ×	
61	Japan					
62	Jordan		× ×		× ×	
63	Kenya					
64	Korea, Republic		× ×		× ×	
65	Kuwait		× ×	× ×	× ×	× ×

Table A9.2 (continued)

		World Bank	Summers and Heston data			
		RGNP 1965– 1984	RGDP 1950– 1981	RGDP 1960– 1981	RGDP* 1950– 1981	RGDP* 1960– 1981
66	Lesotho		× ×		× ×	
67	Liberia		× ×		× ×	
68	Libya		× ×	× ×	× ×	× ×
69	Luxembourg	× ×	× ×	× ×	× ×	× ×
70	Madagascar		× ×		× ×	
71	Malawi		× ×		× ×	
72	Malaysia		× ×		× ×	
73	Mali		× ×		× ×	
74	Malta	× ×	× ×	× ×	× ×	× ×
75	Mauritania		× ×		× ×	
76	Mauritius					
77	Mexico					
78	Morocco					
79	Mozambique	× ×	× ×		× ×	
80	Nepal		× ×		× ×	
81	Netherlands					
82	New Zealand					
83	Nicaragua					
84	Niger		× ×		× ×	
85	Nigeria					
86	Norway					
87	Oman		× ×	× ×	× ×	× ×
88	Pakistan					
89	Panama					
90	Papua, New Guinea		× ×		× ×	
91	Paraguay					
92	Peru					
93	Philippines					
94	Poland				× ×	× ×
95	Portugal					
96	Romania	× ×			× ×	× ×
97	Rwanda		× ×		× ×	
98	Saudi Arabia		× ×	× ×	× ×	× ×
99	Senegal		× ×		× ×	

Table A9.2 (continued)

		World Bank	Summers and Heston data			
		RGNP 1965– 1984	RGDP 1950– 1981	RGDP 1960– 1981	RGDP* 1950– 1981	RGDP* 1960– 1981
100	Sierra Leone		× ×		× ×	
101	Singapore		× ×		× ×	
102	Somalia	× ×	× ×		× ×	
103	Spain					
104	Sri Lanka					
105	Sudan		× ×		× ×	
106	Surinam	× ×	× ×	× ×	× ×	× ×
107	Swaziland	× ×	× ×	× ×	× ×	× ×
108	Sweden					
109	Switzerland					
110	Syrian Arab Republic		× ×		× ×	
111	South Africa					
112	Taiwan	× ×	× ×	× ×	× ×	× ×
113	Tanzania		× ×		× ×	
114	Thailand					
115	Togo		× ×		× ×	
116	Trinidad/Tobago					
117	Tunisia		× ×		× ×	
118	Turkey					
119	Uganda					
120	United Kingdom					
121	United States					
122	Uruguay					
123	USSR	× ×			× ×	× ×
124	Venezuela					
125	Yemen Arab Republic		× ×	× ×	× ×	× ×
126	Yugoslavia				× ×	× ×
127	Zaire					
128	Zambia		× ×		× ×	
129	Zimbabwe		× ×		× ×	

a. × × indicates that the country is excluded from the sample.

of backwardness. In these cases, any gains in productivity from the introduction of new technology may be offset by rapid population growth and, as a result, do not show up as increases in per-capita income.[2]

For each series, three basic regression forms were used. The first is the basic convergence estimating equation:

$$\ln \text{Ratio} = b_0 + b_1 \, \text{RGDP}_0 + \varepsilon, \tag{1}$$

where Ratio = end of period RGDP divided by beginning of period RGDP and RGDP_0 = RGDP at the start of the period.[3] There are five different dependent variables, which are listed in table A9.1. The second form is

$$\ln \text{Ratio} = b_0 + b_1 \, \text{RGDP}_0 + b_2 \, \text{EDUC} + \varepsilon, \tag{2}$$

where EDUC denotes the various variables measuring the proportion of a given age group enrolled in a given level of schooling in a given year. The third form is

$$\ln \text{Ratio} = b_0 + b_1 \, \text{RGDP}_0 + b_2 \, \text{EDUC} + b_3 \, \text{POPGRT} + \varepsilon, \tag{3}$$

where POPGRT = the average rate of population growth from 1965 to 1984.

The Regression Results

The regression results are shown in tables A9.3, A9.4, and A9.5. The first panel of table A9.3 shows the results for equation (1), in which the only independent variable is the initial per-capita income level. In all five cases the coefficient of the initial productivity level is insignificant and the coefficient of variation (the R^2) is extremely low. Thus, over the full range of countries, including both developed and less developed economies, no clear relation emerges between initial productivity level and the rate of growth in per-capita income. This indicates that the catch-up story and the advantages of backwardness are not a general phenomenon and that other supplementary variables are needed to produce a coherent scenario.

In the next panel, the percentage of primary-school-age children enrolled in primary school in 1965 (PRIMARY_{65}) is included as an independent variable [see equation (2)]. The results change dramatically. The coefficient of PRIMARY_{65} is positive and significant at the 1% level in all five cases. The coefficient of initial productivity level is negative in all five cases and significant at the 5% level in the first three of these, which use RGNP and RGDP. These results strongly support our hypothesis that the ability to absorb new technology, and hence the speed of catch-up, is heavily depen-

Table A9.3
Regression of productivity growth on primary school enrollment and population growth[a]

Dependent variable	Constant	Initial RGDP[b]	PRIMARY$_{65}$	POPGRT	R^2	Adjusted R^2	Standard error of regression	Sample size
Panel 1								
R84/65	0.450** (9.59)	−0.091 (0.72)			0.005	−0.005	0.400	105
R81/50	0.849** (10.50)	−0.110 (0.22)			0.001	−0.015	0.379	66
R81/60	0.393** (6.91)	0.589 (1.79)			0.028	0.019	0.389	112
R*81/50	0.736** (8.55)	0.156 (0.31)			0.002	−0.016	0.384	57
R*81/60	0.359** (5.91)	0.622 (1.72)			0.029	0.019	0.410	103
Panel 2								
R84/65	0.141 (1.38)	−0.274* (2.06)	0.448** (3.36)		0.104	0.087	0.381	105
R81/50	0.151 (0.80)	−0.994* (2.02)	0.892** (4.03)		0.205	0.180	0.341	66
R81/60	−0.077 (0.91)	−0.683* (2.03)	0.826** (6.73)		0.314	0.301	0.328	112
R*81/50	0.187 (0.94)	−0.597 (1.12)	0.724** (2.99)		0.144	0.112	0.359	57
R*81/60	−0.081 (0.87)	−0.599 (1.58)	0.791** (5.79)		0.273	0.258	0.356	103

Panel 3

R84/65	0.213	−0.278*	0.419**	−2.19	0.107	0.081	0.382	105
	(1.35)	(2.09)	(2.95)	(0.61)				
R81/50	1.136**	−2.128**	0.437*	−24.41**	0.471	0.446	0.280	66
	(4.84)	(4.69)	(2.19)	(5.59)				
R81/60	0.053	−0.912*	0.806**	−4.08	0.319	0.300	0.328	112
	(0.33)	(2.20)	(6.48)	(0.95)				
R*81/50	1.109**	−1.865**	0.393	−24.17**	0.374	0.338	0.310	57
	(4.09)	(3.43)	(1.77)	(4.41)				
R*81/60	−0.048	−0.661	0.789**	−1.07	0.273	0.251	0.358	103
	0.26	(1.36)	(5.73)	(0.21)				

* significant at the 5% level, 2-tail test.
** significant at the 1% level, 2-tail test.
a. t-ratios are shown in parentheses below the coefficient estimates.
b. For the dependent variable R84/65, initial RGNP is used instead of initial RGDP. Both RGDP and RGNP are measured in units of $10,000s.

Table A9.4
Regression of productivity growth on secondary school enrollment and population growth[a]

Dependent variable	Constant	Initial RGDP[b]	SECONDARY_65	POPGRT	R^2	Adjusted R^2	Standard error of regression	Sample size
Panel 1								
R84/65	0.338** (6.06)	−0.429** (2.73)	0.708** (3.37)		0.105	0.087	0.381	105
R81/50	0.627** (8.98)	−2.391** (4.76)	1.430** (6.84)		0.427	0.409	0.289	66
R81/60	0.335** (6.54)	−1.537** (3.22)	1.290** (5.61)		0.246	0.232	0.344	112
R*81/50	0.566** (7.44)	−2.318** (3.19)	1.470** (5.51)		0.361	0.337	0.310	57
R*81/60	0.318** (5.68)	−1.678** (2.87)	1.386** (4.74)		0.207	0.191	0.372	103
Panel 2								
R84/65	0.199 (1.26)	−0.489** (2.88)	0.907** (3.05)	4.53 (0.95)	0.112	0.086	0.381	105
R81/50	1.150** (6.09)	−2.499** (5.26)	0.821** (2.88)	−16.62** (2.96)	0.498	0.473	0.273	66
R81/60	0.150 (0.90)	−1.422** (2.92)	1.456** (5.40)	6.12 (1.17)	0.256	0.235	0.344	112
R*81/50	1.041** (4.45)	−2.409** (4.09)	0.935* (2.60)	−14.88* (2.14)	0.411	0.378	0.300	57
R*81/60	0.024 (0.12)	−1.470* (2.47)	1.615** (5.00)	9.68 (1.62)	0.227	0.204	0.369	103

* significant at the 5% level, 2-tail test.
** significant at the 1% level, 2-tail test.
a. t-ratios are shown in parentheses below the coefficient estimates.
b. For the dependent variable R84/65, initial RGNP is used instead of initial RGDP. Both RGDP and RGNP are measured in units of $10,000s.

Table A9.5
Regression of productivity growth on enrollment in higher education and population growth[a]

Dependent variable	Constant	Initial RGDP[b]	HIGHERED$_{65}$	POPGRT	R^2	Adjusted R^2	Standard error of regression	Sample size
Panel 1								
R84/65	0.405** (7.88)	−0.255 (1.72)	1.422* (2.05)		0.044	0.026	0.394	105
R81/50	0.820** (10.80)	−1.560* (2.44)	2.536** (3.26)		0.145	0.118	0.354	66
R81/60	0.401** (7.33)	−5.709 (1.16)	2.399** (3.10)		0.107	0.091	0.375	112
R*81/50	0.737** (8.88)	−1.247 (1.58)	2.429* (2.26)		0.088	0.054	0.370	57
R*81/60	0.375** (6.33)	−0.627 (1.08)	2.703** (2.69)		0.094	0.076	0.397	103
Panel 2								
R84/65	0.480** (3.90)	−0.243 (1.62)	1.132 (1.39)	−2.79 (0.68)	0.049	0.021	0.395	105
R81/50	1.496** (12.01)	−2.591** (4.86)	1.416* (2.20)	−25.74** (6.20)	0.472	0.446	0.280	66
R81/60	0.588** (3.86)	−0.899 (1.64)	2.234** (2.86)	−6.43 (1.31)	0.121	0.097	0.373	112
R*81/50	1.487** (9.64)	−2.957** (4.14)	2.270* (2.60)	−27.01** (5.40)	0.412	0.378	0.300	57
R*81/60	0.502** (2.75)	−0.903 (1.30)	2.739** (2.72)	−4.26 (0.73)	0.099	0.072	0.398	103

* significant at the 5% level, 2-tail test.
** significant at the 1% level, 2-tail test.
a. t-ratios are shown in parentheses below the coefficient estimates.
b. For the dependent variable R84/65, initial RGNP is used instead of initial RGDP. Both RGDP and RGNP are measured in units of $10,000s.

dent on the educational level of the population. The R^2-statistic varies from 0.10 to 0.30 among these five specifications. The R^2 is lowest for the regression that uses the World Bank measure of productivity growth, RGNP. This may be due to the greater unreliability of the World Bank data than of the Summers and Heston data. Of the calculations using the Summers and Heston data, the results are stronger for the RGDP variables than for the RGDP* variables. This may be attributable to the fact that the RGDP* measure of productivity growth also includes changes in the terms of trade, which are not directly related to technological change. Finally, the results are considerably stronger for the period 1960–1981 then for 1950–1981. This an important finding, since the 1960–1981 sample includes many more countries and, in particular, many more less developed countries than the 1950–1981 sample. In general, we would expect the results to be stronger for samples that had fewer LDCs. The greater strength of the results for 1960–1981 is probably attributable to the fact that the education variable is the figure for 1965, which more closely aligns with the shorter of the two periods studied.

The same set of regressions was also run using PRIMARY$_{83}$ instead of PRIMARY$_{65}$ (the results are not shown). The results are quite similar. In two of the five cases, the R^2 is greater and the significance level of the coefficient of the education variable is higher, whereas in the other three cases the reverse is true. In all five cases, the coefficient of PRIMARY$_{83}$ is significant at the 1% level.

In the third panel (Column 5) of table A9.3 population growth (POPGRT) is added as an independent variable [see equation (3)]. The coefficient of POPGRT is negative in all five cases but significant only for the two 1950–1981 samples. In both of these cases, the variable is significant at the 1% level. The coefficient of initial productivity growth remains negative in all five cases. However, it is now significant at the 1% level in two cases, the 1950–1981 samples, and at the 5% level for two other cases. The coefficient of PRIMARY$_{65}$ remains positive in all five cases, but its significance level declines in each case. However, the variable remains significant at the 1% level in three of the forms and at the 5% level in another. The adjusted R^2 is now much higher for the 1950–1981 samples but basically unchanged for the other three forms. The best fits are now for the 1950–1981 period. The R^2-statistic is 0.47 for the form that uses RGDP for the 1950–1981 period. This suggests that rapid population growth was an important and significant deterrent to productivity growth during the early postwar period and helps to explain why many LDCs failed to reap the benefits of the advantages of backwardness.

Regression results in which $PRIMARY_{83}$ is substituted for $PRIMARY_{65}$ (not shown) are somewhat stronger than the corresponding equations with $PRIMARY_{65}$. The R^2-statistics are all slightly higher and the t-ratios of the estimated coefficient of the PRIMARY variable are also slightly higher. There is no obvious explanation of this result, except, perhaps, for the reverse causality discussed in note 5.

Table A9.4 shows the set of results corresponding to those in the last two panels of table A9.3, except that the proportion of high-school-age children enrolled in school in 1965, $SECONDARY_{65}$, is used in place of $PRIMARY_{65}$. The results are generally stronger. In the first panel, the coefficient of initial per-capita income level is now negative and significant at the 1% level for each form. The coefficient of $SECONDARY_{65}$ is positive and significant at the 1% level in each case. The t-ratio of the coefficient of $SECONDARY_{65}$ is greater than that of $PRIMARY_{65}$ for the two 1950–1981 samples, lower for the two 1960–1981 samples, and unchanged for the World Bank data. Correspondingly, the R^2-statistic is now higher for the same two 1950–1981 samples, lower for the two 1950–1981 samples, and essentially unchanged for the World Bank data. The best fit, as measured by the R^2-statistic, is now that for the RGDP regression over the 1950–1981 period.

The results for equation (3), displayed in the second panel, show a similar pattern. The coefficient of the initial productivity level is negative in all cases, significant at the 1% level in four cases and at the 5% level in one. The coefficient of $SECONDARY_{65}$ is positive in all cases and significant at the 1% level in four of the forms and at the 5% level in the other. The population growth variable is negative in each case but significant in only the two 1950–1981 samples. Of these, it is significant at the 1% level for the RGDP equation and at the 5% level for the RGDP* equation. The two samples that yield the highest "goodness of fit" are the 1950–1981 samples, and of these, the best is the one which uses RGDP as the measure of productivity. Indeed, the R^2 for this form is 0.50 and the adjusted R^2 is 0.47.

These results suggest, from the significance level of the education coefficients, that high school education is a more important influence than primary education in explaining the ability of a society to absorb new technology. In particular, it suggests that the skills and abilities transmitted in high school are more closely related to the skills that are required for acquisition and utilization of new technology than those taught in primary school. This may have some direct policy implications for education budgeting.

Table A9.5 shows the results when the education variable used is HIGH-ERED$_{65}$, the percentage of the college-age population enrolled in higher education. The results are uniformly weaker than the corresponding forms that use SECONDARY$_{65}$ instead. In the first panel of results, the coefficient of HIGHERED$_{65}$ is significant at the 1% level in three cases and at the 5% level in two cases. However, the t-ratios are substantially lower than those corresponding to SECONDARY$_{65}$. Moreover, the initial productivity level variable is now significant in only one case and at only the 5% level, while the R^2-statistics range from 0.04 to 0.11 and are all considerably lower than those equations that use SECONDARY$_{65}$.

The same pattern emerges in the bottom panel of table A9.5, where POPGRT is included as an independent variable. Initial productivity level is significant in only two cases, those covering the 1950–1981 period. The HIGHERED$_{65}$ variable is significant at the 1% level in two cases and at the 5% level in two others. The POPGRT variable is significant in only two cases, those for the 1950–1981 period. The R^2-statistics are all lower than those for the corresponding forms which use SECONDARY$_{65}$, except for one case where it is essentially unchanged.

The results thus seem to imply that higher education does not confer as much benefit via its contribution to the catch-up process as does secondary education. The skills taught in college and postgraduate school are, apparently, less relevant for the adoption and utilization of imported technology than high school skills. Here, too, there appears to be a lesson for less developed countries that are considering how to allocate their scarce educational funds, suggesting that for rapid productivity growth priority in the use of these funds should generally go to the secondary schools.

In summary, when the initial productivity level is the only independent variable in the equation, no clear relationship emerges between it and productivity growth. When an education variable is included, however, the coefficient for initial productivity level is always negative and is significant for at least the 5% level (two-tail test) in the vast majority of cases. The education variables show a strong positive relationship to productivity growth. In all cases except for one, the coefficients of education levels are significant at the 5% level and in many cases they are significant at the 1% level. When the average population growth variable is added as an independent variable, its coefficient is almost always negative, with its significance level varying widely, depending on the sample and education variable used. In general, the highest adjusted R^2-statistic is achieved in regressions with initial productivity level, education level, and average population growth as independent variables. By sample, the fit of the regressions was generally worst for the World Bank 105-country sample and best for 66-country sample covering the period 1960–1981 and using RGDP.

There is a final matter that merits discussion. As we have noted, the direction of causation between education and productivity also goes the other way. A minimum level of productivity and, hence, per-capita income, is necessary in order for a country to spend a significant amount of its resources on public education. In other words, there is a second equation in our system,

$$EDUC_0 = c_0 + c_1 RGDP_0 + \varepsilon. \tag{4}$$

However, it should be noted that the presence of this second equation does not introduce a simultaneous or specification bias to our first equation, equation (2) or (3). There are two reasons. First, the dependent variable in equation (2) or (3) is the rate of productivity growth. Current education is a function of the current level of GDP per capita, not of its rate of growth. Second, the current education level of the labor force, which is the preferred variable in equation (2) or (3), is a function of the level of per-capita income of 10–20 years *before* the current period.

Notes

1. For example, information on primary school enrollment was not available for Zaire in 1983, and its value was imputed using the mean value for this variable for Sub-Saharan Africa. Regressions were also run where countries with missing educational data were excluded from the sample. The results changed very little. See below for details.

2. If we had actual productivity statistics for the various countries, we could, in principle, separate out these two offsetting effects.

3. For the first productivity series, we use $RGDP_0$.

Appendix to Chapter 10: Derivation of the Propositions on Natural Resource Supplies

The formal construct needed to derive our propositions is quite simple. We employ the following notation:

R_t = the quantity of a depletable resource remaining in time period t.

Y_t = the maximal quantity of output capable of being produced with R_t.

Thus, Y_t is also used as the measure of the *effective quantity of the resource*.

$T_t = Y_t/R_t$ = the average productivity of the resource.

Then we have immediately

$$dY_t/dt = R_t\, dT_t/dt + T_t\, dR_t/dt, \tag{1}$$

where $dR_t/dt \leq 0$. Then (1) will be positive if and only if

$$(dT_t/dt)/T_t > -(dR_t/dt)/R_t.$$

We then have[1]

Proposition 1 There exist consistent time paths involving monotonic depletion of the available quantity of physical resource R_t and monotonic increases in T, which we may think of as an efficiency coefficient, that lead to monotonic and perpetual increases in the effective inventory of the resource Y_t.

Proposition 2 So long as T_t, the productivity of the resource, possesses a positive upper bound, T^*, then Y_t must be constrained by a finite upper bound and effective per period resource consumption, $D_t \equiv T_t(R_t - R_{t-1})$, must ultimately fall below any preassigned but positive lower bound.

Proof of Proposition 1 The following pair of functions satisfies the required conditions (as will be demonstrated next)

$$R_t = R^*(1 + be^{-rt}), \qquad T_t = T^*/(1 + ce^{-rt}), \qquad 0 < b < c. \qquad (2)$$

Obviously, here R decreases monotonically and T increases monontonically, as required. To show that Y behaves in the manner asserted we next obtain

$$Y_t = T_t R_t = R^* T^* (1 + be^{-rt})/(1 + ce^{-rt}), \qquad (3)$$

and writing $Y^* = R^* T^*$, it is clear that as t approaches infinity, Y_t must approach Y^*. To prove that Y_t increases monotonically it is sufficient to show that its time derivative is positive everywhere. Direct differentiation of (3) can be shown, with a bit of manipulation, to yield

$$dY_t/dt = Y^*(c - b)re^{-rt}/(1 + ce^{-rt})^2,$$

which is clearly positive for $c > b$.   QED

Proof of Proposition 2   First we prove that Y_t possesses an upper bound. R_t must decline monotonically, so that $R_t \leq R_0$ for all $t > 0$, and we are given $T_t \leq T^*$, the upper bound of T_t. Thus, $Y_t = R_t T_t \leq R_0 T^*$.   QED

Next we prove the central point—that beyond some $t = t^*$, D_t must lie below any preassigned positive number D^*. For suppose the contrary— that there is no such t^*. Then there can be no last $D_t > D^*$; i.e., for any finite integer, N, there must be N values of t for which $D_t > D^*$. Let S be the highest value of t in such a set of N periods. Then

$$R_s = R_0 - \sum_{t=0}^{s} D_t/T_t \leq R_0 - ND^*/T^*,$$

which must be negative for $N > R_0 T^*/D^*$.   QED

Note

1. We are grateful to Dietrich Fischer for pointing out proposition 2 and for providing the proof of proposition 1.

Appendix to Chapter 11:
Some Modified Total
Factor Productivity
Indices

As was shown in the text of this chapter, the validity of the widely used Divisia index of productivity growth depends upon a number of highly restrictive assumptions—among them constant returns to scale, efficiency in the operation of firms or other pertinent production units, and competitive pricing of inputs and outputs. Several economists, notably Caves, Christensen, and Swanson [1980, 1981], have designed modified measures that permit a productivity growth analysis to avoid some of the most onerous of these assumptions. This appendix describes and discusses some of those substitute indices, which have been used in the statistical analysis in the body of this chapter.

A. Adjustment for Returns to Scale

To measure productive capacity growth in the rail industry, Caves, Christensen, and Swanson [1980] propose an alternative measure to the Divisia index that allows explicitly for nonconstant returns to scale. Their approach uses a general transformation function and its corresponding multiproduct cost function. Differentiation of the cost function leads to a productivity index that is a weighted sum of output growth less a weighted sum of input growth. The weights for output are the elasticities of total cost with respect to the output levels, and the input weights are the elasticities of total cost with respect to the corresponding input prices. Formally, following the work of McFadden [1978], they adopt the following premises:

Assumption 1' The technology of the industry can be represented as an implicit production function of the form

$$f(y_1, y_2, \ldots, y_m; x_1 x_2, \ldots, x_n; t) = 0, \tag{1}$$

where f is an algebraic function, y_1 through y_m are various outputs, and x_1

through x_n are the inputs. This function is used because it is not, in general, possible to assign unique input quantities to each of the several outputs. As a result, the production structure must be defined implicitly as a general algebraic transformation function. As in the case of the Divisia index assumptions, discrete and abrupt changes in techniques are ruled out in this formulation and it is again assumed that technological change is disembodied.

Assumption 2'   The transformation function has a strictly convex structure.

Assumption 3'   Producers are cost minimizers.

Assumption 4'   While economies of scale may be present, their effects can be separated out.

Economies of scale mean that as the output level increases, *measured productivity may increase*—without any change in technology. Roughly speaking, crude productivity (that is, the measured ratio of outputs to inputs) will increase either because of economies of scale or changes in technology. It is crucial to separate out these two influences when measuring productive capacity growth in an industry, since by the latter we refer only to the portion of the change in the measured ratio of outputs to inputs strictly ascribable to *changes in technology*. The Caves-Christensen-Swanson formulation here thus differs from the Divisia index by netting out the economies of scale effect.

Assumption 5'   Prices need not be determined in competitive markets. In particular, as noted above, cost elasticities rather than relative prices are used to weight both outputs and inputs in the Caves-Christensen-Swanson productivity growth measure.

Technically, for this purpose the transformation function represented by equation (1) must first be reformulated as a cost function of the form

$$C = g(y_1, y_2, \ldots, y_m; p_1, p_2, \ldots p_n; t), \tag{2}$$

where g is an algebraic function; p_1 through p_n are the prices of inputs x_1 through x_n, respectively; and C is total cost given by

$$C = \sum_{i=1}^{n} p_i x_i.$$

Next, let the elasticity of the cost function with respect to the price of input, i, η_i, be given by

$$\eta_i = \frac{\partial \ln g}{\partial \ln p_i}$$

and the elasticity of the cost function with respect to output y_i, e_i, be given by

$$e_i = \frac{\partial \ln g}{\partial \ln y_i}.$$

Then it can be shown that assumption 4' yields the following properties: First, the elasticity of the cost function with respect to input price is equal to the share of the input in the cost of the product:

$$\eta_i = \frac{\partial \ln g}{\partial \ln p_i} = \frac{p_i x_i}{C} = s_i,$$

where s_i is the share of input i in total cost. Second, it can be shown that the rate of productive capacity growth, ETFP, is now given by

$$\text{ETFP} = \sum_{i=1}^{m} e_i y_i^* - \sum_{i=1}^{n} s_i x_i^*. \tag{3}$$

B. Adjustments for Returns to Scale and Capacity Utilization

In a follow-up article, Caves, Christensen, and Swanson [1981] provide two advances over their earlier paper [1980]. These are explicit measurement of economies of scale in the railroad industry and allowance for the possibility that inputs are not optimally employed. The measurement of returns to scale uses an analytical procedure similar to the one the authors employed in the earlier article. They begin with a general transformation function describing the structure of production, which is given by

$$H(\ln y_1, \ldots, \ln y_m; \ln x_1, \ldots, \ln x_n; t) = 1,$$

where H is an algebraic function and all other symbols are defined as before.

They argue that in the case where an industry produces only one output, productive capacity growth is defined as the rate at which output can grow over time with inputs held constant (i.e., $\partial \ln Y / \partial t$). In the case of multiple outputs, a "natural" definition of productive capacity growth is the common rate at which all outputs can grow with inputs held fixed:

$$\pi_y^* = \frac{d(\ln y_i)}{dt} = \frac{d(\ln y_j)}{dt} \quad \text{subject to } d(\ln X) = 0,$$

where π_y^* is the rate of productive capacity growth from the output side. It can be shown that

$$\pi_y^* = \frac{\partial H/\partial t}{\sum_{i=1}^m \partial H/\partial \ln y_i}. \tag{4}$$

It is equally "natural" to define productive capacity growth as the common rate at which all inputs can be decreased over time, with outputs held fixed:

$$\pi_x^* = -\frac{d(\ln x_i)}{dt} = -\frac{d(\ln x_j)}{dt} \qquad \text{subject to } d(\ln Y) = 0,$$

where π_x^* is the rate of productive capacity growth from the input side. It can be shown that

$$\pi_x^* = \frac{\partial H/\partial t}{\sum_{i=1}^n \partial H/\partial \ln x_i}. \tag{5}$$

Next, it can be shown that π_y^* and π_x^* are related by the degree of returns to scale (RTS) in the transformation function. RTS is defined as the proportional increase in all outputs that results from a given proportional increase in all inputs, holding the production structure and, hence, time fixed. That is to say,

$$\text{RTS} = -\sum_{i=1}^n \partial H/\partial \ln x_i / \sum_{i=1}^m \partial H/\partial \ln y_i.$$

As a result,

$$\pi_y^* = \text{RTS} \cdot \pi_x^*. \tag{6}$$

The returns to scale factor RTS can be estimated directly from the cost side. If there is a convex input structure and the firm minimizes cost with respect to all inputs, then the transformation function (6) associated with it has a unique cost function:

$$\ln C = G(\ln y_1, \ldots, \ln y_m; \ln p_1, \ldots, \ln p_n; t), \tag{7}$$

where all symbols are as before and G is the cost function. RTS is then given by

$$\text{RTS} = \left[\sum_{i=1}^n \partial \ln C/\partial \ln y_i \right]^{-1} \tag{8}$$

The second major advance of the Caves, Christensen, and Swanson follow-up article [1981] is allowance for the possibility that not all inputs are employed optimally. As the authors argue, productivity growth estimates typically assume that the firm is in a position of static equilibrium—in particular, that the firm is at a position of minimum cost with respect to *all inputs*. That is to say, it is normally assumed that the firm is operating at an efficient point in its production set. In reality, of course, firms often are not perfectly efficient. As the authors note, if the assumption of minimum cost is violated, "then estimates of (crude) productivity growth include the effects of ... movements toward or away from equilibrium, in addition to shifts in the structure of production" (p. 994).

Their way of measuring productive capacity growth when some inputs are not in equilibrium is ingenious. Because the total cost function given by equation (7) will not be satisfied, they do not attempt to use it. Instead, they assume that the firm minimizes cost with respect to a subset of inputs (the so-called "variable" factors of production whose quantities can be changed in the short run), subject to the other input quantities remaining fixed. (These are referred to as "fixed" or "quasi-fixed" inputs.) In this way they can derive a variable cost function

$$\ln CV = G^*(\ln y_1, \ldots, \ln y_m; \ln p_1, \ldots, \ln p_{n-q}; \ln z_1, \ldots, \ln z_q; t), \tag{7'}$$

where CV, the variable cost, is given by

$$CV = \sum_{i=1}^{n-q} p_i x_i.$$

G^* is the new cost function, and the z_i are the fixed inputs. The formulas for output productivity growth π_y^*, input productivity growth π_x^*, and returns to scale RTS must now be modified. It is shown (Caves, Christensen, and Swanson [1981]) that the new equations are

$$\pi_y^* = -(\partial \ln CV/\partial t) \bigg/ \sum_{i=1}^{m} (\partial \ln CV/\partial \ln y_i), \tag{4'}$$

$$\pi_x^* = -(\partial \ln CV/\partial t) \bigg/ \left[1 - \sum_{i=1}^{q} (\partial \ln CV/\partial \ln z_i) \right], \tag{5'}$$

and

$$RTS = \left[1 - \sum_{i=1}^{q} (\partial \ln CV/\partial \ln z_i) \right] \bigg/ \sum_{i=1}^{m} (\partial \ln CV/\partial \ln y_i).$$

It still remains true that

$$\pi_y^* = RTS \cdot \pi_x^*.$$

This formulation of productivity growth is particularly useful when the industry is not operating at full capacity.

References

Aaron, Henry J. *Economic Effects of Social Security*, Washington, D.C.: The Brookings Institution, 1982.

Abramovitz, Moses, "Rapid Growth Potential and its Realization: The Experience of the Capitalist Economies in the Postwar Period," in Edmond Malinvaud, ed., *Economic Growth and Resources, Proceedings of the Fifth World Congress of the International Economic Association*, Vol. I, London: Macmillan, 1979.

Abramovitz, Moses, "Catching Up and Falling Behind," delivered at the Economic History Association, September 20, 1985.

Abramovitz, Moses, "Catching Up, Forging Ahead, and Falling Behind," *Journal of Economic History*, June 1986, Vol. 46, pp. 385–406.

Abramovitz, Moses, and David, Paul A., "Reinterpreting Economic Growth: Parables and Realities," *American Economic Review*, Vol. LXIII, No. 2, May 1973, pp. 428–439.

Aldcroft, D. H., "The Entrepreneur and the British Economy, 1870–1914, *Economic History Review*, Vol. 17.1, August 1964, pp. 113–134.

Altman, Lawrence K., "The Doctor's World: AIDS Recalls Earlier Time," *The New York Times*, July 15, 1986, p. C3.

American Metal Market, *Metal Statistics*, New York: Fairchild, various issues.

Ames, Edward, and Rosenberg, Nathan, "Changing Technological Leadership and Industrial Growth," *Economic Journal*, March 1963, Vol. 73, pp. 13–31.

Ashton, T. S., *The Industrial Revolution 1760–1830*, London: Oxford University Press, 1948.

Atkinson, W. C., *A History of Spain and Portugal*, Baltimore: Penguin Books, 1960.

Baily, Martin Neil, "What Has Happened to Productivity Growth?" *Science*, Vol. 234, No. 4775, 24 October 1986, pp. 443–451.

Baily, Martin Neil, and Gordon, Robert J., "The Productivity Slowdown in the Service Sector: Can It Be Explained by Measurement Errors?" *The Service Economy*, Vol. 2, No. 4, October 1988, Washington, D.C.: Coalition of Service Industries, 1988.

Bairoch, Paul, "Europe's Gross National Product, 1800–1973," *Journal of European Economic History*, Vol. 5, 1976, pp. 213–340.

Barnett, H. J., and Morse, Chandler, *Scarcity and Growth*, Baltimore: Johns Hopkins University Press (Resources for the Future), 1963.

Barro, Robert J., *Macroeconomics*, New York: Wiley, 1984, Chapter 11.

Baumol, William J., "Macroeconomics of Unbalanced Growth: The Anatomy of Urban Crisis," *American Economic Review*, Vol. 57, June 1967, pp. 415–426.

Baumol, William J., "Productivity Growth, Convergence, and Welfare: What the Long-Run Data Show," *American Economic Review*, Vol. 76, No. 5, December 1986, pp. 1072–1085.

Baumol, William J., *Contributions towards Analysis of Entrepreneurship Policy*, Cambridge, MA: MIT Press, forthcoming.

Baumol, William J., and Blackman, Sue Anne Batey, "Unprofitable Energy Is Squandered Energy," *Challenge: The Magazine of Economic Affairs*, Vol. 23, No. 3, July/August 1980, pp. 28–35.

Baumol, Willam J., and McLennan, Kenneth, *Productivity Growth and U.S. Competitiveness*, New York: Oxford University Press, 1985.

Baumol, William J., and Oates, Wallace E. (with Sue Anne Batey Blackman), *Economics, Environmental Policy and the Quality of Life*, Englewood Cliffs, NJ: Prentice-Hall, 1979.

Baumol, William J., and Wolff, Edward N., *Technical Issues in Productivity Growth*, Cambridge, MA: MIT Press, forthcoming.

Baumol, William J., and Wolff, Edward N., "Three Fundamental Productivity Concepts: Principles and Measurement," in George Feiwel ed., *Joan Robinson and Modern Economic Theory*, London: Macmillan, 1989, pp. 638–659.

Baumol, William J., Blackman, Sue Anne Batey, and Wolff, Edward N., "Unbalanced Growth Revisited: Asymptotic Stagnancy and New Evidence," *American Economic Review*, Vol. 75, September 1985, pp. 806–817.

Baydo, Gerald R., ed., *The Evolution of Mass Culture in America, 1877 to the Present*, St. Louis: Forum Press, 1982.

Becker, M. B., "Economic Change and the Emerging Florentine Territorial State," in Molho (1969), pp. 123–131.

Beniger, James R., *The Control Revolution: Technological and Economic Origins of the Information Society*, Cambridge, MA: Harvard University Press, 1986.

Bergsten, C. Fred, *Commentary*. In *Federal Reserve Bank of Kansas City Review*, 1983, pp. 312–320.

Bhagwati, Jagdish N., "Development Economics: What Have We Learnt?" October 1983, unpublished paper.

Blackaby, F., ed. *De-industrialisation*, London: Heinemann Educational Books, 1979.

Blades, D. W., and Sturm, P. H., "The Concept and Measurement of Savings," *Saving and Government Policy*, The Federal Reserve Bank of Boston, 1982.

Bombach, Gottfried, *Post-War Economic Growth Revisited*, Amsterdam: North-Holland, 1985.

Branson, William H., "Industrial Policy and U.S. International Trade," in Wachter and Wachter [1981, pp. 378–408].

Braudel, Fernand, *Civilization and Capitalism, 15th–18th Century*, New York: Harper and Row, Vol. I (1979), Vol. II (1982), Vol. III (1984).

Brems, Hans, *Inflation, Interest and Growth: A Synthesis*, Lexington, MA: Lexington Books, 1980, Chapter 9.

Brown, William M., "The Outlook for Future Petroleum Supplies," in Julian L. Simon and Herman Kahn, eds., *The Resourceful Earth: A Response to Global 2000*, Oxford: Basil Blackwell Publishers, Ltd., 1984.

Bulow, Jeremy I., and Summers, Lawrence H., "A Theory of Dual Labor Markets with Application to Industrial Policy, Discrimination and Keynesian Unemployment," *Journal of Labor Economics*, Vol. 4, No. 3, Part 1, July 1986, pp. 376–414.

Burns, Christopher, "The Evolution of Office Information Systems," *Datamation*, Vol. 23, No. 4, 1977, pp. 60–64.

Carus-Wilson, Eleanora M., "An Industrial Revolution of the Thirteenth Century," *Economic History Review*, Vol. 11, 1941, pp. 39–60.

Caves, Richard E., and Krause, Lawrence B., *The Australian Economy: A View from the North*, Washington, D.C.: The Brookings Institution, 1984.

Caves, Douglas, Christensen, Laurits R., and Swanson, Joseph A., "Productivity in U.S. Railroads, 1951–1974," *Bell Journal of Economics*, Vol. 11, Spring 1980, pp. 177–181.

Caves, Douglas, Christensen, Laurits R., and Swanson, Joseph A. "Productivity Growth, Scale Economics, and Capacity Utilization in U.S. Railroads, 1955–74," *American Economic Review*, Vol. 71, No. 5, December 1981, pp. 994–1002.

Cipolla, Carlo M., "Note sulla storia del saggio d'interesse ...," in *Economia Internazionale*, 1952.

Cipolla, Carlo M., "The Economic Decline of Italy," in C. M. Cipolla, ed., *The Economic Decline of Empire*, London: Methuen and Co., Ltd., 1970.

Cipolla, Carlo M., *Before the Industrial Revolution: European Society and Economy, 1000–1700*, New York: W. W. Norton, 1976.

Clark, Colin, *The Conditions of Economic Progress*, 3rd ed., London: Macmillian, 1957.

Coale, Ansley J., "Demographic Effects of Scientific Progress," *Papers Read At a Joint Meeting of The Royal Society and the American Philosophical Society, April 1986*, Volume I, Philadelphia: American Philosophical Society, 1987, pp. 85–95.

Coleman, D. C., *Industry in Tudor and Stuart England*, London: Macmillan, 1975.

Commission on Minority Participation in Education and American Life, "One-Third of a Nation," Washington, D.C.: American Council on Education, 1988.

Committee for Economic Development, *Productivity Policy: Key to the Nation's Economic Future*, A Statement by the Research and Policy Committee, Washington, D.C.: Committee for Economic Development, April 1983.

Coppock, D. J., "The Climacteric of the 1890's: A Critical Note," *Manchester School of Economic and Social Studies*, Vol. 24.1, January 1956, pp. 1–31.

Corbin, Alain, *The Foul and the Fragrant: Odor and the French Social Imagination*, Cambridge, MA.: Harvard University Press, 1986.

Cowan, Ruth Schwartz, *More Work for Mother: The Ironies of Household Technology from the Open Hearth to the Microwave*, New York: Basic Books, 1983.

Dana, C. W., *The Great West*, Boston: Wentworth and Co., 1857, pp. 140, 174.

Darby, Michael, "The U.S. Productivity Slowdown: A Case of Statistical Myopia," *American Economic Review*, June 1984, vol. 74, pp. 301–322.

Darmstadter, Joel, Teitelbaum, Perry D., and Polach, Jaroslave G., *Energy in the World Economy, A Statistical Review of Trends in Output, Trade and Consumption since 1925*, Baltimore: Johns Hopkins University Press (Resources for the Future), 1971.

David, Paul A., "Invention and Accumulation in America's Economic Growth: A Nineteenth-Century Parable," in Karl Brunner and Allan H. Meltzer, eds., *International Organization, National Policies and Economic Development*, Amsterdam: North-Holland, 1977, pp. 179–228.

Davidson, Caroline, *A Woman's Work Is Never Done: A History of Housework in the British Isles, 1650–1950*, London: Chatto and Windus, 1982.

Dean, Edwin, ed., *Education and Economic Productivity*, Cambridge, MA: Ballinger Publishing Company, 1984.

Deane, Phyllis, and Cole, W. A., *British Economic Growth, 1688–1959: Trends and Structure*, Cambridge: Cambridge University Press, 1964.

De Long, J. Bradford, "Productivity Growth, Convergence, and Welfare: Comment," *American Economic Review*, Vol. 78, No. 5, December 1988, pp. 1138–1154.

De Vries, Jan, *European Urbanization, 1500–1800*, Cambridge, MA: Harvard University Press, 1984.

Diebold Group, "Management Information Services/Telecommunications Budgets, 1982," Document Number 211M, Abstract, p. 10 (also personal communication with David Dell, Director of Research Services, the Diebold Group, Inc., New York, NY).

Douglas, Paul, *American Economic Review*, Supplement, March 1926, p. 22.

Economic Report of the President, Washington, D.C.: U.S. Government Printing Office, 1983, 1984, and 1988.

Fägerlind, Ingemar, and Saha, Lawrence J., *Education and National Development*, Oxford: Pergamon Press, 1983.

Feinstein, Charles H., *National Income, Expenditure and Output of the United Kingdom, 1855–1965*, Cambridge: Cambridge University Press, 1972.

Feldstein, Martin, and Horioka, Charles, "Domestic Saving and International Capital Flows," *Economic Journal*, Vol. 90, 1980, pp. 314–329.

Floud, Roderick, and McCloskey, Donald, eds., *The Economic History of Britain since 1700*, Cambridge: Cambridge University Press, 1981.

Fogel, Robert W., "Nutrition and the Decline in Mortality since 1700: Some Preliminary Findings," NBER Working Paper No. 1402, Cambridge, MA.: National Bureau of Economic Research, July 1984.

Fogel, Robert W., "The Development of the American Economy," *NBER Reporter*, Fall 1985, pp. 1–6.

Fogel, Robert W., "Nutrition and the Decline in Mortality since 1700: Some Additional Preliminary Findings," NBER Working Paper No. 1802, Cambridge, MA.: National Bureau of Economic Research, January 1986 (1986a).

Fogel, Robert W., "Nutrition and the Decline in Mortality since 1700: Some Preliminary Findings," in Stanley L. Engerman and Robert E. Gallman, eds., *Long-Term Factors in American Economic Growth*, Chicago: University of Chicago Press, 1986 (1986b).

Fogel, Robert W., et al., "Changes in American and British Stature since the Mid-Eighteenth Century: A Preliminary Report on the Usefulness of Data on Height for the Analysis of Secular Trends in Nutrition, Labor Productivity, and Labor Welfare," NBER Working Paper No. 890, Cambridge, MA: National Bureau of Economic Research, May 1982.

Frankel, Jeffrey A., Dooley, Michael, and Mathieson, Donald, "International Capital Mobility in Developing Countries vs. Industrial Countries: What Do Savings-Investment Correlations Tell Us?" NBER Working Paper No. 2043, Cambridge, MA: National Bureau of Economic Research, October 1986.

Fuchs, Victor R., *The Service Economy*, New York: National Bureau of Economic Research, 1968.

Fuchs, Victor R., "Economic Growth and the Rise of Service Employment," in Herbert Giersch, ed., *Towards an Explanation of Economic Growth: Symposium 1980*, Tübingen: J. C. B. Mohr, 1981, pp. 221–242.

Fulton, Robert, *A Treatise on the Improvement of Canal Navigation*, London, 1796, as cited in Philip [1985, p. 49].

Furnas, J. C., *The Americans: A Social History of the United States, 1587–1914*, New York: G. P. Putnam's Sons, 1969.

Gerschenkron, Alexander, "Economic Backwardness in Historical Perspective," in Bert F. Hoselitz, ed., *The Progress of Underdeveloped Areas*, Chicago: University of Chicago Press, 1952.

Gerschuny, J., *After Industrial Society*, London: Macmillan, 1978.

Gewen, Barry, "Writers and Writing: Scents and Sensibility," *The New Leader*, December 29, 1986, pp. 12–13.

Gillis, Malcolm, Perkins, Dwight H., Roemer, Michael, and Snodgrass, Donald R., *Economics of Development*, New York: W. W. Norton, 1983.

Gilmore, James Roberts (Edmund Kirke), *Among the Pines*, New York: G. P. Putnam, 1862.

Gimpel, Jean, *The Medieval Machine: The Economic Revolution of the Middle Ages*, New York: Holt, Reinhart and Winston, 1976.

Goldsmith, Raymond W., *Comparative National Balance Sheets*, Chicago: University of Chicago Press, 1985.

Gollop, Frank M., and Jorgensen, Dale W., "U.S. Productivity Growth by Industry, 1947–73," in John W. Kendrick and Beatrice N. Vaccara, eds., *New Developments in Productivity Measurement and Analysis*, Chicago: University of Chicago Press, 1980.

Gordon, Robert T., "The Postwar Evolution of Computer Prices," NBER Working Paper No. 2227, Cambridge, MA: National Bureau of Economic Research, April 1987.

Gordon, T. J., and Munson, T. R., "Research into Technology Output Measures," unpublished paper, The Futures Group for the National Science Foundation, November 1980.

Grabscheid, P., "The Economics of Information Processing," presentation for 1982–83 Chief Financial Officer Seminar Program Series, *Institutional Investor*, 1982.

Griliches, Zvi, "Issues in Assessing the Contribution of Research and Development to Productivity Growth," *Bell Journal of Economics*, Vol. 10, No. 1, Spring 1979, pp. 92–116.

Griliches, Zvi, "Returns to Research and Development Expenditures," in John W. Kendrick and Beatrice Vaccara, eds., *New Developments in Productivity Measurement*, New York: National Bureau of Economic Research, 1980 (1980a).

Griliches, Zvi, "R&D and the Productivity Slowdown," *American Economic Review*, Vol. 70, No. 2, May 1980 (1980b), pp. 343–348.

Griliches, Zvi, "Productivity, R&D, and Basic Research at the Firm Level in the 1970's, *American Economic Review*, Vol. 76, No. 1, March 1986, pp. 141–154.

Griliches, Zvi, and Lichtenberg, Frank, "R&D and Productivity Growth at the Industry Level: Is There Still a Relationship?" mimeo, 1981.

Haveman, Robert H., and Wolfe, Barbara L., "Education, Productivity, and Well-Being: On Defining and Measuring the Economic Characteristics of Schooling," in Dean [1984].

Heim, Peggy, "Living Conditions of a Mechanic's Family in Rural Pennsylvania, 1885 to the Early 20th Century," mimeo 1985.

Helliwell, John F., Sturm, Peter H., and Salou, Gerard, "International Comparisons of the Sources of Productivity Slowdown," *European Economic Review*, Vol. 28, 1985, pp. 157–191.

Hobsbawm, Eric J., *Industry and Empire*, Harmondsworth: Penguin Books, 1969.

Hodges, Richard, *Dark Age Economics; The Origins of Towns and Trade A.D. 600–1000*, New York: St. Martin's Press, 1982.

Hotelling, Harold, "The Economics of Exhaustible Resources," *Journal of Political Economy*, Vol. 39, April 1931, pp. 137–175.

Howard, Ronald L., *A Social History of American Family Sociology, 1865–1940*, Westport, CT.: Greenwood Press, 1981.

Hulten, Charles R., "Growth Accounting with Intermediate Inputs," *Review of Economic Studies*, Vol. 45(3), No. 141, October 1978, pp. 511–518.

Ishinomori, Shotaro, *Japan Inc.*, An Introduction to Japanese Economics (The Comic Book), Berkeley, CA.: University of California Press, 1988 (translated by Betsey Scheiner).

Johnson, D. Gale, "The Functional Distribution of Income in the United States, 1850–1952," *Review of Economics and Statistics*, Vol. 36, No. 2, May 1954, pp. 175–182.

Jorgenson, Dale W., "The Contribution of Education to U.S. Economic Growth, 1948–73," in Dean [1984].

Kendrick, John W., *Productivity Trends in the United States*, Cambridge, MA.: National Bureau of Economic Research, 1961.

Kendrick, John W., *Postwar Productivity Trends in the United States, 1948–1969*, New York: National Bureau of Economic Research, 1973 (1973a).

Kendrick, John W., *Long Term Economic Growth 1860–1970*, Washington, D.C.: U.S. Bureau of the Census, June 1973 (1973b).

Kendrick, John W., ed., *International Comparisons of Productivity and Causes of the Slowdown*, Cambridge, MA.: Ballinger Press, 1984.

Kennedy, Mary M., Jung, Richard K., and Orland, Martin E., *Poverty, Achievement and the Distribution of Compensatory Education Services*, Washington, D.C.: Office of Educational Research and Improvement, U.S. Department of Education, 1986.

King, Mervyn, "The Economics of Saving. A Survey of Recent Contributions" (with comments by Peter Diamond and Mordecai Kurz), in Kenneth J. Arrow, ed., *Frontiers of Economics*, Oxford: Basil Blackwell, 1985.

Kolbert, Elizabeth, "Household Chores, Still Never Done," *The New York Times*, December 5, 1985, pp. C1, C12.

Kormendi, Roger C., and Meguire, Philip G., "Macroeconomic Determinants of Growth: Cross-Country Evidence," *Journal of Monetary Economics*, Vol. 16, No. 2, September 1985, pp. 141–163.

Krantz, F., and Hohenberg, P. M., eds., *Failed Transitions to Modern Industrial Society: Renaissance Italy and Seventeenth Century Holland*, Montreal: Concordia University and Université de Quebec, 1975.

Kubitz, W. J., "Computer Technology, A Forecast for the Future," in F. Wilfrid Lancaster, ed., *Proceedings of the 1979 Clinic on Library Applications of Data Processing: The Role of the Library in an Electronic Society*, Urbana-Champaign: University of Illinois Graduate School of Library Science, 1980, pp. 135–161.

Landau, Daniel, "Government Expenditure and Economic Growth: A Cross-Country Study," *Southern Economic Journal*, Vol. 49, No. 3, January 1983, pp. 783–792.

Landes, David S., *The Unbound Prometheus*, Cambridge: Cambridge University Press, 1969.

Lawrence, Robert Z., *Can America Compete?* Washington, D.C.: The Brookings Institution, 1984.

Lebergott, Stanley, *The Americans: An Economic Record*, New York: W. W. Norton, 1984.

Lee, Valerie, *Access to Higher Education: The Experience of Blacks, Hispanics and Low Socio-Economic Status Whites*, Washington, D.C.: American Council on Education, 1985.

Leontief, Wassily, *Studies in the Structure of the American Economy*, New York: Oxford University Press, 1953.

Levin, H. J., *Fact and Fancy in Television Regulation*, New York: Russell Sage Foundation, 1980 (who cites Federal Communications Commission Network Inquiry Special Staff, *The Historical Evolution of the Commercial Network Broadcast System*, October 1979, p. 176).

Lindsey, Lawrence, "Capital Gains Taxes under the Tax Reform Act of 1986,"

NBER Working Paper No. 2215, Cambridge, MA: National Bureau of Economic Research, April 1987.

Lipsey, Robert E., and Kravis, Irving B., "Is the U.S. a Spendthrift Nation?" NBER Working Paper No. 2240, Cambridge, MA: National Bureau of Economic Research, June 1987 (1987a).

Lipsey, Robert E., and Kravis, Irving B., "Is the United States Losing the Economic Race?" *U.S. Long-Term Economic Outlook*, New York: The Conference Board, 1988.

Lopez, Robert S., "Hard Times and Investment in Culture," reprinted in Molho [1969, pp. 95–115].

MacDougall, G. D. A., "The Benefits and Costs of Private Investment Abroad: A Theoretical Approach," in Richard E. Caves and Harry G. Johnson, eds., *Readings in International Economics*, Vol. XI, Homewood, IL: Richard D. Irwin, Inc., 1968, pp. 172–194; originally published in *Economic Record*, Special Issue, March 1960.

Machlup, Fritz, *The Production and Distribution of Knowledge in the United States*, Princeton, NJ: Princeton University Press, 1962.

Maddison, Angus, *Economic Growth in Japan and the USSR*, London: Allen and Unwin, 1969.

Maddison, Angus, *Phases of Capitalist Development*, Oxford: Oxford University Press, 1982.

Maddison, Angus, "Comparative Analysis of the Productivity Situation in the Advanced Capitalist Countries," in Kendrick [1984].

Maddison, Angus, "Growth and Slowdown in Advanced Capitalist Economies: Techniques of Quantitative Assessment," *Journal of Economic Literature*, Vol. XXV, June 1987, pp. 649–706.

Mansfield, Edwin, "Basic Research and Productivity Increase in Manufacturing," *American Economic Review*, Vol 70, No. 5, Dec. 1980, pp. 863–873.

Mansfield, Edwin, "How Rapidly Does New Industrial Technology Leak Out?" *Journal of Industrial Economics*, Vol. 34, December 1985, pp. 217–223.

Mansfield, Edwin, Romeo, Anthony, Schwartz, Mark, Teece, David, Wagner, Samuel, and Brach, Peter, *Technology Transfer, Productivity, and Economic Policy*, New York: W. W. Norton, 1982.

Marsh, Robert M., *The Mandarins: The Circulation of Elites in China, 1600–1900*, Glencoe, NY: The Free Press, 1961.

Martin, Edgar W., *The Standard of Living in 1860*, Chicago: University of Chicago Press, 1942.

Martin, R., and Rowthorn, R. (editors), *The Geography of Deindustrialisation*, London: Macmillan, 1986.

Marx, Karl, and Engels, Friedrich, *Manifesto of the Communist Party* (1848), London: Lawrence and Wishart, 1946.

Matthews, R. C. O., *Slower Growth in the Western World*, London: Heinemann, 1982.

Matthews, R. C. O., Feinstein, C. H., and Odling-Smee, J. C. (MFO), *British Economic Growth, 1856–1973*, Stanford: Stanford University Press, 1982.

McCloskey, D. N., *Enterprise and Trade in Victorian Britain*, London: Allen and Unwin, 1981.

McCulloch, Rachel, "The Challenge to U.S. Leadership in High-Technology Industries," NBER Working Paper No. 2513, Cambridge, MA: National Bureau of Economic Research, 1988.

McFadden, Daniel, "Cost, Revenue, and Profit Functions", in M. A. Fuss and D. McFadden, eds., *Production Economics: A Dual Approach to Theory and Applications*, Amsterdam: North-Holland, 1978.

McMahon, Walter W., "Comments," in Kendrick [1984].

Miller, L. Scott, "Educationally At-Risk: A Look at Some Data," Presentation to Committee for Economic Development Task Force on the Educationally Disadvantaged, September 23, 1986.

Minicucci, R. A., "Sub-Second Response Time: A Way to Improve Interactive User Productivity," *Systems Management Controls, SMC Newsletter* 82–19, November 1982.

Mishel, Lawrence, "The Productivity Numbers: Of Manufacturing Mismeasurement," *New York Times*, Business Forum, November 27, 1988, Section 3, p. F3.

Mitchell, Wesley C., *The Backward Art of Spending Money*, London: McGraw-Hill, 1937; reprinted from *American Economic Review*, Vol. II, June 1912, pp. 269–281.

Molho, Anthony, ed., *Social and Economic Foundations of the Italian Renaissance*, New York: Wiley, 1969.

Montgomery Ward and Company, *Catalogue and Buyers' Guide*, No. 57, Spring and Summer 1895 (unabridged facsimile published by Dover Publications, New York, 1969).

Moore, Geoffrey H., *Business Cycles, Inflation and Forecasting*, National Bureau of Economic Research Studies in Business Cycles, No. 24, 1983, p. 454.

Morrison, Joan, and Zabusky, Charlotte Fox, *American Mosaic: The Immigrant Experience in the Words of Those Who Lived It*, New York: E. P. Dutton, 1980.

Mueller, Dennis C., *The Political Economy of Growth*, New Haven: Yale University Press, 1983.

Nadiri, M. Ishaq, "Contributions and Determinants of Research and Development

Expenditures in the U.S. Manufacturing Industries," in George M. von Furstenberg, ed., *Capital, Efficiency, and Growth*, Cambridge, MA.: Ballinger, 1980.

National Science Foundation, *Relationships Between R&D and Economic Growth/ Productivity*, Washington, D.C.: Government Printing Office, November 1977.

National Science Foundation, Directorate for Scientific, Technological and International Affairs, Division of Science Resource Studies, "International Science and Technology Data Update, 1986," Washington, D.C., 1986.

Nef, John V., "The Progress of Technology and the Growth of Large-Scale Industry in Great Britain, 1540–1640," *The Economic History Review*, Vol. 5, 1934.

Nelson, Richard R., "U.S. Technological Leadership: Where Did It Come From and Where Did It Go?" New York: Department of Economics, Columbia University, September 1988 (unpublished).

New York Times, "U.S. Gain Is Found in Health Report," January 31, 1986, p. A19.

Norsworthy, J. R., and Malmquist, David H., "Recent Productivity Growth in Japanese and U.S. Manufacturing," in Baumol and McLennan, [1985, pp. 58–69].

North, Douglass C., and Thomas, Robert P., *The Rise of the Western World: A New Economic History*, Cambridge: Cambridge University Press, 1973.

Norton, R. D., "Industrial Policy and American Renewal," *Journal of Economic Literature*, Vol. 24, March 1986, pp. 1–40.

Noyce, R. N., "Microelectronics," *Scientific American*, No. 3, 1977, pp. 63–69, 237.

Ohkawa, Kasushi, and Rosovsky, Henry, *Japanese Economic Growth: Trend Acceleration in the Twentieth Century*, Stanford: Stanford University Press, 1973.

Organization for Economic Cooperation and Development, *Indicators of Industrial Activity*, Paris: OECD, various issues.

Organization for Economic Cooperation and Development, *Labor Force Statistics, 1965–1985*, 1987.

Paik, N. J., "How to Keep Experimental Video on PBS National Programming," in *Independent Television-Makers and Public Communications Policy*, Rockefeller Foundation Working Papers, December 1979, chapter 2.

Palmer, Robert R., *The Age of Democratic Revolution*, Princeton: Princeton University Press, 1959.

Palmer, Robert R., *The Age of Democratic Revolution*, Vol. 2, Princeton: Princeton University Press, 1964.

Patterson, James T., *America's Struggle against Poverty, 1900–1980*, Cambridge, MA.: Harvard University Press, 1981.

Peterson, William, "Total Factor Productivity in the U.K.: A Disaggregated Analysis," in K. D. Patterson and Kerry Scott, eds., *The Measurement of Capital: Theory and Practice*, London: Macmillan, 1979.

Phelps Brown, E. H., and Handfield-Jones, S. J., "The Climacteric of the 1890s: A Study in the Expanding Economy," *Oxford Economic Papers*, Vol. 4.3, October 1952, pp. 266–307.

Phelps Brown, E. H., and Hopkins, S. V., "Seven Centuries of Building Wages," *Economica*, Vol. 22, August 1955, pp. 195–206.

Phelps Brown, E. H., and Hopkins, S. V., "Seven Centuries of the Prices of Consumables," *Economica*, Vol. 23, November 1956, pp. 296–314.

Philip, Cynthia Owen, *Robert Fulton*, New York: Franklyn Watts, 1985.

Ping-Ti Ho, *The Ladder of Success in Imperial China, 1368–1911*, New York: Columbia University Press, 1962.

Porat, Marc U., *The Information Economy: Definition and Measurement*, Office of Telecommunications Special Publication 77-12, U.S. Department of Commerce, Washington, D.C.: U.S. Government Printing Office, May 1977.

Psacharopoulos, George, and Woodhall, Maureen, *Education for Development: An Analysis of Investment Choices*, New York: Oxford University Press, 1985.

Ramist, Leonard, and Arbeiter, Solomon, *Profiles, College-Bound Seniors, 1985*, College Entrance Examination Board, New York, 1986.

Reid, H., *Sketches in North America*, London: Longman, Green, Longmont, and Roberts, 1861.

Repetto, Robert, ed., *The Global Possible: Resources, Development, and the New Century*, New Haven: Yale University Press, 1985.

Repetto, Robert, "Population, Resources, Environment: An Uncertain Future," *Population Bureau*, Vol. 42, No.2, Washington, D.C.: Population Reference Bureau, Inc., July 1987.

Riis, Jacob A., *How the Other Half Lives, Studies among the Tenements of New York*, New York: Hill and Wang, Inc., 1957; originally published in New York by Charles Scribner's Sons in 1890.

Rogers, David E., "The Early Years: The Medical World in Which Walsh McDermott Trained," *Daedalus*, Issue on America's Doctors, Medical Science, Medical Care, Vol. 115, No. 2, Spring 1986, pp. 1–18.

Romer, Paul M., "Increasing Returns and Long Run Growth," *Journal of Political Economy*, Vol. 94, 1986, pp. 1002–1037.

Rosenberg, Nathan, *Perspectives on Technology*, Armonk, NY: M. E. Sharpe, Inc., 1976, "Technological Innovation and Natural Resources: The Niggardliness of Nature Reconsidered," p. 229–248.

Rosenberg, Nathan, *Inside the Black Box: Technology and Economics*, Cambridge: Cambridge University Press, 1982, p. 247.

Rosenberg, Nathan, and Birdzell, L. E., Jr., *How the West Grew Rich, The Economic Transformation of the Industrial World*, New York: Basic Books, 1986.

Rubinstein, W. D., ed., *Wealth and the Wealthy in the Modern World*, London: Croom Helm, 1980.

Sato, Kazuo, "Saving and Investment," in Kozo Yamamura, and Yasukichi Yasuba, eds., *The Political Economy of Japan*, Stanford: Stanford University Press, 1987.

Say, J. B., *A Treatise on Political Economy*, revised American edition, Philadelphia, 1834, (*Traité d'Economie Politique*, 1st ed., 1803).

Scherer, F. M., "Interindustry Technology Flows and Productivity Growth," *Review of Economics and Statistics*, Vol. 64, No. 4, September, 1982.

Schindler, M., "Computers, Big and Small, Still Spreading as Software Grows," *Electronic Design*, Vol. 27, No. 1, 1979, p. 88.

Schumpeter, Joseph, *The Theory of Economic Development* (1911), Cambridge, MA.: Harvard University Press, English translation, 1936.

Schurr, Sam H., and Netschert, Bruce C., *Energy in the American Economy, 1850–1975*, Baltimore, MD: Johns Hopkins University Press (Resources for the Future), 1960.

Scott, Donald M., and Wishy, Bernard, eds., *America's Families: A Documentary History*, New York: Harper and Row, 1982.

Sears, Roebuck and Company, *1908 Catalogue No. 117* (replica published by BDI Books, Inc., Northfield, IL, 1971).

Sears, Roebuck and Company, *1985 Spring and Summer Catalogue*.

Singh, Ajit, "Manufacturing and De-Industrialization, "*The New Palgrave: A Dictionary of Economics*, London: Macmillan, 1987, pp. 301–308.

Smith, Adam, *The Wealth of Nations* (1776), Cannan ed., London: Methuen, 4th ed., 1925.

Smithsonian Institution, *1876 Culinary Exhibit* (display description, 1986).

Solow, Robert M., "Growth Theory and After," *American Economic Review*, Vol. 78, No. 3, June 1988, pp. 307–317.

Stapleton, Darwin H., *The Transfer of Industrial Technologies to Early America*, Philadelphia: The American Philosophical Society, 1987.

Stone, Lawrence, "The Bourgeois Revolution of Seventeenth Century England Revisited," *Past and Present*, No. 109, November 1985, pp. 44–45.

Sturm, Peter H., "Determinants of Saving: Theory and Evidence," *OECD Economic Studies*, No. 1, Autumn, 1983.

Summers, Lawrence H., "Commentary, *"Federal Reserve Bank of Kansas City Review*, 1983, pp. 79—83.

Summers, Lawrence H., and Cutler, David, "Texaco and Pennzoil Both Lost Big," *New York Sunday Times*, February 14, 1988, Section 3, p. 3.

Summers, Robert, "Services in the International Economy," in Robert P. Inman, ed., *Managing the Service Economy*, Cambridge: Cambridge University Press, 1985, pp. 27—48.

Summers, Robert, and Heston, Alan, "Improved International Comparisons of Real Product and Its Composition, 1950—1980," *Review of Income and Wealth*, Vol. 30, June 1984, pp. 207—262.

Summers, Robert, and Heston, Alan, "The International Demand for Services," Discussion Paper #32, Fishman-Davidson Center for the Study of the Service Sector, University of Pennsylvania, January 1988.

Summers, Robert, Kravis, I. B., and Heston, Alan, "Changes in World Income Distribution," *Journal of Policy Modeling*, Vol. 6, May 1986, pp. 237—269.

Taiwan Statistical Data Book, Council for Economic Planning and Development, Executive Yuan, Republic of China, 1980.

Teece, David J., *The Multinational Corporation and the Resources Cost of International Technology Transfer*, Cambridge, MA: Ballinger, 1976.

"Television Financial Data 1980, FCC Financial Figures," *Broadcasting*, No. 6, Vol. 101, August 10, 1981, p. 54.

Terleckyj, Nestor W., *Effects of R&D on the Productivity Growth of Industries: An Exploratory Study*, Washington, D.C.: National Planning Association, 1974.

Terleckyj, Nestor W., "Direct and Indirect Effects of Industrial Research and Development on the Productivity Growth of Industries," in John W. Kendrick and Beatrice Vaccara, eds., *New Developments in Productivity Measurement*, New York: National Bureau of Economic Research, 1980.

Tilton, John E., *International Diffusion of Technology: The Case of Semiconductors*, Washington, D.C.: The Brookings Institution, 1971.

Todaro, Michael P., *Economic Development in the Third World*, 2nd edition, New York: Longman, 1981.

Triebwasser, S., "Impact of Semiconductor Microelectronics," *Computer Technology: Status, Limits, Alternatives*, New York: Institute of Electrical and Electronics Engineers, Inc., 1978, pp. 176—177.

Uchitelle, Louis, "Strength in Manufacturing Overstated by Faulty Data," *New York Times*, November 28, 1988, pp. D1 and D7.

United Nations, *Yearbook of World Energy Statistics*, 1979, 1983, and 1986.

U.S. Bureau of the Census, *Long Term Economic Growth 1860–1970*, Washington, D.C., June 1973.

U.S. Bureau of Labor Statistics, "Family Budgets," *Monthly Labor Review*, January 1980, pp. 44–47.

U.S. Bureau of Mines, *Mineral Yearbook*, Washington, D.C.: U.S. Government Printing Office, various issues.

U.S. Bureau of Mines, Department of the Interior, *The Domestic Supply of Critical Minerals*, Washington, D.C., 1983.

U.S. Department of Commerce, Bureau of the Census, *Historical Statistics of the United States, Colonial Times to 1970, Part 2*, Washington, D.C.: U.S. Government Printing Office, 1975.

U.S. Department of Commerce, Bureau of the Census, *Statistical Abstract of the United States, 1982–83*, Washington, D.C.: U.S. Government Printing Office, 1982.

U.S. Department of Commerce, Bureau of Economic Analysis, "The Input-Output Structure of the U.S. Economy: 1967," *Survey of Current Business*, February 1974 and various years.

U.S. Department of Commerce, Bureau of Economic Analysis, *The National Income and Products Accounts of the United States, 1929–1976*, Washington, D.C., 1981.

U.S. Department of Energy, Energy Information Administration, *Annual Energy Review 1987*, Washington, D.C.: U.S. Government Printing Office, 1988.

U.S. Department of Labor, Bureau of Labor Statistics, *Time-Series Data for Input-Output Industries*, Bulletin 2018, Washington, D.C., 1979 (1979a).

U.S. Department of Labor, Bureau of Labor Statistics, *Capital Stock Estimates for Input-Output Industries: Methods and Data*, Bulletin 203, Washington, D.C., 1979 (1979b).

U.S. Federal Communications Commission, *Annual Report*, various years.

Veblen, Thorstein, *The Theory of Business Enterprise*, New York, 1904.

Veblen, Thorstein, *Imperial Germany and the Industrial Revolution*, New York: Macmillan, 1915.

Viner, Jacob, *The Long View and the Short*, Glencoe, NY: Free Press, 1958.

Wachter, M. L., and Wachter, S. M., eds. *Towards a New U.S. Industrial Policy*, Philadelphia: University of Pennsylvania Press, 1981.

Wells, Robert V., *Revolutions in American's Lives*, Westport, Ct.: Greenwood Press, 1982.

White, Lynn, Jr., *Medieval Technology and Social Change*, Oxford: Clarendon Press, 1962.

Wiener, Martin J., *English Culture and the Decline of the Industrial Spirit, 1850–1980*, Harmondsworth: Pelican Books, 1981.

Williamson, Jeffrey G., "Why Was British Growth So Slow During the Industrial Revolution?" *Journal of Economic History*, Vol. XLIV, September 1984, pp. 687–712."

Willig, Robert D., "Consumer's Surplus Without Apology," *American Economic Review*, Vol. 66, September 1976, pp. 589–597.

Willis, Nathanial Parker, *Hurry-Graphs; or Sketches of Scenery, Celebrities, and Society, Taken from Life*, Detroit: Kerr, 1853, p. 130.

Wilson, Charles, *The Dutch Republic*, New York: McGraw-Hill, 1968.

Wilson, Charles, *Economic History and the Historian: Collected Essays*, New York: Frederick A. Praeger Publishers, 1969.

Wilson, Reginald, and Melendez, Sarah E., *Minorities in Higher Education: Fourth Annual Status Report, 1985*, Washington, D.C.: Office of Minority Concerns, American Council on Education, 1985.

Wilson, William J., *The Truly Disadvantaged: The Inner City Underclass and Public Policy*, Chicago: University of Chicago Press, 1987.

Wolff, Edward N., "The Rate of Surplus Value, the Organic Composition, and the General Rate of Profit in the U.S. Economy, 1947–1967," *American Economic Review*, Vol. 69, June 1979, pp. 329–341.

Wolff, Edward N., "Industrial Composition, Interindustry Effects, and the U.S. Productivity Slowdown," *Review of Economics and Statistics*, Vol. 67, May 1985, pp. 268–277.

Wolff, Edward N., *Growth, Accumulation, and Unproductive Activity: An Analysis of the Post-War U.S. Economy*, Cambridge: Cambridge University Press, 1987 (1987a).

Wolff, Edward N., "Capital Formation and Long-Term Productivity Growth: A Comparison of Seven Countries," C. V. Starr Working Paper # 87–37, September, 1987 (1987b).

Wolff, Edward N., and Baumol, William J., "Sources of Postwar Growth of Information Activity in the United States," in Osberg, Lars, Wolff, Edward N., and Baumol, William J., *The Information Economy and the Implications of Unbalanced Growth*, Ottawa: Institute for Research on Public Policy, 1989.

Wolff, Edward N., and Howell, David R., "Labor Quality and Productivity Growth in the U.S.," *Frontiers of Input-Output Analysis*, New York: Oxford University Press, forthcoming.

Wolff, Edward N., and Nadiri, M. Ishaq, "Spillover Effects, Linkage Structure, Technical Change, and Research and Development," mimeo, September 1987.

World Bank, *World Development Report 1987*, New York: Oxford University Press, 1987.

Index

Aaron, Henry J., 264
Abramovitz, Moses, 86, 89, 95, 164, 171, 174, 175, 310–311n.3
"Advantages of backwardness," 86, 98, 204
Aggregation problems, in multifactor productivity, 250n.3
Agricultural progress, 9
Agricultural revolution, early, 11
Agriculture, U.S.
knowledge and data workers in, 150
productivity growth rates for, 74, 75, 76, 79–80, 128
productivity growth regressions for, 288, 290, 294
sector shares for (1800–1980), 146
Allocative inefficiency, and productive capacity, 237–238
Antitrust suits, and rent seeking, 276–277
Argentina
and convergence hypothesis, 94, 343
productivity growth in (1913–1965), 112
Ashton, T. S., 176
Asia. *See* Far East *or specific countries*
Asymptotic stagnancy, 116, 133–138, 151
basic theorems on, 313, 317–319
Atkinson, W. C., 170
Australia
and convergence relations, 103, 343
defense expenditures in, 267, 268
industry vs. service sector in, 120
labor productivity growth in (1870–1979), 13, 87, 88, 91, 92, 94
labor productivity projection for, 256, 257
output projections for, 259, 260
Austria
and convergence relations, 103, 343

defense expenditures in, 267, 268
industry vs. service sector in, 120
labor productivity growth in (1870–1979), 13, 88, 94
labor productivity projection for, 256, 257
output projections for, 259, 260

Baily, Martin Neil, 71, 72
Bairoch, Paul, 95, 96
Balance of payments deficit, 13–14, 15, 17
Barnett, H. L., 216
Baths, and U.S. living standards revolution, 31, 41, 42, 43–44
Baumol, William J., 65, 116, 124, 144, 185, 203, 211, 216, 260
Becker, M. B., 170
Belgium
and convergence hypothesis, 95, 103, 343
defense expenditures in, 267, 268
and economic leadership, 24
industry vs. service sector in, 120
labor productivity growth in (1870–1979), 13, 88, 94
labor productivity projection for, 256, 257
output projections for, 259, 260
Bell, Daniel, 115
Beniger, James R., 30, 143, 145, 146
Bhagwati, Jagdish, 178
Birdzell, L. E., Jr., 57
Blackman, Sue Anne Batey, 224
Blades, D. W., 186
Borrowing, international, as investment exporting, 168, 191–192n.1
Branson, William H., 6
Braudel, Fernand, 39, 40, 60, 170, 171
Britain. *See* United Kingdom

Broadcasting, television, and stagnancy, 128, 133–134, 136, 138, 139, 140
Brown, William M., 214
Budgets, family, and U.S. living standards revolution, 32–34, 35, 36, 37–38, 56
Building industry. See Construction sector
Bureau of the Census, see U.S. Department of Commerce, Bureau of the Census
Bureau of Economic Analysis, see U.S. Bureau of Economic Analysis
Bureau of Labor Statistics, see U.S. Bureau of Labor Statistics
Burns, C., 135

Canada
capital growth and TFP in, 182, 333
capital growth and GDP/work-hour in, 183
capital-labor ratio growth in, 337
and convergence relations, 103, 343
defense expenditures in, 267, 268
industry vs. service sector in, 120
investment by, 333
labor productivity and capital growth in (1950–79), 262
labor productivity growth in (1870–1979), 13, 87, 88, 93, 94
labor productivity projection for, 256, 257
output projections for, 259, 260
total factor productivity in, 330, 335, 336
total factor productivity vs. labor productivity growth in, 173
Capacity utilization, adjustments for, 361–363
Capital
international mobility of, 184–187
policy proposal for allocation of, 278–282
Capital accumulation or formation, 163, 191. See also Investment; Savings
and convergence club, 165–166
and Industrial Revolution, 176
vs. Innovation in productivity growth, 175
Japanese, 4
and labor productivity, 262, 263–264
and total factor productivity growth, 165, 182–183, 332–338
Capital gains taxation, and savings, 265–266
Capital-labor ratio

growth of (various countries), 337
and labor productivity, 261–263
Capital stock
and output, 166–167
U.S. accumulation of, 188
Carus-Wilson, Eleanora M., 11
Catalogues, mail-order, 44–48
Caves, Douglas, 244, 245, 246, 247, 248, 249, 359, 360, 361, 362, 363
Centennial Exposition, Philadelphia, 36, 39
Chain index, 232
Child labor, in 19th century U.S., 48, 50
Chile
and convergence-education relation, 343
productivity growth data on, 112
China
and convergence, 97, 343
RGDP growth in, 97
savings propensity in, 179–180
Christensen, Laurits R., 244, 245, 246, 247, 248, 249, 359, 360, 361, 362, 363
Cipolla, Carlo M., 11, 169, 170
Clemens, Samuel, 55
Clothing, and U.S. living standards revolution, 42–43
Coefficients of variation, 92
in convergence test, 92, 305–306, 308, 309
Coleman, D. C., 218, 219
Colombia
and convergence-education relation, 343
productivity growth data on, 112
Commission on Minority Participation in Education and American Life, 207
Comparative advantage, and productivity performance, 16, 22, 27n.13
Competitiveness, international. See also Convergence; Economic leadership, world
Britain's loss of, 19
and productivity policy, 10
Competitiveness of U.S.
and deindustrialization thesis, 74 (see also Deindustrialization thesis)
in manufacturing (data on), 106
and postwar productivity performance, 103
and service-economy illusion, 116
Compounding, and savings/investment rates, 3–4
Computation, electronic, asymptotic stagnancy in, 135–136

Computerization, productivity jump
through, 77
Computer prices, postwar evolution of,
321
Construction sector
productivity data for, 76, 128
productivity growth regressions for, 288,
290
as stagnant, 131
Consumer expenditures, taxation of, 265,
266
Consumer goods, nineteenth-century vs.
contemporary, 44–48, 49–50
Consumer preferences, and consumer
welfare improvement, 238
Consumers' surpluses, and welfare
productivity measure, 240–241
Consumption
of food in U.S. living standards
revolution, 34–40, 49
and labor productivity, 227
Consumption expenditures, and economic
takeoff, 166
Consumption-lag hypothesis, 177, 181,
184
Convergence, 85–87, 89–90, 108
and education, 98, 195–196, 203–206
and education (statistical analysis), 341–
355
empirical evidence on, 91–99
explanation of, 99–102
and Japan, 331
and savings behavior, 181–182
statistical tests of, 98–99, 301–310, 331
technological sophistication as base for,
310–311n.3
and U.S. productivity performance, 102–
107, 108
Convergence club, 86, 98, 108
and capital stock growth, 165–166
Cost-disease model, 116, 124–126. See also
Unbalanced growth premise
and asymptotic stagnancy, 133–138, 151
and information explosion, 152–154
and information sector, 143–144
testing implications of, 130
and unit costs, 313
Cowan, Ruth Schwartz, 35–36
Crowding out, 265, 266–267
in Britain during Napoleonic wars, 5
Crude TFP growth, 232, 245
Cultural influences

and rent seeking, 276
on savings propensity, 165, 166, 177
Cutler, David, 275
Czechoslovakia
convergence-education relation in, 343
RGDP growth in, 97

Darby, Michael, 6
Darmstadter, Joel, 213
Data workers and sector, 144–145
employment decomposition in, 155
growth of, 146, 147, 148, 149, 150, 157,
158
as progressive, 151
David, Paul A., 164, 171, 174, 175
Dean, Edwin, 202, 203
Decomposition of employment change,
325–327
Defense expenditures, and crowding out,
267–268
Deficit, government, and U.S. exchange
rate, 26n.11
Deficits in balance of payments, 13–14, 15,
17
Deindustrialization thesis, 15, 19, 65, 115
and convergence relationship, 103, 105
evidence on, 118–124
and U.S. manufacturing, 74
De Long, Bradford, 94, 95, 203
Denison, Edward F., 72, 202
Denmark
convergence relations in, 103, 343
industry vs. service sector in, 120
labor productivity growth in (1870–
1979), 13, 88, 94
labor productivity projection for, 256,
257
output projections for, 259, 260
Depression (Great Depression), productivity statistics for, 70
De Vries, Jan, 169
Divisia index, 233–234
alternatives to, 359
growth in (various countries), 330, 331–
332, 336
in railroad example, 245, 247, 248, 249
Dooley, Michael, 185, 187
Dutch republic. See Netherlands

Economic leadership, world, 23–24
and convergence hypothesis, 86 (see also
Convergence)

Economic leadership (cont.)
   as policy goal for U.S., 254–258, 259,
      260, 282
   U.S. position of, 6, 7 (see also Competi-
      tiveness, U.S.)
Economics, short run vs. long run in, 1–2
Education
   and convergence, 98, 195–196, 203–206
   and convergence (statistical analysis),
      341–355
   gross productivity measure for, 242
   in investment measure, 188–189
   in LDCs, 197, 198, 201–202, 203, 204
   measuring economic benefits of, 198–200
   national differences in, 196–198
   policy proposal on, 277–278
   and productivity growth, 190, 200–203,
      341, 347–351
   and total factor productivity, 172
   and U.S. living standards revolution, 51,
      56
   of U.S. underprivileged minority groups,
      206–209, 277–278
Efficiency, in Japan vs. U.S., 4
Egypt
   and convergence-education relation, 344
   productivity growth data on, 112
Electronic computation, asymptotic stagnancy in, 135–136
Employment change, decomposition of,
   325–327
Energy crisis of 1970s, and resource substitution, 220
England. See United Kingdom
Entrepreneurship, 260
   mobility of, 185
   rent seeking as misdirection of, 273–277
   and technology transfer, 90, 100–102,
      271–272
Environmentalism, 211
Equalization of opportunity, as educational
   benefit, 199
Equilibration process, in international trade,
   21–22
Exchange rate
   fall of for U.S., 26n.11
   and productivity lag, 17, 21–22

Family budgets, and U.S. living standards
   revolution, 32–34, 35, 36, 37–38, 56
Famines
   disappearance of, 58–59

historical prevalence of, 9, 39–40
Far East (Asia). See also specific countries
   and convergence club, 108
   and cultural influences on success, 177,
      180
Feinstein, C. H., 16, 17, 18, 91, 169.
Feldstein, Martin, 185
Finance and insurance sector, as stagnant,
   127, 131
Finance, insurance and real estate sector
   knowledge and data workers in, 150
   productivity growth regressions for, 289,
      291, 297–298
   productivity data for, 75, 76–77, 79, 81,
      128
Financial markets, and rent seeking, 275–
   276
Finland
   and convergence relations, 103, 344
   defense expenditures in, 267, 268
   industry vs. service sector in, 120
   labor productivity growth in (1870–
      1979), 13, 88, 94
   labor productivity projection for, 256,
      257
   output projections for, 259, 260
Floud, Roderick, 170
Fogel, Robert W., 53, 54, 59
Food consumption, and U.S. living
   standards revolution, 34–40
Foreign innovation. See Technology
   transfer
France
   capital growth and GDP/work-hour in,
      183
   capital growth and TFP in, 182, 333
   capital-labor ratio growth in, 337
   and convergence hypothesis, 95, 103, 344
   defense expenditures in, 267, 268
   GDP in 1700, 11–12
   high-tech exports by, 104
   industrial employment share by, 105, 107
   industry vs. service sector in, 120
   investment influence in, 279
   investment rate in, 333
   labor productivity and capital growth in
      (1950–79), 262
   labor productivity growth in (1870–
      1979), 13, 88, 92, 93, 94
   labor productivity growth in (1913–65),
      112
   labor productivity projection for, 256, 257

output projections for, 259, 260
RGDP growth in, 97
savings vs. investment in, 186
socially unproductive pursuits in, 274
total factor productivity of, 330, 335, 336
total factor productivity vs. labor productivity growth in, 173
in world trade, 17–19
Frankel, Jeffrey A., 185, 187
Franklin, Benjamin, 211
Free-rider problem, 270
Frisch, Jack, 216
Fuchs, Victor R., 6, 116
Fuel prices, 217
Fulton, Robert, 101, 227
Furnas, J. C., 29, 51, 52, 55

Germany
capital growth and GDP/work-hour in, 183
capital growth and TFP in, 182, 333
capital-labor ratio growth in, 337
capital-output relation in, 166–167
and convergence hypothesis, 95, 344
industry vs. service sector in, 120
investment by, 190, 333
labor productivity growth in (1870–1979), 13, 88, 92, 93, 94
labor productivity growth in (1913–1965), 112
total factor productivity of, 330, 335, 336
total factor productivity vs. labor productivity growth in, 173
unemployment in, 16
in world trade, 17, 18
Germany, East (German Democratic Republic), and convergence relations, 97, 344
Germany, West (Federal Republic of Germany)
and convergence relations, 97, 103, 344
defense expenditures in, 267, 268
high-tech exports by, 104
industrial employment share by, 105, 107
labor productivity and capital growth in (1950–79), 262
labor productivity projection for, 255, 256, 257
output projections for, 259, 260
R&D by, 269
RGDP growth in, 97
savings vs. investment in, 186

and U.S. productivity goal, 253
Gerschenkron, Alexander, 89
Gerschuny, J., 116
Ghana
and convergence-education relation, 344
productivity growth data on, 112
Gillis, Malcolm, 196
Gilmore, James Robert, 43
Gimpel, Jean, 11
Gini coefficients, in convergence test, 99, 306–310
Godey's Lady's Book, 43–44
Goods sector and workers, 145, 146
and employment decomposition, 155
employment growth in, 147
employment percentage in, 148
as progressive, 151
and unbalanced growth, 157, 158
Gordon, Robert J., 72, 135, 321
Gordon, T. J., 135
Government sector
productivity data for, 76, 129
productivity growth regressions for, 289, 292, 299
as stagnant, 127, 131
Grabscheid, Paul, 135
Great Britain. See United Kingdom
Greece
and convergence-education relation, 344
productivity growth data on, 112
Griliches, Zvi, 268, 269
Gross domestic product (GDP) per work-hour. See Labor productivity
Gross national product (GNP), as market values, 125
Gross productivity, 235, 241–244
Gross productivity index, 225
Growth, productivity. See Productivity growth

Hall's Journal of Health, 44
Haveman, Robert H., 202
Health, and U.S. living standards revolution, 50, 54–56
Heim, Peggy, 31–32
Helliwell, John F., 6
Heston, Alan, 122. See also Summers-Heston data
Hobsbawm, Eric J., 101, 196, 272, 274
Hohenberg, P. M., 169, 181
Holland. See Netherlands
Holmes, Oliver Wendell, 55

Home heating technology, modern improvement in, 59–60
Hopkins, S. V., 12
Horioka, Charles, 185
Hotelling, Harold, 216
Housework, and U.S. living standards revolution, 63n.14
Housing
tax incentives for, 266
and U.S. living standards revolution, 40–42, 49, 54
in U.S. vs. other countries, 189
Hulton, Charles R., 233
Human capital
and convergence, 311n.3
in investment measure, 188–189
Hygiene and sanitation, in U.S. living standards revolution, 43–44, 54, 55–56, 62n.11

Imitative entrepreneurship, 100–102
Income distribution, and living-standards-revolution benefits, 57–60, 61n.11
India
convergence-education relation in, 344
GDP for, 12
productivity growth in (1913–1965), 112
Industrial Revolution, 12
and British labor productivity, 5
and capital accumulation, 176
and convergence hypothesis, 95
innovation in, 5
investment costs in, 12, 25n.3
raw materials use in, 212–213
social class and benefits from, 60
socially unproductive activities impede, 274
"Industrial revolutions," of earlier times, 9, 11
Industry
sector shares in U.S. for (1800–1980), 146. See also Manufacturing sector, U.S.
vs. service in OECD countries, 120
Infant mortality, and U.S. living standards revolution, 52
Inflation
and capital gains tax, 265–266
and productivity policy, 10, 13–14, 15
Information economy view, 143–144
empirical data on, 145–149
and industry/sector breakdown, 149–151
statistical results on, 154–158

and unbalanced growth (cost disease), 151–154, 156, 157–158
Information sector, classification scheme for, 144–145
Innovations
and British productivity (Napoleonic period), 5
and convergence hypothesis, 100–101
of 18th century and before, 11
and historical living standards, 9
and labor productivity growth, 163
and natural resource productivity, 212
and resource utilization, 221, 222
vs. savings/investment in productivity growth, 171–176
and total factor productivity, 165, 172
Input substitution
of information labor, 152–158
and resource utilization, 220
Input-substitution component, 326
Interest rate
and inverstment export, 170
and productivity effect on savings, 180–181
International economic leadership. See Economic leadership, world
International mobility of capital, 184–187
International trade
equilibration process in, 21–22
and productivity growth, 17–22
Investment
calculation of, 329–332
and capital-output relation, 167
conventional vs. broadened definition of, 188–189
determinants of, 165, 264–265
export of, 168, 191–192n.1
French and Japanese government intervention in, 279
in Industrial Revolution, 12, 25n.3
vs. innovation in productivity growth, 171–176
international mobility of, 184–187
and labor productivity growth, 163
and output growth, 261
of past economic leaders, 164, 168–171
and productivity growth, 164
in productivity policy proposal, 263–268
rates of, (U.S./Germany/France/Japan), 3
and saving, 185–186
and saving-productivity growth relation, 180–181

Index 387

of United Kingdom (Napoleonic period), 5
U.S. record in, 187–191
Invisible hand doctrine, 273
Ireland
convergence-education relation in, 344
industry vs. service sector in, 120
Ishinomori, Shotaro, 115
Italy
capital growth and GDP/work-hour in, 183
capital growth and TFP in, 182, 333
capital-labor ratio growth in, 337
capital-output relation in, 166–167
consumption standards in, 181
convergence relations in, 103, 344
decline of and investment export, 169, 170, 171
defense expenditures in, 267, 268
industry vs. service sector in, 120
and international mobility of capital, 185
investment in, 333
labor productivity and capital growth in (1950–79), 262
labor productivity growth in (1913–1965), 112
labor productivity growth in (1870–1979), 13, 88, 92, 93, 94
labor productivity projection for, 256, 257
output projections for, 259, 260
savings vs. investment in, 186
savings-investment record of, 164
and technology transfer, 271
total factor productivity of, 330, 335, 336
total factor productivity vs. labor productivity growth in, 173, 175
in world trade, 17, 18

Japan
capital accumulation in, 4
capital growth and GDP/work-hour in, 183
capital growth and TFP in, 182, 333
capital-labor ratio growth in, 337
capital-output relation in, 166–167
consumption habits in, 181
and convergence hypothesis, 94, 97, 99, 103, 344
cultural influences in, 178
and export of imitative entrepreneurship, 102

high-tech exports by, 104–105
industrial employment by, 104–105, 107
industry vs. service sector in, 120
investment by, 190, 333
investment influence in, 279
labor productivity in (vs. U.S.), 3–4, 5
labor productivity and capital growth in (1950–79), 262
labor productivity growth in (1870–1979), 13, 88, 91, 92, 93, 94
labor productivity growth in (1913–1965), 112
labor productivity projection for, 256, 257
output projections for, 259, 260
R&D by, 269
and rent seeking, 276
savings in, 3, 4, 177, 178, 184
savings vs. investment in, 186
as statistical outlier, 331
and technology transfer, 272
total factor productivity in, 330, 335, 336
total factor productivity vs. labor productivity growth in, 173, 175
U.S. competition with, 82
and U.S. productivity goal, 253
in world trade, 17, 18

Kendrick, John W., 14, 67, 68, 174, 202
Keynes, John Maynard, 1
King, Mervyn, 177
Knowledge sector and workers. See also Information sector
and classification scheme, 144–145
employment decomposition in, 155
growth of, 146, 147, 148, 149, 150, 156, 158
Krantz, F., 169, 181
Kravis, Irving, 167, 178, 188, 189, 190, 191, 264
Kubitz, W. J., 135
Kuznets, Simon, 89, 178

Labor force
costs in building of, 67
effect of poor productivity on, 21–22
Labor force, U.S.
growth of and industrial employment, 105, 107
and information sector, 145–149
and service sectors, 126

Labor Force Statistics, 105
Labor productivity. *See also* Productivity
  growth of (various countries), 12–13
  historical growth of in India, 12
  vs. total factor productivity, 225,
    226–228, 331
Labor productivity growth. *See also*
  Productivity growth
  and capital formation, 262, 263–264
  and capital-labor ratio, 261–263
  convergence in, 91–92, 93–94
  decline of in recession, 67
  ingredients in, 163
  and innovation/savings-investment role,
    171–176
  Maddison data on, 88, 91 (*see also*
    Maddison, Angus, and Maddison data)
  and savings rate, 163, 180–184, 191, 262
  and total factor productivity, 165
  and umemployment, 15–17
  in United Kingdom (Napoleonic period), 5
Labor productivity growth, U.S., 2, 5–6.
  See also Productivity growth, U.S.
  and capital growth (1950–79), 262
  and convergence, 103
  goal for, 252–259
  and information explosion, 152
  vs. Japan, 3–4
  long-term statistics on, 78–80
  Maddison data on, 69–70 (*see also*
    Maddison, Angus, and Maddison data)
  in manufacturing sector, 72, 73–74, 75,
    76, 81, 82n.4
  in nonmanufacturing sectors, 74–77
  projection for, 256, 257
  relative to other countries, 85, 87–89
  sectoral, 72–77, 78–80, 127–129, 320
  statistical tests on, 77–78, 80
  subsectoral, 80–81
  by time period (1870–1979), 13, 88, 92,
    93, 94
  by time period (1884–1969), 14
  by time period (1913–1965), 112
  volatility of, 14
Landes, David S., 12
Latin America
  and convergence club, 108
  and cultural determinants of failure, 177
  education in, 196–197
Lawrence, Robert Z., 6
Lawsuits, as rent seeking, 274–275
LDCs. *See* Less developed countries

Leadership. *See* Economic leadership, world
Lebergott, Stanley, 34, 48, 50
Lee, Valerie, 208
Leisure time, and U.S. living standards
  revolution, 48, 63n.14
Lending
  by Italy/Netherlands/U.K., 164
  international, 168, 191–192n.1
Lerner, Abba, 1
Less developed countries (LDCs)
  and convergence, 86–87, 97–98, 108,
    195
  education in, 197, 198, 201–202, 203,
    204
  U.S. minority groups compared to, 206,
    208
Levin, H. J., 138
Lewis, W. Arthur, 202, 206
Lichtenberg, Frank, 268
Life expectancy
  of British peerage, 59, 60
  and U.S. living standards revolution,
    52–54, 56
Lindsey, Lawrence, 264
Lipsey, Robert, 167, 178, 188, 189, 190,
  191, 264
Living standards. *See also* Welfare
  productivity
  and productivity growth, 10, 24–25
  and productivity-trade relation, 21
  U.K. rise in, 23
  and U.K. trade, 20
Living standards revolution in United
  States, 29–30, 56–57, 61n.3
  clothing in, 42–43
  consumer goods in, 44–48, 49–50
  education in, 51, 56
  family budgets as indicative of, 32–34,
    35, 36, 37–38, 56
  food consumption in, 34–40
  housing in, 40–42, 54
  hygiene in, 43–44, 54, 55–56, 62n.11
  and income group, 57–60, 61n.3
  leisure time in, 48, 63n.14
  life expectancy in, 52–54, 56
  and oral history account, 31–32
  physical stature in, 52–53
  public health in, 54–56
  and rural-urban proportions, 30–31, 56
  travel in, 51–52, 56
  working conditions in, 48, 50–51, 56
Lopez, Robert S., 170

McCloskey, D. N., 20, 170
McCullogh, Rachel, 104
McFadden, Daniel, 359
McLennan, Kenneth, 65
Macroeconomics, and short run vs. long
  run, 1–2
Maddison, Angus, and Maddison data, 68,
  69–70, 77, 87, 88, 173, 253
  and capital stock, 166–167, 182, 183, 262
  and convergence, 91, 92, 93, 94, 103, 112
  on growth rates in leading countries, 12,
  13
  and historical record of growth, 11–12
  on labor-force percentages, 16
  in postwar golden age, 258
  in projections, 256, 257
  and slowdown hypothesis, 71
  and TFP, 92, 172
  on U.K., 19
  on work hours, 48
Mail order catalogues, 44–48
Malaya, productivity growth data on, 112
Malmquist, David H., 4
Mansfield, Edwin, 100–101, 268
Manufacturing sector, U.S.
  and deindustrialization thesis, 115 (see also
  Deindustrialization thesis)
  knowledge and data workers in, 150
  productivity growth regressions for, 288,
  290–291, 293, 294–296
  productivity statisitics for, 72, 73–74, 75,
  76, 79, 81, 82n.4, 128
March, George Perkins, 52
Marginal utility, 240
Marsh, Robert M., 179
Martin, Edgar W., 30–31, 33, 34, 40, 41,
  43, 48, 51, 52, 55
Marx, Karl, on labor, 227
Mathieson, Donald, 185, 187
Matthews, R. C. O., 16, 17, 18, 91.
Measurement, productivity. See Produc-
  tivity measurement
Media, and cost-disease model, 133
Medici family, consumption history of, 181
Medicine, in 1800s, 55
Mexico, productivity growth data on, 112
Military outlays, and crowding out, 267–
  268
Mill, James, 180
Miller, L. Scott, 207
Minerals, See also Natural resource supply
  prices of, 217, 218

reserves of, 215
Mining sector
  knowledge and data workers in, 150
  productivity growth record of, 76–77, 79,
  128, 131
  productivity growth regressions for, 288,
  290, 293, 294
Minority groups, U.S.
  education of, 206–209, 277–278
  poverty of, 207
Mishel, Lawrence, 72
Molho, Anthony, 169
Montgomery Ward catalogue, 44
Morrison, Joan, 50
Morse, Chandler, 216
Multifactor productivity
  aggregation problems in, 250n.3
  TFP as, 228 (see also Total factor
  productivity)
Munson, T. R., 135

Nadiri, M. Ishaq, 268, 269
National Bureau of Economic Research, 67
National Science Foundation, 104, 268
Natural resources supply, 211–215,
  221–223
  and extraction costs, 219, 220, 222
  and opportunity costs, 220–221
  propositions on, 222–223, 357–358
  and recycling, 221
  and resource prices, 215–218
Nef, John V., 11
Nelson, Richard R., 102
Netherlands
  consumption standards in, 181
  and convergence hypothesis, 95, 103,
  345
  decline of and investment export, 169–
  170
  defense expenditures in, 267, 268
  and economic leadership, 24
  industry vs. service sector in, 120
  and international mobility of capital, 185
  labor productivity growth in (1870–
  1979), 13, 88, 94
  labor productivity projection for, 256,
  257
  output projections for, 259, 260
  savings-investment record of, 164
  and technology transfer, 271
Netschert, Bruce C., 217, 218
Newman, Pauline, 50

New Zealand
  convergence-education relation in, 345
  industry vs. service sector in, 120
Nigeria, and convergence hypothesis, 99,
  345
Norsworthy, J. R., 4
North, Douglass C., 272
Norton, R. D., 6
Norway
  convergence relations in, 103, 345
  defense expenditures in, 267, 268
  industry vs. service sector in, 120
  labor productivity growth in (1870–
  1979), 13, 88, 94
  labor productivity projection for, 256,
  257
  output projections for, 259, 260
Noyce, R. N., 135

Oates, Wallace E., 211, 216
Odling-Smee, J. C., 16, 17, 18, 91.
Ohkawa, Kazushi, 178, 179
Oil (petroleum)
  prophecies on depletion of, 213–214
  price of, 217
Oil (energy) crisis of 1970s, and resource
  substitution, 220
Olmstead, Frederick, 41
Organization for Economic Cooperation
  and Development (OECD)
  and convergence, 203–204
  data from, 104–107, 119
  industry vs. service percentages for (by
  country), 119–120
  savings in, 3
  U.S. share of industrial employment of,
  104–107
Organization of Petroleum Exporting
  Countries (OPEC), 216
Output, and capital stock, 166–167
Output, per-capita
  goal for, 252–255, 258, 259, 260
  and labor productivity, 227
Output, sectoral, alternative measures of,
  319–320
Output-composition component, 153, 154,
  156, 157, 158, 327

Paik, N. J. 138
Pakistan
  and convergence-education relation, 345
  labor producitivity growth data on, 112

Palatine, Princess, 60
Palmer, Robert, 39
Peru
  and convergence-education relation, 345
  labor productivity growth data on, 112
Petroleum. See Oil
Phelps Brown, E. H., 12
Philadelphia Centennial Exposition, 36, 39
Philip, Cynthia Owen, 227
Philip of Orleans, 60
Philippines
  and convergence-education relation, 345
  productivity growth data on, 112
Physical stature, and U.S. living standards
  revolution, 52–53
Ping-Ti Ho, 179, 180
Poage, James, 136, 137
Polach, Jaroslave G., 213
Policy, productivity. See Productivity
  policy
Population growth, and industrial employment share, 105, 107
Poverty
  in 17th century Europe, 40
  in U.S. (19th century), 34, 43
  in U.S. (current), 58
  of U.S. minority children, 207
Price index, in service-sector measurement,
  118, 121
Prices. See also Cost-disease model
  computer, 321
  for minerals, 217, 218
  as regulated upward, 275
  resource, 215–218
  and welfare productivity evaluation, 240
Princeton University Computer Center,
  136–137
Producers' surpluses, and welfare productivity measure, 240–241
Production frontier, and productivity
  growth, 235, 236, 237
Productive capacity
  ambiguities in, 244
  program for investment in, 261–268
  vs. welfare productivity, 237–239
Productivity. See also Labor productivity
  concept of, 225
  total factor, 82n.1, 92, 165 (see also Total
  factor productivity)
Productivity growth, 1, 9–10. See also
  Labor productivity growth
  absolute vs. relative success in, 23

alternative measures of, 319–320
compounding of, 3–4
and convergence hypothesis, 85–87, 89–90 (see also Convergence hypothesis)
cyclical nature of, 66–68
economic miracle of, 9
and education, 190, 200–203, 341, 347–351
historical changes in, 10–13
innovation/savings-investment role in, 171–176
and international trade, 17–22
and investment, 164
in Japan, 4
and living standards, 10, 24–25
of natural resources, 212, 223 (see also Natural resources supply)
short- vs. long-term study of, 2–3, 4, 10, 66
and social services, 22–23
total factor, 67, 68
and unemployment, 15–17
volatility of, 14
Productivity growth, U.S., 5–7. See also Labor productivity growth, U.S.
and convergence hypothesis, 85, 90, 102–107, 108 (see also Convergence hypothesis)
in information sector, 159
in knowledge-intensive industries, 156
long-period statistics on, 68–71, 72–73
and minority-group education, 206–207, 209
and slowdown hypothesis, 65–66, 69, 70–71, 74, 77, 81
time series regressions for (1947–76), 287
Productivity-lag component, 326
in information sector, 153–158
Productivity measurement, 225–226, 249–250
conceptual issues from, 234–235
empirical comparisons of, 244–249
and finance, insurance and real estate, 83n.10
labor vs. total factor, 226–228
and productive capacity, 235–237
and service outputs, 117
and tax proposal, 280
and TFP measurement, 228–234
and welfare productivity vs. productive capacity, 237–239
and welfare productivity measurement, 239–241

Productivity policy
and capital-output relation (poorer countries), 167
education as, 206
importance of, 108
limitations of, 10, 13–15
proposals on, 7
Productivity policy, longer-term, 251, 258, 260–261
vs. entrepreneurial rent-seeking, 273–277
failsafe measure for, 278–282
goals for, 252–258, 259, 260
and investment in productive capacity, 261–268
minority education, 277–278
R&D strengthening, 268–271
technology transfer in, 271–273
Progressive service sectors, 117, 124–126, 126–127, 131, 132, 133, 151
and productivity growth measures, 320
Prospective consumption, and labor productivity, 227
"Protestant ethic," 203
Psacharopoulos, George, 201, 202
Public health, and U.S. living standards revolution, 54–56

Quality changes
and gross productivity, 244
and welfare productivity, 239–240

Railroads
as measurement-comparison example, 244–249
and technology transfer, 101
R&D
and cost disease, 116
in investment measure, 188–189
productivity policy proposal for, 268–271
Reagan administration, deficit incurred by, 26n.11
Real estate sector, 127, 128, 298. See also Finance, insurance and real estate sector
Real GDP per capita (RGDP), 96, 258
Recession, and fall in productivity growth, 66
Regression curve, 77–78
Regressions, for productivity growth (1947–76), 287–300. See also Statistical tests

Regulatory agencies
  and capital flows, 279
  and rent seeking, 275
Rent seeking, and policy proposal,
  274–277
Repetto, Robert, 215
Residual, the, 228–229
Resources. *See* Natural resources supply
Retail trade, productivity growth regres-
  sions for, 289, 291
Returns to scale, adjustment for, 359–363
Riis, Jacob, 41–42
Risk arbitrage, 275–276
Rome, ancient, living standards in, 10–11
Romer, Paul M., 94
Rosenberg, Nathan, 57, 85, 86, 195
Rosovsky, Henry, 178, 179
Rubinstein, W. D., 180, 181

Salou, Gerard, 6
Sanitation. *See* Hygiene and sanitation
Satisficing approach, 283n.1
Sato, Kazuo, 163, 184
Savings
  and capital-output relation, 167
  determinants of, 165, 176–180, 264–265
  for domestic vs. export investment, 168
  vs. innovation in productivity growth,
    171–176
  and international mobility of capital,
    184–187
  and investment, 185–186
  in Japan, 3, 4, 177, 178, 184, 186
  and labor productivity growth, 163,
    180–184, 191, 262
  of late-blooming economies, 164
  of past economic leaders, 164, 168–171
  in productivity policy proposal, 263–268
  in United Kingdom, 4–5
  in United States, 3, 163–164, 187–191
Say, J. B., 178, 180
Scherer, F. M., 269
Schindler, M. 135
Schooling. *See* Education
Schumpeter, Joseph, 100, 271
Schurr, Sam H., 217, 218
Scott, Donald M., 55
Sears Roebuck catalogue, 44–48
Self-interest, and social value, 273
Sella, Domenico, 169
Service economy
  and national wealth, 121–124

and stagnant services, 139
  statistical test for, 130–132
Service sector, and gross productivity,
  241–244
Service sector(s), U.S., 115–116, 117. *See
  also specific sectors*
  and cost-disease model, 116, 124–126 (*see
    also* Cost-disease model)
  and deindustrialization thesis, 115, 118–
    124
  employment decomposition in, 155
  growth of, 118, 147, 148
  knowledge and data workers in, 150
  measurement of outputs from, 82n.6,
    117–118
  prevalence of, 119–120
  productivity data for, 72, 74–75, 76, 79,
    128–129, 131
  productivity growth regressions for, 289,
    291, 298–299, 300
  progressive vs. stagnant services in, 117,
    124–126, 151 (*see also* Progressive
    service sectors; Stagnant service sectors)
  rate of movement toward, 107
  sector shares for (1800–1980), 146
  and unbalanced economic growth, 126–
    133
Shipbuilding, and technology transfer, 101
Singh, Ajit, 6
Slowdown hypothesis, on U.S. productivity, 65–66, 69, 70–71, 74, 77, 81
Smith, Adam
  on mobility, 186–187
  on value of self-interest, 273, 274
Smithsonian Institution, commentary by,
  36
Social rate of return, 269
Social services, through productivity
  growth, 22–23
Solow, Robert M., 261
Spain
  convergence-education relation in, 346
  industry vs. service sector in, 120
  productivity growth data on, 112
Spillover effect, 269
Stagnant service sectors, 117, 124–126,
  139, 151
  asymptotic, 116, 133–138, 151, 313,
    317–319
  basic theorems on, 313–319
  knowledge sector as, 151, 159
  and productivity growth measures, 320

and unbalanced growth premise, 126–127, 130, 131, 132, 133
Standard of living. *See* Living standards; Welfare productivity
Stapleton, Darwin H., 272
Statistical tests
for convergence-education relation, 203, 341–355
for convergence using Summers-Heston data, 98–99, 301–310
on productivity data, 77–78, 80
for quality of minority education, 208
regression curve as, 77–78
for service economy, 130–132
on Summers-Heston (convergence) data, 98–99
for unbalanced growth premise, 130–133
Stature, physical, and U.S. living standards revolution, 52–53
Steamship, and technology transfer, 101
Stone, Lawrence, 274
Sturm, Peter H., 6, 186, 264
Summers, Lawrence H., 6, 275
Summers, Robert, 116, 122
Summers-Heston data, 12, 96–97, 98, 258, 259, 301–310, 341, 342, 352
Supply, effective, 219
Swanson, Joseph A., 244, 245, 246, 247, 248, 249, 359, 360, 361, 362, 363
Sweden
and convergence relations, 103, 346
defense expenditures in, 267, 268
industry vs. service sector in, 120
labor productivity growth in (1870–1979), 13, 88, 94
labor productivity projection for, 256, 257
output projections for, 259, 260
Switzerland
and convergence hypothesis, 95, 103, 346
defense expenditures in, 267, 268
industry vs. service sector in, 120
labor productivity growth in (1870–1979), 13, 87, 88, 94
labor productivity projection for, 256, 257
output projections for, 259, 260

Taiwan
and convergence hypothesis, 99, 346
productivity growth data on, 112
savings in, 177, 179

Takeover activities, as rent seeking, 275
Taxation
capital-allocation proposal on, 280–282
and savings, 264, 265–266
Technical change, and productivity growth, 235
Technological innovation. *See* Innovations
Technological sophistication, as convergence base, 310–311n.3
Technology, and post-WWII productivity growth, 70
Technolgoy transfer, 271–272
and convergence hypothesis, 85, 90, 100–101
in productivity proposal for U.S., 272–273
Teitelbaum, Perry D., 213
Television broadcasting, and stagnancy, 128, 133–134, 136, 138, 139, 140
Terleckyj, Nestor W., 269
Texaco-Pennzoil lawsuit, 275
TFP. *See* Total factor productivity
Third World, income growth in (1970s), 5, 12
Thomas, Robert P., 272
Tilton, John, 101
Time periods of productivity growth
1930s (Great Depression), 70
World War II and after, 70
1960s, 69, 73, 77
1960–1979, 70
1970s, 69, 71–72, 74, 77
1980s, 71, 72, 72–73, 77
Time series regressions, for productivity growth (1947–76), 287–300
Törnqvist-Divisa index, 332
Total factor productivity, 82n.1, 92, 165, 172, 228
calculation of, 329–332
and capital accumulation, 165, 182–183, 332–338
growth of (United States), 67, 68
growth of in seven countries (1870–1979), 92–93
and innovation/savings-investment role, 171–176
vs. labor productivity, 225, 226–228, 331
measurement of, 228–234
modified indices of, 359–363
Trade, international. *See* international trade
Training. *See* Education

Transportation, in U.S. vs. other countries, 189
Transportation and public utilities sector
  productivity growth regressions for, 288,
  291, 296–297
  productivity statistics for, 76, 79, 81
Transportation and warehousing
  knowledge and data workers in, 150
  productivity growth for (1947–76), 128
Travel, and U.S. living standards revolution, 50, 51–52, 56
Triebwasser, S., 135

Uchitelle, Louis, 72
Uganda, and convergence hypothesis, 99,
  346
Unbalanced growth premise, 126–127. See
  also Cost-disease model
  and information sector, 151–152, 156,
  157–158
  statistical tests of, 130–133
Unemployment, and productivity policy,
  10, 13–14, 15–17
United Kingdom (England; Britain)
  absolute vs. relative productivity growth
  of, 23
  capital growth and GDP/work-hour in,
  183
  capital growth and TFP in, 182, 333
  capital-labor ratio growth in, 337
  capital-output relation in, 166–167
  consumption standards in, 181
  and convergence hypothesis, 95, 97, 346
  cultural influences in, 178
  decline of and investment export, 169,
  170–171
  as deindustrialization forerunner, 119
  economic fall of, 2–3, 108, 169
  and economic leadership, 23–24
  education in, 196
  GDP of (1700), 11–12
  high-tech exports by, 104
  income growth in (Industrial Revolution),
  5, 12
  industrial employment share by, 105, 107
  industry vs. service sector in, 120
  and international mobility of capital, 185
  international trade of, 17, 18, 19–20
  investment of, 333
  investment of (Napoleonic period), 5
  labor productivity and capital growth in
  (1950–79), 262

labor productivity growth in (1870–
  1979), 13, 87, 88, 91, 92, 93, 94
  labor productivity growth in (1913–
  1965), 112
  labor productivity projection for, 256,
  257
  output projections for, 259, 260
  peers' life expectancy in, 59, 60
  savings vs. investment in, 186
  savings-investment record of, 164
  savings rate of, 4–5
  socially unproductive pursuits in, 274
  and technology transfer, 271–272
  total factor productivity in, 330, 335, 336
  total factor productivity vs. labor productivity growth in, 173, 175
  unemployment in, 16, 19
  and U.S. shipbuilding technology, 101
United Nations, data from 213
United States
  as borrower (19th century), 168
  capital growth and GDP/work-hour in,
  183
  capital growth and TFP in, 182, 333
  capital-labor ratio growth in, 337
  capital-output relation in, 166–167
  and convergence, 97, 103, 346
  defense expenditures in, 267, 268
  education in, 196
  education in (underprivileged minority
  groups), 206–209
  exchange rate fall for, 26n.11
  high-tech exports by, 104
  industrial employment share by, 105, 107
  industry vs. service sector in, 120
  international trade of, 17, 18
  investment in, 333
  labor productivity growth in, 2, 5–6, 14
  (see also Labor productivity growth, U.S.)
  output projections for, 259, 260
  productivity growth in, 65–66 (see also
  Productivity growth, U.S.)
  RGDP growth in, 97
  rent seeking in, 276
  savings and investment in 186, 187–191
  and shipbuilding technology, 101
  and technology transfer, 271–273
  total factor productivity in, 330, 335, 336
  total factor productivity vs. labor productivity growth in, 173, 175
  unemployment in, 15–16
U.S. Bureau of Economic Analysis, 72, 80,

289, 292
U.S. Bureau of Labor Statistics, 33, 36
U.S. Department of Commerce, Bureau of
  the Census, 32, 35, 38, 42, 51
USSR
  and convergence relation, 97, 346
  productivity growth in (1913–1965), 112
  RGDP growth in, 97

Variation, coefficient of, 92
Veblen, Thorstein, 143
Viner, Jacob, ix, 9, 220
Vogeley, William, 215
Voltaire, on history, 171–172

Wages, and exchange rate, 22
Weber, Max, 203
Welfare productivity, 235, 239
  measurement of, 239–241
  vs. productive capacity, 237–239
Wells, Robert V., 48
White, Lynn, Jr., 11
Wholesale trade
  productivity growth regressions for, 288,
    291
  productivity statistics for, 76, 79, 128
Wiener, Martin J., 178
Williamson, Jeffrey, 12
Willig, Robert D., 241
Wilson, Charles, 11, 169, 170
Wilson, William J., 195
Wishy, Bernard, 55
Wolfe, Barbara L., 202
Wolff, Edward N., 93, 116, 144, 174, 268,
    269, 320, 338
Woodhall, Maureen, 201, 202
Working conditions, and U.S. living
    standards revolution, 48, 50–51, 56
World Bank, data from, 197, 267, 268, 341
World War II, productivity growth during,
    70

X-inefficiency, and productive capacity,
    237–238

Yugoslavia
  and convergence-education relation, 346
  labor productivity growth data on, 112

Zabusky, Charlotte Fox, 50